THECOMICSJOURNALLIBRARY6
THEWRITERS

THECOMICSJOU

THE

NAL**LIBRARY**6

WRITERS

Fantagraphics Books
7563 Lake City Way
NE Seattle, Washington
98115

Publishers **Gary Groth and Kim Thompson**
Managing Editor **Gary Groth**
Editor **Tom Spurgeon**
Editorial Assistance **Kristy Valenti**
Cover & Book Design **Jacob Covey**

THANKS TO
Mike Dean
Dirk Deppey
and especially
Ema Nakao

FANTAGRAPHICS BOOKS
First Edition: January 2006
ISBN-13: 9781560976967
ISBN-10: 1560976969
Printed in Canada

THE WRITERS.

Contents...

EDITOR'S NOTE

The period 1965 to 1985 in American comic books was marked by seismic shifts and shocking reversals up and down the status quo which had been entrenched since the industry's start. Comics reoriented its sales emphasis from newsstands to comic-book shops. An industry of several publishers providing a variety of material became dominated by two companies, Marvel and DC, and their approaches to basically one genre: superheroes. Companies changed hands and began to act more like corporate entities than ragged start-ups. The first generation of creators began to fade in favor of a generation of talent who looked to past comics for inspiration just as much as they did pulp novels or the movies. The audience narrowed and a portion of it grew older and more demanding. Creators began to question standard industry practices like work-for-hire and being removed from freelance projects by capricious editorial whim. Television and licensing exploitation of the characters started to press its way into an important part of the business. The undergrounds gave way to an alternative comics movement that fought the mainstream for shelf space. It was a heady time, two boom periods sandwiching a stretch that almost saw the entire business fade into history.

You can see the modern comic-book industry taking shape in the conversations reprinted here with several of the most popular, talented mainstream comic-book writers of the period. Reading them talk about their favorite characters, their dissatisfaction with one company or another, their desires to move into different fields, the joy they found in their work, gives you an idea of what it must have been like to be one of the few dozen personalities around which an entire industry revolved. And when you get mini-debates about the near impossibility of 250-page comic books, or the burden one might be forced to shoulder moving from comics into a different form of writing, you can see how much distance the industry has traveled, even when so many of the complaints, backstories and expressed hopes sound the same then as now.

The best thing about the following interviews being gathered together in one place is less about specific content and more about how reading them at once allows you to settle into the past and listen to the way a group of creators felt about themselves and their work. You begin to realize there was a time when comics writers and artists seized for themselves the right to be taken seriously as creative artists – not by sacrificing a generation in a holy war for creators' rights or by becoming an entrenched part of an unfair system, as a few had been able to do in the past, but by demanding that respect for what was special about their work, assuming it was due.

— TOM SPURGEON

VOICES FROM THE RE-BIRTH OF
AMERICAN COMIC BOOKS, 1975-1985...

Steve Gerber

CHANGING COMICS' COURSE

INTERVIEW BY GARY GROTH: Steve Gerber is the creator most emblematic of the concerns and opportunities unique to American comic books from the late 1960s until the early 1980s. He began work at Marvel in 1972, and soon settled into a style unlike any other writer's in the industry: a voice favoring offbeat characters and satire, resistant to the well-worn patterns of most superhero books. It found expression in *The Defenders* and *Man-Thing*, a horror feature (running first in *Adventure Into Fear*) that among its various zany goings-on briefly introduced a loudmouthed character named Howard the Duck. Howard would become Gerber's signature creation, and one of Marvel's most popular, during an eponymous series run that saw the character campaign for president, change briefly into a human, learn kung fu, and run afoul of society's more censorious elements. Gerber was also the co-creator of *Omega the Unknown* and the driving force behind the best-selling Kiss comic book.

Gerber left Marvel in 1979 and fought the company over the rights to Howard, a case that was eventually settled. In the minds of many fans, Gerber was the individual creator standing up against corporate power and claiming a right to something on the basis that he and only he could have made it, changing the way comics creators thought about themselves and their value to such companies. Gerber would enjoy long runs working on successful animated television shows such as *G.I. Joe*. In 2001, he wrote a *Howard the Duck* miniseries for MAX, Marvel's imprint for mature readers, and today co-writes *Hard Time* at DC Comics, a comic that helped launch, and then survived, their Focus imprint. His impact and influence since the 1970s cannot be overstated.

This interview by Gary Groth (TCJ #41, August, 1978) catches Gerber just as he's left Marvel over a dispute concerning the Howard the Duck character, and opens with the text of a Gerber letter.

Writer: Steve Gerber Artist: Val Mayerik *Howard the Duck* #23 April 1978 [©1978 Marvel Comics Group]

Dear Gary:

I've been deliberating with myself for several days now just what sort of public statement I wanted to make regarding my parting of the ways with Marvel. Obviously, I've also been thinking about the matter itself for a great deal longer than that, and frankly, it's become a bother and a bore to discuss it.

There's a potential mountain of mud to be slung, but very little point in slinging it. So, rather than present a long, laborious and largely speculative account of just what happened, suppose you, your readers, and I settle for the following.

I was dismissed from the *Howard the Duck* newspaper strip in a manner which violated the terms of my written agreement with Marvel. Marvel was advised that I was contemplating legal action which would likely result in my ownership of the Howard the Duck character and all rights therein. As a consequence of the notice given Marvel by my lawyers, the company chose to terminate my contract on the comic books as well. Marvel's action was not unanticipated, and my only regret is that, for a while at least, the Duck and I will be traveling separate paths.

Those are the facts, stated as simply and plainly as possible. Aside from the above, the only statement I can make with complete certainty is that the situation was, and is extremely muddled.

I know nothing about the status of the proposed $1.50 HTD Magazine, nothing about the future of the four-color comic, nothing about the future of the strip.

No lawsuit has been filed to date.

And that about sums it up. What matters now is tomorrow, and that's more than enough to think about.

Best,

Steve Gerber
Burbank, CA
5/26/78

GARY GROTH: Was writing the Howard strip important to you?

STEVE GERBER: Yes, it was, both financially and because the strip reached at least 10 to 20 times as many people as the *Howard the Duck* comic book.

What did you want to do in the strip that was so important to you?
Phrased that way, it's a difficult question to answer, because actually we had to be a lot more inhibited with the strip than with the comic book. Newspaper editors are very squeamish, even more so than the Comics Code. There are things we have done, lines that I have written, for the ordinary 35-cent Code approved comic that I could not do in the comic strip. But there are precious few strips on the newspaper comics pages right now that address themselves in anything other than the very

stale gag-a-day type material. *Howard* was something different, and in most of the cities where it was run, it acquired a rather devoted following. I hate to see people robbed of it. Also, I thought the strip to be a very important advertisement for the comic book – or for that proposed $1.50 magazine. I wanted the strip to reflect the content of the book to whatever degree possible.

Now, in Marv Wolfman's version of the strip, about all that remains of the feel and thrust and the general artistic direction of the magazine are the names of the characters. It has descended into simple-minded parody. They've amputated its social commentary as if it were a vestigial tail. It has been lobotomized. There is no content to the strip any more. It's entirely without substance. Marvin's first episode, the one running now, is a parody of *Close Encounters*.

I'm surprised you had to be more conservative with what you did in the newspaper strip. Presumably, it reaches an older audience – working men and women who read the paper over a cup of coffee in the morning, etc.

The problem with the newspaper is that, like television, it's supposed to be for everybody. There is only so far they will let you go, because not only Daddy and Mommy, but also the little kids look at the comic strips, to check out *Dennis the Menace*, or whatever.

What would you do that might damage their minds?

The story we did on Beverly inheriting a massage parlor stirred up a little furor. Even though the material, to look at it, is perfectly innocuous, there were editors who objected to the use of the words "massage parlor" in the strip. On the other hand, that particular episode also evoked a lot of positive reaction from senior citizens. The premise of the story was that the old folks were using the massage parlor as a front for a nursing home in mid-Manhattan. It was a turnaround on an old Damon Runyon story in which the bookies used an old folks' home as the front for their betting operation. Our thesis was that it was easier, more acceptable to put the corruption up front.

Because of the shifting morals?

Sure. And because a nursing home in the middle of Manhattan would be a target for, as some of the old ladies in the strip put it, "anyone who ever lusted after a Social Security check." By hiding behind the camouflage of a massage parlor, they blended into the neighborhood. They were not harassed by cops or street people, and they were able to live out their lives in relative comfort while maintaining financial independence, because they had a profit-making operation going on also. A group called the Senior Citizens Anti-Crime Network wrote a letter to the *New York Post*, which appeared in their letters to the editor column, praising the story.

But it's the kind of so-called "controversy" you have to be careful about in a newspaper strip, whereas we would utilize a massage parlor without fear in the comic book. The only restrictions would be in terms of what we could graphically depict. The very mention of it on the newspaper page, though, stirred up a little bit of controversy.

And now we'll be subject to parodies of *Close Encounters*?

Yeah. Parodies of just about everything that isn't controversial, I imagine. I am very, very sad about what they're doing to the strip.

What is the difference between a parody of *Close Encounters* and your parody of *Star Wars* in *Howard* #23 and #24? I was pretty unimpressed by those issues.

Actually, I wasn't too happy with them, either. The story needed a more unifying element about it. And in fact, the *Star Wars* parody happened almost by accident. I was going in an entirely different direction with it when I plotted the first half, and then suddenly realized that I had Man-Thing, who was the Chewbacca figure, and Korrek, who was the Han Solo figure, and the Princess Leia, as portrayed by Jennifer, and Howard as the Luke Skywalker figure, and the temptation was irresistible.

The difference, though, is that rather than settle for simply parodying the *Star Wars* movie, we took the premise on another level, satirizing the commercialization of the *Star Wars* phenomenon, the commercialization of the universe, with the Death Store and the various other elements tossed in – the idea that Berserk Joe, the villain, intended to transform the universe into a gigantic shopping mall. Marvin told me that he does not even intend to go this far with the strip. It will be *Mad*-type parodies, basically, except the Duck will be the star.

Would you have preferred writing a magazine-format *Howard* over a 35-cent comic book?

Yes, definitely. It's a format aimed at the readers who are much more likely to appreciate Howard. Older readers, excluding hardcore fans, just don't browse through the comic rack – people who would buy the *National Lampoon* or *Heavy Metal* on the newsstand, I think people would notice it. Canceling the 35-cent book in favor of the $1.50 magazine would have been a very smart move on Marvel's part. In fact, I suggested it to them last July. At the time, they told me that I must be insane.

Who is They with a capital "T"?

They is Stan [Lee] with a capital "S." They didn't think – Stan didn't think it would be feasible to cancel the 35-cent book at that time. They wanted to do both magazines, the four-color comic and the Super-Special format. Their master plan was to convert the regular comic into a slightly more sophisticated funny-animal book. And I was opposed to that. I felt it was a bastardization of the concept, and really didn't want to see it done. The decision was made at that time to stay with the 35-cent book. Now, almost a year later, they are considering exactly what I proposed. So I wouldn't have been unhappy with it at all. Better this than *Howie Super Stories*.

I assume that's next.

I have no idea. I'm not privy to much inside info from the House of Ideas these days.

One of my major criticisms with the *Howard* book is that you've aimed at obvious targets: violence in media, the Moonies, *Star Wars*, etc. It is all essentially social satire, and I think it's been done better in other media, though I don't discount its importance in comics – since it's not been done in comics at all.

I both agree and disagree. I don't think anyone else has ever examined the fascist implications in a movement like Anita Bryant's on television, for example. Or the Moonies, except perhaps on a news program or a talk show. If they try to tackle these subjects in situation comedies, the results are just ghastly. The seriousness of the phenomena, the potential danger, is always sacrificed to the one-liner. But in essence, I know what you are saying; I've been going for obvious targets. That is, perhaps, true. But I think *Howard* has gone much farther than any television show, in terms of setting those potshots within a dramatic structure.

The *Howard the Duck* strip is not merely a series of comedy sketches. It's also a continuing storyline about a group of characters living out their lives. In that sense, comics have a far greater freedom than the television medium. Our characters can change; things can happen to them that affect their subsequent behavior. They can go through stage of development, physically and psychologically. The Howard character today is not the same character that appeared in *Fear* #19. He couldn't be, after having been through what he's experienced in this world.

This could be debated, but I have the feeling that with the Howard strip and book, that the readers got more of a sense of real people living through those incidents than they would have from a television series.

I had a feeling that what you were really waging war against was the superficiality and hypocrisy at the core of the American culture through popular media stars like the Moonies and Anita Bryant.

In a sense, that's what the whole *Howard* series was about. And I don't know if that's such an easy or obvious target. I do know that it's not a target that you can attack in a single issue of a comic book. You'd almost have to look at the whole run of the magazine before you could understand that that's been the general theme through the series since the very beginning. And it makes no difference, really, whether the target in any given issue is 200,000 decency crusaders bent on saving our children from reality, or barbarian comic books, or the various mindfads like est. Each is just another manifestation of a deteriorating culture. Each little idiocy offers a slightly different peephole into the core insanity.

Writer: Steve Gerber Artists: Carmine Infantino & Klaus Janson *Howard the Duck* #21
February 1978 [©1978 Marvel Comics Group]

One of the themes I'd been playing with since the *Star Wars* parody was that Howard himself, in order to deal with this world, has had to function on a more superficial level than he would have liked to. In "The Night After You Save the Universe," he finds himself walking the streets, wondering why he doesn't have any opinions about what's happening to him. In the next several issues, 25-27, circumstances force him to confront all those depth-emotions that he has been suppressing since his separation from Beverly. It's a very serious sequence, and there is no external, sociological target at all. Instead, we employ the Ringmaster and his Circus of Evil as a metaphor for the various influences on everyone's lives, and in particular, for the recent events in Howard's.

Wasn't it a one-note strip, then? Even with American culture being what it is, you may run out of satirical targets.

I don't think so. The culture keeps on coming up with so many new aberrations. It might have been true if we had a one-dimensional protagonist, but I don't think we did. Howard is a very real character to me, as are most of the rest of the characters in the strip. Beverly, certainly, Paul and Winda to a somewhat lesser degree, because I just haven't had the opportunity, or perhaps the inclination, to develop them as fully as they could be. But, no, I don't think we would have run out of material. The characters themselves were story matter.

Could you explicate a few of your feelings on some of your targets? For instance, *Howard* #3 deals with violence in the media. Could you tells us exactly what you think of violence in media? Obviously, you think it's a bad influence...

No, that's not true. I don't think so. As a matter of fact, I think a group like Action for Children's Television, while they certainly have the right idea, are going at the problem from a totally wrongheaded approach. I don't think it's the depiction of violence itself that's the bad thing. It's the question of how the violence is presented, the artistic rationale behind it, and how much of its consequences are shown. Then, too, the nature of the violence itself, and the even more basic question of honesty – are these actions and emotions representative of human behavior in the context of this set of events, or are they contrived? It's a very complex question, and you may be interested to know that violent actions are not the only concern of ACT and similar groups. They're also opposed to the presentation of violent emotions.

I have it on good authority that one of the major problems with the new *Fantastic Four* cartoon series has been the characterization of the Thing. Now get this – they are afraid that his nasty temperament and his arguments with Reed and Sue Richards will "encourage sibling rivalry." The networks and the various pressure groups hope, with the tool of television, to wipe out a complex pattern of human behavior that dates back to Cain and Abel by excising strong emotions from the *FF* cartoon show. What frightens me, given the statistics on the viewing patterns of today's kids, is that it may actually be possible. The Soofis' Blanderizer machine may be television.

The problem with many comic books and with much of children's television is that the effects of violence are rarely presented honestly. The buildings the Hulk would tear up were always abandoned warehouses; Spidey and Doc Ock can punch each other in the face for 38 consecutive panels and neither gets a nosebleed. An impressionable child might be misled to believe that punching, kicking and maiming were all good clean fun – and that he or she *could get away with it*, that the violence would have no ramifications, that no one would really get hurt, least of all himself. Prettied-up violence is, to my mind, the most vile of all.

But now we have a whole host of other questions to consider! What about that cannon that backfires on Wile E. Coyote? What about Elmer Fudd running down Bugs Bunny with that steamroller? The coyote is charred for a few frames; Bugs is flattened, but snaps back to three dimensions. Is that violence without consequence, too? Personally, I don't think so. I believe a child can distinguish between Bugs Bunny and a human being. I could at that age, and I never expected the physical universe to conform to the laws of reality as presented in the Warner Brothers cartoons.

On the other hand, you have the kung fu movies that we were dealing with in *Howard #3*. The best of them depicted violence as a kind of poetry, a savage, exotic kind of ballet. In the worst of them, violence was presented as a near-sexual means to gratification. Worse, the gouging, jabbing, and chopping were treated as acceptable, and not even extraordinary, forms of behavior – as something everyone takes for granted, because we all know there's a martial arts expert lurking around every corner in New York City, and you'd better be prepared, because he's going to beat your brains out.

There was a real-life incident that stimulated the story in *Howard #3*. Originally, I'd planned to do a parody of the *Master of Kung Fu* book, with Howard doing the first-person narration, and so on. Then, Mary Skrenes and I were sitting in the Market diner at 44th Street and 11th Avenue in New York, trying to work out that plot and a couple of others, when some sort of incident took place out on the sidewalk. We couldn't even see clearly what was happening, but by the time we got up and left our seats to see what sort of insanity was going on out there, a kid came staggering into the diner, his face bloodied, stab wounds all over his body, and collapsed on the floor. We were told by one of the waitresses the next day that he had died. It was at that point, after that incident, after walking up and down 8th and 9th Avenue and Times Square in New York and seeing the kids play with their nunchaku sticks as if they were squirt guns, that I decided a story like "Four Feathers of Death" had to be done. It meant something to me. I don't know how well we carried it off, if it produced the desired effect, I mean. A lot of people liked it, a lot of people didn't. But the idea of using the Duck in that fashion, of making him the target of that kind of brutality, was a valid and important one. No one expects to see a "funny animal" bleed. It was a very, very graphic way of making a point about what those films were saying, how easy it is to become inured to violence when it's presented in that fashion.

But I am definitely not in favor of the elimination of violence from television, from film, from any medium. First of all, that would be utterly unrealistic and dishonest. Secondly, I grew up watching *Roy Rogers* and George Reeves' *Superman* and *Sky King*, and they certainly didn't turn me into a rampaging monster… opinions differ on that matter. [*laughter*] But, no, I mean, I was a conscientious objector. None of the supposedly violent programs I watched made me a more violent person. None of the current films that utilize violence for artistic ends would really have that effect on anyone who wasn't already severely disturbed.

How would you differentiate using violence for artistic ends, and…

It's much easier to give examples. It's essentially the difference between *Taxi Driver* and *The Street Fighter*.

Street Fighter I haven't seen.

Don't bother. It's Sonny Chiba ripping out people's tongues and tearing off their genitals. With *Street Fighter* the violence *is* the entertainment. In *Taxi Driver*, it is there to make a very important character statement about Travis Bickle. Although the scene in *Taxi Driver* is incredibly bloody and incredibly violent and difficult to watch, its intent is entirely different. It's the act of a man who cannot express his emotions any other way, whereas, for Sonny Chiba, it's all in a day's work – and Chiba is presented as the hero of the picture. There is no similarity at all between the two films, and no similarity in the meaning of the violence.

The Dr. Bong episodes confused me. Who or what did Dr. Bong represent?

That story started out, too, as something very different from what it became. It began as a parody of *The Island of Dr. Moreau*, with an attempt to create a villain for Howard of the stature of Dr. Doom or the Red Skull, someone we could bring back periodically. The origin of the name is funny, too. I was over at Gene Simmons's apartment – this was during the time we were working on the Kiss book – and he was showing me some of the group's fan mail. Someone wrote them a very strange letter that said, "Come over to the house. We'll have some good music, some good wine and some bonging." Whatever that meant. Gene didn't know, and neither did I. We had different assumptions about it. But it struck me as very funny, and it stuck with me, and when it was time to create this new villain, Dr. Bong was it. Marie Severin and I designed the costume with the ding-dong school bell on his head, and the clapper on one hand. It began, really, as nothing more than an exercise in silliness, combined with a number of my own dream images. *Howard* #15 was comprised almost entirely of strange images from my own dreams.

Then, a fellow by the name of Bob Greene, with the Chicago *Sun-Times*, wrote an incredibly vitriolic article about our Kiss book – prior to its publication, with no solid, factual basis for the criticism except his own negative attitude toward the group. The article was syndicated to some 100 newspapers around the country, and the mail began pouring in to Marvel from outraged people who, though they hadn't seen the book either, were certain we were out to corrupt the moral fiber of the nation's young. They warned us they would never buy Marvel comics again if we dared publish the book. They vowed to burn every copy that reached their neighborhood newsstands. It caused a great deal of trouble for me with Marvel. So I decided to have a little fun.

Bob Greene had previously written a book called *Billion-Dollar Baby*, about his experiences touring and performing onstage with Alice Cooper. Knowing nothing of Greene's past other than that, I set out to construct a character as loathsome as Greene was in my eyes at that time – a former yellow journalist who utilized the power of the press amorally to his own ends.

Strangely enough, Greene's brother, who lives in Colorado, is a Duck fan and brought *Howard* #17 to Greene's attention. Greene loved it, called me up again, and wrote a very favorable article about *Howard the Duck* in which he gave me a chance to rebut some of his statements about the Kiss book. So Mr. Greene and I are now on, I think, fairly good terms. He said it was a lifetime ambition fulfilled, becoming a comic book villain.

That's everyone's ambition.

I've done it myself. *I* was Winky-Man.

You also put your friends in the strip, didn't you?

Friends, enemies, unsuspecting strangers off the street. The Beverly Switzler character was based very loosely on Mary Skrenes; Arthur Winslow was a kind of Don McGregor type. The Kidney Lady is real, I encountered her on Times Square. Other characters were either combinations of various persons, or, in many cases, just pure invention. Iris Raritan, who appears in the Ringmaster stories, is a character not so much based on any one individual as on a trend I've perceived in people lately – the feeling that they have absolute license to monkey around with anyone else's life by whatever means they choose, basically for their own amusement or to satisfy their own needs. It's a logical extension of the "Looking Out for Number One" concept.

What do you say to people who accuse you of being too negative, and of disparaging great institutions like shopping malls and television violence?

I don't know. I just know I never apologize… I think all the explanation that's required is contained in the stories themselves.

I think something has happened to this country in the past 10 years or so. We've become much more willing to accept anything – again, it's hard to escape the clichés – Madison Avenue or the Government shoves down our throats. The truth has become unbearable to contemplate. There's a terrible apathy that's engendered a new movement back to the Self. The society seems to have accepted the notion that by simply becoming oblivious to what's happening in the world outside our skins, the horror will go away. It's not going to go away.

Isn't that the nature of escapist entertainment?

It is, but I think we are being deluged with escapist entertainment.

Aren't comics escapist entertainment?

Not exclusively, no. Not by definition.

Virtually they are, don't you think?

Virtually, yes. Most of the Marvel line is, yeah. And DC, and the rest. You're certainly not going to find a great deal to think about in the average issue of *Casper the Friendly Ghost*. But I think there's enough of that stuff around that we have room for a magazine like *Howard*, maybe even a need for it. There are other books that deal in social criticism and serious characterizations. *Howard* may differ from *Master of Kung Fu* or various strips that McGregor and Englehart wrote, because of the presence of the Duck, the inherent humor of that character. We may have found a format in which these kinds of stories can be made more palatable, a little easier to swallow.

It seems paradoxical that you're working in an industry that specializes in escapist entertainment, and yet you cited escapism as a bad trend.

No, I don't mean to say that. I think there's definitely a place for escapist entertainment. Films like *Star Wars* or *Close Encounters*, or a comic book like *Marvel Team-Up*, definitely have their place. You can't have social commentary jack-hammered into your head constantly, either. It becomes a case of sensory overload after awhile. There's only so much of it you can absorb at a time. I don't think there's anything wrong with getting way from it all occasionally. But *most* American entertainment is escapist – movies, television, most magazines, paperbacks, comics, all the way down the line, and I think there's a glut of that kind of material. I think something else is needed. What amazes me is that so many people find one itsy-bitsy comic book like *Howard* so threatening.

Do you think *Howard* is an important book because of your willingness to tackle social issues head-on?

No, I don't think that's the major breakthrough with *Howard*. To an extent, we dealt with social issues in the *Defenders*, in *Man-Thing*. The main contribution, if any, that Howard has made to comics has been its departure from the standard formula of comic-book storytelling – of what can constitute a comic book, what it can do, what it can say, and what it can mean.

Glance through a typical Marvel or DC book, you'll find that, regardless of which character the magazine features, the material will be arranged in roughly the following way: a three-page fight or chase scene to open; about two pages of the character in his secret identity; three more pages of the character back in costume, either engaged in a second fight with the villain or swinging around the city looking for the villain and encountering other little obstacles along the way; a couple more pages of the alter ego; and then the big fight scene at the end. That's the formula for the DC books.

All of it looks alike. All of it reads alike. The pacing of every story is virtually identical. I think that formula has just about outlived its usefulness. Largely, the sales figures, except on the most established characters, back me up on that. *Spider-Man*, *Superman*, *Hulk*, *Thor*, and *The Fantastic Four* – all of them still do very well. But when you start moving below that crème de la crème of comics characters, you will find that most of them are just limping along, both in sales and in terms of readability.

Where do you think they'll go if the formula does indeed break down?

Frankly, I don't know. I don't see any evidence on the part of either company to explore any vastly different kind of story. Well, actually, that's not simple. That's the basis of everything. I'm not talking about different kinds of characters, or tossing out the superhero format entirely, or anything that superficial. The very nature of the stories being told may have to change if the medium is going to survive. That's all-encompassing, really.

What do you mean by the nature of the story?

Well, all right. I think the time is coming when the kids are not going to be willing to settle for about six pages of Peter Parker's neverending, never-changing problems with Aunt May sandwiched between two fight scenes with the Vulture. That era is rapidly drawing to a close. It's a style that became a formula accidentally. It was, I think, the natural way of writing comics for Stan Lee in the very beginning. Something that he did instinctively. I don't think it was anything he ever wrote down as Ten Rules of How to Write Comics. He followed certain guidelines – snappy opening scenes that involved the reader immediately in the action, major climactic scenes around page 17 (when comics were 20-page stories). It was no more than the same basic dramatic structure one would apply to a play, a film, or anything else. You build to a climax, the climax occurs, and you resolve the conflict.

What has happened, though, is that over the years that simple dramatic structure has ossified into a page-by-page formula that has become so predictable and so mind-numbing to the readers that it's hard to tell, except by the colors of the costumes – and they've all begun to look alike, too – whether you're reading *Ms. Marvel* or *Spider-Man*. The formula today doesn't merely dictate an exciting opening scene. It requires the hero, in costume, as the largest central figure on the page. In cases where the hero cannot appear on page one, some or another representation of the hero – a phantom figure, a statue, a newspaper photograph, whatever – must be present. Theoretically, this is supposed to help sales. That's just one example.

Not only do the books read alike, they all look alike. This also was an accident that, I believe, had its origins in Stan's wanting certain artists to emulate certain very good things in Jack Kirby's work. As progressively less creative types took the reins at Marvel, this mutated into a slavish imitation of Jack, and later of John Buscema, to a degree where all the artists are becoming indistinguishable from one another.

You're starting to sound like Gil Kane, Steve.

I read the Gil Kane interview. He and I agree on certain points, but not all. My major argument with Gil is his assessment of the writing in comics. Gil considers it far below the level of the artwork. In my opinion, the majority of it is *exactly* at the level of the art, and that's the problem. You have a situation now where most comic-book artists do not know how to draw human beings. They know how to draw Kirbyesque machinery and the ray guns and the conventional muscular heroic figure, one stereotyped watermelon-busted female figure, and about six facial expressions. And that's it. The exceptions to that rule can be counted on the fingers of both hands – without using up the fingers.

For me, Gene Colan is probably the most fabulous exception to it. Gene has a way with nuance in facial expression, body movement, camera angles, and lighting – I've never seen an artist who could touch him on that. There are more dynamic artists, some who are better storytellers, but there is no one in the field that can match Gene's subtlety. Unfortunately, a lot of it is lost in the printing process and in the inking. That's not a comment on the inkers; it's just that some of the stuff Gene does relies so heavily on delicate pencil shading that the effect cannot be duplicated in opaque ink.

My feelings about what Gil had to say – God, we could do a whole interview on that – I disagreed with him profoundly on a number of things. I don't believe that a comic book is just a collection of pretty pictures. I don't believe that the pictures alone can or should tell the story.

Do you agree with Gil's assessment that the writer is just as important to a comic as the artist?

Did he say that?

Yes.

I must have glossed over it. I didn't see that. But I think the writer is at least 50 percent of the book.

At least?

At least, yeah. Possibly more, for the simple reason that that's where the story originates.

Let's talk about the nature of the medium.

All right. Before we move on to that, I want to say that there is a strange rivalry between artists and writers in comics. I wouldn't call it bad blood, but sort of semi-spoiled blood between the two divisions. It would be impossible for the writer to do what he does in comics without the artist. That's absolutely true. The artist plays a gargantuan part in it. Percentages, I don't think mean anything. There are some cases where I've had to do 80 percent of the work, because the storytelling was so bad, the artwork was so muddled, that I found myself explaining what was going on in the pictures as well as just trying to advance the plot and delineate the characters. There have also been cases, and it's always a bonanza when it happens, when the pictures have spoken as eloquently as the words. When that happens, it's not less work for the writer, it's the writer being able to concentrate, say, less on narrative than character development, being able to do something else better, because the art has done part of the job for him. As I say, it's like 50 percent, 20 percent, 90 percent – none of that means anything. It has to be a true collaboration for it to work, and that's the bottom line.

Now, about the nature of the medium. Another thing that Gil said – to use this as a kind of jumping-off point – where I think he's really wrong, is that the writers in comics are writing comics because they can't do anything else. Again, I have to say that in a lot of cases, that's true, but I don't think the real story will be told for another 10 years or so. Watch what I, Wein, Wolfman, Conway and the rest of the current bunch – Doug Moench and Don McGregor and so on – look at what we're doing 10 years from now, and then we'll know the score. I think it's too early right now for the final tally. But some of us, certainly, have been working in comics because we like the medium. There are things that comics can do that no other medium can; there are things other media can do that comics can't.

Can you give us some examples?

Let's start with the very basics, all right? A comic book page measures about 7" x 10". We're working with a limited amount of space. Those 7 x 10 inches are divided into, say, usually three to six panels per page. Those panels contain artwork, and they contain lettering. There is only a certain amount of reproducible detail, due to a really rotten printing process, that can be presented on a comic-book page. There are only a certain number of words that can be written for that page without covering up all the pictures. This sounds very basic, but it's strange how few people think about it. For these reasons, the medium has developed, and, in fact, is really a kind of literary shorthand. You don't get the depth of characterization that you can find in a 1200-page Russian novel. It cannot be done. The quality of the reproduction, the general quality of the art – this goes back to what I said earlier about the probability that your artists will only be able to do about six facial expressions – the fact that the images do not move, the fact that there is no supplementary text to give you any indication of how these lines are being spoken... the best indicators or vocal intonation you have are balloon shapes – the icicle balloon; the thick, wavy balloon; the mechanical balloon; the burst balloon; the news-flash balloon (the one they use to represent radio or TV voices)…

Aren't there other alternatives? For instance, couldn't you have descriptive narration with dialogue under or over the panel? In other words, instead of a balloon containing the words, "But, Howard, this exit leads to the tower," you could place the words at the bottom of the panel to read, "But, Howard," she said with urgency, "this exit leads to the tower." Or would that approach ruin the nature of a comic, because the picture should express that urgency?

There are several answers to that question. First of all, at that point it becomes something other than what we know as a comic. I've tried doing this in various stories.

In *Man-Thing*?

In *Man-Thing*, "The Book of Edmund" [*Giant-Size Man-Thing* #4], in the *Howard* book – not issue #16, I don't even want to discuss that; if you want to bring it up later, OK, but I don't consider it an example of this – but there was a page in one story where we did a news conference [*Howard* #8], part of Howard's presidential campaign, where we were able to fit literally about three times as much dialogue as we could have if they had been hand-lettered balloons. I've made other attempts at this. Other writers have tried it, too. Reader reaction is varied. My own feeling is that it works in certain contexts, but not always. It worked with "The Book of Edmund," because the book was a story-within-a-story, self-contained. And it worked with the news conference, because that was like reproducing a transcript of the news conference. It worked in "Song-Cry of the Living Dead Man" in *Man-Thing* [#12], because that was a piece of prose written by a character in the story and intended to be read as such.

I think in cases like these, it can be done successfully, but to try it on a regular basis for a comic book – number one, I don't think it would sell. I think that's something that has to be taken into consideration. Number two, the words are still limited by space; the depth you could achieve would still be limited. You would lose a lot of the continuity and storytelling techniques from panel to panel that we've developed over the past 20 years, roughly since the advent of *The Fantastic Four*. I don't know. I could see a book done that way. It might be an interesting experiment. I'd like to see what would happen with it. I would not be inclined to do it. My own inclination is not to tamper too much with the nature of the medium, but more with the content.

(Incidentally, I am aware that the format we're discussing here isn't exactly revolutionary. The text-below-pictures thing is, of course, *Prince Valiant*. The indisputable success of the strip notwithstanding, I'm still not sure it would work in a comic *book*.)

We hear catchphrases like "good storytelling" bandied about everywhere. Could

you tell me exactly what good storytelling means?

Yeah, all right. Very simply, it's the continuity and flow of action from panel to panel, page to page. No, wait – that's just a definition of "storytelling." *Good* storytelling would include the phrase "immediately apprehensible" in there someplace. If the artist has done his job really expertly, anyone should be able to get the gist of the story simply by looking at the unlettered pages – not necessarily the entire story, Lord knows, but the outline of the plot, at least.

I remember that in the Soofi/Anita Bryant satire [*Howard* #21], Soofi was throwing Howard into a washing machine. In the first panel, Soofi held Howard with her left hand, and in the second panel she threw him in with her right hand, the entire perspective changes before our eyes.

It's crazier than that. The crown also disappears from Soofi's head. I'm not positive about this, but I think the door on the washer opens two different ways. It's weird. It looks like one of Mort Weisinger's April Fool stories. That's bad storytelling. Strangely, throughout the rest of that issue, Carmine [Infantino], who is generally a very good storyteller, did a very good job. The flow from panel to panel and page to page in that story is generally excellent – with the exception of that single page, and those come under the category of annoyances, not atrocities. I should have spotted them myself, and they should have been corrected by the inker at my instruction. I'm writing the stuff now from Xeroxes rather than from the original art – one less chance for something getting lost or delayed in the mail between New York and Los Angeles. Dependent upon how many books they have to get out of the office in a given day, whether the notes I make on the Xeroxes are ever carried out into action – art changes, coloring done the way I ask – it's always unpredictable. Anyway, the Soofi would be one example of very obvious bad storytelling. Another kind would be an entire page, for example, consisting of long shots for no reason, or an entire page consisting of essentially the same medium shot of two characters, for no reason. These are mechanical things, they're craft, and they have to be learned.

I was just looking at one of the Marvel classic adaptations the other day. I don't remember which one it was, whether it was *A Connecticut Yankee in King Arthur's Court* – it was some Mark Twain story. The cover copy was straight out of the *Incredible Hulk* or *Thor* – "Thou wilt not do this, varlet! So swears" – whoever it was – Huckleberry Finn. [*laughter*] That kind of thing appalls me. There are some stories comics are not suited to tell, because they seem ridiculous when reduced to the shorthand. *Hamlet* may be one. You certainly couldn't tell it in Shakespeare's terms, and I wouldn't want to be the one who took on the task of editing Will to make him conform to Marvel's house style.

I was involved in interviewing Denny O'Neil several years ago, and he said this about adapting classic works like *Hamlet*: "I think the combination of poetry, the spoken word and an actor's resources measure up to more than the combination of word and pictures, which is all we've got to work with. Ditto movies."

Ditto movies? What does he mean by that?

Let me quote a little more. "Ditto movies. I think movies are potentially the most complete art form, because they can combine an actor's presence, an actor's skill, a writer's skill, painting, and music, and they can make a single entity of it. So, potentially, movies are the best art form ever until we maybe find a way to plug directly into somebody's brain with telepathy and create experiences with no middleman at all."

Whew. Again, I agree and disagree. The problem with movies and television – some of the same criticism applies to both – is that they do not require the participation on the part of the audience that a novel does, for example. Movies and television are a much more intimate form of storytelling. I think that's true. But, as Gil [Kane] pointed out, you can't turn back to a previous scene in a movie to check out the nuance as you can with a novel, or even a comic book, because there's no way to turn back the "pages" of a movie to see what you missed, or if you missed anything, or reread a scene to savor it without going to see the entire film again. You're at the mercy of the technology. So I think each one of those media has its own distinctive advantages and disadvantages. I tend to agree with Denny, though, that films and, potentially, television, are two of the most powerful that we have, and both of them are more powerful than comics. Although each has its own individual peculiarities.

There are certain things about the comics medium that will not change, that cannot change. However they're arranged on the page, you're still limited to words and pictures; in combination, hopefully; in harmony, hopefully. Or in interesting discord, for that matter. But movies – when you consider the size of the screen, the fact that the actors move and talk, the fact that you have a choice between color and black and white, an open-ended length, no enforced limitation on the amount of dialogue, the addition of music, sound and optical effects – movies are just much less limited than comics. It's true.

On the other hand, someone who has told a story in a comic book that has moved you, or pricked your brain, to the extent that a movie can, may have done a much more difficult job than the screenwriter's, because of all the obstacles he has had to overcome.

When is a comic book not a comic book? Can you put too many words on a page?

No, no, I don't want to think about it in those terms. There are no strict rules. There are too many words on a page when you can't see what's going on in the pictures. But that's the only rule I would like to impose. The copy shouldn't dominate the page, force the artwork into the background by its sheer weight.

When does it become an illustrated story? Take *Chandler*, for instance…

The thing that Steranko did?

Yeah. I think anyone would be hard-pressed to call it a comic book. The illustrations were juxtaposed with the copy.

I don't think that's a comic book. That *is* an illustrated story. It may have more illustrations than your typical illustrated story. It strikes me – and I'm going to get fried for saying this – as the B-movie, pulp equivalent of a Little Golden Book. A novel shouldn't need pictures.

These forms may be interesting in and of themselves, they may be valid, but they're not comics. They're something else, whatever else they are. That's not meant in a pejorative sense.

Do you think the comics form is capable of producing work on the same level as a novel or a film?

I can only say that I've never seen it attempted. It's certainly not been done. But, wait, before we even say that – the term "novel" is rather all-encompassing. Robert E. Howard wrote novels. Unquestionably, to me, what Roy Thomas, John Buscema and Barry Smith have done with Conan is so far superior to the stuff that Howard turned out… so I suppose a certain kind of novel very definitely *can* be done in comics.

What about mainstream novels, or SF novels that contain the best aspects of mainstream literature?

I don't know. I think comic books are most adaptable or amenable to the kind of story that relies very heavily on plot, and not on characters or inner dialogue – this despite the fact that I have been accused of ignoring plot entirely to concentrate on character on virtually every strip I've ever done. But there is no question that because of the current format in comics, meaning the physical format, the amount of space for story and art in each issue, one element – plot or character – always suffers as a result of emphasis on the other. There is not time to linger over a character bit in a comic book. Although, ideally, the two elements should work together. They should not be in conflict. The definition of plot, in fact, is characters in action; the interaction of character traits *is* the plot, and for that reason the two should never have to come into conflict. With comics they do because of the types of story we have traditionally tried to tell – in which character traits are reduced to "good person" and "bad person," hero and villain – or because of the emphasis on what one editor used to call "density of incident" – a lot of things happening in as few pages as possible.

Could you expand on the advantages of film over comics?

Given a company of really fine actors, an excellent screenplay, a good cameraman, a good director, a cooperative studio head, and a lot of money, movies can virtually outdo comics at anything. Almost anything. Compare the *Star Wars* movie to the *Star Wars* comic book, just to take an extremely obvious example. The same sense of wonder is not and cannot be created in the comic book as in the film. In the film, you're actually seeing it happen. It's a well-known fact that an artist can draw anything.

To see a man flying through the air in a comic book is no big deal any more. I would suspect that the effect of the same action on the screen, when they release the *Superman* movie, if they've done it right, is going to be breathtaking. But flying has become almost a casual thing in comics. Hawkman, I think, failed for that reason. That's all he did! He just flew around. On film, that character would probably scare the shit out of an audience. It's an extremely powerful image. But you have to stretch the element of the fantastic to the point of absurdity before it really engages anyone's imagination in a comic book.

I thought a very good example of that was Marvel's *Close Encounters* adaptation, which lost so much in translation.

I haven't looked at that closely. There are a lot of problems with it. The fact that the UFOs in the film were all done in lighting effects, basically – they were not solid objects – to try to convey that in a comic book panel is next to impossible. I think what Walt [Simonson] did with it is amazing under the circumstances. Also, none of the things that happened in the movie, in terms of comic books, are very fantastic at all.

Can you imagine what it would cost to construct Jack Kirby's version of the Kree Empire for a movie set? Comics have already, in certain ways, so surpassed films in terms of sheer spectacle that a movie like *Close Encounters* becomes very dry, very dull reading on the comic-book page, a pallid imitation of what the comics themselves excel at.

It looks to me like comics may be moving out of the production ghetto they've been in with the slicker magazines from Marvel.

Yeah, but they're making mistakes there, too. The idea of dropping the black-and-white format and going to these color books is a very, very good one. But, unfortunately, again they've made the mistake of trying to concoct an instant line of books rather than to focus the necessary attention on one magazine. The one magazine could eventually be expanded upon, but the whole scattershot technique of comic book publishing and distribution have come into play again, and they're not working on one magazine, but five. So we're going to get the same old stuff again – there's going to be a horror book, there's going to be a Western, there's going to be a science-fiction book, there's going to be a barbarian book, there's going to be a duck book, y'know… [*laughter*] My God, we've glutted the market already, and haven't even got one book on the press!

What would you suggest?

I would suggest Marvel's answer to *Heavy Metal*, a book that could contain all of those genres and sell for $1.50, and be able to maintain itself well enough by demanding high enough advertising revenue so that it could continue to print quality stuff, and a lot of it, without having to raise its cover price for a long, long time. A book that fairly reeks prestige, uniqueness.

None of the comics companies – and this astounds me, that they haven't seen this to this day; we're not talk about Marvel exclusively, here, it's all of them – none of the comics companies has ever been able to sustain itself on the strength of one publication. The reason for that is that none of the books has ever become a "class" advertising vehicle. *National Lampoon* has, *Rolling Stone* has, and *Heavy Metal* is well on its way. They can command more dollars for a page of advertising at this point in some cases than Marvel dares ask for a page in its entire four-color comics line – 40 publications, a readership of a couple million per month!

Maybe those advertisers don't make enough money from their x-ray specs…?

That's part of it. If Marvel or DC were able to charge $25,000 per page per book, each book would instantly become a gigantic moneymaker. The one problem has been – you used the term "ghetto" a moment ago, and I think it's apropos – they've been a literary and *commercial* ghetto for a long time. The demographics on the books – sorry, we have to haul these in – indicate that they are not an advertiser's route to his prime market. Both *Heavy Metal* and *National Lampoon* certainly are. So they get the Seiko ads, and we get Count Dante.

What you're saying is that comic books don't operate on the same principle that the entire magazine publishing industry does.

Only because it's never been tried. Only because no attempt has ever been made to reach that audience. Only because they never believed it was possible until *Heavy Metal* and the Kiss magazine. What Marvel discovered with the Kiss book is that it *is* possible, even for them. We sold out damn near a half-million copies of that magazine. It was a virtual sell-out. The sales figures must be somewhere near 80 percent. It actually went back to press for a second printing after the initial quarter-million sold out. There has not been a sale on a comic book like that in recent history, and that's including the so-called "phenomena" like *Howard* #1. Percentages of that kind have been non-existent in comics since the 1940s. Initially, no one at Marvel believed we could price a magazine – other than the tabloid size – at $1.50 and sell it. It was felt that comics had no business dealing with rock 'n' roll personalities. It was felt that the most efficient way to promote comic books was to advertise them in other comic books – house ads.

All of those theories were proven wrong by that Kiss book. There were a number of reasons why it succeeded: First and foremost, the fact that a group who sold seven or eight million records had its logo reproduced on the cover. In addition, we traded off for advertising space in three or four of the major rock magazines. Aucoin Management bought a full-page color ad in *Circus* magazine to promote the book. We did a lot of advance publicity on it. Kiss's public relations people were turning out copy on it. The Bob Greene article, I suspect, helped. [*Laughter*] In general, the product was marketed in an entirely different way from anything comics have ever done before. It is of interest to note that because of the Bob Greene article, not one ad for the Kiss magazine ever appeared in the Marvel line of color comics. They were so panicked and so afraid of what it would do to the "Marvel image" that they dropped the ads from the comics.

Who do you mean by "they"?

By "they," I mean the powers-that-be, the editorial people, Stan, whoever was in the editor's chair at that time, and I assume, Jim Galton, the president of Cadence Publishing. They thought it would reflect badly on Marvel. So this comic book sold with just one squib in the Bullpen Bulletins and four or five ads in various rock magazines, and on the strength of the Kiss logo and the popularity of the group. The mail came in enormous quantities. For a while, they had one drawer for Kiss mail, and another drawer for all the fan mail on all the other Marvel books, at the office.

This indicates something to me, not just about the viability of these rock 'n' roll crossovers, but about the means of promoting a magazine. Incidentally... the trade-off ads were my idea, I was the prime advocate of doing the book, and Sol Brodsky and I virtually invented the physical format, even to picking the paper stock. I personally supervised everything from writing and editing to the selection of the typography – which was a bad choice; my mistake; I learned something – and the layout of the text pages and the selection of the photos. I even wrote that "Welcome to the Marvel Universe" ad, the first bit of sophisticated ad copy for itself that the company has ever put before the public. I'm not boasting here. Dave Kraft put the Beatles book together the same way – and *all* of the new color magazines should be receiving that kind of attention, every one, every issue. It's necessary to produce a classy book. That's my point. Someone has to do a little thinking. You can just set the production line in motion as they do on the 35-cent comics.

Do you think the Kiss magazine sold because of its quality or on the strength of Kiss?

Oh, no, it sold primarily on the popularity of the group. But a crappy-looking book might not have sold as well. The fact that it was a classier publication in terms of paper stock and printing and so on certainly helped it. People could look at it and say, "This is *worth* $1.50. I'm going to plink down that much money and take it home with me." From that standpoint, obviously, it couldn't sell on the strength of the story or the artwork, because people would not have that much time to look at it before buying it. A magazine that sells on the basis of its quality has built that reputation over time. A second Kiss book may sell even better than the first, because all the care and time and work that went into the first issue managed to show through. That, and the better printing process.

I'm not going to try and defend the content of the book in terms of the art or this particular story that was written for it. There were good things about it, there were bad things about it. In a strange way, given the nature of the project, it's probably some of the straightest superhero material I've written for Marvel in the past three years. What was important, paramount, to me about the Kiss book was the concept of doing a book in that format with that marketing strategy. If it could be duplicated with other publications, not necessarily movie adaptation s or presentations of rock 'n' roll groups, I think Marvel – or whichever publisher is smart enough – might eventually be able to abandon the 35-cent books almost entirely in favor of a small line of magazines – say six different magazines – that would make more money for them while producing better quality material.

What kind of material would you like to see in a line of magazines?

Everything. Absolutely everything. My plan for the proposed *Howard the Duck* magazine was to present a wide variety of features, not exclusively Howard. It would have been roughly 35 pages of Howard each issue and various backup features, no other series. I'd already done one crazy three-page thing that just came to me, a little humor spot. I was encouraging other writers at Marvel to submit ideas to me for anything they would like to do. *I* didn't want a regular backup feature in that magazine. I think that would have been death. Marvel was pushing for a regular Man-Thing backup. Here again, it's the instant impulse to shoot for the easiest possible thing. So immediately we'll have five or six more fossils on the stands, all of which have a regular lead feature and all the backup features designed and planned before the magazines ever hit the stands, I think that's a terrible mistake.

Obviously Marvel doesn't.

No, but I think you have an editorial team up there that doesn't know what else to do, and so they're very possibly incapable of producing any other kind of magazine if the situation were to demand it. There are very few people left up there capable of independent thought, let alone creative, innovative thought. Rick

Writer: Steve Gerber Artists: Gene Colan & Steve Leialoha *Howard the Duck* #13
June 1977 [©1977 Marvel Comics Group]

Marschall has just joined the staff. Ralph Macchio certainly has an appreciation for some of the more unusual material. Whether he'll be able to actualize that in his editorial capacity on this new line of magazines remains to be seen. Dave Kraft, who is handling the rock 'n' roll books, has got imagination – Dave's got a lot of talent he can bring to those books, if they let him. And there are a handful of others fully capable of this, but right now I think the general trend, the main thrust of Marvel's whole editorial policy is homogenization, to make everything so much like everything else as humanly possible.

I guess their strategy is that if it worked once, it will again – or still.

Very sound reasoning. I mean, nothing else has changed since the 1950s, has it? Why should comic books? Speaking of movies again, there's now what I call the Peter Bogdanovich syndrome, where –

It sounds horrible.

Yeah. It amounts to a vain and futile attempt to recapture past glories. *Nova* is an example. *Nova* was supposed to be cast in the old mold of the early 1960s Marvel Comics, and it bears no resemblance whatsoever to those books. It's basically a fan's interpretation of what those books were like. To compare *Nova* with the early Ditko or Romita *Spider-Man* is fatuous. All the evocative elements are completely lost. It's an attempt, again, to formularize what was done in the early '60s. Every attempt at that has fallen just short of pathetic. What can I tell you? *Nova* is one particular book; there are others. *Nova*, strangely, when it first appeared, had its own interesting charm about it. I liked the first couple of issues. And then the degeneration was rampant and apparently irreversible. It didn't fool anybody.

I'll tell you the truth. I look so little at the Marvel line of the past couple of years that I couldn't tell you what's going on in the books. I don't know. I don't read them any more. They're dull to me. They bore me.

One title I happened to pick up the other day that interested me was "Seeker 3000" that Doug Moench and Tom Sutton did. That was at least a nice attempt at something. Here again, one of the funniest things about comic books is their literal interpretation of everything. Se we have a book called *Marvel Premiere* in which each issue *must* be a premiere. We cannot do two issues of the same characters, because then it's not a premiere any more. So, we're left with this Seeker 3000 bunch, which was one of the more interesting science-fiction efforts in the comics over the past couple of years, and God only knows if we'll ever see them again, because it would not be permissible to do a second issue of something in a book called *Premiere*. It's a little ridiculous.

This business of literalism says something not only about the nature of the medium, but also about a lot of the people who work in it, the thinking of a lot of the people. Something you cannot do in comics is have a character say one thing and *mean* something else – unless you slap a virtual Archie or Jughead smirk or the face of the dissembling character as the broadest possible indication that he or she is lying. There is no subtlety, no nuance in this medium.

Isn't the lack of subtlety and nuance a result of the comics' target audience – young kids?

No, I think it has more to do with the nature of the medium, the rotten reproduction process; even if the artist were to capture that nuance in facial expression, it would probably be lost by the time the plastic plates were stamped out.

Aren't production values so shoddy because the target audience – young kids – only has 35 cents to 50 cents to spend?

And the fact that the writers and artists only have about 35-cents' worth of imagination – and they're not paid for more than that. The system rewards quantity of output, nothing else. The fastest artist or writer is the best, the most valuable.

Anyway, even when some very good people have attempted to do subtler things, they've almost always died. The one I can point to, and take the blame for, is *Omega*. That strip was an attempt to depict a certain ambiguity about a lot of the characters and a lot of the situations that were occurring – and it fell flat on its face. Everyone, anyway *most* everyone, interpreted everything we did literally.

Comic readers have been programmed to do that, haven't they?

Oh, yeah! One of the most amazing cases of this, for me, had to do with the Howard character. In *Man-Thing* #1, I think, we showed him grabbing up a gun and firing at some demons, quacking something like, "You better watch it, you guys! I happen to be a crack shot! (ha ha)." Later, much later, we had Howard using a gun again, firing wildly, and several readers wrote in to ask, why is Howard having so much trouble handling this gun when we know from *Man-Thing* #1 that he is a crack shot!

Because you couldn't hear how the Duck spoke the line in *Man-Thing* #1, and because there wasn't enough on his face to indicate the vocal intonation – the statement was interpreted literally by an embarrassing number of readers. You can't even do an obvious bluff in a comic book without it being taken literally.

Omega was, then, a massive artistic failure and too small a financial success. The book was actually making money. The fact that they felt another book would make *more* money, combined with the fact that nobody in the editorial office liked or understood the book, contributed to its demise.

What can we expect from Steve Gerber in the future?

Expect nothing, and you won't be disappointed.

No, actually things seem to be happening too quickly to keep track of them all. I've been approach by one independent publisher already to do a limited edition comics-format book. I'm working on a nonfiction book about the comics. Mark

Evanier and I have been discussing a couple of magazine projects we'd like to do together. I'm writing some straight funny-animal comics for one publisher and having a ball at it. I've gotten the go-ahead from DC on a three-part Dr. Fate serial for *Adventure Comics*. And I still owe Marvel 20 or so pages – which will probably take the form of a "Lilith" story.

Then there's the stuff I've already written for Marvel that's yet to be published, including four issues of a *Shanna the She-Devil* color comic, and one last *Howard the Duck* story I dialogued from a fill-in plot by Mark Evanier.

What do you see yourself doing 10 years hence?

I can't answer about 10 days in the future. I don't really foresee my staying in comics much longer.

Why not?

Several reasons, actually. The limitations of the medium, as we discussed, is one. I think my work already – this has nothing to do with the quality of it, only with the nature of what I'm trying to do, I don't want to get too self-congratulatory – it's already – the balloon is about to burst in terms of how much further the medium can be stretched. If I ever wanted to do the stories that Howard is currently appearing in, but without a duck, there would be no way to do them in comics.

That's very discouraging.

It is. Unless I was willing to put someone with long underwear in the lead. That would be the only other way of doing the stories. I'm trying hard to avoid sounding pretentious, folks. My artistic expansion can't be contained by this medium any longer.

How pretentious!

How pretentious. I agree. Y'know, it's just a matter of enlarging the scope of the subject matter, regardless of how good the material is. Comics just cannot contain it. Another factor, and at this point I'm willing to be absolutely frank about it, I don't like the way business is conducted in this industry.

In what way? Can you elucidate?

Yeah. There's very little in writing. Very few people are willing to live up to their promises even when they *are* made in writing. Because of the publishers' – publishers', that's plural – because of that lack of courage Paul Levitz talked about in his interview and their unwillingness to try new formats which could be, ultimately, financially more beneficial to them, the pay scale is going to remain at peon level. A person could do, at this point, virtually the same kind of material they're writing for Saturday morning TV and literally earn three times the money. And as crass as that may sound, it is a consideration. The really silly nature of the business – I don't like the way that professionals have been treated in this industry, what I've seen over the past five or six years.

How have professionals been treated poorly?

Well, Paul Levitz brought this up, too, in his discussion of the GACBAE – the Great American Comic Book Exhibition – that never came off. There is really a kind of cloying paternalism interlaced with an essential plantation mentality, but it's so stifling…

Whoa! A cloying paternalism interlaced with a plantation mentality?

Yeah. I mean, I don't need a surrogate father. I don't want to be strung up by the wrists and whipped until I confess I'm not Steve Gerber, but that my name is really Toby. I don't need this. But essentially, that's the way it works. You're told to work for the good of the company, and then when the company returns your favors in less than honorable ways, you're expected to smile and take it like a good nigger, because essentially, they feel they own you, there's nowhere else for you to go.

What disgusts me even more, though, is that I think the writers and artists have largely brought this on themselves. They don't want to know about the business end of comics. They prefer to remain ignorant. They've allowed the publishers to convince them that they're a bunch of no-talent bums surviving on the goodwill of the companies. Very few people in this industry really believe that their work has any artistic merit, or that it's salable elsewhere. Or that they deserve more than they're getting. You will actually hear them defend the publishers' ownership of their creations, the low page rates, the cowardice of the companies to explore new markets. That's why it's startling when someone like Gil Kane or Neal Adams or Don McGregor or Barry Smith – or Steve Gerber – shoots his mouth off. People in the industry find it disturbing that one of their number might actually take his work seriously, take pride not only in being fast and dependable, but in the work itself. They're so completely brainwashed into thinking they're creating throwaway culture…!

Is it different in other media?

Yes, it is. Certain things are, certain things are very, very different in other media. I'm not saying that there isn't as much dirty dealing in the movies or television or book publishing or magazine publishing, because there certainly is. But there are also more buffers. There's a Writer's Guild. There are agents. There are lawyers. There's a classic story about one publisher who refused to negotiate a contract with a writer, because the writer dared to bring his lawyer into the publisher's office.

This is in comic books?

This is in comic books. I won't say which publisher. I won't say when it happened. But it's true. The publisher was so outraged that the writer couldn't accept the company's word, that he felt he had to have a lawyer, that the contract could not be discussed. Actually true. This would be so outrageous in television or film that nobody would even believe it. It's almost beyond the imagination of people who work in other fields of entertainment.

Do you think that will ever change in the comics industry?

I don't know. It won't change until the nickel-and-dime mentality of the publishers changes.

What about independent publishers? Do you think there is any hope there?

I think that may be the only hope. But magazine distribution, as Gil Kane told you, and he's correct about this, is so difficult, and there are so many influences of savory and unsavory kinds operating in it, that unless the venture is backed with a lot of money and an already established name, chances are very, very slim. Not hopeless, but slim.

Jesus, this all sounds so miserable.

It is! And yet, at the same time, there are ways all of these things could be circumvented. There are people with large amounts of money who might be willing to invest in a magazine of this kind. And who might be willing to do it on the basis of the demonstrated success of *Heavy Metal*.

Where are they?

That would be telling. But there are people who have no interest in controlling the editorial matter, who simply want to get into it as an investment. These people exist. Could it compete with Marvel or DC? You betcha. You betcha. It really could on a large scale. All it takes now is the bankroll. Marvel is losing a lot of their talent to some very ratty publications just because they're offering more money.

What ratty publications are these?

Oh, let's not mention names. They're spin-offs of the various skin magazines. That sort of thing. But when an artist is suddenly offered $600 a page, which is comparable to what he could earn in advertising…

He's not going to be drawing *Marvel Two-In-One* for long.

Not really. He's not going to worry about whether he wants to draw *Marvel Two-In-One*, if that's been his life's ambition. It's just not enough to make somebody stick around anymore. But that's what the companies have fed off since the early '60s – the fan mentality. I was tempted to say "psychosis." Many of them, the artists and writers, are still up there solely because it's always been their ambition to write or draw whatever characters – Spider-Man or Dr. Strange, or whatever it may be.

What do you mean by the fan mentality?

Again, Gil did a nice job of outlining this for you. First of all, it's a result of most of the current comics professionals – the third generation, as they call it in rock music – now having been raised almost exclusively on comic books, not looking very far afield for new stimulation. So they're still reacting to the books and the publishing business as comics fans. The publishers love this! It allows them to think of their eight-to-14-year-old audience and their employees as one group… Even I've lapsed into the habit of calling the Marvel editorial staff "the kids at the office."

Actually, though, it has both desirable and undesirable elements, both artistically and financially. On the one hand, you need dedicated people, people who enjoy what they're doing, if you're going to produce material of any quality at all. Quality is another word I don't like to use very much. I mentioned in a letters column that it sees more appropriate to apply that word to meat rather than art. Let's say work of merit, rather than quality.

I'm not sure I understand the difference.

"Quality" assumes an objective scale for judging a comic book. "Merit" is a purely subjective judgment. We can discuss the quality of the printing and paper, but not the story matter.

Isn't artistic or literary merit difficult to define?

Yeah, absolutely. But the one thing that's certain is that given a bunch of hacks in the office – were that to be the situation, I don't think it is – any literary or artistic merit in any of the books would be purely accidental. Dedicated personnel is the positive side of the fan mentality.

But dedication to comic books – a total immersion in them – can produce some pretty weird side effects. You can't read that stuff, extensively and exclusively for many years, without absorbing some of its explicit and implicit assumptions about the way the world operates. And that's going to be reflected in the stories, too. Writers write about what they know, and hat many of these people know, is comic books. It's an artistic cul-de-sac.

Then, there's the consistency bug. They're likely to become more obsessed with whether Thor's polka dots are arranged correctly in one panel than about the literary or artistic values of an entire story. I have seen this happen, not with Thor's polka dots, but with other things. There's a sequence in an old "*Our Gang*" film that has Alfalfa arguing with, I believe, Porky, and the dialogue consists of: "Flash Gordon is too stronger'n Tarzan." "No, Tarzan is stronger'n Flash Gordon." On and on, interminably. Sadly, this about the level of much of the conversation day-to-day at the Marvel offices.

The fan mentality also produces an extreme resistance to change. They are resistant to any kind of expansion of the medium. The Kiss project was viewed with horror around the office for a long time. It was felt to be a pollution of the Marvel mythos. As was the Superman/Spider-Man book, which was one of the most ingenious ideas I have ever seen – regardless of how well it was carried off, and

I think it could have been much, much better. But it was a stroke of genius both in terms of marketing and in terms of just an event. People were tearing their hair out over that. A certain amount of it is jealousy.

You mean just because of the DC character?

Yeah, right, because of the DC character crossing over into the Marvel Universe, or vice versa. That was the major objection to it. The other, unstated, reason was that a current Marvel writer was not scripting it, or co-scripting it. Similar objections were not heard over at DC. The third was that each individual himself was not writing it. At the same time they were bemoaning the idiocy of the project, there was a mad scramble to get their names on it, somehow – consulting this, advisor that. It was pathetic. Funny, but pathetic. As I said, there's a lot of petty jealousy in this business, much more than I would like to see.

It becomes a sad little contest. Who is the most popular, who is getting the best fan mail, who got the interview spot in this month's *Comics Journal*, who got quoted in the *New York Times*. Certain assignments take on a prestige that others supposedly don't. It's some sort of honor to be writing *Spider-Man* or the *Hulk* or the *Fantastic Four*. That's status. They don't *pay* any more for writing those books, but that's status.

The big sellers, the major books, are rarely fought over, though. There's never much argument over who's writing the FF on a given month. It's whoever Stan or Shooter have decided will write it. Seeing as those four or five books – plus *Conan*, which no one else ever writes – are beyond question until the anointed writer vacates, all the other books become targets. It's amazing. There are several writers at Marvel who are known, through political maneuvering, to leap onto a book that's doing well in sales or is a fan favorite and abandon ship at the first sign of a drop. So they're never around to take the flak when the book goes under. This happens constantly.

You will hear people say – I'm picking this character out of thin air; I don't want anyone to assume it's a special case – "I deserve to write *Dr. Strange*" or "I deserve to write *The Defenders*," or that sort of thing. I got to the point where I was ready to say, "Well, listen, if you feel that strongly about it, you probably do."

It's incredible what goes on. Every time a book comes along whose success they can't explain – and we all know which book we're discussing now – the place is in an uproar about who could do it better. No – who could do it *right*. There have been people who have been trying to get their hands on *Howard the Duck* for I don't know how long. They will mark this down to paranoia on my part. It is not.

Frankly... no, no, I better not mention names. When I lost all those other books at Marvel – *The Defenders*, "Guardians of the Galaxy," the whole complement of books I was doing besides *Howard*, back at the time when *Howard* was just getting started – if there had been a way to take the Duck away from me, they would have. But it would have been a serious public relations problem. Who would've believed that I'd given up the Duck to concentrate on… whatever. That's the usual Bullpen Bulletins drivel that's handed out. The Ministry of Information version of history.

As I said, I'm accused of rampant paranoia, of being crazy. I don't know how many times I've heard the words unreliable, undependable, lunatic, latent berserker, all of these things applied to me. They all think I'm Travis Bickle for some reason. Maybe it's the *Man-Thing* stories. Well, nothing could be further from the truth. I'm sweet. I'm gentle. *And if you don't print that I'll kill you!*

No, no. People like to create stories about me more than some others. I don't know why. I find a lot of it amusing. It wasn't until recently, since moving to California and talking to people out here, that I became aware of the extent of the legend. I found out that people at Marvel were physically afraid of me. I am so gentle, I don't understand why. If I see a cute little animal caught in a trap in a forest, I will immediately stomp its head to put it out of its misery. [laughter] These are all jokes. There has never been a physical incident between me and anybody in that office, ever. I don't understand where these stories come from. But everyone I met out here acted peculiarly toward me at first – as if they had expected to meet something else, like whatever knew fear would burn at Gerber's touch, that I was this mindless, shambling creature, capable only of reacting, not acting. Bizarre, really bizarre. If Don McGregor were six inches taller, they probably would have feared him in the same way. I don't know. When I first heard about it, I was in hysterics, laughing. I couldn't believe it. It's a source of great amusement to me.

A lot of the time I think, seriously now, that comics people are unable to conceive of anger taking any other form than a punch in the mouth. Which is essentially the way that emotion is expressed in comic books. That expectation has been internalized in these people. I mean, when was the last time you saw Spider-Man go to a lawyer to sue J. Jonah Jameson for libel?

God, the material you're getting out of me!

Yeah, this will be a juicy one, all right.

Really. Really. Do I get approval of any of this before it goes out?

Yeah, I'll send you a copy.

No, no, wait a minute! Oh, all right, print it. Who the hell cares? Other people's work is out there just as mine is, and it's open to criticism from all comers. But launching personal attacks is another question entirely. I don't think I've done that.

People are very sensitive to criticism.

Oh, yes. Actually, except when I'm feeling very insecure, I'm less touchy about that than most people. I find the criticism very useful. And I've always done my own letters pages for that reason. I like to read all the mail that comes in, particularly on a book like *Howard*, where I was very deeply concerned with the subject matter. About the only kind of criticism I can't listen to is the variety that tells you something you're doing should be more like something else. Virtually anything else I'm open to and eager to discuss, whether it comes from fans or from people in the business.

I think that it would be impossible to maintain a consistently high level month after month.

It *is* impossible. We're human beings.

Denny O'Neil once told me that 20 percent of his scripts he's proud of, 50 percent fall into the level of mediocrity, and 20 percent he doesn't want to think about. I'm not sure if I've quoted the percentages correctly, but it struck me as a realistic view of a working professional.

It's probably like that for me, too. I would consider myself unusually fortunate in the fact that of the *Howard the Duck* series, I think there are more than 20 percent of the scripts that I'm proud of. But it's true. I've written a lot of tripe. So has everybody. I'm not excusing it. Again, particularly given the quantity of material a comic writer has to turn out to make a living, it's amazing that more of it isn't crap. Or is that possible?

TCJ

marv

wolfman

COMING UP
THE HARD WAY

INTERVIEW BY KIM THOMPSON AND HEIDI MACDONALD WITH GARY GROTH: Marv Wolfman has fashioned a long career for himself in comics through a knack for character creation and the ability to write books for companies that move against the grain of their previously published output. A comics fan growing up, he broke into the field in the late 1960s. He moved to Marvel in 1974 and worked as both a writer and editor; he was one of several writers to hold the editor-in-chief position between Stan Lee and Jim Shooter. Although Wolfman enjoyed a number of fruitful runs on top characters at both Marvel and DC, the work that is most fondly remembered is the horror title *Tomb of Dracula* and his revamp of second-tier superhero book *The Teen Titans*, signature American mainstream comic books of the 1970s and 1980s, respectively. Among the characters Wolfman created or co-created are Nova, Blade, Raven, Starfire, Cyborg and many enduring *Teen Titans* villains. Wolfman penned the *Crisis on Infinite Earths* miniseries, DC Comics' attempt at a must-read "event" combined with an in-story clean-up of the company's complicated and convoluted history. It would prove to be the blueprint for any number of major efforts to come from both Marvel and DC. Wolfman has since gone on to write for television, and has kept his hand in with the occasional comics-related project. In 2000, Wolfman lost a two-year battle to Marvel over ownership of the Blade and Deacon Frost characters, the protagonist and antagonist in the first *Blade* movie.

The following interviews, the first a portion of a longer piece with Kim Thompson (TCJ #44, February, 1978) and the second with Gary Groth and Heidi MacDonald (from part two of a two-part interview in TCJ #80, March, 1983), finds Wolfman on either side of the runaway success with the *Teen Titans* book. The first interview includes honest dialogue about the realities of the shrinking late-1970s comics market and a young writer's struggle to remain consistent in that system. The second interview is a textbook example of a discussion about a direct market darling superhero book.

Writer: Marv Wolfman Artists: Gene Colon & Tom Palmer *Tomb of Dracula* #44 May 1976 [©1976 Marvel Comics Group]

INTERVIEW I

KIM THOMPSON: I have seen from you spectacularly good material and absolutely terrible material, and the divergence annoys me, because it indicates that you are capable attaining a much higher level than you are currently reaching.

MARV WOLFMAN: OK. All I can say is, I write *Tomb of Dracula* for a very different audience than I write *Nova*. I write *Nova* at about the youngest age level Marvel has. I did not intend it for an older audience. Right or wrong, it's not intended for that particular audience. I write *Tomb of Dracula* for a slightly different audience than I now write *Spider-Man*. *Fantastic Four* may be on a closer level to the *Tomb of Dracula* as far as writing a slightly – you know, that kind of storyline, because of the way the *Fantastic Four* has always been. I don't think that my *Spider-Man* sounds anything like *Nova*; in fact, a lot of people didn't want me to write *Spider-Man*, because when people saw *Nova*, they thought I couldn't write *Spider-Man*. The same people now like the book.

I don't think that a book that is written for a younger reader cannot be read by an older reader; I don't think you have to disqualify the older ages just because you're aiming at a younger audience.

I agree with you. There was a middle ground with *Nova*, beginning with about issue four, and it lasted about a year and a half, then I totally lost the character. There are reasons for that, totally unimportant to what we are discussing. I could go into problems you have with the book, on characters; the Marvel staff knew that because I'd constantly be picking brains to find out what I was doing wrong on the book. I knew what I intended on the first issues; I totally lost it. And I agree that you can make a book work on both levels.

***Spider-Man* certainly did.**

The structure – I'm a very structural writer, because I'm not a very good dialogue man – the structure of the *Nova* series is not nearly as detailed or as complicated or as resolved as my other material because I was specifically going for a different audience.

The artists you work with have a lot to do with it. With Gene Colan, you can play on the facial expressions, so what happens within two issues, the *Dracula* book was very heavily an emotional book, because I finally was able to find an artist who was able to do that. It's the type of material I enjoy writing. I like writing character studies, character pieces. Now, Sal Buscema is an action artist; I could not get strong facial characterization that I felt worked. So the *Nova* book stayed clear of that. That was a mistake, and I knew it was a mistake, but because I could not get what I wanted, I did a different type of storyline; consequently, the material was not as good as it should have been. I think the stories have started to pick up – very slowly – it's getting better, now with Carmine's art, because Carmine does better facial expressions.

Why are you dropping [*Tomb of*] *Dracula*?

Very simply, Gene Colan dropped it the other day – he wants to be put on various different books. He's been on *Dracula* now for seven years, he would like to be put on, I guess, more what he feels are high-prestige books. He feels that in many ways the *Dracula* books don't give him the prestige he feels he wants. For various reasons. He also feels that he's a little bit tired of it, after seven years of drawing it, and would like to go on to something else. He's asked to take over *The Hulk* and *Starlord*, but I don't know if that will happen...

So Gene asked to get off the *Dracula* book, to get off *Howard*, get off everything he is currently working on. Now we went through this once before, about three years ago, and quite frankly, at this particular time, in my own life, I just decided I didn't feel like fighting. I tried to convince him; I'm sure I could have convinced the Marvel staff to insist that Gene Colan draw *Dracula*. But I've never believed in that. As an editor, if an artist was tired of a book, he went off it, whether or not he was best suited. You're dealing with people. I didn't feel like having major fights because I have an incredible respect for Gene's talent. When I spoke with him and tried briefly to convince him otherwise, he said he just felt tired. You can't argue with that. He's been on the book month after month for seven years.

And it is an absolutely astounding run.

Yes, we reached several major records with that particular book. It was the longest-running mystery series in the history of comics, longest-running artist, writer and inker team in the history of comics, as far as I know – certainly at Marvel, let me put it that way. We were almost at the point of beating Stan and Jack on the *FF*; about two more years and we would have done it. If we were monthly, we would have done it by now, or come very close, because Jack lasted I think 103 issues. And we've been bimonthly for the last year and a half and so... But another two years and we would have beat their record. And since Tom [Palmer] and I are absolute fans of the book, neither one of us would have gotten off. Up until now, because of Gene's desire, we could have made it.

I think it's an absolutely astounding book, and I enjoyed reading it from the time you took over 'til now.

Thank you. I'm very sorry to get off it; I won't do the book with anyone else, it would break the feel of the book, and quite frankly, though I have a great respect for a number of artists, and would love to work with an awful lot of them, I don't think any one of them is right for *Dracula*. Then again, I wouldn't put Gene Colan on *Spider-Man*, because as much as I respect Gene's material...

I heard there were plans to cancel *Tomb of Dracula*.

When I walked in and told them that 72 will my last issue, what I did was plot the last two issues, and send it off to Gene, and then announce that those would be the last two, because Gene agreed to stick on 'til the end of the storyline, however long that would be. When I spoke with Jim [Shooter], Jim said, if that's the case, he'd try to push to cancel it. I would never have considered that, quite frankly. I appreciate it greatly. I've only done that once: we did that with the last issue of *Man-Thing*.

Oh, that's why it got canceled?

Yeah, it was gonna be continued, we had bought the next issue, by Steve Skeates, and it would have been continued for three more months, then it would have been canceled, because the book wasn't doing well, but it was supposed to be canceled with whatever number, I don't remember, and we just decided to leave it with Steve's last, rather than wait a couple of issues and bring down the quality.

Not to detract from this artistic integrity displayed by the higher-ups, but both books were pretty low sellers, weren't they?

Not *Dracula*. *Dracula* reached a low, but every book did. There were incredibly bad sales, but then again, at the worst sales of that run, we did not fall below *Spider-Man*. But that was last winter. *Dracula* has not been as popular as it was, but the sales were respectable enough not to be canceled. In fact, when we went bimonthly, we had to fight to get it made bimonthly because the sales were good enough to keep it monthly. It's one of those situations, as soon as a book is bimonthly, I mentioned to somebody, "Well, I think this is gonna kill it," because the book is aimed as a monthly book and could not survive as a bimonthly title. The types of storylines that I do in it prevent the bimonthly approach. I tried to change it around so it would work bimonthly, but it doesn't. Not only that, but ever since we went down to 17 pages, I think the book has started to suffer.

I think just about all the books suffered from the reduced size.

Yes, tremendously. *Dracula* more than most because the subplotting was so vital to the book. You can get away without subplots in a lot of books, and have a lot of fun, but in the *Dracula* book, the plotting was the structure of the book and the action was there just to keep the younger readership still in.

There were certain points where the subplots would be two panels, continued next issue. At one point, I was thinking of doing a parody, having four [consecutive] issues of *Tomb of Dracula*, four covers of *Tomb of Dracula*, like a stop-motion picture, two seconds apart...

You could have done that. That's not because I wanted it to be two panels, but because every time we got to it, there was less and less pages and it took the 17 pages for me to realize you couldn't do it that way and I had to come up with a totally new concept as to how to handle the book which wasn't as strong, but which wasn't, I think, as bad as it could have been under the situation.

The circumstances were really terrible.

Yeah. I'm very pleased with the run on *Dracula*; I think that the next couple of issues, I think the last four issues are about the best four issues I've done. Issue #69 has probably the most horrifying story I've ever written, as far as I'm concerned, just a very, very nice story. I liked it.

I'd like to interject here: How does the Code feel about your *Tomb of Dracula* series? Did you have any problems?

Ohhhh… every issue. I have not had an issue, almost, go by, since I introduced Domini into the storyline that I haven't been censored by the Code in one fashion or another. The entire "Dracula-speaking-to-the-Christ-painting," there is not one line of copy in any of those pictures of Dracula and the painting, that was what I wrote. I did all the rewriting, but that is not the initial copy.

The relettering is often noticeable.

Yeah. Sometimes we'd get someone like Jim Novak or an Annette Kawecki, who could mimic the other letterer – they were correcting it – but more often than not it was somebody who did not take the patience to imitate John Costanza's lettering, but there was not one single balloon that went through as written originally. And not that anything was in there that should have been censored; every single one of them was Dracula realizing as he's speaking to the picture of the Christ that he's losing and that he was being defeated and that there's no way for him to fight. And as I've tried to point out more than once to this Code, it's perfectly permissible to show Hell and Satan and damnation, but you can't show God winning.

It's a very strange double standard.

Yes, incredibly strange. We also got perhaps the best story on *Dracula* recently when about a year and a half after Domini as introduced the Code finally realized what "Domini" meant, and asked that her name be changed. We indicated at that particular point that Sorry, the character has been around for a year and a half and we're continuing it, and they said, OK. The fact that nobody up there knew that domini meant "belonging to God" and that it was a verbal pun right form the beginning, astounds me. It's part of the prayers, "domini."

But then, again, one of the strange reactions I received in speaking with Len Darvin, whom I happen to like, I just think that his job is a job that should not exist, is that I'm Jewish and he's Jewish and he's telling me that it would offend Catholics. Now one of my friends happens to be a very religious Christian and I usually checked out things with him first because my knowledge of the Christian religion is probably one step below my knowledge of Judaism, which isn't great… Anyway, he approved of everything, and I've gotten letters from priests who've agreed with what I've written. I spoke with some other religious people who are comic-book fans and they have all felt I was handling the Christian religion positively, and yet, one Jew is telling another Jew, "That's not good." I couldn't argue with him, because you couldn't point that out. It just doesn't work. It just doesn't work at all. It bugs me, 'cause I'd like to do a religious storyline and with *Dracula* I think it's vital that religion be mixed into the storyline. There's a possibility we may do one more *Dracula* as a full-color magazine; if we do, I may finally be able to do the religious storyline I've been wanting to do.

Nobody ever accused the Code of sanity.

No. But they serve a very viable purpose; but, because they've never had to deal with a book in the history of comics quite like *Tomb of Dracula* I don't think they quite understand how to handle it. The fact is that the mail on *Dracula*, I have yet to see – and I read it – more than one negative letter in the last two years. If there's one that I've missed or have forgotten, that's strange. I have not seen virtually any negative mail. The last time I got negative mail was on the issue where Janus was first introduced, just as the angel, and the only reason I got negative mail was a lot of people thought it was Christ. However, one priest wrote, realizing it wasn't Christ, because of the way he spoke, and said he appreciated it as a fantasy book. He said it wasn't a religious thing, it didn't even approach being accurate as far as a religious tome, but he appreciated the fantasy book and was not offended. So yes indeed, I got into trouble, constantly.

I just got into trouble with the *Fantastic Four* and the Comics Code because I have Doctor Doom, in issue #200, saying he's sorry he can't stick around and watch Reed Richards die. I mean, the line's only been done, maybe 200 times. "I wish I could be here as you reach your final death, but I must be elsewhere." That sort of a line.

"… so that you may escape."

Yeah. So the Code said that displayed… what was it?

Disrespect for death?

No, just an enjoyment for terror, or something like that. It was some very vague term that just… Jim Shooter called them up and said, "Wait a second; forget it." That was so stupid. Jim could possibly tell you more about it. That's the only time I've been involved with a Code problem off *Dracula*.

I think I got in the points I was primarily interested in on the other… I disagree, obviously, with the reaching a potential. I believe I try to reach my potential on most of the stuff I do. You have problems with it, but because the Dracula book is inherently more an adult book, I think that as an adult you appreciate it more. I once asked Stan if we should worry as much about it, because he got some letters on it at various points, from parents and stuff, and he said, he basically felt we didn't

have to worry about what we did that much in Dracula because most parents, looking at the title, will realize that Dracula is a vampire who kills people, so they could censor their kids right from the beginning.

I assume that when you took over *Tomb of Dracula* you didn't expect to be doing it for seven years.

Put it this way: I took it over just because I didn't want to be fired from Marvel. I'd never seen a Dracula movie, I do not read vampire stories, I have no love or care for vampires at all in the slightest. I don't write a vampire comic book. The only reason I took it over… I asked for *Doctor Strange*; I was on *Captain Marvel* at the time and did an incredibly bad issue of *Captain Marvel*.

God, yes. I remember.

The art was hideous to begin with, and even the bad stories that I wrote, [the artist] didn't follow. The story was just appalling. My lack of ability at that particular time – that was seven years ago – was horrendous. How I even got it, I don't know. I was at a party and Roy was there, and I said, "Please take me off *Captain Marvel*, I don't know what to do with the stupid thing. I'm awful on it." He said, "What do you want?" I said, "*Doctor Strange.*" Gardner Fox was on *Tomb of Dracula* and *Doctor Strange* at the time, and Roy made the comment that he wanted to see what Gardner did on *Doctor Strange* but if I'd like *Dracula*…

As I said, I never read or saw horror movies. I don't see horror movies today. I can't stomach 'em. I'm very queasy about horror; I can't stand the sight of blood at all. Really. I'm very strange. I walked out of *The Exorcist*. In fact, when I was the only one left to do a parody of it for *Crazy*, I had to go see it again, and Len Wein had to give me tranquilizers to sit through it, because I felt nauseous during the whole thing. I really cannot see horror stuff.

But I read the Stoker novel at that point, when I was told that I'd write *Dracula*

Writer: Marv Wolfman Artists: Gene Colon & Tom Palmer *Tomb of Dracula* #44 May 1976 [©1976 Marvel Comics Group] and I had no other choice. I fell in love with it. I had never read the book previous to that; I only knew Dracula from the knowledge of him – without ever having seen a movie of him, you know who the character is. Christopher Lee had never seen the previous [movie] and he knew it. Naturally, the first thing I was assigned to do at Marvel when the [black-and-white] magazines came, was to write a review of all the movies. I explained to Roy that I had never seen them, but I still had to do it, and I did it, which is a story in itself. But that's how I got involved with *Dracula*, simply to keep my job at Marvel. I had no other work at that particular point and I had just been married, so I needed a book and I read the novel, fell in love with the novel, and it's still, to this day, virtually my only basis. I've seen the two Dracula plays recently, because I happen to be a Frank Langella fan, and Bob Hall, who co-produced, gave me tickets to see the other Dracula play, *The Passion of Dracula*, and it was very nice. He told me, when we went out to dinner afterward, that he used *Tomb of Dracula* as the character inspiration. So it was a very strange thing. But my only interest for the character is based on Stoker's novel, which I think is just great. Because it's a novel told – I don't know if you've ever read it.

I read Roy Thomas and Dick Giordano's adaptation of the book, and part of the novel.

Ah. As you know, it's told solely through diaries, and what I instantly appreciated by it was the fact that the *Dracula* book did not feature Dracula that much. It basically was a book about people and how they reacted to evil, and that's basically what I was interested in. If there was any sort of background in the occult that I had, it was that I enjoyed *Paradise Lost*, which is one of the same sort of situations since that has to do with Satan – Milton's *Paradise Lost*. I read that in college, and, you know, boingg! Just beautiful writing, I had no expectation that *Dracula* would last two weeks, let alone outlast every Marvel horror book. But I think that's only because I'm not a horror fan.

Steve Gerber claims he hates horror.

I could believe it.

Maybe the best horror writers are those who don't like horror.

Most likely. Steve was not writing a horror book either, he was writing a people book, he was writing a story about all the people the Man-Thing met; in fact, the only difference – the reason I say Steve's not a good comic-book writer but he's a good writer is that commercially, he did not make use of the star of the book, whereas commercially, I did make use of the star of the book. I'm not as good a writer as Steve, but I think I have a better commercial instinct for comic books. I could not be as good a novelist – Steve could write circles around me; he could write circles around almost everyone in comics, but again, he's one of those who I'm really sorry is no longer doing comic books, but I can't wait to see his "real" writing, where he doesn't have to disguise it in the terms of a character or a duck, or anything else, just be him.

He says the same thing.

Oh, yeah, I think it's the best thing for him. I wish that it had come when he was a little better off, financially. You know, he had been down to very few books. I wish it had come when he was writing an awful lot of books so he would have had a better bank balance, but at least now he's not gonna have anyone really tampering with his work as far as trying to reach a mass market. I think he'll reach it because he'll be writing something that people will be interested in. Not have to deal with the little kids who are both the bane and strength of comic books all at the same time. [*Laughter.*]

I wanted to comment on his comment; I looked through his interview.

I expected you might want to.

I agreed with everything he said as far as I'm concerned, I agreed with virtually everything he said as far as Marvel and everything he said about the books. I agree with [his comments on] *Nova*; he liked it in the beginning. I liked it – I think I'm getting back now, just on the books plotted, to what I had started to do. So I agree. He fell into the same trap that most people do – he believed those little promo pieces. I never intended *Nova* to be the next *Spider-Man*. I just intended to have the fun I enjoyed in *Spider-Man*. But I agree with him saying it was lost very quickly.

As far as the duck goes, there was such an anti-Gerber reaction on the strip because it began with very healthy sales for a strip as far out as *Howard the Duck*; it was in about 80 newspapers, they were making good money at that point, Steve and Gene were doing quite well. Because of the type of storyline he was giving, they lost an awful lot of newspapers; Steve's stuff is far too intellectual for the *Podunk Times*.

I was told that part of the reason they were losing so many papers is that they were so late.

Well, that's the other thing. There were two reasons; at least, that's what I was told by the syndicate. One, that nobody understood the stories – now, that doesn't mean that people reading the newspaper didn't understand the stories, but that the *editors* didn't understand the stories, and they're the ones who buy the strip. They were getting an awful lot of bad reaction on the storylines. The second thing is, they were six days ahead of print date. The *New York Post* and a couple other people were getting the strip by some sort of a machine – you put it in on one end and it comes out the other. That's how they were delivering it – that's how late they were. When I took over the strip, it was very, very strange: I was told on Thursday that I would take over the thing, do it as a gag strip, try and change it as much as you can, see if you can stop the tide. Now I'm not a gag writer; I can write comedy but I'm not a good setup gag man. That's a totally different talent. I figured, OK, give me a couple of days, and I'll start making up my first story. I came into the office early Friday, because I have to go someplace, and Jim Shooter says, "Come in here." I go into his office; Alan Kupperberg is sitting there. [Shooter] says, "We need three Sundays by Monday." This is on Friday afternoon. I hadn't even – now, you have to understand, you put Sunday around your story – I hadn't even come up with a story.

Alan and I did it, somehow, and it's obvious that first story suffered from both the deadline problem and the wrong handle for the strip. But we continued. During the second story I was called into Stan's office and I sauntered in. He said, "The *Duck* strip is really the worst thing I've ever seen." Very friendly. Not a condemnation, just fact. We talked. I said I was producing the best I could do on a gag strip. He said he wanted it done straight, with humor. I asked who was the boss on the strip, the syndicate or Marvel, and he said Marvel, and he asked me to make changes immediately, which is why halfway through the second story the entire tone of the strip changed.

The third story, the first done to Stan's specifications, and, by the way, the first done the way I wanted to handle the Duck, was the Clone Ranger piece which I feel is as good as anything done in the strip by Gerber. Frankly, I was glad Stan told me to make the changes because writing gags took four times as long as writing it straight.

The strip ended, then they asked us to do another month. So I had to rush out the final sequence overnight.

As for why the strip died. Well, we didn't lose any papers while I was on it – or if we did we picked up others, because the royalty statements remained pretty much the same. But I figured out at one point that Alan and I were making more than Marvel was getting. We were down to some 20-odd papers when Gerber left, and that wasn't enough money for a three-way split.

If Steve had been on time, if his stories were a bit simpler and he had taken his audience into account, I think the strip would still be around, by him. With me, if I hadn't done the gag storyline I don't think anyone would have cared if I wrote it or Steve wrote it. It's just that the gags were so bad that it made my stuff look miserable.

INTERVIEW II

HEIDI MacDONALD: I'm sure you're sick of this question, to start off...

MARV WOLFMAN: Since I haven't really been interviewed much about the Teen Titans, you can ask anything but how much money I make.

GARY GROTH: Are you serious? You haven't been interviewed much?

Not about the Titans. It's a book that's received no publicity. We are finally coming out with a poster with issue #30, but we received no advertising. We just appeared on the newsstands and that's it. And it's become a success but there's been no push either by DC or in the fan press. We've had no reviews, except for the year-end review in [*Comics Feature*] and it was one of 45 reviews. But considering the popularity of the book, I've been very surprised the book hasn't been reviewed or dissected or taken apart or ripped to shreds or praised over or anything.

I felt like it was almost virgin territory. I want to ask what you think is the main difference that sets the Titans apart from all other groups?

If there is a difference it's just in the people who are doing it. My interests are different from other writers', therefore I aim the book differently. Although everybody says it's like *The X-Men*. I don't see any similarities, and I never have. And in fact, if you go back far enough, you can say *The X-Men* was a rip-off of *The Legion of Super-Heroes*, and the Legion was a rip-off of the Boy Commandos or the Young Allies; it goes right back to the past. I'm sure there were a bunch of teenage Greek Gods running around, too. I think it's just the interests that George and I have that make the book different.

The heroes, as with any superheroes that exist today, are fairly straightforward. There's no intrinsic difference between Raven and Mr. Fantastic [*Laughter*] in the sense that they are hero characters. What makes them different is the attitude that we take with the character, that we bring to each specific person. The way I handle the Teen Titans would be very different than if, say, Roy Thomas had written the same book and created the same characters.

So it's just you and George [Pérez], there's no real thematic difference?

Again, the thematic difference is something that is imposed on us by the title. Originally, we had talked about dropping the word Teen and making it The Titans, but the fact that we couldn't because Neal Adams had a trademark or something on the word Titans by itself forced us to use them as teenagers. And that is the strength of the book now—they are now teens. The X-Men are all adults now. With the Legion, it's never mattered one way or the other what age they are. But the Titans has been played very strongly on the fact that they are teenagers.

With the X-Men meeting in *X-Men/Titans* , there were so many differences…

And I think there was room for even more differences. And when George and I do ours next year, Christmas '83, we will try to bring our sensibilities to bear on the team-up.

Did you have any input on the current one?

Yeah. I had a little bit, I suggested the Terminator and just a couple of minor things. They plotted the story. We were just trying to figure our how to get a Titans villains in there, and we went out to lunch one day and talked about it. Technically, we really can't do too much mingling on these books so it was just sort of a friendly conversation. I was getting phone calls regularly from Chris

[Claremont] and Walt [Simonson] to answer questions like "would the Titans do this?" "how would they react to that?" "what would they be wearing here?"

Were you surprised to see your characters handled by someone else?

No. I've been in the business now for 15 years, and that sort of thing doesn't bother me as long as they are handled correctly. Some of the dialogue wasn't the way I'd write it. Starfire did not sound at all like Starfire. She was the most different, strangely enough because Chris likes writing macho women, and I think he failed on that particular one. But I understand that there are differences and I'm sure there are going to be differences when I handle the X-Men characters, because I see the X-Men the way it *seems* to be to me, rather than the way Chris writes it.

It's difficult to pin down, but just how old are the Teen Titans?

Let's see, Changeling's 16; Terra is 15 turning 16; Raven, oh, boy, I have this written down; Cyborg and Robin are 18, and the others I believe are 17. No, I'm sorry, Wonder Girl and Cyborg are 19.

In some ways it's really kind of hard to believe that they are kids.

It depends. I've seen some teenagers who you would never know. I mean you look at the Playmates in *Playboy* and they're 19, and they look older than the Teen Titans.

[*Groth*] Depressing, isn't it?

Yeah. [*Laughter.*] I used to look forward to being that age so I could meet them. Now, they're half my age. And I cry. My time has passed; I have to wait for the geriatric version.

I don't know, the Titans all seem about 20 to me.

The differences between the ages 18 and say, 25, are pretty nebulous, I'd say. Kid Flash is obviously younger even though he's the same age as some of the others. Robin because of his background thinks differently, he's more logical. Wonder Girl, who's my favorite character, was raised in the best situation and therefore probably has the personality and the wherewithal and understanding of herself that a far older person would have. Which is why her boyfriend is 10 years older than she is.

[*Groth*] Hasn't Robin been in college for about 10 years?

Oh, yeah, I'm sure he has. [*Laughter.*] But then again, that's the way things age. I assume someday we'll keep mentioning that they have birthdays and never refer to the fact that they are 19, 21, 22. But that will come with time.

They can stay within that nebulous region.

Especially if they drop in and out of college for awhile. They could be in college forever.

Writer: Marv Wolfman Artists: George Pérez & Romeo Tanghal *The New Teen Titans*
#20 June 1982 [©1982 DC Comics Inc.]

Well, what can you do with Robin?

Now, a lot, but not that much in the beginning. Let me rephrase that. In the very beginning I was able to do anything I wanted because I was also writing *Batman*. When I got off *Batman* and someone else was in charge of that, I couldn't do it. Gerry [Conway], however, is introducing a new character into *Batman* that will replace Dick Grayson as Batman's partner, which means I now have total control of Dick Grayson. And that allows me to do what I want. We're furthering the romance between Starfire and Robin and we're pushing the character a little bit further and taking him where I couldn't have six months ago. Where we will go with the characters is still a question. There are several places that I've outlined but George and I haven't had a chance to talk about all of them.

You don't think he'll be moaning for Batman? [*Laughter.*]

No, no. He has a very strange attitude in my mind. He was raised by Batman, taught by him, knows him, wants to be as good as the Batman and knows he never can be. Because he's not psychotic and Batman is. Batman has this mission he has to do, Robin doesn't. So no matter how hard he tries, he will never be that good. But as far as I'm concerned, he won't think too much about wanting to go back there.

I don't understand why, in the beginning of one of the issues, after they came back from Tamaran, everyone was so upset about Robin and Starfire. It seems to me the other Titans were just busybodies. [laughter]

People are gossips. I look at the way we talk up here about the risings and fallings of various people, and I assume that other friends would too. More of it would be concern for the characters and whether or not they are making the right decision, than being against it. It's very possible that Robin and Starfire are not very well suited for each other because they are very different in their thinking. Starfire is very quick to emotion and Robin tries to fight that, even though he is too.

Well, Changeling always says, "Go for it guys!" [*Laughter.*]

[*Groth*] He's young.

Well, Changeling is young, and we don't have a lot of winners in the group, which is bothersome to me, outside of Wonder Girl, Starfire – Cyborg is getting there. Changeling puts on a big pretense because he wants to be like the others. He is three years younger than Cyborg and there is a difference between 16 and 18, where there isn't much between 18 and 25. So he's pretty much a braggart about most of the stuff he says. His romantic escapades are pure fiction. The Changeling miniseries story is the only one where I go out of my way to show that what he says isn't really what happens. But that's been my attitude from the very beginning. What he's been saying for a 16-year-old kid is totally outrageous. And if it weren't for the fact that everyone knew he was just talking through his hat and that he's 16, they wouldn't put up with it.

If he's only 16, why doesn't he go to school?

He does. We haven't shown it yet. It's one of the problems of moving the stories along as quickly as we have; we haven't lingered as much. I've tried to make no story last more than three issues, usually two issues, and one of the problems has been in not showing their private life enough. At least these characters have private lives. Very often in the team books, you don't know what they do outside. We have to do a little bit more on Changeling and we have, to do a little bit more on Wonder Girl. We're starting Wonder Girl now, finally. We're moving her. In issue #30, Terry Long proposes to her and we are going to be doing some changes in her soon.

And the guy who was running Changeling's father's company seemed to be coming to Changeling for advice...

The Questor character. The father was gone and by rights, by whatever they set up, Changeling was the next one to agree to things and he didn't want to.

Well, for a 16-year-old kid...

I have to tell you, some of the stuff that we did in the very early issues I would love to forget because there were a lot of mistakes. You learn the characters as you go on, and you work out the story structure. You become more familiar with writing each character. I'd love to forget that happened. I'd love to forget that Starfire learned the language by kissing Robin. [*Laughter.*] It made things too convenient. But I don't mind that they are there, and I wouldn't edit them out, but I don't think I'll refer to a lot of that stuff ever again.

What possible rationalization is there that Changeling cannot change into a human?

The fact that the people who created Changeling said that? [*Laughter.*]

There is none?

There is none. George and I have talked about this and said that even if he could turn into a human, he'd turn into a human who was green, so unless he was becoming the Hulk, it wouldn't make much sense. We'd rather just keep it to animals, for whatever reason. He was bitten by a monkey and he was injected with this monkey juice. [*Laughter.*]

Hey, we didn't create him. The only thing I wanted to do when I used him was to change his name because I though Beast Boy was a really stupid name, and to handle the character for fun, with the underlying problems that he has, because he had this really awful origin. Every set of parents he ever had was killed. So we try to avoid that and put that away and say he only turns into animals and the larger the animal, the fewer changes he could make because it tires him out faster, but those are things that came about later.

George and I didn't think in those terms. We had him turning into dinosaurs and all sorts of things in the early issues and he keeps changing into stuff. Later on, we decided that we would only allow him to change into certain mass and at that point, if it's too large, he can't make another change for 24 hours or until he recuperates. So again, these are things you learn. All series do that. I mean, in *The X-Men*, Moira MacTaggart began as a housekeeper and now she's a doctor, so you get a complete change and it's probably better for the strip. But you have to do those things.

So Wonder Girl's your favorite character and you're going to be doing more with her?

Oh, yeah, I always intended to. The problem was that I didn't want to center on the original characters up front. I wanted readers to understand who all the new characters were before we got to Robin, Wonder Girl, and Kid Flash. Kid Flash we probably did more with because he's the character I like the least.

To get the worst out of the way first?

[*Groth*] Why is Kid Flash your least favorite?

Because if you think logically, all he has to do is see the villain and the fight's over. He moves too quickly. I like his personality very much because I like playing his middle class, Midwest personality against the others. But as far as his power goes, I don't like it.

[*Groth*] Too inconvenient?

Much too inconvenient. If used correctly, he's really too powerful.

[*Groth*] Have you thought of reducing his powers somehow?

We're going to play some games with him. Probably move him out of the book for a few months and then decide what to do with him when we bring him back. But we haven't yet decided how to handle him. And the best thing to do is to drop him for a few months in a logical fashion and fortunately the setup has been to do that anyway. And all the characters have been moving toward this one storyline. It will be about issue #40 or #41.

But the reason I played him up the most is that I tend to work harder on characters I don't like or don't feel comfortable with. When I was at Marvel, I was assigned *Fantastic Four* and *Spider-Man*, so I wanted the *FF* and didn't want *Spider-Man* and I spent all my time on *Spider-Man* until I got to like him. And I didn't care about the FF. So I was hoping by working very hard on Kid Flash, I'd be able to conquer the problems, resolve the problems I was having with the character. Unfortunately, I still haven't.

He's a very sympathetic character…

He's a good character. I like his personality. It's just that his powers are a very big problem. He just moves too fast.

Raven's powers are very vague.

Not to me. She's the empath who can cure some illnesses, some problems. She can't cure death, or any major disease. She failed when trying to cure the Russian Starfire's girlfriend. If it's small pains or hurts at least she can cure them, but it affects her. She can move through dimensions, which is the effect of teleportation.

How far can she go with that?

I would say about 100 miles. That's about it. We really haven't played with it or have her go more than 10 miles at any given point. But I'd say 100 is about the most. But it's not really teleportation, I was trying to get away from that. If Raven comes from an interdimensional place, I wanted to play on her origin. What else can she do? Her soul-self, that's the part of her that's Trigon, her father, the evil part of her, and that's also the part that's the aggressor, the one that actually stops all the villains. She's not able herself to fight. But the soul-self does most of that for her, because it has all her aggressive tendencies.

And just what happens to those people when they get inside there?

Usually they are either sent away, teleported away, or they fall down and faint, or she learns something from them.

It's not very nice in there, is it?

No. It's awful. [*Laughter.*] In fact, in issue #29, I believe, because of what happens to the Brotherhood of Evil, the character Phobia who sets up her greatest fear – she sees Kid Flash as her father and the soul-self goes after Kid Flash and virtually kills him. Raven's not very happy about that.

OK, now this question goes back to the beginning when you didn't know what you were doing.

We knew what we were doing, we just developed it further. I had all the origins worked out and I actually knew where they were going, but I didn't have the characters firmly set in mind. I didn't have any speech patterns in those early issues. I've got them all but two now – I still haven't differentiated Wonder Girl and Robin. The only difference between them is what they say, not how they say it. All the others have very specific phrasings in my mind. I hear their voices. Wonder Girl and Robin are the only two that I can't yet hear a difference.

What I meant was that Raven was crying an awful lot and it seemed like she was crying every time she turned around.

Again, early developmental characters.

And she cried recently, I think. When Starfire almost died.

I'll have to be honest, I don't recall the incident. In my mind and in George's she tries to suppress the emotions, and when she lets them come out, she releases Trigon. And that's the one thing she fears the most. So she doesn't want that at all.

Yeah, but I didn't think she'd really be crying all over the place.

Well, those are accidents. [*Laughter.*] As I said, things we'd like to forget.

And of course Trigon will come back?

Not until I find a story.

You mean you don't have it all plotted out?

No, I haven't come up with something that's worth it. I like the character so much that I don't want to do one of these endless "Let's bring back Galactus" stories. He has only appeared once as well as the miniseries — but that was a flashback. He will appear in images for awhile, but I haven worked our a story yet.

You tend to plot a long time in advance, though.

Rough plot, I should say. I know what's happening with the characters for the next year and a half, but I don't know who the villains are five issues from now. Actually, five I do, eight issues I don't.

But you know generally where they are going emotionally and so forth?

What you try to do is to create the high points and low points for each character, where they are going to be at various stages so that one person's problems actually affect somebody else's. And you're trying to milk each person's emotions the best you can. So you don't want all the characters resolving their major crisis within four issues of each other. You want to build them as sort of stepping stones and so there are a lot of high points in the series. You just don't end it at one specific point.

Just like a soap opera.

Yeah, very much.

When a soap opera goes wrong, all the plots end at once, and I saw it happen…

And that's why the cast is changed, or the writers, or whatever.

You had all the origins fleshed our from the beginning and I thought it meshed rather well.

That's from the Dracula training. The book was plotted, every story specifically, two and a half years ahead of the book ever coming our. I had complete paragraphs on everything that was going to happen in the book including all the breaks, and I'm trying to bring some of that to the Titans. I just started about a month ago to outline the next year and a half very clearly, juggling things back and forth, taking things our of this issue, moving them to that one, so that each one paces, but that took a long time to plot out correctly.

And now you're going to have a new Titan, right?

Two new Titans. Terra becomes one of them. She becomes a member in issue 30. And we'll be introducing another character, set for issue 38 or 40, but I may move him back because I've got something else I may want to do first. I indicated who the character was way back when. It's the Terminator's other son. It was mentioned only once, but that will be the other character.

Terra's obviously the youngest.

She's 15 and three-quarters. But should be turning 16, in the book.

I don't want to beat a dead horse, [*laughter*] but now that you are bringing in a young girl...

[*Groth*] Marv leers...

I know what you are going to say. [*Laughter.*]

They are going to say it's because the X-Men brought in a young girl.

I know. [*Laughter.*] I can't wait until they see what we have planned. I told Chris about this a while ago, before anyone knew we were doing Terra. "Wait until you see this, everyone's going to say 'Kitty Pryde.'" And just wait until you see, that's all I'm going to say. I'm very pleased with what we are planning with her. Chris knows, and I hope he doesn't say anything.

She was very well planned out in the beginning, and very specifically, I've been doing something for my own self. I've been leading readers for the last six, seven months to the typical comic book cliché that everyone expects, and then twisting it at the last second. Terra is one of those.

What would be another?

Honestly, I can't think at the moment, but I have like five or six of them, of leading you one way and taking you right back. Because very often, everybody assumes certain things in comics, and I'm trying to get the readers not to accept a status quo on the book. I have a very short attention span, so to keep myself interested, I have to keep playing games, and this is one of my little games to keep up my interest, and I think it will keep up the readers too. It will be revealed what happens to Terra about seven months after she finally is made a member. And I hope everyone accuses me of ripping off Kitty Pryde. [*Laughter.*] Oh boy, do I hope it! [*Laughter.*]

Getting back to killing off old characters, you didn't have the guts to kill off Komand'r. [*Laughter.*]

No, I didn't. I like her. It would have been simple, even obvious to make it look like we were killing her off. There were dozens of ways that we could have brought her back, but I opted to do something that was obvious in this particular case. Primarily because I didn't want anyone to think that she really was dead. Readers know that. And I want the character used at least once more. I haven't worked out the story yet. Because I don't want to do another space story within two years of the last one. But the next time she appears, it will probably be on Earth. But I never wanted her dead. Other characters will die.

And you didn't kill off Ron, the guy who fell off the U.N.?

Actually, that was a mistake, because I intended him to die.

Well, they haven't found his skeleton...

Well, we may bring him back and then kill him off to make it clear.

And also you didn't kill off Marcy.

I recognize the name but you'll have to tell me who she is.

Victor's old girlfriend.

Oh, no, she's dead. She was blessed and we saw her burial. She is pushing up daisies. [*Laughter.*] Singing the last chorus eternal. [*Laughter.*]

[*Groth*] For a second here, I thought Marv wasn't reaching his kill quota. [*Laughter.*]

You don't want to kill off everyone. I think killing off everybody is stupid, and it becomes "who are you going to kill off next?" I don't want the big Titans epic to be "Who in the Titans is going to die?" I would like it to be based on something else.

But isn't it just a cop-out? If they are not really dead, why not show that they aren't?

I thought by saying that they didn't find her body that you'd know Komand'r wasn't really dead. There are a lot of ways to artificially boost sales in comics today because the fans seem to want to buy everything.

[*Groth*] Is that why you think Marvel is doing it?

I think that's one of the reasons.

[*Groth*] Which characters are you talking about specifically?

I'm thinking of all the publicity they gave Ka-Zar, and the fact that he wasn't dead, that they were actually thinking of doing it. You can do double-sized issues as opposed to two issues of the regular comic.

And so far we've avoided that. We will have one double-sized issue and that's it. And that's issue 50. We've waited an awful long time. Considering that everybody in the office would love to have us do as many as we can... they would love to have us go double-sized every month, because the Titans sells that well. But neither George nor I want to do that. And we don't want to kill off every character. There are things you can do other than killing off characters. I resented Chris killing off Rachel Van Helsing for no apparent reason. I resented half a dozen deaths over there, for no purpose other than to kill off a character because "I didn't like them," whoever that "I" is. Or "we want better sales." My view is that you can use a lot of these characters and if you can't make them work, find other ways. But you can, indeed, kill them, when they absolutely have to be. If that's the only place you can go.

But, let's face it; there are a lot of characters who really aren't worth the space they take up. Although a good writer can change any character.

I think so. A lot of people seem to like what we do with Robin and *The Teen Titans*, who haven't liked what's happened to Robin in other books. Not every character can be saved. We didn't bring back half the old Teen Titans because there was nothing we could do. But I don't want to indiscriminately kill off everyone. I just think that's a mistake. And I know George doesn't either.

How about those old Teen Titans? Will they just be popping up, or...?

None of the middle ground Titans will pop in and out because George and I don't like any of them. [*Laughter.*] We think that most of the characters are fairly silly.

[Groth] Which ones are you talking about?

Harlequin, and Bumblebee, and people like that.

I have one old *Teen Titans*, from '72, and it's just so embarrassing to read it. I don't know who wrote it. It doesn't have any credits on it, so they must have been pretty embarrassed too.

The one or two issues that I wrote have credits.

[*Groth*] Are these the hip, mod Teen Titans?

Yeah, every other line the black guy [Mal] says "I'm black, I'm angry, get out of here you honky." And the women all say, "Get out of here you male chauvinist pig. I'm a woman."

That's one of the things that we were trying to avoid. As far as I'm concerned, I didn't want to have Victor say "I'm black" in every story. In fact he never has. I mean, it's obvious he is, his background is from a scientist so he's not very street-oriented. None of the women go around parading for any specific cause or whatever. They act like those characters should act. And I think that's more important than whipping out machine guns and all that stuff some of the other characters do.

I'M GONNA MAKE A FORTUNE *RECYCLING* THESE INTO *LAMPS!*

IT'S REALLY A PLEASURE *MEETING* YOU. I JUST CAN'T *BELIEVE* IT.

I'M NOT SURE *WE* CAN, EITHER. JUST ONE QUESTION, THO--

--*WHO ARE YOU?*

POST NO BILLS

HI! I'M MARV!

I'M A WRITER!

HI! I'M STARFIRE!

I'M A SUPER-HERO!

YOU'RE *GORGEOUS!*

HI, GEORGE.

BUT, JUST AS MARV'S SMILE FADES INTO A QUIVERING MASS OF RED JELLO...

ZAP!

ROBIN! THEY'RE *GONE!*

SOMEHOW, STARFIRE, I DON'T FEEL ALL *TOO* BAD ABOUT THAT!

WHAT'S *HAPPENING* TO US, *GEORGE?*

CAN'T YOU *GUESS?* WITH ONLY *FOUR PANELS* LEFT TO THIS STORY...

...WE'RE RETURNING *HOME.*

AND JUST IN TIME TO WATCH *"THAT'S RIDICULOUS"* ON *TV.*

I'M GLAD YOU'RE SO *UNDERSTANDING,* FLUFFY.

IT WON'T *EVER* HAPPEN AGAIN.

MARV. GEORGE. YOU'RE *LATE* ON YOUR NEXT TITANS STORY.

NO *PROBLEM,* KAREN. I GOT AN *IDEA!*

THIS ONE'S *FAN-TASTIC!* IT'S THE GREATEST IDEA SINCE *DC* PUBLISHED *"THE GEEK!"*

DON'T *WORRY,* GUYS...

I'LL MAKE SURE HIS STORY *WORKS...*

...AS *USUAL.*

AND I HAVE TO *COLOR* HIS BOOK, SHEESH!

I TELL YOU, GEORGE. I MUST BE *BRILLIANT* TO COME UP WITH THESE STORIES. YOU HEAR ME? *BRILLIANT!*

YES, MARV. OF *COURSE,* MARV.

POOR, DELUDED *FOOL.*

DEFINITELY THE END!

5

Writer: Marv Wolfman Artists: George Pérez & Romeo Tanghal *The New Teen Titans* #20 June 1982 [©1982 DC Comics Inc.]

You said earlier that one of the reasons the Titans were different was because of you and George. Where do your interests converge on the Titans?

Amazingly, we are very similar. There has been more than one instance where George has called me up and said he has a great idea and he wants to do this and I'll say, "You're not going to believe this, I just typed it up, it's in our next plot." We have done this constantly. First of all, our interest is to produce a fun comic book. One of the interesting things in your review was that you said we're not blazing any new territory, but it's just a good comic book. That's all we ever intended to be. We're not setting the world afire as far as new concepts in panel layout or story structure. Though some of the stories within the structure ate a little bit different, like the Brother Blood sequences, things like that, in terms of using religion, or runaways or thing like that. We just want to produce a comic that is very professionally done that we have fun doing and getting involved with. We did not set our to change the whole face of the comic-book world.

[*Groth*] But where do your interests converge so that you can accomplish that?

Where they converge is that we tend to have a lot of fun. We like the characters. Virtually everything I've wanted to do with the Titans, George has wanted to do as well and vice versa. In other words, if he's just gotten in the mood to change something about a character, such as forget the fact that Wonder Girl has a magic lasso, and just make it a regular lasso. I hadn't realized that he hadn't been drawing the glow around Wonder Girl's lasso for months, he had just dropped it. And I happened to write into a plot that somebody asks Wonder Girl if her lasso was magic like Wonder Woman's. She said "no." And when George got the plot, he said, "You didn't notice that I had already done this?" and no, I hadn't. So all the character bits are very similar. We keep wanting to do the same type of stuff.

[*Groth*] A very symbiotic relationship.

Incredibly so. It's remarkable.

[*Groth*] But the two of you have vastly different backgrounds.

George is more street background and I'm very much lower-middle-class Jewish background from Brooklyn; he's from the Bronx, and in that case, we're both New Yorkers.

That's funny because his work is so idealized, and yours is more human.

I don't know, some of the best sequences in the comic in terms of human emotion are George's bits. For instance the scene that everyone comments on in issue #8, that had Cyborg and the kids, I just had him there with the kids and getting involved with them. And George came up with the little kid who picked up the ball. That was his. And it was such a human touch. George has a very very warm side to him. He's this big burly bear and everyone assumes that all he's good for is punching holes through brick walls. And he's a hell of a fun person, hysterical to be with. He says all the things I'm thinking but don't dare say. He's outgoing. I'm nervously quiet.

How about in the "Runaways" story? Was that both of you?

I tend to work, for the most part, with a fairly complete plot. You can always tell when George and I come up with a plot together, because the credit reads co-plotters. And there will be a separate credit that say co-creators. George gets the plots and does what he wants with them, takes away scenes, adds scenes. He never changes the story, but he will pace it his way, change the fight scenes around and whatever else and add what he wants. With the "Runaways" story he completely followed the plot. I don't think there was a single change. He tells me that I caught without knowing it a relative of his very closely, and it made him care about the story even more. It's the first issue of the Titans that he did full pencils, he used to do layouts on the book. And he liked the character Louis, it was very close to one of his relatives and very similar in a lot of the setup, and I was just taking it from my own talks with runaways.

I detected either restraint or constraint in that story. Did you have any Code problems with that?

No, no. We were prepared to go without the Code symbol. We submitted into the Code as we always do, and assumed that they would reject, but they didn't. The only correction they made was we misspelled a word that they spotted. I was very much surprised. Our idea was not to hit the readers over the head with the message. I don't like those type of stories. I just wanted it to be there, where you judge for yourself and make your own decisions. The only concept that I wanted to get through was letting people know about runaway shelters. Otherwise it was a fairly straight story.

Did you do a lot of research on runaways?

Yeah. Len [Wein] and I went to a runaway shelter here [in Manhattan]. They just loaded us down with material. And took the story from that point.

You did it again, the bad parents and the kids.

You know, that is a problem because it is a problem with runaways.

Yeah, even though it worked in that story…

I couldn't avoid it there. We did try to have with Louis, good parents and a bad kid. So the parents were really loving and caring, but the kid wanted freedoms that the parents in all honesty knew he wasn't ready for, as proven in the story. The parents were good there. One of the biggest problems we discovered with runaways is not kids running away, but kids being thrown out. So in the case of the girl who was pregnant, for instance, she was actually tossed out. So a throwaway is as much of a problem as a runaway. And we could not avoid the main concept, that most kids are running away because the situation at home is bad. They are not running away for fun. It's not taking to the rails like the bums.

How come you write so many issues where one of the Titans is missing?

Because it's real hard juggling seven characters. When you have the group fighting against a villain, it's seven against one. And one of the things I'm trying to do now is to break up the group so that all seven characters aren't in each issue. It gets very very hard. That's why we tend to have them fight large groups of characters, the Fearsome Five, Brotherhood of Evil, and Trigon – but he had all the superpowers. We've had to in the past, and I'm trying to avoid it by breaking up the group; there are just too many heroes and too few villains. And you can't keep blowing apart the world, so if you want smaller stories and more emphasis on characters, we have to have the group not be in force all the time.

Don't you think it upsets the readers, say, when Changeling or another character isn't there?

I'll avoid that in the future by not saying that they aren't there, as opposed to just having them show up. Or as in issue #29, you watch the characters go apart so that when it comes time for the big fight, the only ones left are Speedy, Kid Flash, and Frances Kane, and they have to defend Titans Tower by themselves.

One of the things about Titans Tower, do you suppose that if they all ran over to one side, the thing would tip over? [*Laughter.*]

It's not based on a real building but there is a building that looks like that. It's in Flushing Meadow Park. It's huge. What happened when I designed that – because I designed the Tower – I was just trying to get a double T shape, the outer shape of the building being a T and the windows forming a second T. Trying to be cute, "Teen Titans" and all that stuff. And after I drew the thing I realized that it looked like Terrace on the Park, which is in Flushing Meadow Park.

You mentioned that you did the whole story about Starfire going back to her planet by phone.

Yeah, George handled most of the plotting…

Because there were a lot of little gaps in there…

I wasn't able to tie some of the stuff together. And I think George did a phenomenal job. At that specific point, I had just taken a staff job here, I was writing my full load of comics, I was doing a special project for DC that took months to do, and two or three other problems going on all at the same time. And I found that I had instantly backed up on everything. And that's something I hate doing, because I write out long plots. As George says, my plots always have to be cut because I tend to cram 32 pages of material into them. So we worked virtually all of that over the phone, or in person, George lives about a half-mile from me. And George handled the majority of it and I think he did a phenomenal job considering the sketchy material I gave him.

It hung together very well considering.

Oh yeah. George is the only person I've ever worked with that I trust to do that. He and I think so much alike about the group, that I would never give that open feeling. I would have been there for any other artist, but for George, I knew that he would be capable of doing it. He's so strong and a good plotter. He's a perfect pacer for the material and I just love working with him.

It must be a nice feeling to be able to trust someone.

It's incredible, because I know he'll change stuff, but he has never changed anything for the worse. Very often he has changed things for the better. Sometimes he's not available and I won't know why he made a change and I'll write it based on what I think he wanted. And we seem to have some incredible sort of mind-sync on this book.

Maybe it's from living so close together?

Oh, it's very strange. The whole time we were both at Marvel we only did one story together. The *Titans* is the only time we've actually worked together. I've known George, liked George, and since become a friend of George's, but we really were not close the entire time we were at Marvel. So I just find working with him an absolute dream. And if the story didn't hold together as tightly as it might have, it's because I wasn't there all the time. George is not a writer, but he was able to take very sketchy material, like I did have the origin of that whole galaxy and X'hal all set, typed out, so he knew what I wanted there, but he did so much of that story himself that I'm just astounded that it did work that well. The mail reaction was phenomenal.

I understand all that, but the one thing that really bothered me is that when Raven has the big breakdown from all the emotions and Kid Flash rushed to her side, and you wrote that, but there wasn't a picture of him running to her side. And that would have been a very nice romantic thing.

I don't know why. It's too late. Very often when these things are being done, a lot of people will not tell you that deadlines are a major problem. We try to do the best we can. I am very happy that we can produce a book as good as it is, month after month, considering the rush deadlines that we have. The fact that we try to do even more helps. George and I and [inker] Romeo [Tanghal] are very much dedicated to the book. And one of the reasons I'm leaving staff is so I can go back to spending more time as a writer. I just spread myself a touch too thin, and I don't want to do that. George has cut down a lot of his outside commitments, he was doing an awful lot of special projects work and he's not doing that any more. He still does some Atari stuff but that's about it. We want to spend more time on the Titans, it's the book that we cared about the most when we started it. And we don't want that to drift just because it popular. You'll notice, I think, in the whole batch of stories that are coming out now, that we've really recommitted to the book. Issues 29 and 30, I'm very very pleased with.

Let's talk a little about that. Terra...

Terra becomes a member with issue #30. Strangely enough, Mike Barr and I came in with identical characters, the same day. Mike is doing a book called *The Outsiders* and I wanted a new character for the Titans, and he came up with a guy who had earth powers [Geo Force], and I came up with Terra who has earth powers. And we both came in the same day so we couldn't say who was first, and I came up with the idea of making them brother and sister. So Mike and I have cooperated to make these characters work between the two books. And Terra will be a regular character, for how long I will not say, because that ties in with some of the things we have in mind.

Where we are moving is that Wonder Girl will be getting married, and, shock of shocks, she will not be leaving the Teen Titans, and it will not affect her work in the Teen Titans. She's marrying somebody outside the team, who's not a superhero.

That's probably a first.

Probably. He will never be a superhero.

I thought he was going to be Vigilante; that was my first guess.

No, I had determined from the beginning that he would be normal and stay that way. He will not get involved with any of the crimes or anything else. But George and I both thought that we would have one of the characters get married, without any affect. Just because somebody gets married, it doesn't affect their job. And, essentially, the Teen Titans is their job. So why should it affect Wonder Girl to that extent? She does what she does, she has her photography work, and she's married. She'll be getting married in issue #50. That will be the double-sized issue. And, shock of shocks, there is not going to be a big fight at the wedding. [*Laughter.*] That's another thing we determined not to do.

Raven and Kid Flash's relationship will come to an end. It can't continue, because Raven can't give Kid Flash what he wants, ever. And it's going to change; as I said, she virtually destroys him. And at the same time, Frances Kane comes back – that's the girl with the magnetic powers – and they'll all get involved with the Brother Blood storyline for a few issues. But then Kid Flash will probably leave with Frances.

Robin has his own set of problems because of various things that are happening with the Titans that I set up, and working out at the same time in Batman so it worked out very well, introducing this new Robin character. Robin is pushing himself because he's trying to be Batman. And he's basically having a nervous breakdown. He can't work to the extent that he wants to. He can't do 12 different things. And he keeps thinking he can. How that's going to affect Koriand'r is very very important to where we are going to go.

Wonder Girl will begin the tracing of her parentage. Where we are going to go on that I don't want to say. Vic is having his own problems because he always assumes his relationship with Sara Simms is more than it is, and he meets her fiancé. He never expected that. So the characters will start moving and developing, and introducing other supporting characters. Again, we are only entering issue #30, we are very young in the history of the book.

The Fantastic Four didn't start getting really good until about issue #50. I think that since I am leaving staff and George has been cutting down, and we've been spending more time, and I've been setting down the next year and a half, two years worth of storylines, that we will actually get much better stories now, because we will be able to take a little more time on it. I've been happy with some of the last six or seven months. I haven't been happy with all of it. I don't think issue 28 is as strong as it could have been. It's too much character without enough plot mixed in. It's just a bunch of characters sitting around talking.

But that's the best kind of story there is…

But there isn't a story to go with it. Unlike issue #8, which had a story.

[*Groth*] "My Dinner With Robin." [*Laughter.*]

It just didn't work for me. Also, that was at the worst point in my schedule and I did not like my copy on it, and I did not like my pacing of the plot or anything. That's what finally got me to leave staff. I just could not do all that I wanted to.

What about Changeling?

Changeling will probably undergo the biggest change [*Laughter.*] because of what happens with Terra. We will probably be bringing back his old girlfriend. Despite the fact that I've had Changeling serious at times, I've been playing him more as a punctuation mark or point to the joke. And he's been there to serve whatever I needed for that panel. As opposed to being more realistic in a superhero vein. So we'll be making slow changes with him based on the Terra storyline. And he won't be spouting off constantly, every line won't be a Woody Allen one-liner or whatever else. We're trying to lace that with some sensibilities.

I've been meaning to ask you, you meant his humor to be terrible, I hope. [*Laughter.*]

Oh, of course. A 16-year-old kid has got to have bad humor. There are a couple of lines he's done that are good, but most of them have been pretty bad.

What's the new character going to be like? Is she going to be a tough-guy or what?

Terra? To say too much about Terra would give away too much of our plans. By the time this comes out, people will have already written in saying we ripped off Kitty Pryde, so I want them now to know before we reveal what it is.

[*Groth*] You're taking perverse pleasure in this.

Yes, I am. [*Laughter.*] I have to have fun.

You always have a lot of plotlines, there's Thia…

There's a guy up in space…

Yeah, what's going to happen to the guy in space?

What happened there… that was a mistake in that everybody else didn't pick up on it fast enough. I was creating a character for all DC to use, and I told every-body what it was, but they didn't pass it on down to their writers. So I have to reintroduce him. I want a character who's available, who's called the Monitor, who keeps track of everybody and he sells information. And any writer could use it.

You mean like The Watcher as a blackmailer?

Yeah. I had the character about 18 years ago. I called him the Librarian then because I didn't have a good sense about names and thought that it would be a neat idea to do that. You know, one villain that the whole company could use. I didn't have to sell it to Marvel, because they already had one universe, but when I came back to DC I indicated that I wanted to do it here. Everyone liked it but forgot to hand out the sheets I gave for their writers. So I have to redo it indicating how far you can take the character from month A to month B. Like for three months you can only show this much and after six months you can show that much, and at the end of a year we can reveal who that character is and start getting into interesting stories that all the writers can pick up on.

So he's going to be all around?

Oh yeah.

He's not specifically Titans?

Oh no.

One of the things that bothers me about comics is that when you have 27 guys in leotards come in they always say, "Joe is right. Tom, see what George thinks" and you solve that by just having the heads with the names underneath.

You have to occasionally do that. One of the things, the first time a character is introduced, I try to say their name, after that, I try to drop it from that point on because most people don't talk to each other using their names. The main thing that I try with my copy is never have the copy refer to what's happening in the picture. Nobody repeats what's going on in the artwork. There's no caption that says, "As Superman flies over Metropolis" and Superman saying, "I'm flying over Metropolis." That's the one rule that I have and insist that all my writers do as well. If they have copy that says what's in the picture, I take it out. The only time I write copy that explains what the picture is is when I want to convey the scene correctly.

But you save a lot of grief by doing that, because it's so simple, so nice.

But I think even in copy they would at least mention each other by name once, the first time.

One of the things that readers picked up on was when they were in the devolvo chamber Starfire turned into a cat.

And nobody noticed that Raven had four eyes. That was George's bit. As was the four eyes on Raven. They were both his. That's what I mean; he adds these little touches. And at no point has it ever not worked our.

You don't like secret identities much, do you?

I think they are useless. I love playing with Wonder Girl because she makes no pretense at hiding her secret identity, but we never talk about it. So somehow nobody has ever spotted that this is Wonder Girl. And that's okay with me.

You don't feel this burning need to have all these secret identity plots?

If you'll notice, all the characters that I created don't have secret identities. Kory, sort of, but if anyone thought twice, they'd know that she was an alien.

Why do your characters say "God" so much?

Because I do. It's a mistake.

They never say "Jeez."

Because I think "Jeez" is phony.

[Groth] You think "Jeez" is phony?

Yeah, because I'd want to go all the way and have them say "Jesus" and they wouldn't let me.

But you know what they are saying is "Jesus Christ."

Of course, but I can't get away with that. What I'm probably going to do is just cut the "God"s. One thing I can say about the Titans, and I've said this as a joke around the office about the Brother Blood stories, and that's that the Titans is finally getting as good as the readers said it was. I enjoy it, George enjoys it and we're having a hell of a lot of fun producing it. The first superhero series that I've really loved writing. It's not, to me, the world's greatest book, it's not the be all and end all of what comics should be. It's just a good fun comic book.

I would love to see a ton of comic books produced with the dedication and professionalism that we have for the most part. We're not trying to create new records in creating designs or stuff like that. We're just trying to have fun and let the readers enjoy the book. And there aren't enough books that are enjoyable to me. Three years ago I read every comic that came out and it turned my mind to mush. And I can't enjoy three quarters of the comic books any more. There are few I like, very few.

[*Groth*] Why do you think that is?

Because most of the people who have been in the business have either tended to lose the ideas after a certain amount of time. After five, six, seven years you get real tired, and most of the top professionals have been in the business 15 years, about the same length I have. If I have any strong points it's that I didn't learn what I was doing for the first six years. Other people began very good very quickly and now are just hacking it out. I didn't know what I was doing for an awful lot of those years. So I am just now coming into my prime as a comic-book writer. And I'm just learning superheroes. For the most part my reputation has been on mystery comics.

Spider-Man was the first superhero I thought I did well. *Teen Titans* is the first book that I'm really enjoying. I loved doing *Spider-Man* because it taught me an awful lot. But the *Teen Titans* is the first superhero book I'm feeling free on. And knowing what I'm doing and able to plan it, it's not all happening to me. I'm actually creating it and pacing it the way I feel it should be paced. A lot of the things I've done in the past just came crashing in on me and I didn't know how to juggle it and all I did was keep throwing all these plotlines in the air. I know where I'm going with this book. We enjoy it. And I hope that the readers do. We're enjoying it and now making a lot of money on the book, which is nice, but George and I put in all the effort before royalties so we were doing it for ourselves in this particular case and just having fun with it.

Do you ever find the characters surprising?

Raven specifically because she was the one character I didn't want to do originally. Len asked for a female mystic and I've been quoted elsewhere as saying that I came up with Raven to answer the problems. But I've never felt comfortable writing a mystic character despite the fact that I've done all these mystery books. So she surprises me. Who else? Cyborg, because every time I start having him go one direction, I realize he has a lot more depth in a different direction. We keep trying to Mickey Mouse him, in a sense. Mickey Mouse began as a troublemaker and he was made into this happy smiling character and we've been making him [Cyborg] too nice and too sweet and too happy, and we finding that he has a lot of strength pulling him back the other way now.

I sense a lot can be done with that character.

Yeah, he's a real strong character to me. Starfire hasn't got as much surprise yet, but I'm working on that. That's part of my plan to really make that character tick, and explode in my head, so that it works. The rest of them are fairly straightforward characters. Gar, as I said, I have to explore a little bit more, to make him work. And we're going to take Kid Flash our for awhile until we come up with the best way of handling him.

Break his legs or something.

When I was on *Dracula*, I removed Blade from the book. He was a character I'd created. I really liked him, he was my favorite character, but I took him our of the book for a year and half because I didn't have a way of handling him correctly and letting him grow. I have yet to figure our how to let Kid Flash grow as a character and yet keep the essential strong points of him. So we'll rake him our and when we come up with something we'll do it. He may come back for a guest appearance here and there just so people don't forget.

Seriously, how could Starfire be a model? [*Laughter.*]

That's the silly side of me. She sees nothing wrong with it.

She's just not built like one.

I guess she is a little too zaftig. She's been in jeans ads, so it's OK. She has a good rear.

That's one thing that bothers me, the standard superhero woman pretending to be a skinny model.

That's just a little bit of fun. We're poking fun at some things, and occasionally we throw in things that make absolutely no sense just for fun. The day George and I stop having fun I don't want to do it any more. When it becomes a chore, it becomes boring.

Are Starfire and Robin going to be continuing their relationship? Are they going to be fighting a lot?

Uh, no, right now... The interesting thing is that we've finally – I mean, should I say this, since the Code will see? – we had them go to bed in one of the issues. Robin couldn't do much for Starfire and he sort of feels guilty right about now.

[*Groth*] How sad.

That'll be cute. [*Laughter.*]

Yeah, he's not a teen wonder on all occasions. Robin's having his own problems trying to be Batman. And Starfire can't understand why he can't be himself. She hasn't got those problems. Whatever appeals to her. She really likes him, and she can't understand why he doesn't like himself.

Brother Blood's going to be coming back.

Yeah, I really like him. He's the strongest character I've...

He's not very nice.

He gets worse. The Terminator is coming back. The only ones I haven't got planned at the moment are the Fearsome Five, and I'll have to throw them in some issue I just have to mark time with. You wanted death. I'm thinking of killing of Dr. Light and having someone female wear his costume. Since all his powers are in his costume, anyone could wear it. Unstable molecules. It's skintight.

Is it tough to write gods?

I almost never do. You'll notice the one book at Marvel I never touched was Thor.

Well, Superman's a god.

No, I don't think of Superman that way.

I just stopped to think the other day, what would really happen if there really were superheroes.

We probably wouldn't be in the situation we are today.

These guys are gods!

You have to constantly come up with the reason why Superman doesn't end all wars. If you want to play this seriously. John Byrne and I got into a real big "argument" – not a real argument – on Superman's powers. He's trying to give all these pseudoscientific explanations, I said it was fairy dust. As far as I'm concerned, you have fun with the material. This stuff is not real. You make it as realistic as you can to give it enough for people to accept it, and you give the characters semi-real problems, because nobody has to face villains and worry about those things, so you have the human side of it, that's probably the biggest difference between comics today and comics in the '40s.

I was going to say practically everything has been done with superheroes. It's been done seven, eight, nine, 10 times.

More than that. I say that to all the tryout writers coming in on the tryout book, you're not going to show me anything that hasn't been done, so the only thing you can do is make the characters interesting. And if we try to analyze the superhero's powers, you bog yourself down in so many things that you can't make the book enjoyable. I don't care that Superman's powers are psionic, robotic, or whatever. To me, fairy dust is a good enough explanation.

He can jump high: okay, red sun. Red sun to me is fairy dust. It means nothing. But that's the explanation. Where does Batman throw his line when he's swinging through the city? There are no buildings that tall. There was one story once where he was swinging past the Empire State Building, and the line was going up. To what? The thing is for fun. I take my work seriously, but I don't take all the stories seriously. I take the stories to have fun with and to move them around. I don't believe that giant robots are going to – come down or statues are going to turn into gods or any of the other stuff, but that's where you put your superheroes, you face them against that. Then you have the fun part of the story. The part that's interesting to write is the characters, but the fun is the action. The real enjoyment is writing the character stuff.

Superman was the first superhero and he can do everything and every superhero since then can only do one thing.

It's one of my jokes about the Legion of Super-Heroes. Each character has to have one new power and I keep thinking that if I were in charge of an intergalactic police force I would want a hundred characters with superpowers. I would want a hundred Mon-Els because you could do anything. I don't want someone who can eat metal. Who cares about him, let me have a hundred Mon-Els. But those are givens and I sort of accept it. I approach the stuff with a lot of fun because I still enjoy comics as a writer if not as much as a reader, unfortunately.

TCJ

NOTES ON AN
INDUSTRY IN PROGRESS

INTERVIEW BY GARY GROTH: The writer and essayist Harlan Ellison has written few comic books, but his presence among comics writers of the 1960s, 1970s and 1980s is impossible to dismiss. Not only did he befriend several of the writers featured in this volume, he paid attention to their work and provided an example of a sometimes-scriptwriter, sometimes-prose author career that many no doubt aspired to. Ellison also cut an intriguing figure in the then-closely related field of science fiction, with a strong, forceful personality and a tendency to speak bluntly and to the point.

The following interview with Harlan Ellison by *Comics Journal* Editor Gary Groth was a milestone in comics culture. It rambles mercilessly, careening from science fiction to literature to television to movies, but does so in a way that reminds how much comics at that time struggled with an artistic identity in a period where it had become clear art wasn't highly valued in any medium. Consider it a prediction of comics' own movie boardroom dramas and outrageous behavior to come. Ellison, as a famously contentious writer and critic but one who didn't always want to apply stronger standards to comics, provided an interesting model for *and* contrast to the more demanding attitudes of comics fans who were in increasing numbers continuing to read the medium into adulthood. Comments within this interview led to a lawsuit by writer Michael Fleisher against both the interviewee and the interview's publisher. The defendants won in court, but the Ellison-Fantagraphics relationship was soured forever.

That's a lot riding on one interview. In his original introduction (TCJ #53, 1980), Groth wrote a fair introduction to Harlan Ellison the writer and fandom figure, here in part:

Harlan Ellison was born May 27, 1934 in Cleveland, Ohio. Prior to becoming a professional writer, Ellison's life was characterized by restlessness and a desire to move on, always to move on: He has worked as a tuna fisherman, an itinerant crop-picker, a hired gun for a wealthy neurotic, a dynamite truck driver, a short order cook, cab driver, lithographer, book salesman, door-to-door brush salesman, department store floor-walker, bridge-painter, porno salesman on Times Square, trash collector in Manhattan parks, singer, and stand-up comedian. Ellison attended Ohio State University in 1954-1955, was told he had no talent by his creative writing professor, and was eventually thrown out of the school. In 1957 he was drafted into the U.S. Army, escaped three courts-martial, and was honorably discharged in 1959. ... Ellison has gone on to become one of the most respected and honored writers in the SF community. He has written novels, short stories, television, and films. He has professionally reviewed films, TV, and music.

The interview begins in the middle of a discussion, featuring arguments that in many ways began early in the history of comics and continues today, even if the identity of the speakers has changed.

[As the tape begins, Ellison is discussing then-current comic book writers.]

HARLAN ELLISON: Dennis [O'Neil] has got the fatal flaw that I think is shared by many of these fellows. They pick the wrong idols. They worship at the wrong altars. When you're a kid and you pick for your idol Jonas Salk or Charles Lindbergh or Babe Ruth, then you've really got something to shoot for. When you pick for your idol Jack Kirby – I mean, as nice a man as Jack is, he's a comics artist. He's top of his profession, but it's a very rarefied kind of thing, and even Jack has finally gotten out of it, into other artistic areas. But there's a thing about your dreams when you're a kid... In some way, I don't know how, [Mike] Friedrich and Denny [O'Neil] and [Steve] Gerber and all of those guys got burned out in their brains. They worshiped the idols of childhood and never made the transition when they became adults to understand that success is having the dreams you had as a child but in adult terms. If when you were a kid you wanted to be a cowboy, you grew up and became a rancher – you don't become a cowboy. If you wanted to be Superman, you grew up and became a pro football player – I mean, that's as close as you're going to get in this life to being Superman.

Dennis is one of the nicest and finest people I've ever known – I'd like to think he's a very dear and close friend – and I really weep about it sometimes, I mean not really weep, but it makes me very sad to think about it because Denny could have been anything. Could have been anything. He's got one novel to his credit, not a good one. Dennis had the ability to really go to the top of the mountain, and you say, "Why didn't he? What the hell's he doing at Marvel, and what the hell was he doing at DC for 10 years?" I wish to Christ he were out of comics. I wish to Christ he were writing things that…

GARY GROTH: **I have a feeling he does, too.**

Yeah. I mean, he did a piece for – was it *Oui*, or *Penthouse*?

The one on Vaughn Bodé?

No… it was a piece in *New York* magazine. It was very good; he really is a fine writer. I mean, God only knows whether he'll ever be Dostoevsky, but a lot of years and a lot of visceral material has to be expended behind the typewriter before you can ever hope to be read five minutes after you're down the hole. And Dennis has spent a lot of time writing a lot of stuff that even at its best – and Dennis to my mind is the best writer that's come out of comics in the last 30 years.

The stuff he did for *Batman* in the '60s, man, the *Green Lantern/Green Arrow* stuff, was important stuff. He and Len Wein are the two best writers that I have ever read in comics. The best. Len doing *Swamp Thing* and Denny doing *Batman* and *Green Lantern*; that was heaven. That was a time to read the comics, for Chrissake – what a leaping, boundless joy. Pick up the crap today, man, I just – psheeeww. I mean, it's silly. And the best you can hope for is less silly.

Wouldn't you say that most of the writers in comics have more or less reached their proper position in life in a way?

Yeah, I suppose. That's a tragic thing. I know a lot of them.

I'm not talking about Denny. I'm talking about others.

Right. There are some guys – I mean, I have no doubt that Len Wein and Marv Wolfman will be out of that in a few years, will be into something else.

Really?

Absolutely. I think they're too good. I mean, I'm more familiar With Len's writing than with Marv's, but I recently met Marv again. I had met him briefly before, but he and Len came out to the house and hung out and shot some pool and went and had a funny dinner and all. They're lovely guys, and I think their aspirations are higher, and I think they're good hustlers. A good hustler is not going to stay in a little pond if he has access to a bigger one. They're already packaging these novels for Pocket Books, so they're in an entrepreneurial configuration, if you'll pardon the jingoism, already, and I think they're going to go on from there. I really think they're going to become less writers and more entrepreneurs of some sort. I don't know how… Time is very strange. I mean, the first time I met Gerry Conway, who the hell would've known that Gerry Conway would single-handedly ruin the entire comics industry. He's a classic example of the deification of no-talent in all industries. He's not good, but he has it in on Thursday. And that's all they care about. You know, fill them pages.

That kind of attitude seems to pervade almost all popular entertainment – television, comic books, even book publishing.

Absolutely. They've got endless hours of prime time to fill, and they don't care what they fill it with, because the drones in this country will sit and watch it, and they don't give a shit whether they're watching *The Merry Wives of Windsor* or *Charlie's Angels*; they see it all as one and the same thing. And that's one of the reasons taste in this country has almost totally vanished. There is no sense of discrimination. Good and bad alike are lauded and they applaud garbage on the grounds of, "Well, it was entertaining." And they suddenly raise to the level of deification absolutely mindless and empty posturing poseur-kind of stuff like *Coming Home* and *Heaven Can Wait* and *Black Sunday* and *Manhattan*, all of which are really empty, pointless, silly, stupid movies. And a film like *Apocalypse Now*, which is breathtaking, a genuine work of high art, is treated as if it's some kind of brobdingagian freak because it took so long to make. They don't understand that high art occasionally takes time to perfect, that you cannot constantly have the script written by Thursday, that you cannot constantly have 64 pages of bright, fresh, and intelligent comic-book story written by Thursday, that high art demands clean hands and composure, as Balzac said.

When I was much younger, when I was just starting to write, I had a lot of respect for writers who could get it in on time, and then suddenly I realized, "Wait a minute, what the hell is this, 'Get it in on time'?" I owe no allegiance to publishers or producers or networks. Even if they paid me staggering sums of money, I owe allegiance only to the work. Only to the work. And if I give them shit on time, then I have cheated them. If I take six months longer than they expected, or five years, or 10 years longer, and give them something that no one else could have given them, then I've honored the obligation to them. Whether they see it that way or not, that's the way I see it. I've become totally irresponsible in that respect.

People say, "When is *The Last Dangerous Visions* coming out?" and I give them the same answer that Michelangelo gave to the Pope: "It'll be done when it's done." And of course they scream and they yell, and Fred Pohl runs around and tells terrible stories about me. Fred Pohl was running around at SeaCon and telling everybody that *The Last Dangerous Visions* wasn't going to come out because everybody was withdrawing their stories. People were pulling their stories left and right. Fred is an old acquaintance and periodically we have been very good friends, and I tell you, for the record, in no uncertain terms, Fred Pohl is full of shit right up to his earlobes. Not one single writer has pulled a story from *The Last*

Dangerous Visions, Nobody – no one has pulled a story from *The Last Dangerous Visions*. Every single story that I had for the book is there. It's going to be in very soon, in a month or two, and it'll be done.

It's been a huge job writing over 100,000 words of introductions, because the book is 750,000 words; it's 120 stories. It's a three-volume boxed set. It's the biggest anthology ever done, of any kind – it'll certainly be the biggest science fiction anthology – and it's the final block in that edifice called *Dangerous Visions* and it's state of the art. It's bloody state of the art. Somebody says, [in an idiot's voice] "How can it be state of the art? Some of the stories you bought ten years ago." Doesn't matter. Doesn't matter. It's still state of the art today. It's where it is, as far as I can tell, now. Because things have been kind of laying low, they haven't done much in the last five or six years. There are a lot of new writers, and I've gotten those as they came along. I don't know why Fred would say a thing like that. I mean, he may be mistaken, he may have been being funny, he may even be malicious, who the hell knows? All I know is that the book is going to press exactly with the table of contents that I had all along. The only story that was removed was one I removed a while ago from a writer who gave me a hard time, so I said "Fuck you," took the story out and gave it back to him, because he was playing Mr. Moneybags. He'd had one little successful thing happen to him and all of a sudden he thought his shit didn't stink, and he started siccing agents on me. And I said, "Hey, man, fuck you! Here's the story, keep the advance I gave you, piss off! You know, roll it up and insert it up your tozz!" And I got a substitute story of exactly the same length from P.J. Plauger, and it's a very very fine story, and the book's the same length. It was just that one thing. But it had nothing to do with everybody pulling for any reason. Everybody's stuck by me; they understand.

And I've had a tough year anyhow. I spent an entire year, from November of the year before last to last November, writing *I, Robot* for Warner Brothers. It was a full year; it just fucked up my health, fucked up all my relationships. The woman I was going with just one day wandered up into my office and said, "Forget it! I didn't sign on for this!" I'd gone days without washing, without brushing my teeth, without shaving. I was like an animal. She would make me lunch and I'd come down and eat it with my hands and grunt at her and then go back to the typewriter. It was monstrous. I was like some sort of crazed vampire bat who would come out in the dead of night to suck up dinner and babble meaningless lunacies at her and then crawl on all fours through broken glass back to the typewriter. And this went on for day after day after week after month after… for a full year. I finally got it all finished, handed it in to Warner Brothers. They said, "It's a work of genius" – that's a direct quote – "it's a work of genius, it's brilliant… we'd like a few changes." So I passed on that, I wouldn't do the rewrites, so they took me off it and gave it to four other writers in the last 10 months. A week ago they crawled back on their knees and said, "Would you go back on the script and do it?" I said, "If you stay out of my way. Get out of my fuckin' face and then I'll do it." They said, "Uhh, I was waiting for you to say, 'I told you so.'" And I said, "I don't have to tell you

'I told you so,' asshole. I was right to begin with. You don't pay me $150,000 to write a goddamn movie that you couldn't get made in 15 years and I do it and you tell me I have to change this character for this, and this character for that." I said, "We're not going to change Susan Calvin into Rocky just so the assholes who sit in these four-in-one theaters can applaud. Fuck the assholes, man. If they don't like it, let them go see another *Smokey and the Bear* movie – *Smokey and the Bandit*," whatever the hell it is.

I'm getting crankier in my old age. Have you noticed that – ?

I thought you were mellowing until now.

I did too. I swear to God, just one day I'd like to get up and not be angry. Just one goddamn day in this life I'd like to arise and not be fuckin' pissed off at the world.

I spent an entire day today in deposition. I'm suing ABC-TV and Paramount for three million dollars. The lawsuit was filed two years ago; we're going to trial. We've got pre-trial hearings on October 25, we'll probably be in the courts in December. They ripped off my *Brillo* story and teleplay, which I did for ABC, and was then shown to NBC, to a guy who is an executive at NBC, who then went to Paramount and put together *Futurecop* and sold it back to the same people who had rejected *Brillo* at ABC!! And we got them on access, and… The sum total of their case is that "Ellison's hands aren't clean, because *Brillo* – the story I had in *Analog*, with Ben Bova – Ellison stole the idea from *The Caves of Steel* by Isaac Asimov." Now, anyone who's ever read both of those damn things will know how berserk that whole thing is. I mean, even the suggestion that I would steal from Isaac, who has been one of my closest friends for 25 years – I mean, you don't steal from your friends. And if I were going to steal, I would really have to be some kind of a great schmuck to steal from a book like *The Caves of Steel*, that everybody in the world has read, right?

But what happened was… I mean, they don't even know from *Caves of Steel*. What happened was, those putzhole attorneys, "Ahh, we've got a nuisance suit here." It's not a nuisance suit; I promise you, it's not a nuisance suit. I'm going to have those fuckers' hides on the wall and I'm going to drive it through their brains.

So they said, "We've got to find an expert on this and find out about Ellison." So they go to somebody who works at ABC, somebody who's a Trekkie, and they say, "What do you know about Harlan Ellison?" "Ohhh, Harlan is a terrible man, he insults *Star Trek* people, and the first time he met Isaac Asimov he insulted him, ohh, he's terrible." They said, "Well, do you know the story *Brillo*?" "No." "Well, then go read *Brillo*." So the person goes and reads *Brillo* and they say, "Well, is there anything else like this in science fiction?" and he says, "Well, there was a robot in *Caves of Steel*." "*Caves of Steel*, okay, let's write that down." So they say that I stole *Brillo*, Ben Bova and I – Ben Bova, are you ready for this, the ex-editor of *Analog*, the fiction editor of *Omni*, stole from Isaac Asimov. That's wonderful; I love that.

So they say I stole *Brillo*, which was published in the August 1970 issue of *Analog* from three sources: from *The Caves of Steel*, which I read when I was 15 years old in 1953 – or however the hell old I was then – and I didn't even think of it when we did *Brillo*. I also stole it from David Gerrold's book *When Harlie Was One*, which, strangely enough, was published three years after *Brillo*. But I clearly saw into the future, and I saw that book and I said, "Aha!" And the third book is Michael Crichton's *The Terminal Man*, which doesn't even have a robot in it, but why deal with logic here – which also, oddly enough, was published four years after "Brillo." Now these schmucks are so stupid that they don't even go and look up the fuckin' publication dates on these things, and they bring this stuff into deposition and I sit there and I giggle at them! They're such dummies! But arrogant, because they've got a big insurance company behind them and they figure they're going to paper me out – that's what they call it in the law industry – they're going to paper me out with depositions and discovery and all that bullshit. It's already cost me over $36,000 and it will probably cost me another 35 or 40 [thousand] before it's finished but I'm going to *get 'em*!

By "papering you out" do you mean that they hope you can't afford to fight it?

Right, exactly. The attorney's fees are going to kill me, and they're going to depose this person and they're going to depose that person and they're going to take all these depositions and I'm going to have to pay for all that, and blablablablablablah, and they don't understand. They don't understand, man. I'm a snapping turtle. When I fasten, I'm on, I'm on to the grave with my teeth in their throat. They don't understand that. They think it's money. They already tried to settle. They tried $165,000, whatever the fuck it was they offered, and I said, "Put it up your snout! I don't want it! Forget it!" The money is only to make them hurt a little. What I want is public admission. See, they don't understand what ethics are. They steal out there constantly from writers and very few writers can afford to have the chutzpah to fight them. I can do it because I'm untouchable. Nobody can write like me. They've gotta hire me. I don't worry about that. If they don't hire me, fuck 'em. I do my books. I make a lot of money and I'm safe, man. And even if they fuckin' blacklisted me and killed me in the publishing industry – I don't write TV any more anyhow – but in every industry, I can go back to being a bricklayer. I mean. I've still got my ticket. And if they broke my hands, for Chrissake, I could sing on the street for dimes. They cannot scare me and they cannot… The worst they can do is kill me.

By "they," you mean the television networks, the executives?

Yeah, yeah. The great military-industrial complex. You know, "them" out there. And if somebody reads this, he's going to say, "Ho ho ho-o, has this poor fucker gotten paranoid." No, I'm not paranoid, I just know that industries and corporations and machines like the movie studios, huge, giant corporations that are owned by conglomerates are no longer human beings. They are mechanical things that are run by insurance companies and fidelity reserves, corporations, and things like that, who have insured them, and they say, "This is a nuisance suit." They don't know… They don't have the common sense to say, "Jesus Christ, we did steal this. Let's take care of this with this guy." And I would settle tomorrow for the attorney's fees and time that I've spent – reimbursement for that and for Ben to get a chunk of change – for public admission, and I mean big public admission, not a line at the bottom of a newspaper. I want a full-page ad in *Variety*, I want a full-page ad in *Hollywood Reporter*. "We had our hands in this man's pocket and he caught us cold. We stole from him and he made us pay for it. Signed, the President of Paramount Pictures, the President of NBC Television Network."

And I want a billboard on Sunset Boulevard. I want that. They won't give me that, of course. I mean, they'll give me all the money in the world because money is what they give you to shut you up. They can afford to give money to you. What is it to them? It's another drop in the bucket. But boy, they wont give you the admission, and that's what I'm going to take them to court for.

Is this kind of casual theft that goes on malevolence, or ignorance, or stupidity, or what?

Arrogant stupidity is the base of it. First of all, they do not understand that it is *wrong* to *steal*. A man like Glen Larceny does not understand that it is *bad* to rip off *Smokey and the Bandit* and do *BJ and the Bear*. It is *wrong* to rip off *Butch Cassidy and the Sundance Kid* and do *Alias Smith and Jones*. It is *wrong* to rip off *Star Wars* and do *Battlestar Ponderosa*. It is wrong to do these things. He does not understand this. He says [*in cloddish accent*], "Wu-ull, it's a viable idea." That's the wrong use of the word "viable," but that's the kind of language a jerk like him uses. They don't understand.

I once had a meeting with a producer for a film, and he said, "I've got a terrific idea for a movie. You remember the giant ant movie? Well, we've got a whole new terrific idea: it's a giant grasshopper," and he goes on, to tell me about the giant grasshopper and I say to him, "That won't work." He says, "Why? Why? Why not?" I said, "There's something called the Inverse Cube Law" – Square-Cube Law, whatever the hell it's called – "as the mass grows, the weight grows, and a grasshopper has hollow bones, and it will collapse under its own weight. So you can't have it, it won't work." "Oh, oh, oh, that's all right, we've got a lot of other ideas, I've got a lot of ideas over there," and he pointed to a stack of old science-fiction magazines. He said, "Pick any one of those! Take any one of those!" I said, "Those belong to writers, those are stories you have to buy." "Why? Why? They're just ideas!" They simply don't understand. Now, the people who are at the networks, who are in charge of creative…

I mean, the things I'm hearing at these depositions are terrifying to me. We've been taking depositions from people at the highest levels at Paramount and ABC. One guy, who was in charge of creative development for the entire ABC network, his entire credential for being in that job was that he had gone to business college and had graduated and had been the executive assistant to the chairman of the board of RB Furniture. Now you say, how does a man like this wind up telling me what to write? How does this happen? Well, it's because businessmen can talk to businessmen. They don't trust artists. And they have producers who have been artists of one kind or another on a very low level, guys like Glen Larceny, are the interface. They are the axemen. They are the whistlers who come in between you and the merchants. And they get you to write this shit and they corrupt you and writers are turned into more hacks. I won't do it any more, but there are plenty who... Almost everybody in comics, every, one of them would give his arm to be able to go out there and write shit. They're dying to do it. There are guys like... I've brought out a couple of guys on my own.

The usual excuse is that they'll make a lot of money and then they can get out.

Yeah. But they don't, of course. You know, I'm firmly convinced that writing shit is like eating bad food. Eventually, you will be unable to eat good food. You write shit long enough and it will corrupt your talent, if you have any. There are guys who've got very minimal talents and it doesn't matter whether they corrupt it or not. I could name them and would happily name them, but why bother? There's no sense kicking cripples. I mean, all you have to do is open up comic books from Marvel and DC and take a look at them. You see these guys have a very minor-league talent and. to say, "Well, these people are wasting their talent" is ridiculous. I mean, they're never going to be any better. What's the name of the guy who used to do... over at Marvel... he used to do... [*Pause*]... the worst artist in the field.

Don Heck?

Don Heck. [*Laughter.*]

This is going to look good.

Well, of course. You say, "Who's the worst artist in comics?" "Don Heck!" Of course. Absolutely.

I'll tell you a true story: A very high-positioned editor at DC told me three weeks ago that he respected Don Heck very much.

Because he turned in the work on time? Of course. That does not deserve respect. I mean, a dray mule can do that. You know, for whatever other flaws and faults Neal Adams has, and God knows he has many – he's driven almost everybody bugfuck at one time or another – Neal is an artist, and Neal is conscientious and Neal cares, and when they rush him Neal turns out dreck and he hates it and he hates himself for it because he has the soul of an artist and he's been a seminal influence and he's a man capable of good work. Jeff Jones was driven away, Bernie Wrightson was driven away, Barry Smith was driven away, [Michael] Kaluta was driven away. All the really good guys, they vanished. They couldn't take it any more. And of course, the industry says, "Well, man, they were irresponsible." Irresponsible is what the fuckin' river merchants call artists who will not kowtow to artificial fuckin' deadlines.

That's what they call them – irresponsible, crazy, hard to deal with, impossible. Five thousand Don Hecks are not worth one Neal Adams. And I don't know Don Heck. I'm not even sure I've ever met Don Heck, and I mean him no harm when I say this. I'm talking about his work, talking about what I see on the page. Who was that guy who did *Nova*? Was that Heck?

No.

That was Ayers?

Wolfman wrote it, and who the hell drew that? I don't know. It was awful.

Awful! Wasn't it Heck?

Dick Ayers or someone.

Yeah, it was somebody like Dick Ayers. It may have been Dick Ayers.

[*The artist in question was Sal Buscema.*]

It's all the same.

Yeah. And even guys like Gene Colan. There's a man who had an interesting talent – on time, on time, on time – and he pissed it away.

Gene Colan and Don Heck: Isn't it just a matter of Colan having a little more talent but being totally unwilling to channel that talent in any meaningful direction? I mean, Colan's the better illustrator, but that's about all.

Yeah, well, that's what I say, there's a genuine talent there which he's never done anything with. He got to a place and he did a thing and that's all he did. And it's like Neil Simon. People talk about how great a playwright Neil Simon is. Neil Simon bites the big one. He's the worst fuckin' playwright put on this planet. He writes cheap, shallow shit. He found himself a niche and he can do it and he can do it facilely and he does it and that's what's happened to Gene Colan.

The secret is what is the secret of all great art, I believe, which is taking risks, running into the mouth of the fire, walking the tightrope, trying the thing that nobody. Even if you fail dismally, goddammit, that's what it's about. You can't be safe. The minute you're safe in what you're doing, you are dead. You have stagnated. People write comments – well, they don't do this any more, I've taught them enough lessons – when I say "they," I mean just the general audience, the mindless wad that's out there. They didn't pay any attention to me for a while, and then somehow I started making a lot of noise, and I did "Repent, Harlequin." So it won a Hugo and won a Nebula. They said, "Oh, wow, terrific story, terrific story." So then I sat down, and my next story was "I Have No Mouth and I Must Scream," and they said, "Ahh, what a piece of shit, man, why don't you write something terrific like 'Repent, Harlequin,' why don't you do that again?" Well, then that won a Hugo and so then the following year I wrote "Pretty Maggie Moneyeyes," and they said, "Oh, Christ, what garbage! Why don't you do something like 'I Have No Mouth and I Must Scream'? I mean, that was terrific!" I never go the same place twice. You may be able to detect things in my style that I enjoy doing, but I'm never... You can hit a sitting target. That's why, when they imitate me, when people do parodies of my work, they're parodies of things I wrote 10, 15 years ago, because they don't know where I am today, man. I mean, "Jeffty Is Five" is not like anything I wrote 15 years ago, a completely different kind of story, and next year I'll be somewhere different. But they don't do that in comics. They just don't do that. The last time risks were taken was in the '60s. They did "relevance," and most of that was bullshit because nobody really believed in it, except for guys like Denny and Len and a few others, who really came out of the streets.

Wouldn't you say, though, that if even Denny's stuff, the _GL/GA_ books, were written as a book, or in any other medium, it would be laughed at?

Oh, sure, it was very sophomoric, but that's what comics are. Comics are sophomoric. I mean, even when they're doing some kind of great experimental thing like "Weirdworld," I mean, Jesus, what imbecile, childish, adolescent bullshit. That's the kind of stuff I read in the public library in Painesville, Ohio, when I was a ten-year-old child. You know, stories about fuzzy-footed little creatures. I mean, if that's the big, bold new development in comics... and I'm sorry to say it to you, because it was on the cover of your bloody magazine. The "Bold New Direction." You ought to be ashamed of yourself, for Chrissake.

Well, I think we were more impressed with the technological aspects of it. For what it is, I mean, it's a little elf tale...

But it's banal! It's imitation! It's bad, cheap, silly imitation Tolkien! And Tolkien is imbecile shit to begin with. And God knows how many letters you'll get on that [_high-pitched whine_]: "How _dare_ he speak nyeh nyeh nyeh...."

I was at the Second World Fantasy Convention and Michael Moorcock, who's been a real close buddy of mine, was the guest of honor, and they expected Michael to say all the things they wanted him to say. He got up there and sat down and he proceeded to tell them what shit Tolkien was, that he hated Tolkien's stuff, that he thought it was absolute dreck and garbage, and that if they wanted to read good fantasy, they ought to go and get _Gormenghast_, the Mervyn Peake trilogy, which is brilliant. I mean, that's high art. And right next to me was a woman who suddenly leaped up and said [_indignant woman's voice:_] "You're a terrible man" – and this was not even a little old lady in varicose veins and support-hose, this was a woman in her 20s or 30s who should have known better – "You're a terrible man and they should never have made you guest of honor. You ought to be ashamed of yourself and you aren't even fit to carry Tolkien's typewriter," his hernia case, or whatever the hell he has, and she ran out of the auditorium and people were applauding her and booing Michael. Now this is a man who is considered a natural, national treasure. This is a man who has won the Guardian Prize, for Chrissake, which is the equivalent of the Pulitzer over here. This is a man who is mentioned in the same breath as Graham Greene and C.P. Snow and he understands literature and he says to all of these slobbering, bucolic, tunnel-visioned, terminal-acne fans, "You deify shit! You worship garbage!" As John Gardner said in his book *On Moral Fiction*, there is room in the world for trivial art, but it is only because high art exists and is recognized and is worshiped and honored that the world is safe for triviality. But in a world of nothing but triviality, there is nothing to anchor to, there is no place to look for a firm foundation, and as a consequence you get worse and worse and worse and taste gets further and further bastardized. And none of these people will take the risk.

Let me tell you something: Jenette Kahn is a nice woman. I've met her a number of times and she's a nice woman. One day, paging through a DC comic – and it had never dawned on me before, and I have been reading comics since I was a very little boy, I mean, I was Supersnipe, I had all the comics, man – I suddenly looked at an ad for Crossman rifles and I suddenly thought, "Oh my God – I've been looking at these all my life." It was an apple exploding and when I looked at it, I didn't see an apple, I saw a kid's head. I said, "Holy shit! A kid with a BB gun could shoot an apple and explode it, and if he's ever read William Tell he's going to put it on the head of another kid." And I said to myself, Wait a minute, the condition in this country of macho craziness, where we wind up honoring an asshole like John Wayne, a fascist eggsucker like that, comes out of this whole tradition of guns. And where do kids get their guns? They're brought up with them in comic books. "Dad will buy me a Daisy." I mean, – I remember wanting a – I probably had one – a Ryder, a Daisy Red Ryder BB gun, and I said to myself, "This is terrible. This is terrible…" And I wrote to Jenette Kahn and said, "I'm a member of the Ban the Handguns Coalition, and it just dawned on me, and I'm not sure if you've ever thought of this, but it is infinitely painful for me to see a medium that I have adored since I was a kid be used for the promulgation of this kind of bad thing." I said, "Do you really need these ads this much? Couldn't you, out of a spirit of social responsibility, say, 'No more gun ads, no more war toys ads,' and seek other kinds of ads?" God knows they've got plenty of them these days, they've got the television networks and the candy companies, and *Grit*, Burpee seeds, and all that good shit. She wrote me back a note and said, "I'm going to look into this," and for a couple of months there were no gun ads and I thought, "My God, I have been a force for good in my time." And then of course they started up again and I realized that it had just been a couple of months where there were no gun ads. They simply don't give a shit. They have no corporate sense of social responsibility. And I'm not sure anyone has ever mentioned this in print before, but I hope that whoever reads this article will take it and stuff it under Jenette Kahn's nose and say I'm aware of the fact she didn't do anything about it. I'm aware of the fact that she probably went to the moneymen, and [*greedy voice*]: "Well, you know how many hundreds of thousands of dollars worth of ads they take in our comics over the years, blablablablah." That's always what it is – it's the fat burghers who make the bucks, and they don't give a shit what you put in the comic. They don't give a damn.

I assume you're advocating this kind of moralizing only when it has to do with children. Do you feel similarly toward ads for pornography, or, I guess, guns in magazines like *Esquire*…?

Having been someone who has had a very violent life… I have guns around my house. They're all locked up; I haven't used them in years, for Chrissake. I used to go out and hunt predators, and I've shot gophers in my back yard. I mailed one of those to the comptroller of New American Library. He wouldn't let me out of a contract so I sent him this dead gopher by fourth class mail.

It must have taken three weeks to get there.

Oh, it was ripe. It was in bad shape. There was also a recipe for Dead Gopher Stew in the package, a Ted Cogswell recipe that was in Anne McCaffrey's book, *Cooking Out of This World*. You've got a dead gopher that's redolent and covered with maggots, you've got to do something with it, you can't just let it go to waste, So-o-o…

I've never seen pornography ads in comics, but I'm against guns. I really am.

Don't you think that people should be able to make their own choices as far as what they see and buy?

Yeah…

Be it stupid or otherwise…

I suppose I do…

In other words, there's a dilemma here.

Yeah, there's a First Amendment dilemma and given a choice of censorship or letting the gun ads run, I would say, Let the gun ads run. Let anything run. Don't start thinking for other people. You can't legislate morality. You just can't. Ordinarily, when I hear people talking about [whining voice:] "Well, we can't let pornography get into the hands of children"… I don't know what children they're talking about. You go past a high school, you look at 13-year-old girls, and they look like a casting call for *Irma La Douce*! There's a young woman, just turned 17, who has been on my back to get in bed for months. I can't get rid of her, and I keep telling her, No! I'm not one of those guys who's a dirty old man who likes young girls. I've nothing to say to young girls…

Send her to Roman Polanski.

Whatever, yeah… He's a creep. We were talking about protecting children. Most people who talk about protecting children are just a bunch of goddamn anal-retentive bluenoses who are terrified of sex themselves and are also terrified that someone else is going to have a good time. So I don't make that brief on pornography, because I'm not really sure what pornography is. I really think I would blanch to put a copy of *Hustler* in the hands of a 10-year-old kid, but then, what the hell is it going to hurt? I mean, aside from the brutality in *Hustler* – the bit-off nipples, and the penises guillotined and the blood and shit like that, and the debasement of women and the debasement of men, too, the feces-humor – that's really in terrible, tacky taste, but that's not going to hurt a kid's mind any more than my mind was hurt from seeing *Dick Tracy* serials when I was a kid. I mean, shit, I was brought up on all that stuff and I turned out to be a very moral and ethical person who is "against that kind of thing."

But I think it cannot hurt if you have a series of options, if you can take an ad for candy or you can take an ad for kites or you can take an ad for any damn thing, for clothing, anything you can take an ad for, and God knows they've got very sharp advertising departments, both at Marvel and at DC – I mean, DC is Warner, and they've got a lot of clout, they've got a big, big sales force and they can go and say, "Okay, let's start exploring some other areas." I think it demonstrates a lack of social responsibility. I think there are some things in our culture that are basically destructive and negative in tone and one of them is this whole "We should be able to bear arms" bullshit, which is as sick and twisted to me as the taboos against homosexuality. They've just discovered, according to Tripp's book, *The Male Mystique*, or *The Human Matrix*, or something like that…

The Homosexual Matrix.

The Homosexual Matrix, that there is more homosexuality in societies where there is a taboo against it than in societies where there's not a taboo against it. In societies that don't give a shit, people seek their own level and do what they want to do. And there's always the Anita Bryants of the world who want to govern for us. And if I sound at all like that by saying that I'm pissed off about gun ads, I really don't mean to.

The reason I bring up this point is because the *New York Times* proved their great moral responsibility by refusing to accept porno ads.

Yeah, and they run ads for Néstle, who are poisoning babies all over three different continents, and they run ads, without checking out verifications, for shyster car dealers and fast scam artists. This whole high moral tone that people affect strikes me as an enormous pain in the *tuchis*. All it is is a leftover from the Puritan ethic, which was nothing more than a hand-me-down from Torquemada anyhow.

How would you describe your own moral tone?

I have no moral tone. I have an incredibly high ethical tone, but no moral tone at all. I would fuck chickens in the window of Bloomingdale's if I felt like it.

How would you differentiate ethics and morals?

Well, every time I've tried to do that, someone says to me, "Well, that's a very fuzzy definition," and it probably is. Ethics is to me… I'm trying to give you a for-instance, to explain what I mean, and I can't even do that. For morals I say fucking chickens in the window of Bloomingdale's, but for ethics I guess I mean…

Would you say ethics is more of a universal standard and morals are society's conventions?

Yeah. That's very good. You're a wiser man than I, because I would not have been smart enough to think of that, but that's what I mean. I know it is ethically correct for me to defy the war in Vietnam, to go to jail. Now people say, "Well, that's your moral conscience." Maybe it is, but I consider that ethics. It is ethical for me to take the vast sums of royalties that have come in from the *Dangerous Visions* books over the last 12 years and make sure that every single penny goes out to those writers. It is ethical for me to fight ABC and Paramount, not just for myself, and not to make the buck. If tomorrow they said, "We'll give the public admission, so that other writers can see what we did, and all we're going to do is pay your attorney's fees and you're not going to make one penny off it," I'd go for it. I'd go for it in a hot second. They won't. They'll never do that, but that would be a very ethical act for me. That whole thing I did with the ERA in Arizona, that's ethics. It's a sense of belonging to the community of humanity and knowing that you have a responsibility, and not just to yourself, to make yourself feel good and to get the best for yourself, but if you've got any kind of strength and any kind of clout and any kind of courage, to fight for other people, goddammit.

I tell you this in strict seriousness, in dead seriousness, in earnest seriousness, in serious seriousness:

People say, "How do you see yourself?" And I finally figured out how I see myself. I see myself as a cross between Jiminy Cricket and Zorro. That's me, man. In my wildest dreams, I see myself precisely that way. I'm able to do a lot of fighting for a lot of people, because I'm known as a pain in the ass…

For instance, Mystery Writers of America has for years had their MWA anthologies, to which MWA writers are supposed to contribute their stories. The money goes all to MWA, usually to put on a banquet and pay the office staff in New York. I got very pissed off at that. I said, "Wait a minute! How dare an organization that's supposed to be a service organization for writers screw writers out of the money for their work?!" "Well, it's tradition…" "Don't give me tradition. I don't want to know tradition, man; that fucks over writers. I don't want to hear that." And I made a big stink. Finally, they took it to the board of directors of MWA and said, "Oh, Ellison's making noise again, he's screaming and yelling," and one guy on the board, one guy, Otto Penzler, who is the mystery editor at Gregg Press and publisher of *The Armchair Detective* and has got the Mysterious Bookshop here in New York – he's a very good man, we're friends – he said, "Dammit, Ellison is right. He's right. Science Fiction Writers of America, they pay their writers for the stories that go into the Nebula Awards book every year. Why aren't we paying our people? Even if it's just an honorarium?" So they're paying some ridiculously incredible stipend like $15, $25, but it's a breakthrough. And of course the Board of Directors has taken all the credit for it: "We've decided that it's not right..." Right? Nobody remembers and nobody will acknowledge that it was this deranged, crazed loon from Los Angeles who screamed in their ears and said, "Goddammit, do this." And that's OK. When the great book is written, they will say, "This little fucker did a lot of good." And that's OK, because I know what I do. And that's fine.

I've got a reputation for being a terrible man and a brutal, ruthless, rotten human being. A woman I know said, "I was afraid to meet you. I heard you brutalized women." I said, "I do, I do... you know, I beat them with big sticks, I tear out their eyeballs, I imbed them in walls – I'm a rotten human being. A rotten human being." The stories they tell about me serve a very good and very worthwhile end. I love 'em, man. I love to hear the crazed mythology that comes back to me. I love it when they say I threw somebody down an elevator shaft – and they believe it! They believe it!

[*ELLIOT BROWN*] Did you really punch Irwin Allen in the face on the top of the table?

No! I never touched Irwin Allen! It was the head of ABC Network Continuity that I punched. Irwin Allen was just sitting to the right. Yeah, well, that's absolutely true. And actually, I would have kicked him in the face. See, I didn't mean to punch him in the face, I meant to kick him in the face, but I ran down this table and it was a 10'-long table and it had been highly polished and I slipped and fell and I slid on my stomach and when I came at this guy I hit him and caught him in the mouth and he went over backwards and fell off his chair and this model of the *Seaview* fell off the wall and broke his pelvis. That's what happened.

Since this has been brought up, can you tell us why you punched this guy out?

Yeah. They did an article about it in *TV Guide* a few years ago. It was a man named Adrian Samish who was at that time the head of ABC Network Continuity, which is the censors. He was a gibbering gargoyle who was a failed advertising man, a failed college man, and a failed homosexual – he couldn't even make it in that area – and they put him in as head of censors and he came on at a story conference for my script for *Voyage to the Bottom of the Sea* and insisted that I make a lot of stupid changes. And I said, "Those are stupid! And you're stupid for asking for those things. I mean, I don't know who you are, but I'm a writer. I have no idea what you are!" But I wouldn't make those changes, and he says, "You'll make them all right." And I said, "No, you don't understand, I will not make them." And he said, "Writers are toadies. You'll do as you're told." And I went bananas.

We were at this long conference table in Irwin Allen's conference room. Irwin was to the right of me and there were 26 yes-men all up and down. I jumped up on my chair because it was the quickest way to get to him. It was a narrow room and everybody had their chairs back, and their chairs forward, and I would have had to go around them and I saw blood red and I wanted him then. I didn't want to have to go around anything, so I just took the straightest route, which was right down the middle of the fuckin' table. There were papers and everything, and I slipped on them and went right on my gut and just slee-ee-ee-id down the length of the table and as I approached him it was like one of those Alfred Hitchcock dolly-in shots, and POWWW! I tagged him a good one right in the pudding trough and zap pow over he went, ass-over-teakettle, windmilling backwards, and fell down and hit the wall and Irwin had this big, six-foot long model of the *Seaview*, which I guess they had used as a miniature on the series, and it came off its brackets and dropped on top of him and just busted this dude's pelvis.

It sounds like a Road Runner cartoon.

Yeah, that's exactly what it was. It was a Road Runner cartoon. And I went for him. I was still going, hanging half off the table, my ass on the table. I'm swinging and I can't quite reach him, and three guys grab me and drag me into another room, and I'm doing an adagio. You know, Lemme at 'im! I'll eat the fucker's eyeballs! I'll tear out his heart! I'll spit in the milk of his mother! Piss on him and the snake he slithered in on! I was crazed. They put me down on a chair, you know, "Take it easy, take it easy." Oh, he was going to sue Irwin, he was going to sue me, he was going to sue 20th Century Fox. Irwin settled out of court; I don't know how much he gave him, but he settled out of court on the thing.

Anyhow, yeah, so that kind of thing does happen, but I've never thrown anybody down an elevator shaft. And no one ever stops to say, "Well, wait a minute. Is the body still down there? Who was this guy? Didn't his family worry about what had happened to him? And if Ellison threw someone down an elevator shaft, isn't that murder? Wouldn't the police be here investigating?" I mean, they never stop to think about these things. I sat in a room where they didn't know I was there and somebody was having them tell Ellison stories and I heard guys lie and say, "Well, this is a true story because I was there and saw it happen. Ellison dropped a chandelier on 200 people at a convention in San Diego." You know what happens if you drop a chandelier on people? They die. They die. There are a lot of people who go to hospitals. Jesus. But see, it's good…

It promotes you, right?

No, it's not the promotion. I'm not worried about the promotion. That kind of promotion doesn't do diddly squat. That's not going to make any one of my stories any better. In the final analysis of the work, that kind of promotion is only good if you want to do TV talk shows.

But the work doesn't sell it. I mean, it's the promotion that sells it, isn't it?

Well, no. You see, there are 200 paperbacks that come out a month. You have exactly 14 days – that's the lifetime of a paperback on the newsstand unless you're Harold Robbins or *Jaws*, and I'm not. Which means that my audience is an audience that comes to me and to my work because they like my work. My books have never been promoted. Have you ever seen an ad for one of my books anywhere? Except maybe in science-fiction specialty magazines?

No.

No. There was not one single ad taken for *Strange Wine* in the paperback edition. Warner Brothers brought it out and took not one single ad. And yet the book sells very well. To whom does it sell? It sells to people who know my name and read my work. Now even if I was the most colorful fuckin' character in the world they wouldn't come back to read a bad book from a bad writer. You don't do that. You just don't go back. So it's the quality of the work that eventually sells it. Because I'm a word-of-mouth, underground writer, really. I won't be that two years from now, I promise you. There's something in the offing. Two years from now, I will be on the top of the best-seller list, and everybody will know the name and everybody will buy the book. Every asshole who reads under a hairdryer or while sitting with a can of beer in his hand is going to be buying and reading the book that I will be writing, the novel that I'm writing and that will be top of the best-seller list. I promise you. Number one best-seller in the nation. God knows how long it will be there, but it will be the number one fiction best-seller in the nation. Your brow is furrowing and you're saying, "This man is really out of his mind with egomania."

Do you have this planned?

It's planned to be… I mean, I'm not going to write it any less than I write anything else I write. I write one way: I write for me. But the book that I'm writing is a natural best-seller idea. It's got to be a runaway. I mean, it's such a simple, terrific idea you say, "Oh Christ, why didn't I think of that? Why didn't anyone think of that?" I thought of it. And I'm going to write it.

It's possible to reconcile best-sellerdom with art?

I think so. *Lolita* was a best-seller. *The World According to Garp* is flawed, but it's a good book. *Ragtime* was a best-seller and a brilliant piece of work. Sometimes it happens. Sometime it slips through. I ain't gonna write a Peter Benchley kind of book, I ain't gonna write Jacqueline Susann or Erich Segal or Sidney Sheldon; I mean, I'd rather cut off my hands than do that. But it's a contemporary novel.

Could you verbalize the difference in values between *Ragtime* and Harold Robbins or Jacqueline Susann? I mean, it sounds like a sophomoric question, but I think it might be important to…

It's hardly a sophomoric question. It's just that it's a very difficult question to answer in any kind of codifiable terms.

I know. That's why I asked it.

I think… You see, they all say, "We-e-ell, you know, Harold Robbins, Jacqueline Susann, Erich Segal, it's just to entertain." Well, that's what they said about *Star Wars*. That's how they validate *Star Wars*, that's how they validate *Moonraker*, that's how they validate *Charlie's Angels* – it's just entertainment, as if intelligence and entertainment could be separated. And so as a consequence, the word "entertainment" has come to be bastardized and to mean the cheapest, lowest possible common-denominator of entertainment. I find Kafka vastly entertaining. Shakespeare is entertaining to me. Not high-minded and uplifting; it's entertaining. I mean, I can read Shakespeare and just laugh or cry or feel morose or feel great angst – I am touched by it. Because great art does that: It touches you and reaches you on an absolutely human level. And I think that the difference between a book like *Ragtime* or *One Day in the Life of Ivan Denisovitch,* or anything else that had been a best-seller that one can say has a claim to art, is that apart from being high-minded, as opposed to cheaply entertaining, to appeal to the lowest common-denominator of entertainment, there is an artistic sensibility at work that speaks to the human condition, that in some way uplifts and enriches. We should come away from the work better than when we went to it. Whereas books like Harold Robbins's and Irving Wallace's and people like that are anti-human. They deny humanity. They postulate templates, clichés, cheap, ready-made answers to human emotions. They're like an old-time Western; they're black and white in some ways. And they are, for that reason, negative. They are anti-human. Does that answer your question?

Yeah. I think that's a good answer.

I'm not sure I've ever said that before, because I'm not sure I ever thought about it in those terms, so you probably have some…

It's a difficult thing to make concrete.

And it also sounds very pompous, and yet *Ragtime* is a very bright book, and funny, and light, and yet it…

That wasn't one of his best books, though, was it?

I am in awe of *Ragtime*.

Really?

Yeah. I think *Ragtime* is one of the most important books of the last quarter century. That book is an amazing tightrope walk. It's strictly and severely plotted, and has so many things going for it. It's a watershed work in terms of using real history and real people and weaving them in and out. It's a fantasy. Very few people realize that it's pure fantasy. I'm knocked out by that book. I mean, I like *Welcome to Hard Times* and… uh…

Book of Daniel.

Book of Daniel, but *Ragtime* really blew me away. I read it, I think, about six or seven times.

Let me follow up on some of the things you talked about. One is this wretched condition in which we live, where the most trivial, vapid crap is glorified as entertainment. How do you think we have reached this state of affairs?

It has always been so. It has ever been so. At the highest peak of the Roman civilization, bread and circuses were their entertainment. The popular entertainment was throwing Christians to Protestants, or whatever they threw them to, and legalized prostitution, the public brothels, and bear-baiting.

What I'm about to say will not fall well on the ears of many people. We, in this country particularly, have always totemized the Common Man, which I've talked about endlessly in my essays. This nebulous concept of a noble savage who will always in the last ticking moment rush up and say, "You cannot lynch that man! It's not the Amurrican way!" and take him down, when in fact the Common Man has always been the slobbering, no-nose, prognathious-jawed, slope-browed yeti that formed those lynch mobs. And the Adlai Stevensons of the world and the Isaac Asimovs of the world and the Jonas Salks and the Ralph Naders and Florence Nightingales of the world have been in the minority. As I say, this will not fall lightly or happily on the ears of a lot of people. I deny the nobility and honor of the Common Man. I think to be common is to be base. I think it is closer to the animal state than to be uplifted and noble. I think that I'm clearly an elitist and that has always been the worst thing you can call someone. I mean, you can call someone an incestuous child-raper and it is less offensive to the monkeymass than being called an elitist, because what it says is, "I'm better than you." And there are people who are clearly better than the rest. No one can convince me that Albert Einstein was not better than everyone around him when he was alive. Clearly, Galileo – better! Clearly, Jesus – better! Better because brighter, quicker, faster, stronger, more able to think properly, inventively. Louis Pasteur said, "Chance favors the prepared mind." These are the people who move the world. These are the people who risk it all and who usually condemned and driven mad by it and are usually killed by it, crucified in one way or another. Driven to the madhouses, as Dylan Thomas said. And they are the ones who move us, micromillimeter by micromillimeter, off dead center, who push us into the future to, one hopes, a better world. The mass always, if left to its own devices either because of genetics or situation, will go for ease and comfort and non-involvement and non-responsibility.

Why is it, for instance, that so many women in urban areas these days are clearly going bugfuck? Women, as I perceive them today, are more irrational than they have ever been. You know why? Because for the first time in the history of this planet, they have demanded for themselves a kind of equality that is not only just their right – it is due them, it is long overdue them – but accompanying it comes a concomitant responsibility for their lives and because they have for thousands of years not borne that responsibility for their lives in the way that they're asking of themselves and their sisters, they are going crazy. Why is there such a rise in cigarette smoking among women? The rise in cancer among women is something like 200 percent in the last five years. It's because they are more nervous; they are edgier. All the old templates have been broken. This kind of responsibility that we ask of people, to live in a better world, to make it a better world, to be more responsible, to stop driving cars, to stop paving over the world, to stop chopping down trees to provide paper for attorneys so they can do more and more briefs. That's the thing that drives me crazy about this lawsuit. I see the amount of paper they're using. Fuckin' acres of woodland are going into this. They do everything in five or six Xerox copies. They make a mistake, they throw it in the wastebasket; they don't even turn it over and use it for scrap paper. It drives me mad. Do you know that one hundred acres of timberland is used every year to make McDonald's wrappings? One hundred acres. It's a terrifying thought.

Anyhow, to tie off that thought, the monkeymass, the wad, the great sleeping wad, all it wants is to be comfortable and fat. All it wants is its television and its car and it doesn't want to be infringed upon. It resents the gas crunch only because it can't have off-road dune buggies to tear up the land and get out in the woods and start fires with their fuckin' campfires, and be as fat and happy as they've always wanted to be. The pursuits of intellect, the pursuits of the godlike state, are beyond them, and to them go all of these joys and treasures. Not just in literature, but in television, in cinema, in terms of fast-food chains that have pushed good dining out the window. Kids are brought up now to believe that a good meal is to go to McDonald's. And they push and shove at Mommy and Daddy and Mommy and Daddy justify it to themselves by saying [*in whining housewife's voice*]: "Well, you know, they're very nutritious meals. I couldn't give them this nutritious a meal at home." What do you mean, you can't give them this nutritious a meal at home? What the fuck are you doing all day that you can't give them a nutritious meal, Mommy and Daddy?

Let me ask you this: What do we do with the stupid people, the people who are too dense to learn?

What do you do with the stupid people?

Yeah.

They're in the majority. We don't do anything with them. We just kind of skulk around ourselves in the deep grass and hope that they don't spot us and kill us. It's the green-monkey syndrome. You take a monkey that's lived in a cage with all these other monkeys for years, and you take him out and spray him with vegetable color, you spray him green, and they'll tear him to pieces within moments when you put him back in. They hate us. I've said these things on television and they've gotten thousands of telegrams and letters saying, "Who the fuck does he think he is?" Well, I'll tell you who I think I am, schmuck: I'm the guy who'da run Anita

Bryant out of town, that's who the fuck I am. I wouldn't keep her from working, but I sure as shit wouldn't let a crazed loon like that get a foothold and infringe on other people's rights. You don't do anything with the stupid people. You just hope to Christ they don't kill you before you've lived out your tenscore and seven, or sevenscore and 10, or whatever it is. Ninescore and four. [*Giggles.*]

Is the reason for our wretched state of culture that there are too many stupid people who refuse to learn and refuse to upgrade their lives? These two facts seem woven together.

Well, they are, they're inextricably linked. But you see, it's almost impossible to try and blame them for their stupidity, because they've been programmed that way. I mean, we are taught to be cowards all our lives. They start teaching it to you in kindergarten: "Don't stick your head out above the crowd, you won't be well-liked, the kids won't play with you." You're taught to be liked. Well-liked and secure are the two things that you're taught are the highest possible goals you can have. To be on the football team, to get in a fraternity, to get that piece of paper that will get you a job, to get into the organization, to rise in the organization, to get two cars in the garage and 2.6 children and a house in the valley, and these are the things that you're taught and they're drummed into your head in every possible conscious and unconscious way, through full-color lithography and phosphor-dot television, and subtle pressures put on you by church and school and family. Your parents, God love them, run these numbers back at you because these are the values that were instilled in them. God forbid you grow a beard and say, "I want to publish a comics fanzine." They say, "Ahh, he's a bum, he's a bum. Why doesn't he get a nice job as a bagger at the Safeway?" Those are the same people who would drive past on the freeway and not stop when someone's lying there bleeding. They're the same people who – what was it, 10 kids got on a bus here in New York and robbed 65 people on the bus. By the time the cops got there, there were only four people left on the bus and nobody wanted to get involved. You bow down to that kind of thing, man, and they will enslave you! Because the outlaws are always there and they don't give a shit.

"The Whimper of Whipped Dogs."

Yeah, exactly. You either become a willing supplicant at the altar of street violence and brutality and dehumanization, or they eat you alive. You have no other choice! There's my choice, which is to fight back, and they do you no honor for it. Because it makes them nervous. As long as they don't have – and when I say "they," I mean the monkeymass, the wad, you know, the scuttlefish – as long as they don't have before them a living example of courage they can con themselves into believing that cowardice is discretion, is judicious behavior, is the better part of valor.

As a critic, a television critic, do you feel a responsibility to teach, or do you write to those people who are already enlightened?

I don't know the answer to that. I've wondered about that, too. I've done all the TV work I'm ever going to do. I don't write for TV any more, nor will I ever again. They cannot buy me, there's no amount of money they can offer me, there's no inducement, either. They can't say to me, "Yeah, but gee, you'll put something good on," because my belief is, it doesn't matter what's on. It's the medium that drives you crazy. As long as it's on, you're watching it, you're a passive clone sitting there and letting this shit seep into your brain. The better the stuff is that they put in, the more intriguing it is and the more people will sit and watch it and the more they'll turn into Jukes and Kallikaks and illiterate babbling boobs. And I don't want any part of that. As for my criticism, I did two full books; I did the column ["The Glass Teat"] for two and a half years. It's a massive compendium of everything I could say about TV. If you can't say everything you've got to say about TV in two and a half years, you shouldn't have started in the first place. The books are constantly being reprinted, *The Glass Teat* and *The Other Glass Teat* are being taught in universities in this country along, in the media classes – media classes, whatever the fuck that means "Media," another one of those babble-words…

Dreadful-sounding. I took them in college; they're dreadful things.

Psychobabble. They talk about, "Yes, television is a fine media." [*Laughter.*] And I say, "No, you simp, it's called 'medium.' 'Medium' is the singular."

There are two corrections to be made in that sentence. "Fine media…"

[*Chuckles.*] Yeah, well, it's mutually contradictory. Well, in any case, they just reprinted the introduction to my book, *Strange Wine*, which is my most recent statement about TV, in which I said many of the things I've said here. It's called, "Revealed! At Last! What Killed the Dinosaurs! And You Don't Look Too Terrific Yourself?" And it's all about how TV is turning us into a nation of illiterates and with statistics to prove it. I mean, this is no longer even up for grabs any more; it's not even in contention. We've had TV for 40 years now. We know what it does to people. We know what it does to children. We know what it does to the social order. For the first time in the history of the planet, we have a universal curriculum. The child in Beirut and the child in Bayou, New Jersey both get the same picture of the young, the old, the rich, the poor, men, women. I mean, once you start working with templates and clichés, everything blands out, and there is no room for the individual any more. When there is no room for the individuals, you do not get the Jonas Salks, you do not get the Ralph Naders, you do not get the Wilbur and Orville Wrights, you do not get the Mary Wollstonecraft Shelleys. You don't get those any more. Or if you do, they die young.

So they reprinted it in the newsletter of the Television Critics' Association. Well, the shit-rain fell, m'friends. Because these suckers make their living off that. I mean, they suck at – the neck of this hideous goblin, television, this behemoth that bestrides the land. And they cannot face that they are pimps and whores for a basically destructive force. They cannot face it. And so they will offer all of these off-the-wall and absolutely irrelevant reasons why TV is good or why it's worthwhile, or the worst delusion of all, [*pompous voice*] "Well, I'm helping to change it by writing relevant crit-icisum," which is about as valid as the schmuck who works in the mail room at NBC saying, "Ah'm gonna change it from within." I lied to myself that way for years so I could make the money, and then one day I couldn't lie to myself any more. I said, "This is fuckin' evil! I can't be a party to this!" I get really messianic about it. It's about as close to religion as I come. So it is not the fault of these people, because it is comfortable to be stupid. It is comfortable to be cowardly…

Stupid people are happy.

I'm not sure about that. I've got another theory. I've heard all my life: "Ignorance is bliss." I've got another theory. Here we go; fresh theory: I think that human beings are all basically the same, the smart ones, the dumb ones, me, you. I'm the same as the poor devil living in a slat-back shack in the redneck mountains in Virginia. I'm the same as he. But I know why I'm unhappy. They've got the same angst; the world is crushing them too. They've got to pay bad taxes, they get bellyaches from bad food, their children are getting fucked up and they don't know how, they can't find any enrichment, their marriages are going bad, they long for and hunger for better things, they don't know the nature of these better things, they don't know who they want to be. They've tried to live the way their fathers and grandfathers and forefathers lived and it doesn't work any more, because it's a different world. There's a guy out there with a button. He can push the button at any time. They don't understand why it is they're dying from black lung, they don't understand why it is their children are born with two heads, they don't understand that somebody put pollutant into the air in Tibet, which has now floated down to wherever the hell it is, Decatur, Georgia. But they know they're not happy. There's tremendous subliminal, subcutaneous unhappiness there. The difference is, they don't know who's doing it to them. The don't know they're being manipulated by television and by big corporations that want them to buy cereals with sugar in it and another new car that is worth maybe a thousand dollars and they're buying it for 10 thousand dollars. They don't understand the nature of dishonesty. They look at a schmuck like Ronald Reagan, and he tells them they're unhappy. They say, "Yeah, I'm unhappy," and he says, "Well, wait a minute, you know who's making you unhappy?" It's the Jews, or the communists, or it's the big business, or it's the Democrats, or it's Jimmy Carter. "Yeah! Yeah! That's who's making me unhappy!" They'll take anybody. They don't give a fuck.

But they're no happier than we are. They're no happier just because they're stupid. They're in pain too, for Chrissake – they're human beings! They burn, they hurt, they bleed, they cry – they just don't know where it comes from. They don't know what to do to relieve it. So what they do is, they get drunk, they go to football games, they fuck each other's wives and husbands, they drive fast on the highways. You've got it in New York – people who go to the goddamn New

York Experience and Studio 54, they're just as stupid as the slatback rednecks. The only difference between the dope in Paswell, Virginia and the dope in New York is that in Paswell, Virginia it comes out of the mouth of Ernest Angley and the PTL Club and the 700 Club and Billy Graham and Oral Roberts, you know, "Gimme a snake!" and here it's coke. They dance 'til they drop, and they fuck 'til they're blind, if they can get it up, and this is high life to them. A big evening is being in the same room with Truman Capote, who's 'luded out...

Did you read John Simon's essay on TV?
No, where was that?

It was in *TV Guide*. He bought his first TV, and he ended it by saying that it wasn't a total loss because he could put plants and things on the TV set and he wouldn't have to bend down to pick them up off of a night table.
Right, and all the stupid letters from the schmucks in Pittsburgh. You notice how the schmucks always write from Pittsburgh? (*Whining nasal voice:*) "Who the heck does he think he is, nyeh nyeh nyeh nyeh, just because he uses big words doesn't mean he's smarter than..." Yes it does, lady, it means he understands the English language. It's a tool and he uses it well. I admire John Simon enormously. I think he's one of the few people in the world who has standards that are high. And occasionally he's wrong and occasionally he makes a fool of himself, but what the hell, he runs the risk, he really plays the tightrope act.

He has the courage to do it.
Yeah. And I love it when he uses words I've never heard of. I rush to the dictionary to find them. I mean, it's nice. John Simon is one of our natural resources. He's a very nice man. We've exchanged a couple of phone conversations. He did a review of a movie I'd had something to do with, that was based on one of my stories, and he panned the shit out of it, and he said, "If I had not known how good a writer Harlan Ellison was, I would have thought that he was responsible for this abomination, but it clearly is not his work." And it was so nice, and I said, "Thank you ever so much." He's very evenhanded and very fair-minded. And people attack him for attacking Liza Minnelli on her looks, but when that's what you're selling... First of all, the woman is a ghoul and a grave robber. She's been living off the corpse of her mother for God knows how many years. She's also a virtually talentless young woman. I mean, she looks like a baby bird dropped out of its nest and all the feathers have been plucked out by vultures. and as far as singing is concerned, I have heard Drano going down a tube better.

I listened to a lecture he gave at the New School, and it was quite good. There was the ritualistically obligatory crazy woman who screamed at him and it was really very funny.
I get that when I do my lectures too.

You get loonies too…

Oh! They took a shot at me in Billings, Montana on the stage. In Ohio, at Wittenberg College, they got me on the subject of religion, and only damn fools do that. The audience was apparently full of Jews for Jesus and other freakos like that, Children of God and all those wackos, and I paraphrased Mark Twain: I said, "If you truly believe that there is a divine entity who oversees it all, and you look at the condition of the world, you are forced to the inescapable conclusion that God is a malign thug." And this young woman leaped up in a balcony and screamed, "You're the Antichrist! You're doing the Devil's work!" And she flipped her Bic – literally, a Bic lighter – and set her hair on fire, tried to immolate herself and all of her friends leaped up and began screaming and beating at her head and she ran up the aisle and out with all her friends running after her. It was a moment like in *The Producers*, where everybody's sitting there with their mouths hanging open, and then the audience turned to me and I said, "That was terrific. That was sensational. I mean, this is the best evening I've ever had! I mean, how do you follow that act?" Here's a leper. Rrrripp! Throw an arm out at the audience. It's terrific. I've had some heavyweight evenings. And I love doing it. I love doing it. People say to me, "Well, you only do that to shock." And I say, "Absolutely. Abso-fuckin'-lutely. What did you do, come in here to sleep?" It's my intent to run around the outside of the circle like a sheepdog, as loud as I can, make as much noise as possible, and keep the sheep from being eaten by the wolves if at all possible. This may be an egomaniacal attempt on my part to rationalize and ennoble my own troublemaking, but that's what I am. I'm not even a gadfly; I'm a troublemaker.

One thing I wanted to get through is *The Illustrated Harlan Ellison*, because that's what sort of spawned this…

Triggered it, yeah.

You took exception to the review.

Well, I've taken exception to a number of reviews. Dan Steffan did a review of *The Illustrated Ellison* in *Thrust* and he did the same kind of thing that you did in *The Comics Journal*, whoever it was that did it.

Pierce Askegren.

Right. And I could not make head nor tail of his objections to the book. I must tell you, I'm very pleased with *The Illustrated Ellison*. Now, there are a lot of guys who – and I understand Chip Delany has backed off some of the things he said in his piece about *Empire*. I understand that is the case. I don't know for sure.

He sent us a letter.

My objection goes to – see, it's happened to me, and I can spot it happening to somebody else. You go through periods where all of a sudden everybody's down on you. For no reason in particular, it's just that you are considered shit. Like, you take a Don Heck, there's a reason why everybody thinks he's shit, that's because he's shit. But…

You mean it's sort of trendy to feel that certain people…

… are doing the wrong thing. Now, we're talking here about Byron Preiss. I too have got my beefs with Byron Preiss on a number of levels, and Byron sends me these long letters in which he justifies himself, and I wish he wouldn't do that. He doesn't have to do that because I would say, *en somme*, Byron Preiss is anal-retentively ethical. The kid really – I call him a kid. but I shouldn't. He's a man, but I think of him in that way because of his ebullience, I suppose. Byron Preiss goes way the hell out of his way to be conscientious. Whatever else you may want to say, he really has had a marked effect on what's being done in the visual media.

It takes a lot more than just being conscientious, though.

Well, yeah, but that's the beginning. There is a tendency in the things I've read about Byron, particularly in your magazine, and not once but many times, and a lot of it is subtle, and some of it may be valid I don't deny that, but a lot of it is crazy. And a lot of it is written by people who have seemingly no understanding of the simple mechanics of putting a thing together. To do *The Illustrated Ellison* took him, as coordinator, a couple of years, working with 10 crazed artists. Neal [Adams], for instance. I love Neal, but Neal strung us out for the longest damn time. Neal was supposed to do "Riding the Dark Train Out." He never did it. Bernie [Wrightson] was going to do something. He never did it. For whatever reason. I'm not putting them down, I'm not saying they were bad guys. Bernie got involved in the *Frankenstein* project; he just couldn't do it, that's all. Neal's got nine million projects going. I understand that. Christ, I do it myself. And you can't say they're bad guys. Their energies are elsewhere. Nonetheless, Byron put together what I, as the subject of the book, think is one hell of a good book.

There are some things in the book I'm not fond of. I'm not going to say what those things are because there's no reason why I should. There are some things in there that I think could have been done differently there are a couple of things I find very strange that Byron wanted to do. But he was, in fact, the editor on the book. Byron's agreement with me was that I'd see everything before it would go. I would see the scripts, I would see the roughs of the art, I would see the finishes. He tried very, very hard to do that. A lot of times he couldn't because of production deadlines, the artists were late, the artists were crazy, whatever. But there are things in this book – for instance, it is a stroke of genius on his part – absolute genius! – that he got Overton Loyd to do "I'm Looking for Kadak." I want to tell you, I could not have visualized the Jewish aliens in that story better than Overton Loyd did. I had never even heard of Overton Loyd in my whole life. He looks like Robert Grossman, but better – better! – than Grossman. I was just approached to do a piece for the *Heavy Metal* movie, and they said, "What artist would you like

Writer: Harlan Ellison Artist: Overton Loyd "I'm Looking for Kadak" collected in
The Illustrated Harlan Ellison [©1978 Byron Preiss Visual Publications, Inc.]

"There's always Kadak," he said. His voice came from a nowhere spot in the air about a foot above his body, which was on a table in the yeshiva.

"This is getting us nowhere," said Yitzchak. "The gonifs come in a little while to take away the planet, we can't stay, we can't go, to Bromois."

"Kasrilevka," said Avram.

"Kasrilevka," Yitzchak agreed, his prop-arm, the one in the back, curling an ungrammatical apology.

"A planet of ten million Snodles," said Yankel.

"There's always Kadak," said Snodle.

"Who is this Kadak the oysvorf's babbling about?" asked Meyer Kahaha. The rest of us rolled our eyes at the remark. Ninety-six tsuris-filled eyes rolled. Meyer Kahaha was always the town schlemiel; if there was a bigger oysvorf than Snodle, it was Meyer Kahaha.

Yankel stuck the tip of his pointing arm in Meyer Kahaha's ninth eye, the one with the cataract. "Quiet!"

We sat and stared at each other. Finally, Moishe said, "He's right. It's another tragedy we can mourn on Tisha Ba'b (if they have enough turns on Kasrilevka for Tisha Ba'b to fall in the right month), but the oysvorf and the schlemiel are right. Our only hope is Kadak, lightning shouldn't strike me for saying it."

"Someone will have to go find him," said Avram.

"Not me," said Yankel. "A mission for a fool."

Then Reb Jeshaia, who was the wisest of all the blue Jews on Zsouchmuhn, even before the great exodus, one or two of them it wouldn't have hurt if they'd stayed behind to give a little help so we shouldn't find out too late we were in this miserable state of things because Snodle seized up and died, Reb Jeshaia nodded that it was a mission for a fool and he said, "We'll send Evsise."

"Thanks a lot for that," I said.

He looked at me with the six eyes on the front, and he said, "Evsise. Should we send Shmuel with one good antenna? Should we send Chaim with a defective hop? Maybe we should send Yankel who is older than even Snodle and would die from the journey then we'd have to find two Jews? Moishe? Moishe argues with everybody. Some cooperation he'd get."

"What about Avram?" I asked. Avram looked away.

"You want I should talk about Avram's problem here in front of an open Talmud, here in front of the dead, right here in front of God and everyone?" Reb Jeshaia looked stern.

"Forget it. I'm sorry I mentioned," I said.

"You made your point. I'll go. I'm far from a happy person about this, and you should know it before I go. But I'll do it. You'll never see me again, I'll die out there looking for that Kadak, but I'll go."

I started for the burrow exit of the yeshiva.

Then I rolled, hopped and unwound my way up the tunnel to the street, and went looking for Kadak.

to have?" and they named a whole bunch of artists, and I said, "I want Overton Loyd. He's the one I want."

The 3-D experiment with Steranko and "Repent, Harlequin, Said the Ticktockman," whatever you may think of it, there are people I know, I swear, with very, very highly developed artistic sense, I mean, they are people who have hanging in their homes Mark Rothkos, Picassos. I mean, they know art, they are not dilettantes, and they look at the Steranko stuff and they say, "This is fine." Other people say [*in a weasely voice*]: "What the hell is this? I don't understand it." I have a beef on the plates in the special limited edition portfolio [of "Repent, Harlequin, Said the Ticktockman"]: The Thoreau quote was cut. I mean, you can cut my words if you want to on those damn plates, but for Chrissake, you don't cut Thoreau. You don't edit Thoreau because the lines don't fit. And we can't really figure out whether it was Steranko who did because he didn't like the art layout or if Byron allowed it... But it doesn't matter. It happened. So, I have my minor beefs, my minor cavils.

But, I really like that book. I am pleased and proud of it. And Byron Preiss did it. He was the one who did it, dammit. He ramrodded it, he put it together, he babysat the goddamn crazy artists, he sat with me through my crazinesses where I insisted on things. It's a book that I'm pleased to add to my oeuvre. And I read these incredibly pompous, sententious, powder-pigeon martinet analyses by schmucks I never heard of. God knows what the fuck they do for a living. They pack ice cream at Baskin-Robbins or something and in their spare time they write you a review. And they sit there and judge those who are their betters. Because Byron Preiss is one of the best, man. You know why I think he's one of the best? Because he takes the chances. Byron did the *Weird Heroes* series, Byron did *Empire*, Byron did *The Stars My Destination*, Byron did *The Illustrated Ellison*. Byron did all these things. Some of them may be failures, but goddammit, he did them! He didn't just sit down and do fuzzy-footed little creatures for "Weirdworld." And I think he is deserving of respect and deserving of respectful attention for the intent and for the execution. If he fails, it's possible to say, "This was an attempt, it was an interesting attempt, it failed. It failed for these reasons." That's OK. But the shit I read that's directed toward this guy gets me upset and it gets me upset because it's an echo and a resonance of what was done to me and has often been done to me. I'm very serious about my work. No fuckin' around. I don't take me particularly seriously, but I take my work very seriously. I have been dismissed by snots. And it hurts me to see it happen to somebody else who's trying. One of Byron's greatest flaws is that he is so defensive. He gets very defensive and very crazy and he tries to fight back, and I shouldn't be pinning him for it because I do it too. Someone says to me, "Why do you bother to respond to that stupid letter in a fanzine? Who gives a shit? They have circulation of 200 and you're on the *Tomorrow Show*. What the hell are you doing? What is this?" For me, it's a very different thing. I need the bile. I need the exercise. My childhood idol was not Charles Lindbergh or Babe Ruth. It was Sheridan Whiteside, the man who came to dinner. He was modeled after Alexander Woolcott, one of the great figures of the Algonquin Roundtable. I wanted to be an acerbic wit, I always wanted to write the great letters that would cut and slice and burn. And I do that. It's great fun for me. Byron it hurts. And it makes him look like a fool sometimes to respond to these things.

I think [Preiss] is a truly creative man. Whether this is a major creative talent or merely an interesting entrepreneurial packaging ability, I don't know. I'm going to say things Byron is going to get unhappy with, but it isn't going to be all positive. I don't think Byron's much of a writer. I think he means well and he tries, but I think he's a damn fool for doing as much of the writing as he does. I think he should turn that over to writers, whether they're young writers or older writers. He should exercise his creative intellect in the areas where he can.

But, he's the first guy who came along and said, "Let's really expand the parameters of the equation." And he did. There are a lot of things being done today that Byron pioneered, which I give him credit for. The whole thing in the pocketbook format. That was Byron. He's given a lot of young writers breaks. He's gone with a lot of people with no credentials.

I think a lot of this [criticism] is irrational bullshit and it's nice and trendy to pin Byron to the wall. I think it's good that people try to keep him straight. I don't mean that he's crooked, I mean if he goes off on a project, someone may say, "Hey, this was a bummer." But I've never really seen any of his things praised. None of them! And some of them are terrific. Not all of them, but some of them I like. The Steranko *Chandler* novel was a very interesting experiment, a lot of very good stuff in that. Jim [Steranko] likes it, he's happy with it. And, as I say, *The Illustrated Ellison*. I'm foursquare for it.

I don't intend to knock Preiss, nor do I intend to speak for the people who write reviews of his books, because I didn't write any of them. I would say all the reviews of his books were written taking into consideration the merits of those particular books.

Well, I'm not sure. If you were to give me a copy of the review that guy did. I don't have it in front of me...

I didn't bring it.

I wish you had because I would point to it and give you line-for-line and chapter-by-chapter where the guy was really off-the-wall. A lot of things seemed to be incredibly arbitrary. I understand a critic is going to give his opinion and that's what a critic does, but in some cases, particularly in that last review, because that's the one that spurred me to get in touch with you about this [interview], I think the opinions were utterly unjustified and could not be backed up in terms of acceptable standards of art. They were irrational, and, for the most part, very picayune. And the good things, the positive things, [the critic] didn't talk about.

I mean, Byron went way the hell out of his way to satisfy my demands. When it came time for the limited edition, he asked what artist I wanted for the plates.

I said, "I want Don Punchatz." Don Punchatz does not come cheap. A lot of money went into getting the Don Punchatz plates and they are sensational. I wish the printing on them were better because the originals, which I own, are unbelievable. I mean, they are major pieces of art. I've got them framed in the house. They're good in the hardcover, but they're not as good as they could be. I asked for Michael Whelan for the cover. He got me Michael Whelan for the cover.

The interesting thing is that when they do these reviews, like on *Empire*, they say, "Chip Delany is without error and without flaw and he's a good guy, and we know what a giant talent he is, so obviously this piece of shit is not his responsibility. And we can't really attack Howie Chaykin. Howie Chaykin is a wonderful man" – and he is a wonderful man and a fine artist – "so, if it's a piece of shit, then it's got to be Byron Preiss who made it a piece of shit! Wrong! First, there was the word. If it reads like shit, it's Chip's responsibility. If the artwork isn't good, it was Howie Chaykin's responsibility as a creative intellect to say to Byron Preiss, "Goddammit, Byron, this layout will not work! I am a partner in this project and I don't want to do it that way." I did it. I did it. He had a couple of artists lined up for various things and I said, "Absolutely not. I will not have this artist in there." A few things I didn't like scraped through, but… I mean, they say, "Ellison is such a giant talent, and he's so good we know this book is not shit because of him, it can't be him, and there are great artists in there, so it's obviously Byron Preiss." He's the fall guy.

Well, talking about *Empire* for a moment, the fact is it was Preiss's layout and Preiss did rewrite 39 percent of the copy.

Then it was Chip's responsibility to say no. See, I make no brief whatsoever for writers who are always talking about being screwed, but who are too schmucky to know how to do a contract properly so that they protect themselves or who are too cowardly to fight the publisher, because they say [*mumbling*]: "Oh, I won't get published –" Or they might be too lazy, or they're off on another project. They're like a writer who writes a TV show and then is off on another one and then complains because it's been turned into a piece of shit by other people. If you care about the work, goddammit, you hag-ride it all the way to the finish line. That's what you do if you care. I don't know whether Chip did or not. But if somebody tried to rewrite 35 percent of me, I'd bust their fuckin' fingers off.

But would you do it before it saw print?

Absolutely. You insist, by contract… I have a contract with Byron that says nothing will be done until I have put my initials on it. For the most part, that's what happened. A few things did slip through because of deadlines and Byron just had to go with them.

I see your point. I don't know, though, if Preiss can totally escape responsibility for rewriting things, for designing the layout.

I didn't say he escapes responsibility. But, you see, producers are producers. That's what Byron is – he's a producer. Producers have to get the product out. The artist should be concerned about the quality of the art. Byron mistakes himself. He divides himself. He thinks he's an artist. He's not. He is a creative producer. It's his job to put the package together, to sell it, to produce it in the way that is most rewarding. And to do that he must be overseen by the artist and the writer working in collaboration with him. And if they want to do something that can't be done, he should say to them, "It can't be done. Sorry, I can't do that. We'll have to find a way around that." And if they care about the work they will find a way around it. So, I'm not saying he escapes responsibility. No, Byron probably should not have rewritten. Except Byron will now come back and say, "I had to rewrite! There wasn't space, or it wasn't this, or it wasn't that." He probably has what he thinks is a perfectly valid reason for it. We look at it and say, "Jesus, what terrible layouts." Or Howie Chaykin would say, "Gee, what horrible layouts." But Howie Chaykin did the layouts! I mean, those lines didn't appear on paper magically. Byron didn't put them there. Howie did it. Howie Chaykin is not a weak, simpering... What we're postulating here is this monstrous Simon Legree-like character, Byron Preiss, who locks Howie Chaykin into a dark closet and beats him with a cat-o'-nine-tails until he does shitty layouts. C'mon, folks.

I think it's more of a case of Preiss giving Chaykin the layouts and saying, "Put drawings inside these panels. And if you don't do it, I'll find someone who will."

Well, then that's what Howie should have said. But I don't think Byron would ever say that. I cannot conceive of Byron saying, "If you won't do it, I'll find someone else who will." Byron's not like that. This is a terrible thing to call him, but Byron frequently is a pussy. If you are firm, and you say, "No, Byron, I'm sorry, this will not go, and I do not want this this way. Now either I do it, Byron, or cancel the project," Byron will find another way to do it.

I do know Howard would have preferred to do his own layouts on *The Stars My Destination*.

Then Howie should have done them. I mean, if Howie Chaykin is the great creative artist that we know him to be – and I have nothing but respect for Howie Chaykin, as does Mike Moorcock. I mean, Mike holds him in the highest esteem, and he says he's a very fine man personally. I'm not sure I ever met Chaykin, but I've talked to him. Howie Chaykin should take the responsibility too. Because it's his name on it. Y'know, 10,000 years from now when the cockroaches take over and they dig up that book, what do they know from Byron Preiss? What do they know from the guy who did the review and said, "This is shit"? They know from Howie Chaykin, and they know from Alfred Bester. A guy gives something over to be adapted, I mean, that's happened to me a couple of times. I didn't know any better in the first few things... Gerry Conway did an adaptation of "Delusion for a Dragon Slayer" – I thought I'd die. I thought I'd fuckin' die, man. I couldn't believe it. It was beyond belief and beyond redemption. It was just terrible.

One more thing. I suppose what I'm speaking to in this apart from my saying that Byron Preiss has almost always played fair with me, and when I say "almost always," there have been a couple of times that things have happened that I have been unhappy with. Byron found himself in a box and he had to do things that I was not happy with, but I can understand the boxes he was in. And I am not a terribly forgiving person, as you know, but I hold no beef against him. He's a good guy as far as I'm concerned. What I guess I'm talking about here is artistic responsibility. Again and again I return to that word. Responsibility. And courage. Responsibility and courage. Ethics. I cannot separate the artist from the responsibility of the art. These reviews praise the people who are the current good guys and pillory the ones who don't have the cachet. Byron Preiss has never written a *Swamp Thing*; Byron Preiss has never drawn an *X-Men*. All you see is the stuff that comes out, finally. And if it's good, it's good, if it's great, it had to be great because of Philip José Farmer or Steve Fabian or Overton Loyd, or whomever. And if it's bad it's got to be Byron Preiss. And I think this is really unjust. In the final analysis, the artist, whether it's an artist or a writer, must be responsible.

Actually, I think all the reviews of Preiss's books have taken the artists and writers to task. Certainly that's true of the Zelazny book. Gray Morrow didn't escape unscathed. Chaykin and Delany were criticized for *Empire*, not Preiss.

It's the overall tone I'm talking about. Specifics can be leveled at him. Absolutely. I think the Zelazny book is a piece of shit. I mean, it really is. For whatever reasons. It's the overall tone that I'm talking about. It's this ambience of "This schmuck Preiss who has wandered into our holy and sanctified grove and is pissing on the trees," and I don't think that's fair. I know you're bored with this and you want to move on, but that's all right.

Well, I disagree, and there's not much point in saying I disagree.

Well, what do you think of Byron Preiss, man? Let's have it from your face?

To be perfectly honest, I was thinking of writing an editorial actually praising him, not necessarily for what he's done, but for what he's trying to do. I think he's got a totally derailed esthetic sensibility. The Zelazny book made no sense. There were tiny drawings and small blocks of type, and it was like watching a movie and reading the movie's dialogue on another screen simultaneously. The layout in *Empire* was confining. Here you have a comic- book page with dozens of possibilities to integrate the text with the pictures and he has a very strict format.

He made bad choices.

I thought *Chandler* was a mess.

Really?

It was abominably written. Every hackneyed cliché in the book was thrown in there. And I didn't think the story was terribly interesting. I guess it was clever, coordinating the text with the little drawings, but I saw no particular advantage to it.

I liked *Chandler*.

Why?

I don't know. I just liked it. It was a pleasing exercise to me. I would never confuse it…

I have not read Raymond Chandler, but I did read Steranko's *Chandler*, and I thought if Chandler was anything like that I was very fortunate.

It was a pastiche on Chandler. If you like Chandler then it has greater consequence for you. And it did for me. I like Chandler. And I liked Steranko's *Chandler*. I mean, it was not great literature. As I was going to say, I would not confuse it with *Remembrance of Things Past*. But, I thought it was a nice, good exercise and an interesting thing to do. I mean, I don't see you sitting down and doing an editorial on the last 25 issues of *Wonder Woman* or *Super Friends*. I mean, you wouldn't bother with it because there's no one trying anything. I mean, here's *Chandler*, and he tried something, he may not have succeeded with you, he did for me. But, it's a very different kind of thing. I mean, I'm sure that Byron could put together a comic book for DC or Marvel, but he never has. He's never taken that easy way out. What am I arguing with you for? You were telling me what you thought of *Chandler*.

Well, I am interested in seeing comics elevated to certain standards, and almost nothing is being done in that regard. Preiss is taking very popular SF authors like Chip, Zelazny, yourself, Bester, and he's illustrating them, but he's not really…

Breaking out?

Breaking out of the science fiction/fantasy/comic-book mold. It seems as though he wants to divorce himself from comic books. He wants to produce something akin to illustrated stories, he wants something better than a comic book, and he's demolishing the idiom of the comics form for something else, something Preissesque. And it doesn't seem to be making any esthetic impact at all.

It's a little diffuse at the moment, I would say.

I haven't read *The Stars My Destination* yet. I found a few screwy things, though. There's one page filled with little circular panels, numbered, maybe three quarters of an inch in diameter each, and he has corresponding numbers with text. It looks like something a university would sponsor.

Well, posterity will tell. However, here are you, the publisher of a magazine that deifies silly comic-book stuff. I mean, every issue you have a drawing of the Hulk in there one way or the other. Every issue you've got a webslinger in there one way or another. And, you know, you pander to children. You're not trying to uplift them too much. Or are you?

I think we are.

So is Preiss.

I don't deny that.

I saw [on the cover of TCJ #48]: "At last! A great breakthrough! 'Weirdworld!'" And I hadn't seen "Weirdworld" yet. Hey, at last: the breakthrough. I knew someone was going to make the breakthrough. Let's see what this is. And I look at "Weirdworld," and I think, "This is the great breakthrough? This dreck?" But you did it! You bought the party line. You went along with it. I think *Moon Knight*…

I don't think we endorsed "Weirdworld" as a breakthrough in terms of story or theme…

All I know is, your front cover said, "The greatest thing since sliced bread, folks, here it is – 'Weirdworld.'" Special issue devoted to it. You did it. And it's no nobler than *Starlog* praising the worst fuckin' films month after month after month after month. If it's got any fantastic elements, if it's got any bright flashing lights, they do a big article, because you're selling to children. And the children want to see that and you know which side your bread is buttered on. So, don't tell me it's not noble for Byron Preiss to protect his livelihood when you do the same thing.

I never said that.

Unless your hands are very clean you really can't take that uppity an attitude, it seems to me. See, I can do it. I don't sell out to anybody. They'll say [*in an idiot's voice*]: "Well, you wrote a *Flying Nun*." That's because I wanted to write a *Flying Nun*, and I wrote a terrific *Flying Nun*. And when they fucked it up, because I had the responsibility for it, I put my pen-name Cordwainer Bird on it. You know, *sprrritzzz* flip them the bird. I stand behind everything that has my name on it. So I'm above reproach. I'm like Caesar's wife, my man, you can't touch me. But, you! Ah-ha! We can get you like crazy. Comes the day that you put out a headline, "The Hulk is adolescent bullshit and hasn't been well-written in 10 years. Gerry Conway ought to be nailed to a cross somewhere."

I think it has been said in our pages.

It sure hasn't stopped him, though.

Well, no.

Gerry's gonna love this when he reads it. I really don't bear Gerry any malice.

I think there's a big difference between an entity such as a magazine and one man acting as a critic.

Why is there a big difference?

Because if I put out a magazine that appealed exclusively to my taste, it would sell maybe 30 copies.

Why? Why can't it be done?

Because I could not make a living at that.

Ah! So the fat burghers are with us – again.

Except that we do attempt to provide intelligent criticism of the medium. My point was that there is simply a tremendous difference between expressing your opinion and putting out a magazine...

Isn't Byron Preiss expressing his opinion when he sets up the layout? I mean, he is the editor. It's his attempt to try to say something new and different and be balanced. And you sit off there on the side and watch it and you've got this guy reviewing *The Illustrated Ellison*, and he reviews... I mean, did he ever talk to Byron Preiss to find out the background on any of these things? Did he ever call me to ask me how I felt about this stuff? No. Occasionally someone will say to me [*in cornball accent*]: "Everybody is entitled to his opinion." And I respond to them, "No. Everyone is not entitled to his opinion. Everyone is entitled to his or her enlightened and informed opinion." Without information, without valid reasons for saying things, all it is is the babble of chimpanzees, and I would as soon listen to children as listen to someone who thinks he understands... I mean, I have read things... You have published, because I have read reviews where you knew very goddamn well that the reviewer was saying something totally illogical in terms of the business, that what they were saying was impossible. They would be saying something like, "Gee, why wasn't this done in color?" when you knew very well why it was done in black and white, but you didn't arrange it. You didn't alter it. You let them have their say. You knew it was insane to let them say that. Now that seems to me a lack of responsibility on the part of the editor. I mean, you wouldn't let them publish a thing in there that said, "Harlan Ellison stole *Caves of Steel*." You know very well that I would sue your ass off for that. But you let them say these other things...

Aren't critics utopians and aren't utopians given that leeway?

We aren't talking utopians. We're talking about people who are informed enough to have a valid opinion. Someone who is totally off-the-wall, who lives in Decatur, Georgia, and doesn't know what the realities of the industry are – and I'm not saying those are excuses for doing something wrong, I'm just saying he might say, "Gee, why did he do this story, why didn't he do that story?" and there might be a very good reason why he didn't do this or that. The critic just sat out there in

Cloud-Cuckoo-Land and wrote this thing. He looked at it and said, [*in cornball accent*]: "Gee, ah don't lahk this so ah'm gonna say ah don't lahk it. Now, whah don't ah lahk it? Ah know ah don't lahk it… Oh, an know whah ah don't lahk it, ah don't lahk it cuz the art isn't any good. Whah isn't the art any good? Well, the layouts is shitty." He gets the theory and then he gets the facts to fit it. And you know better than that, Gary. You're a bright man. And you're a good editor, too. And when the magazine is good it is very good indeed. And when it's slovenly, it's indefensible.

But, is a critic responsible for knowing every facet of every book, every film, every comic book?

There is a difference between being a professional critic who makes his living from criticism and has to have the facts at hand to explain it, and even if he's only doodling up the reasons out of whole cloth and couching them in sophisticated terms so they sound good, that's still his livelihood, and he's going to have to stand or fall on that reputation. The guy who wrote the piece on *The Illustrated Ellison* is, y'know, Sidney Schiobo from God-knows-where. I mean, I don't know who this dude is. Where are his credentials to say *anything*? Has he ever drawn a painting? Has he ever produced a book? Has he ever written a story? Who is he? If he's a 13-year-old kid who's writing about art, I mean it's very nice that he got published and I wish him well and he should go back and teethe a little and when he reaches puberty…

But somebody's background wouldn't make his opinions, if they were inane, any more palatable. I mean, it stands and falls on that review, not who he is, or how old he is.

Absolutely, but one feels a little more secure in trusting the opinions of someone who can say, for instance, the register is very good on the art. Has anybody ever bothered to point that out – good or bad register, which can ruin something? If you get a thing in the review that is knowledgeable then you feel you can trust him for the whole review, whether you like what he said or not. You can say, "Well, that's an informed opinion." But I found nothing in that review of *The Illustrated Ellison* by this guy that led me to believe this guy's anything but a schmuck. Isn't this some guy who said, "Let me review that? Let me review that?"

Uh…

Or did you say. "Hey, this is a major piece…"

I think he was assigned to it.

I would like to thank you a great deal for that. Maybe next time you can get a one-nostriled, hunchbacked dwarf who speaks in Urdu. What does this guy do?

He writes for Warren. He's a comic-book writer. I don't know what else he does.

Anybody who would work for Jim Warren is automatically beyond the pale.

You worked for him.

Once.

Well…

It took once to learn the lesson. Who was it – was it La Rochefoucauld? – who once said something about homosexuality – if you try it once it's curiosity, if you try it twice, you're a pervert. Anyone who works for Jim Warren more than once, which is long enough to get screwed by Jim Warren, is a damn fool. I'd just as soon not say anything about Jim Warren now. The risk you run with Jim Warren is that if you speak candidly about him he will do something that will cause you trouble. I mean, he'll never pull it off, it never really comes across, you're always able to stop him through attorneys or something. He's the sort of person you just stay away from, you want nothing to do with, because he always means trouble to you. You will always wind up on the short end of the Jim Warren stick. I gave him the opportunity to do it to me once, which I was a damn fool for doing, but it was early on in my knowing him, and he introduced me to my second wife, and I had never worked for him, and I didn't expect that kind of treatment. I thought I was above that. Well, nobody is above that. Anybody can be screwed by Jim Warren.

The comics industry and the people in the comics industry vastly amuse me. You know why? They talk a very big tough game. [*In a credulous idiot's voice:*] "This one's a shit and that one is a rip-off artist." And the dumb fuckers are still having their art stolen from them, they're still working for disreputable publishers who steal their work and reprint it overseas and don't pay them anything and just use them and use them and use them. And they're in the same rut they were in in 1940. They couldn't even get together a goddamn union! Neal [Adams] and the rest of those people put themselves on the line and tried to get a union started, said, "Hey, let's goddamn well get together," and don't you know all the old fuckers said, [*in senile voice*]: "Ah, I gotta make my living, and support my 13 children" or whatever, "my fuckin' coke habit," or whatever it was. And a lot of young guys did the same goddamn thing. It was Me-Firstism. They looked after Number One. Do an article sometime. Go around to everybody in the industry and say, "Hey, when was such-and-such cowardly? Tell me about that." And they'll all rat on each other, because they have no fuckin' sense of ethics, any one of these assholes. They're cowards. They're cowards and little yellow McCarthyite bastards, all of them. Not all of them, but almost all of them. Even the guys who lay themselves on the line at some point or another really chicken out. There's never been a firebrand who's gone all the way… Neal [Adams] is as close to someone like that as I can think of… He's got himself a terrible reputation for being a troublemaker. But Neal did, in fact, get Siegel and Shuster money. He did, in fact, get them recognition. He was a force for good. It's an important thing. Once in a while a Zorro in the crowd is a good thing to have.

There was one point I wanted to make because you sort of implied that because I wasn't publishing the magazine I wanted to entirely, I was sort of selling out or something like that...

No...

The one point I did want to make is that I think the editor of a magazine has to have more ecumenical tastes than the very personalized vision of a critic and that is because the magazine acts as a forum for ideas, and there might be those ideas that are intelligently presented that are different than my own.

Absolutely, no question about it. In *The Last Dangerous Visions* I'm publishing a story that has a fascistic point of view written by a guy who really believes it, and I've also got a story written by a sexist, and these are philosophical concepts that I find abhorrent in the extreme, but they're good stories, and they express the viewpoint intelligently. No. What I was saying was...

You were saying I was pandering, and I wanted to dispute that. I don't consider it pandering if it's a point of view intelligently presented.

No, I wasn't talking about pandering in that sense. I was talking about pandering in terms of your obligatory crotch-shot of Wonder Woman, you have your obligatory hard-nippled picture of Spider-Woman.

They're illustrating articles on those subjects.

Gary, I don't mind if you think I'm an asshole; I resent it when you talk to me as if you think I'm an asshole.

If you run a review of Spider-Woman, pro or con, it's logical to run a drawing of Spider-Woman.

Yes, I understand that. Do you have a copy of the magazine with you?

No.

You just don't happen to have one... [*Laughter.*] We happen to know that every issue has a big green Goliath smashing down the wall. I rest my case. Because the kids want to see a Hulk picture. That's pandering. You may want to run a Hulk picture, that's fine. I don't put you down for it. I just say, don't get this uppity, my-shit-don't-stink attitude, particularly when talking about Byron Preiss, who panders no less than you...

I don't think my criticisms of Byron are mitigated by your criticism of *The Comics Journal*.

They're not intended to. There's a parallel...

I'm not sure what your point was.

I said certain things had to be done for business reasons or for expediency, and you said, "Well, I don't think that's a valid reason for doing it," and then when I say it to you, you say, "But I have to make a living from it." So, it is a parallel.

But in that sense, it isn't valid even when it pertains to me.

As long as we understand that and you don't take a lofty, mountain-peak attitude toward me, everything's fine. This is called forensic debate.

Let's talk briefly about _The Illustrated Ellison_. I have a general question that pertains to the whole book. Your short stories were simply edited down so that they would fit into the prescribed number of pages. Sentences and paragraphs were chopped up. Isn't there a particular idiom to the comics form that requires the story to be written for the comics form? There are rhythmic patterns to words – you know this very well, I'm sure – there is a pattern to sentences, paragraphs, to the story as a whole, and when you chop this story up, doesn't this do something esthetically derogatory to the story?

Absolutely. The printed versions of the stories in _The Illustrated Ellison_ are clearly and obviously less than their originals. Of course. My hope is that the illustrations fit into that empty space in the story, where things have been cut out, so that illustrations provide the additional... It's not called a comic book, it's called _The Illustrated Harlan Ellison_, which means it's illustrated Harlan Ellison stories, and they are in fact just that – illustrated stories, with the text as much maintained as possible.

What, then, is the purpose of publishing something that is an inferior product? Your own stories were superior in their original form and you sort of co-conspired to put out an inferior version.

Well, one does not co-conspire to do an inferior product. One co-conspires – I love the phrase "co-conspire," that's not too loaded – one _joins_ in a project that one hopes will be an equal but different version. If it is in fact inferior, there is no reason to do it. Now, some of the stories in here are inferior and are failures. A couple of them, more than a couple of them, are superior in a couple of ways. Particularly I keep going back to "I'm Looking for Kadak." The editing on that, I think, is rather skillful. Byron did the editing on it. He sent it to me and I looked at it. It's painful to me to see my words being dropped, because I wouldn't have done those words if I didn't think they were necessary to the story.

But the drawings by Overton Loyd are so extraordinary that they add a dimension to it. They really do. I think it's really a very worthwhile thing to have. "Deeper Than the Darkness" – God knows your critic tore it to shreds, and so did Dan Steffan [in _Thrust_ #12] – I liked. You have to understand something. The stories that Byron picked, with the exception of – let me look at that [_Ellison pages through a copy of_ The Illustrated Harlan Ellison] so I don't pass over anything. [_Pause._] "Repent, Harlequin, Said the Ticktockman" is almost totally there. He did not fuck with it.

I couldn't find any cuts.

There may be one or two small deletions, but essentially that's the whole story. So, that is a way of presenting the story with illustrations. That stands up. "Shattered Like a Glass Goblin" and "Croatoan" are two stories that I consider serious stories of mine. It happens that – here it comes – I am not happy with either of those, for any number of reasons, not the least of which is that they have been edited. I don't like the art in "Croatoan." I just don't like the art. I didn't like it when it was in *Heavy Metal* and I just felt miserable about it, particularly since *Heavy Metal* ran the last page first, which was insanity. Bil Stout was really conscientious about doing "Shattered." He really cared about it. He even went and tried to find the house I talked about in it. [His version] just didn't fit my particular esthetic taste about that story. That was the story I wanted Bernie Wrightson to do. I think Bernie would have been perfect for it. But, again, the art is good. It's good art. I don't think it's bad art. There is stuff in "Shattered Like A Glass Goblin," particularly on page... The pages aren't numbered. I just noticed that.

Byron doesn't number the pages. That's another one of my complaints.

You're kidding. I never noticed that. Jesus Christ. There's a kind of triptych of a man falling; it's the acid trip he goes on. I think that's inspired. Absolutely inspired.

I thought so too.

And there is stuff all the way through it. It's what Gully Jimson said in *A Horse's Mouth*: "It's not the dream I had," or "It's not the vision I had," meaning that the art is not the kind of art that I saw for it. But, since Bernie couldn't do it or wouldn't do it or wasn't able to do it, whatever happened, Bil Stout was a good choice. And he really worked hard at it. The story, basically, is not very deep. It is not one of the great literary works of our time. Nor are "Deeper Than the Darkness," "The Discarded," or "Riding the Dark Train Out." Or even "Looking for Kadak." "I'm Looking for Kadak" is an entertainment which I think was done splendidly well. The others, it seems to me that we're not talking about maiming great literary classics. We're talking about stories, such as "The Discarded," which is one of my earliest stories for Chrissake. "Deeper Than the Darkness" was maybe the fourth story I ever sold. And I think it was one of the reasons why they were picked – because they were easy to adapt. It would be difficult to try to adapt "Adrift Just Off the Islets of Langerhans" or "The Deathbird," for Chrissake. Those are serious, high-minded works with serious intent and they would be diminished by this kind of thing. "Deeper Than the Darkness" is a simple fable; "The Discarded" is basically an adventure story. I can't get very upset because they were edited down. If they are diminished I suspect they were diminishable. They were capable of being diminished.

I don't see these as inferior representations of the stories. They are, in a way, an introduction to my work in another form to people who might not know my work. For instance, Byron didn't have to put in this Dillon series, the "Ellison Tapestry." He did it because he's an admirer of good art and the Dillons and I are associated and affiliated with one another – they've done so many covers for me and I've written so many things around their artwork. And he put it in as a responsible act. I mean, this is a non-pandering thing. There's nothing in here that the kids are going to get off on. And the reproduction is flawless. I mean, this is like Swiss printing. Does that answer your question?

I'm not sure. Do you remember what the question was?

Yeah: The question was, "Why co-conspire in a project that's going to publish diminished or lesser versions of my work." I think the ones that deserved respect were left alone – three or four of them. The others [weren't] hurt any.

What is the value of an illustrated story that truncates the original story?

The reason for doing an illustrated book is the same reason that they have done illustrated books for children or for adults all through history. I just bought a new edition of *War and Peace* illustrated by Feliks Topolski. I've read *War and Peace* three or four times, and what the hell am I going to get out of having some pictures by Topolski? I'm going to see someone else's vision of what was written there. Now, it wasn't chopped up. It's the full *War and Peace*.

But if we accept the implied subtext of what you're saying, which is that it is not valid to do an illustrated version of a story that's going to chop it up, then that also means we can't have movies made from books. It seems to me they are absolutely the same thing. There are books that have been turned into movies that I think were a disaster to do. We were talking about Ridley Scott earlier. Ridley Scott flew in from England to ask me if I would write a movie he is about to direct. The movie is *Dune*. I said I wouldn't touch it. I wouldn't touch it on a number of counts, not the least of which is that I don't think *Dune* should be a movie. I didn't think *Moby Dick* should be a movie. There are some books that are books, they were written as books, and there is no possible way you can capture it without changing it. Orson Welles did Kafka's *The Trial*. It was certainly not Kafka's *The Trial*, it was Orson Welles's *The Trial*, which is a very different thing, and people hate the movie. There are some books that should be left absolutely alone. But, we are a species that likes to have our little pictures dance. We really believe One Picture Is Worth A Thousand Words. Nonsense. That's absolute nonsense. And movies which are moving must be worth a million words, according to the schlumps. I don't believe that. But, if you want to deny a thing like *The Illustrated Ellison*, then you have to deny movies as well, it seems to me.

You're talking only about those movies based on books.

Yeah. Originals like *Apocalypse Now* are fine. But even that is based on a book.

The theme is based on a book.

Yeah, right. He took *Heart of Darkness* and he said, OK, I'm going to do it.

I'm not sure if Coppola was as successful as Conrad.

I'm in awe of *Apocalypse Now*; I think it is a masterpiece. I don't think there's a thing wrong with it at all. I think it's perfect. It's not *Heart of Darkness* and it isn't intended to be *Heart of Darkness*. It's an interpretation of the theme of *Heart of Darkness* and it is in the truest sense [a case of] literary feedback. It is one artist giving to the other artist, saying, "OK, you run with this idea and do your version of it." It's very different from *Heart of Darkness*. There's no plagiarism there at all. It's a very true homage.

The horror.

Yeah. "The horror. The horror." Into the mouth of the demon. But, even *Apocalypse Now* is based on a book. So you've got to deny that. The only thing you can do is an original, written for the screen and intended to be a film. And what have you got? At the best you've got *Citizen Kane*. At the worst you've got *Love Story*. You've got to give that some thought.

But, why do an illustrated book? To have an illustrated book that you like. If you like the story, you have an illustrated version. If you feel ripped off because the story was changed, then you go back to the original, read that, and then look at the pictures. But, for me, the Uncle Wiggley books wouldn't be Uncle Wiggley books without those wonderful George Carlson drawings. They're integral.

Shouldn't the illustrations embellish the story, add something to the story? In many cases, the drawings were almost superfluous. For instance, in "Shattered," Bil Stout added four panels on the bottom of a page, which weren't hinted at in the original story.

Oh, which are those? Show me. Ooh, this is good. I'm finding out things I didn't know. [*Groth shows him the page.*]

It's a flashback scene. It's apparently the protagonist's stint in the Army, but it isn't followed up on in the text.

Huh! I wonder what those are. What the fuck are they...?

It's as though it foreshadows something that isn't followed up on.

Oh, no, I see what it is. Look. It's very interesting. He's looking at the cops.

Authority.

Yeah. They're the same figures. He's remembering the Army, he's remembering the mouths. He talks back to the cops and sends them away. He stands up to them, which he was not able to do in the Army, or something like that, I gather. Up here is the reference to the Army, and down here it's obviously memory because there's a screen over it. No, it isn't in the original, but I'm willing to let the artist take a little license. It's interesting. I'm not wild about it, but I can see a valid reason for his doing it. The more I look at it, the more I like it, actually. Because I had my head set for Bernie Wrightson, I have not been fair to Bil Stout, who's a fine artist, and a fine man. He's a friend. I'm sure he's not going to be a terribly happy with my comments about this. I should state over and over again that it's only because I had my head set for Bernie Wrightson...

[dangling The Illustrated Harlan Ellison *in front of him, allowing the pages to fall haphazardly from the book, still held in his hand, to the floor*] **This is called perfect binding.**

Well, if it's called perfect binding, what I would do – do you go up to Baronet Publishing occasionally?

Never. I don't think they'd like to see me.

Give it to Byron.

No, I'm only kidding.

No, no, no. Perfect binding is called perfect binding because the pages don't fall out. On the record – and, Byron, you're going to read this interview: The man, as he's sitting here talking to me, holding a book with "perfect binding," the pages fell, out in his hand. That is not perfect binding. If you're going to sell something as perfect binding, goddammit, it better be perfect binding. I want you to replace every single defective copy of everybody in the world who bought one of these. Everybody: You herewith have my permission to send them back to Byron Preiss and I will give you Byron Preiss's address, which will be published with this interview, send them to Byron COD, and ask for a new copy. [*Laughter.*]

It's like talking to a vast, unseen audience. You know they're out there... And, if there's anybody crazier than science-fiction fans, it's comic-book fans. I mean they are really nut cases. Is that the interview?

Oh no. That's only this part of it. Now we go on...

Oh, now we go on to the greater work. You know, we've only been at this... It's one o'clock. It's one fuckin' o'clock [a.m.].

[*Intermission. Ellison goes to pour himself a drink. As the tape resumes, he is explaining the nature of* The Comics Journal *to a friend who sat in on the interview. Her question: Is it like* The Armchair Detective?]

In a way. Except *The Armchair Detective* is much more literary and it's about something of greater substance. I mean, what they're basically talking about is comic books. Comic books. Whether, in fact the Hulk is a modern representation of the Faustian legend. Or, does Spider-Woman – I'm being deadly serious – does Spider-Woman more perfectly represent contemporary woman's search for self-identification and self-fulfillment than the traditional image of Wonder Woman? This is the kind of thing they're in. Or Steve Gerber: "Why They Threw Me Off The Howard The Duck Strip."

Steve Gerber is crazy as a bed bug.

Is he?

Yes. He's as crazy as a bed bug. And if he isn't, Mike Fleisher is. Did you find that review in *Publishers Weekly* [of Fleisher's new book, *Chasing Hairy*] that I told you about?

No, I couldn't get the damn issue.

I read it to Len and Marv when they came out to the house. Their hair stood on end. I want to tell you something. The *Publishers Weekly* review said, "This is the product of a sick mind. It is so twisted and nauseating, it has no – absolutely no – redeeming social value." It's a book about a couple of guys who like to beat up women and make them go down on them. In the end they pick up some woman – a hippy or whatever the fuck she is – and set fire to her and she loves it so much she gives them a blow job. Which is essentially what the review said about the book. It said, "This book is so fuckin' twisted, there is no point even in discussing it. It is beyond the pale." Who is the publisher?

St. Martin's.

They're an A-1 publisher. I mean, they're not a top rank, but they're a very reputable house. Fleisher, when he was doing the Spectre – and I guess he did *Aquaman* too, didn't he?

No, I don't think so. Steve Skeates did *Aquaman*.

He did the Spectre and he did something else.

And he does *Jonah Hex*, which is really twisted.

Oh, yeah, right, right. This is a guy – it's like looking at the paintings of Giger. There is a genuine, twisted mentality at work here, and it's fascinating to look at. And I understand he's a very nice, pleasant man.

I understand he looks like an accountant.

Aren't all Texas Tower snipers like that? [*In cornball accent:*] "He went to church every Sunday. He loved his mother. I have no idea why he cut up those 135 people and mailed parts of them off to other people COD. I don't know why he did that. But he's a good boy, a good Christian boy." Fleisher – I think he's certifiable. That is a libelous thing to say, and I say it with some humor. I've never met the man. But, what I see in Fleisher's work and in Giger's work... I mean, Giger's clearly deranged. I mean, look at [his work]. Show [his work] to any psychiatrist. All of his visuals for *Alien* are sexual and psychosexual in nature. All of it. Endless vaginas

THE STUFFED CORPSE OF JONAH HEX UNDERWENT A STRANGE ODYSSEY AFTER THAT. IN 1923 IT LAY IN THE BACK ROOM OF A MUSTY OLD ANTIQUE SHOP SOMEWHERE IN THE MIDWEST...

AND WHEN THE ANTIQUE SHOP WENT OUT OF BUSINESS IN 1949, ITS CONTENTS WERE CONSIGNED TO A DINGY WAREHOUSE IN DOWNTOWN DETROIT...

JONAH LAY THERE UNNOTICED UNTIL 1972, WHEN HE WAS PURCHASED BY AN ENTERPRISING BUSINESSMAN, REPAIRED, REPAINTED AND INSTALLED AS PART OF THE WILD WEST DECOR AT THE *WESTWORLD AMUSEMENT PARK* ON THE OUTSKIRTS OF NEW YORK CITY...

IS THAT A *REAL* MAN, MOMMY?

OF *COURSE* NOT, DARLING! HE'S ONLY A *DUMMY!*

YOU'VE PROBABLY SEEN THE COMMERCIALS FOR THE PARK ON TELEVISION...

TAKE *THAT*, *BADMAN!* BANG! BANG!

WE'D BETTER GET BACK TO THE *CAR*, TIMOTHY! IT'S STARTING TO *RAIN!*

BEFORE YOU TURN THE PAGE, STOP TO SAY GOODBYE TO HIM: JONAH HEX, BORN 1838. DIED 1904.

BANG! BANG!

THE LAST BOUNTY HUNTER.

30

Writer: Michael Fleisher Artist: Russ Heath *Jonah Hex Spectacular* Fall 1978 [©1978 DC Comics Inc.]

and fallopian tubes and burning penises, and all kinds of fascinating stuff that makes life worth living. But, I mean, he's really a nut case. His personal life, too. He's got the skeleton of his second mistress in his home. I'll tell you what's really scary. Dan O'Bannon told me how [Giger] claimed the body [of his mistress] – apparently there was nobody to claim the body, so he claimed it. At that, you say, "OK, he loved her. He'll bury her." No, he doesn't bury her. He takes her and he had the flesh taken off. You know how? Carpet beetles. You know what carpet beetles are?

They eat flesh?

They eat flesh. They're used by museums to clean the flesh off skeletons. And they pick it to the bone. They're like piranhas. He used carpet beetles to clean her off and he's got her now as an artifact in his apartment. Cute. Cute.

Did you read the Jonah Hex story where Fleisher had Hex killed and stuffed in the end?

[*Laughter.*] That's fascinating. What's interesting is that the thing that makes Fleisher's stuff interesting was the same reason Robert E. Howard was interesting and nobody else can imitate him. Because Howard was crazy as a bed bug. He was insane. This was a man who was a huge bear of a man, who had these great dream fantasies of barbarians and mightily thewed warriors and Celts and Vikings and riding in the Arabian desert and Almuric, Conan, Kull, and all these weird ooky-booky words. He lived in Cross Plains, Texas in the middle of the Depression, and he never went more than 20 or 30 miles from his home. He lived with his mother until his mother died and then he went down and sat in the car and blew his brains out. Now, that's a sick person. This is not a happy, adjusted person. That shows up in Howard's work. You can read a Conan story as opposed to – I mean, even as good as Fritz Leiber is, Fritz is logical and sane and a nice man. Or take the lesser writers, all the guys who do the Conan rip-offs and imitations, which are such garbage, because all they are are manqué. They can't imitate Howard because they're not crazy. They're just writers writing stories because they admired Howard, but they don't understand you have to be bugfuck to write that way. Lovecraft – you can tell a Lovecraft story from a Ramsey Campbell story, from all the rest of those shlobos trying to imitate him, all the nameless yutzes shrieking like Lovecraft, they still have not got the lunatic mentality of Lovecraft. And the same for Fleisher. He really is a derange-o. And as a consequence, he is probably the only one writing who is interesting. The Spectre stuff was fuckin' blood-chilling, which it was supposed to be. I mean, he really did the Spectre, man. For the first time since the '40s, that goddamn strip was dynamite. And the first time they looked at what they were publishing, they said, "My God, we have turned loose this lunatic on the world," and they ran him off. And that was a shame because Fleisher should have been kept on the Spectre *forever*. It was just the most perfectly nauseous ghoulish thing for him.

[*Laughter.*] What an absolute fuckin' booby hatch this whole industry is.

Aren't you glad you're not in it?

Yeah! I mean, I'm writing a *Batman* story for Julie Schwartz...

You've been doing that for six years, haven't you?

I know. I plan on getting it done before Julie retires. I really do. But, every time I get around these people, if they're in L.A. and they invite me to their Comic Guild artist thing, and I look at some of these people, and I know them socially, and I say to myself, "Do I really want to go sit in a room with these people?"

They're all a little bonkers, aren't they?

Oh, yeah.

Have you met professionals in the industry you've felt were, comparatively, normal and well adjusted?

Yeah.

Denny [O'Neil] is pretty normal.

Denny's fairly normal. But, Denny's got his oddnesses, too. Denny's self-image is Orson Welles in *The Lady from Shanghai*. Black Irish. That's what he thinks he is. That's a little deranged for a man his age.

Who do you think are abnormal and what are their particular traits?

I think anybody who works for Jim Warren is a card-carrying righteous nutcase who ought to be put away...

There's a great animosity between you and Warren, so your opinion is probably flavored quite a bit...

Well, the animosity is because he screwed me. And he's got a very small mind.

He's not an unintelligent man, wouldn't you say?

Well, wait a minute. There's a difference between cunning and intelligence. He is a cunning man, he is a clever man, he is articulate to serve his own needs. Even when he gives out some great bit of largesse, it's like the saints and sinners who tell nothing but scatological jokes and then give milk to children to justify it. Jim Warren is a self-server, always has been, he'll be the first to admit it if he's candid about it, and I don't like his business ethics, and I think he's an outright liar. He has lied to me. He has screwed me. And he had no need to. You see, that's the mark of a stupid person. There are certain people I will not fuck with because I know goddamn well that they are trouble. They mean business. It is better to have them neutral to me or not aware of my existence than feeling inimical toward me. Warren gratuitously, for pennies or for pique, who knows, fucked me over. I will give him this: He got away with it. He is one of the very few who got away with it. But, as a consequence, he made a dread, living enemy of me. And I have done him great disservice that he knows nothing about, that he will never know, and have cost him thousands of dollars, thousands of dollars. Where film companies have come to me and asked me questions, and I have given them an absolutely candid answer. I could have been politic and just said, "I really don't know anything about him." But I told them the truth. I didn't lie. I never went out of my way to do it. It's just that I'm in a position… there are certain people who are going to be in your line of sight and if you fuck them over, somewhere down the line they're going to get you, not by even doing something malevolent, just by not doing something generous. And I have no reason to be kind or generous to him. And so I don't.

I was just disputing the validity of your statement that anyone who works for Warren is stupid. That's like saying everyone who works for television is stupid.

No. I would say unethical. Jesus Christ, do you know anyone who has ever worked for Jim Warren who has not come away from the relationship saying that he was screwed? Anyone? Name me one who hasn't. [*Silence.*] Rich Corben. Will Eisner.

No, I'm not going to defend Jim Warren.

It's hardly possible.

I'm just saying that he sounds like an intelligent man. A devious schemer, perhaps, but an intelligent man.

There are levels of intelligence. You're a much more intelligent man than Jim Warren will ever be. I mean, he has a cunning, he has an animal ferocity, he has a way of working deals, but that's not intelligence. I don't see that as intelligence. I mean, intelligence leads to high-minded ideals and a broadening of your world and a bettering of your world with other people. Jesus Christ, look at *1984*. That's wretched.

It's true pornography.

Yeah, exactly, it's true pornography. It's a comic magazine filled with sex and violence of the most offensive sort. The cover of the second issue I couldn't believe when I first saw it. Rich Corben did it. It was horrible. It was a rocket. You're looking down on like a V-2 rocket, one of those big phallic rockets, and there is a naked woman with huge, bulbous breasts, as if they're pumped full of cellulose, they're like big round balloons, with gigantic, protuberant nipples, all detailed, and all of this in a kind of three-dimensional art so it looks airbrushed and real. And she is tied with ropes – ropes – to the bulk of the rocket, up near the tip, and you're looking down on this… I mean, the sexual implications… I never opened the magazine – was there anything inside the issue that pertained to the cover?

No, but everything inside was worse in terms of the stories. Even I was offended by that.

Is Warren still publishing it?

Yeah. The audience must be composed of idiots.

No, no, no. Young kids who are coming into puberty, for Chrissake, and who are getting off on it.

I don't know about that. I believe Warren has taken marketing surveys and the average age of his reader is around 18 years old.

Don't you think that retarded adolescents – that's exactly what their age is, for Chrissake. Eighteen years old. God knows why they aren't buying *Penthouse* and beating off with that.

They probably are.

Penthouse is probably harder to come by for kids.

Not 18-year-old kids.

No, not 18-year-old kids. Have you every done an analysis of *1984*?

Oh, yeah. [*The Comics Journal* #40]. You don't remember it?

I didn't read that. I didn't see it. How does Warren justify it? Did you talk to Warren when you did the piece on it?

No. I interviewed him once many years ago and asked him why he publishes such crap and his position was basically, "You say it's crap but our readers don't, so who are you to say otherwise?" There's not much to say to that.

He's like a Polish bowling league idea of a lower case Hugh Hefner. What surprises me is... I mean, Bill DuBay has got to be as sleazy as he is. Can I tell you something? I love *The Spirit* and I love Will Eisner. As you know, I did the treatment for the *Spirit* movie. It was incredibly painful for me each month to buy *The Spirit*. I couldn't not, but I swear to God it just galled me to do it. But, when I wanted *Spirit* binders or *Spirit* posters, I would not send him money. I would call a friend of mine at Warren and say, "Pssstt, slip 'em out and send 'em to me," and they did. Of course if he ever found out who it was, he'd fire him, so I won't tell you. Jim Warren is the only person I know who leaves a moist trail where he walks. He's a petty Napoleon who's lucked on to a small publishing idea. He's found a way to milk adolescents out of their lunch money by selling them monster masks and other useless garbage. I mean, he really is in the great tradition of American obsolescence. You may print all of this. And instead of having a little humility about him he comes on like Billy Rose. He thinks he's running the Ziegfeld Follies or something when, in fact, all he's got are these silly, dumb magazines that print pictures of crazed monsters. Anyone who makes a living off publishing pictures of people with pustules and running sores on their faces is in no position to be talking about art or anything. And he really babbles on like some sort of Kansas Elmer Gantry selling feces. [*Laughter.*]

He's sort of like the character on *Saturday Night Live* played by Gary Busey who dives into a pile of shit for 25 cents and then charges $50 to leave the area. He was called a muck-jumper.

[*Uncontrolled laughter.*] What a great analogy! I love it! You've got to run this! I mean, put the words in my mouth if you want to. If you're embarrassed, put them in my mouth. It is so wonderful!!

He is so loathsome. He is so fuckin' loathsome. He's like a pimple that keeps coming back again and again.

Would you say he's more loathsome than Stan Lee?

Oh, I like Stan Lee. See, I like Stan. I'm sorry, man; I like Stan.

Why? He's built this giant conglomerate that grinds out pap every month that pollutes the stands. He has a factory outlet for vapid crap.

Is it any more vapid than the shit that was being published in 1940 when he was just a writer for them?

No, but that's irrelevant.

It is?

To our assessment of Stan Lee as a human being I think it is.

OK. Let me tell you my assessment of Stan Lee as a human being. Stan Lee is a very fine man as far as I'm concerned. Stan Lee has never treated me with anything but respect and mutual civility. The few times that I've been up to the Marvel offices, Stan has... It may be because I have some kind of rep, so he does that. I know he has a thing for people who have a rep. But how can I dislike a man who has never done anything wrong to me?

I'm not talking about personally disliking him.

But I don't know anything commercially that he's done either. I don't understand.

You must see his comic books on the stands.

Yeah.

You shudder when you see them.

I do?

I believe you implied that.

Well, I buy…

You certainly don't think the latest issue of *Godzilla* is any particular cultural achievement?

No, but then I didn't like *Super Friends* either. I remember *Prez*. What was that other wonderful thing?

Geek?

[*Laughter.*] *Brother Power, The Geek*, right. I remember that very well. That, I think, is the lowest moment of comics. I mean, that's even worse than the latest issue of *Scooby-Doo*. [*Uproarious laughter.*] I mean, it just bites the big one. It's incredible. I can't even describe this comic. It's just amazing. It made no fuckin' sense at all. How could they even put out one issue? I mean, that's all they put out, one issue. And *Prez* had two? Two or three. But, they must have looked at the first issue and said, "What the fuck is this?" It's like when you wake up in the morning and your hand has turned into a claw, and you say, "What the fuck is this?" [*Uncontrolled laughter.*] You cut it off immediately, you don't put it out. But, the interesting thing is if they put that out, can you imagine the ones they haven't released?

But, Stan…

Stan hasn't displayed a serious thought in his head in the 40 years he's been in the comics industry.

I don't know what I'm defending Stan Lee against. What are the indictments?

Well, he's at the pinnacle of this pyramid that grinds out so much crap every month. He's the Freddy Silverman of comics.

As opposed to the wondrous stuff that comes out of DC?

Not at all.

Well, where are you finding excellence? There are only two companies as far as I can tell.

There are a lot of alternative publishers. Are you familiar with Craig Russell's work?

Yeah.

Russell's *Parsifal* is an example of excellence.

Yeah, but it's not a major work.

[*NOTE: it became apparent later in the interview that Ellison was thinking of* Arik Khan: *as a result, his remarks on* Parsifal *should be read with that in mind.*]

That hardly matters. What do you mean by major?

I see a lot of the undergrounds, and they're all garbage as far as I can tell.

There are a few bright spots, certainly light years away from the *Incredible Hulk*.

I said most of them. How many years can you keep doing Robert Crumb kind of protuberant nipples, funny animals, and Inner City Garbage – I mean, that's way over the hill. I'm not one of those people who did the Movement in the '60s and still talks about it [*in senile voice*]: "Yes sir, I marched with Martin Luther King," like an old wobbly from the 1920s saying [*in senile voice*]: "The union, the union forever!" Times past are times past.

But, I see *Star*Reach*. And I don't think much of *Star*Reach*.

I think *Star*Reach* has published a few interesting things.

Well, yeah, there are always a few interesting things everywhere that have been published somewhere, which is nice, but I don't see it as a great artistic breakthrough.

Comparatively speaking it is.

Andromeda seems to me to be a pretty good magazine. They've done stuff with intelligence and wit and they bought a story of mine 900 years ago. They may even get around to doing it. One never knows. They keep doing all the biggies like Walter Miller and James Tiptree and Arthur Clarke, the heavyweights. Maybe they'll get down to us lower-rank shits…

What were we talking about?

We were talking about Stan Lee and how he's at the pinnacle of shit. Yeah, I suppose that should bother me. It doesn't, really.

I thought it might because you've inveighed so heavily against television, an industry which displays the same sort of sensibility.

I suppose it does. But I can't get very upset about comics because a) I don't take them that seriously, and b) it's people reading things. Even reading anything is better than sitting and watching the Drone Tone. I suppose I make that distinction, which I shouldn't. But I do.

Personally, about Stan – and I've never said this to Stan because I'm not sure Stan and I have ever had a serious, meaningful conversation…

It might well be impossible.

Well, I don't know. I'm sure Stan talks to his wife or talks to someone – everyone has someone to whom they unmask. Stan Lee has never been anything but nice to me, polite to me, complimentary to me, not only privately, but from the public lecture platform where there was no percentage in doing it. I mean, he did it, because, I gather, he felt like doing it.

Let me give you a footnote: On a number of occasions, not one or two, but a number of occasions, I have suddenly looked out into an audience at a college, in an auditorium lecture of mine, and suddenly seen Stan Lee sitting there, with no coterie, no nothing. He may have had his wife with him, he may have been alone, he may have had a friend with him, but Stan sitting and listening to me lecture. Now, I've thought to myself, "What the hell is Stan Lee doing out there? Why would he be going out of his way to hear me speak?" Well, Stan has a very well-developed platform presence. He makes a lot of money doing it. One of two things occurs to me. It is either Stan Lee coming to hear me because he likes to hear me speak, or it is Stan Lee picking up variations or other ways of doing lectures. Because I have an individual way of speaking on a platform, too, and I can work a crowd very well. I think Stan may have been interested in that from a technical point of view, or it may be a combination of both. But, that is, to me, a very genuine compliment. My ego is easily as big as Stan's, although it doesn't manifest itself in the same ways perhaps. So, I say, how can you dislike someone who likes you? That's all it takes to get me to like you. If you like me I'll like you. If you fuck me over – to the grave. Or if you fuck over one of my friends… I'm very loyal.

I remember the very first time I went up to the Marvel office for some reason. I was going to pick up some kids, some friends of mine who were working there. It may have been Gerry Conway. And Stan heard that I was there. I didn't even know he knew who in the hell I was. He invited me into his office, he sat me down, we talked for a while. He was very pleasant. So, I can't dislike Stan Lee because of the product, because I don't see his product as being particularly harmful.

Isn't banality harmful in any form?

Absolutely, absolutely.

Really, here is a man running from college campus to college campus, equating Shakespeare to his stable of writers, talking to impressionable college kids, who are sucking this up.

C'mon, man, they're mostly assholes in college and you know it. They're there because they don't want to get into the job pool. And if they're fools enough to go and sit and listen to a man who writes comics, and let him tell them about Shakespeare, then they're no better than boobs to begin with.

I don't see that as much of an excuse for his behavior.

What is his behavior? Here is a man who has, for wrong or right, for bad or good, changed the face of comics. He was a germinal influence, no question about it. He wrote things that hadn't been done before. Yes, that was 20 or 25 years ago, whatever the hell it is, and times do change. But, he was also the first one to hire the kids. That's something else in his favor. I don't see that those magazines are any better or worse than the bulk of what's being published. Yes, there are a few peaks – there's *Andromeda*, and there's a few things in *Star*Reach*, and there's "Harlan

the Duck," which is possibly the greatest work of literary excellence of our time, dwarfed only – perhaps – by *Gravity's Rainbow*, *Huckleberry Finn* and *Moby Dick*. Other than those, "Harlan the Duck" is in the first rank.

There's something else in your comments. There's the same animosity toward Stan Lee in what you say that I have toward Jim Warren.

I don't know Stan Lee. I met him only once and very briefly.

Really? That's interesting. I'll tell you, I like the Marvel comics a hell of a lot better than the DC comics. And that pains me because I like the DC characters better.

There seems to be more vitality at Marvel than at DC.

Absolutely. I've always liked the Justice Society, and God knows what was done to them by Gerry [Conway]. I've always liked Batman, I've always liked Aquaman, the Flash, the Spectre, Dr. Midnight, Hourman, Starman. Those were the ones I grew up on, and to see them back, even in their altered, bastardized, corrupted, wretched, crippled, paraplegic form is some small pleasure. But I find that I can't read the goddamn things. They are just imbecile. I read them and think, "Oh,

Writer: Harlan Ellison Artist: James Steranko "'Repent, Harlequin!' Said the Ticktockman"
published in *The Illustrated Harlan Ellison* [©1978 James Steranko]

Christ." And the thing that annoys me even more is that they take a paranoid, pathological interest in integrating everything, so that everything joins up. Y'know, every story – "That villain was in the background of panel three in World's Fair Comics in 1939" – what became *World's Finest* – and "Now he's back again! The Villain You Thought You'd Never See!" Who knew from this villain – Piss-Face is back, after 40, 50 years, Piss-Face is back to fight his old nemesis, Flash. [*Snores.*] Who needs that?

I find your lax attitude toward comics strange insofar as you've always attacked the second rate or the mediocre. Mainstream comics are such repetitious banalities I find your thoughts on comics a little contradictory.

Do you? Do I contradict myself? I contradict myself. "I am large. I contain multitudes." Walt Whitman, *Song of Myself.*

If you're opposed to the second rate, falsity, vapidness, why excuse it in the comics form?

Well, we must deal with realities here. Television had the potential from the git-go of being the greatest tool for the education of the masses the world has ever known. As all mass-anything, it sank to the lowest possible common denominator as quickly as possible. It fell over itself getting there. If it had roller skates, it would have done that. It now does a lot of damage, a lot of active damage, daily, day in and day out, hour in and hour out. While we sit here, the human race is being destroyed by television. I firmly believe that. Maybe I'm being Anita Bryant-messianic about it, but I really, truly believe that. Active harm is being done, night and day, to people's minds by television, which will eventually result in the watering down of the gene pool so completely that we will sink beneath the morass like the dinosaur.

Comic books, on the other hand, even though they are absolutely banal, absolutely pointless, kids grow out of them. They grow out of them very fast. Very few kids stay with comic books forever. There are very few like us. [*Laughter.*] I mean, people come into my home – I'm an adult, I'm 45 years old – on one wall they'll see a Hundertwasser and over there they'll see a Rothko, and over here they'll see a statue by Brancusi, and right next to it is a wall full of comic books. And they'll say, "Gee, do you collect those?" And I'll say, "Yeah, I still do, but I don't read them any more. Once in a while I'll read them." What they don't know is that I buy them because I want to buy them, because I always bought comic books and I always had comic books, and I always believed in comics. We are the exceptions. We are the exceptions. Most normal children grow out of comic books very fast. Whether they graduate to something else – one hopes. And in that way comics become primers for children. So, even if they're banal, they're a way of seeing words and teaching linear construction and they have very positive teaching aspects, which have always been understood about comics. I think comics are very positive for kids, depending on what kind of comics they are. They're not going to get into any trouble reading *Godzilla*, as bad as it is. They're not going to learn anything really bad. Except the thing that they learn in other parts of society equally easy, and that is that articulate vocabulary of a punch in the mouth. That you can solve all problems by throwing the bad guy up against the wall. Well, if they don't learn that in comics, they'll learn it in movies, and if they don't learn it in movies they'll learn it in television, and if they don't learn it on TV, they'll learn it in the schoolyard. So, I'm sure that's not a bad lesson to be learned.

I didn't mean to imply that comics were destructive to children.

No, but in terms of banality and mediocrity.

Of course, adults read these childish comics.

Those are adults who are far gone already. There is nothing to be done for them. Any adult who would read comic books...

One of my dearest friends is Arthur Byron Cover. Arthur is an amazing man. His newest book, *East Wind Coming*, is a Sherlock Holmes-kind of pastiche. He's a fabulous writer, a brilliant young writer. He reads comics, reads them faithfully. After I'm done with my *Comics Journal*, I give it to him. He reads it and keeps it. Arthur reads comics the same way, literally, that he reads Dostoevsky. He's an authority on Russian literature. This is a man whose intellect operates at the pinnacle of literature. We're talking about *The Possessed*, we're talking *The Idiot*, we're talking Turgenev, we're talking Chekhov, people like that. At the same time, he does not miss an issue of a DC or Marvel comic. He reads them all. He doesn't read the love comics or the war comics, but he reads all the superhero comics, every one of them, cover to cover. And can tell you anything you want to know about them. And I say to him, "Why, Arthur, why do you do that? I mean, I have the same sensibility about comics as you do. I find them great fun." I have a voracious need to know everything. I have a house with 37,000 books in it. In a given month I will read *Science News*, *Scientific American*, *Playboy*, *Atlantic*, *Harper's*, *Time*, *New York*, *New West*, *American Film*, *Armchair Detective*, *TV Guide*, *Partisan Review*, *National Review*, *New York Review of Books*, *Intellectual Digest*, which is no longer being published, sadly, *Esquire*, *Omni*, *National Geographic*, and a smattering of others.

The American Spectator?

What's that?

That's a right-wing magazine, like *The National Review*.

Oh, no. I read *The National Review* to keep abreast of those people, not because I like any of it. Also, they do have some very, very well-written stuff, and a lot of interesting people who are not necessarily of their political persuasion do write some interesting things.

But, anyway, I buy comics the same way: Because I need to know everything. I just need to know everything. I guess it's a fatal need to be hip or some stupid thing like that.

You read them more to know what's in them…

… than for enjoyment, yeah. I keep up with comics to know. Also, when I go out on a college campus, it's good to be able to mention whatever is going down currently. For a long time *Howard the Duck* was very good coin on college campuses. You try to establish a rapport with an audience anyhow, so you talk about whatever it is they're doing, and since they're only doing dope and beer what the hell else is there to talk about? It's hard to get people to trust you on a lecture platform. I mean, they'll listen to you and maybe believe you, but they won't trust you, and I work off trust.

So, I think anybody who takes comics seriously as an adult is already pretty far gone. I can't take them that seriously. When we talk about mediocrity, I say, "Yeah, but they were always mediocre." The very few that were not mediocre – things like *Doll Man*, the Lev Gleason comics, Eisner's *The Spirit*…

But, you see, Eisner's *The Spirit*, that's the true pinnacle. I can go back to those things and read them again and again and again. They are not only intellectually valid and enriching, but visually they are startling. The cinematic techniques in there! When I started writing the treatment for the *Spirit* movie, I had talked to Will a number of times and I described to him the opening scene that I was going to do. The opening scene is a terrific scene: The camera coming in in long shot, dollying down the length of a fog overridden river. High up above in the darkness you can see a bridge going across from left to right. Camera starts to come up, it's right at the level of water, coming through the fog, and you come up on the bridge, and the bridge is very high up – it would be like if you were down at the water line of the Brooklyn Bridge looking up at it – the camera starts to come up. As the camera comes up, it moves very quickly up into the air, up toward the bridge and you see two figures up there. Suddenly there's a flash of light, and one of them has lit a cigarette. He hands some papers to the other one. The other one tears the papers up, throws them over the bridge, the papers begin to fall as the camera is going up. The papers float past; the camera goes to the two figures as the one who has torn the papers suddenly lifts the guy bodily and throws him over the bridge. Camera holds as the body falls past. The camera goes with it. As the body falls, the camera tracks down through the paper and the paper spells out "The Spirit" in little pieces of paper. The camera follows the body as it falls into the water followed by the cigarette, which falls and extinguishes in the water. That's the opening shot.

In the Eisner splash panel, you know how "The Spirit" is spelled out in a funny way. And there's one of them where there's paper falling. I told that to Will and he said yes, absolutely. He said, "How did you come to that opening sequence?" I said, "Well, it was very easy. You drew Fellini. The film has to be Felliniesque. And you drew Fellini and I will write the film Fellini." And we were in heaven together for a few minutes until Friedkin ran amok. He's a real creep. And he has so many projects going that he just couldn't get to it, he didn't want to get to it; he's like a butterfly. He kept poor Will hanging and hanging and hanging. Will finally got the rights back. Anyhow, it's a nice treatment. It's got corrupt politicians, and all of them with funny names. One of them is named George Jerrymander, that kind of thing. There's an alien, one of [Eisner's] funny little bald-headed aliens. There's a femme fatale, Ebony's in it. Not only Ebony, but the other little kid with a lollypop always sticking out of his face. It's got Dolan and Ellen. There's a wonderful scene with Dolan where somebody comes in the door and threatens Dolan with a gun. It's really funny. Dolan hits him with a lamp. And The Spirit is The Spirit. It's Jim Garner 20 years ago, with that wry expression. It's Terence Hill without an accent. I don't know who else could do it. It's a wonderful treatment. I'm so fond of it.

What did you think of Eisner's new book, *A Contract With God*?

Very strange, very strange. I think it's an important book. I really do. I think it's an important book. I think Eisner is one of the few men of whom you can say he has an individual vision with touches of genius in it. And he's a nice man, too. But, God, his ego's as big as Stan Lee's. It's just that he's a beloved old figure. He's not around so much, so I don't see him, but Will has a well-developed ego.

But he's got talent.

Oh, yes, his talent is impeccable. He could be a monster; he could burn babies and still be beyond reproach. So, we're talking there about a pinnacle. We're talking about George Carlson – *Jingle Jangle Tales*, "The Pie-Faced Prince of Pretzel." That's genius, that's high art. I think Carlson is high art, I really do. And he's been almost totally ignored. But, Jesus, Maurice Horn didn't even mention him in the Encyclopedia.

He left out a lot of people.

Yeah, a very incomplete book. Those are the pinnacles as far as I'm concerned. Walt Kelly is a pinnacle for Chrissake.

McCay?

Winsor McCay, absolutely.

Herriman?

George Herriman, of course. Absolutely. Harold Foster, Alex Raymond.

Do you like Segar's work?

Yeah, oh yeah. I'll tell you what I liked even better. I loved Ed Wheelan and the *Minute Movies*. I think they were just spectacular.

Which?

Did you ever see Ed Wheelan's *Minute Movies*?

No.

Did you ever get that series of books from Hyperion Press?

Some of them, not all of them.

You should've gotten Ed Wheelan's *Minute Movies*, because that's one of the really remarkable ones. He had a repertory company of players who did stories, movies, screenplays, that he would make up. One time there would be a good looking guy, and there would be a beautiful girl, and there would be a villain, and there would be an old man, there would be an old woman, and he would have their names: He would say Minny Starbuck as Aunt Emma in *Sheik of the Desert*. One time he would do a desert story and another time he would do a Captain's *The Cloud* story, and they were all the old templates, and done with wonderful... I mean, they had John Barrymore physiognomies.

Percy Crosby did *Skippy*. *Skippy* was brilliant. That's a staggeringly brilliant book. The book is a genuine work of art. *Skippy* was the biggest thing in this country for 25 years. Everybody knew *Skippy*. Jackie Cooper won his first Academy Award for the movie – his only Academy Award. There were Skippy toys, Skippy premiums, Skippy suits, and Skippy hats, Skippy everything. Percy Crosby was a multimillionaire. He was making more money than the President of the United States. Ten years later he was in an insane asylum, committed by his family. No one visited him for something like 20 years, and everything gone, everything lost. Now nobody remembers. And the strips are wonderful beyond belief. They're so joyous, there's so much life in them, and such incredible movement! He has an understanding of movement. Those pictures of the kid riding down the hill in a drawer with the wheels on it, cartwheeling – just startling stuff. He hung in the Louvre. Now, today nobody knows him.

It's interesting, isn't it, that most of the best comic art has had a great deal of humor in it?

Yeah, yeah.

The Spirit. I'd put Barks in the category of the best.

Oh, yeah. Carl Barks. Definitely.

Of course all the humor strips are obvious. Kurtzman who was with *Mad* after his war books.

Do you remember the little magazine he put out three issues of?

Trump?

Trump, yeah. That was wonderful. "Hey Look!" is great stuff. Kurtzman's wonderful. But, see, those are, to me, the pinnacles. I don't see any of that in *Parsifal*.

I really thought *Parsifal* was outstanding. Beautifully told and intelligently written.

I'll have to go back and take a look at them. I think I've only seen one or two issues.

There was only one issue. In full color.

Maybe I don't even know what you're talking about.

It was 32 pages in full color. Craig Russell drew it.

No. What am I thinking of? It's done by the people who do *Andromeda*. What the hell is that called? I didn't know what you were talking about at all. Oh – "Something Khan," that's what it is.

Arik Khan. That's just a barbarian thing.

I was saying to myself, "Why is he so high on that?"

To go back to the original thing with Stan Lee, I can't get upset about it because I don't think it's important.

It's as though he doesn't want to do anything but this juvenile crap.

He doesn't. What the hell does he care?

He doesn't. Freddie Silverman doesn't care. Nobody seems to care...

Hypothetically, if he cared, what could be do?

It would certainly be possible with Marvel's resources to publish an adult magazine.

To what end? Who would buy it?

I think there's an adult market out there.

It's called *Heavy Metal*.

I'm not talking about adults tripping out on acid once a month. Preiss is trying to publish adult material. I'm talking about a mature story told in the comics form. People look at me incredulously when I say this. All an adult comic is is a mature story told in the comics form.

You mean like *Classics Illustrated*?

Yeah, right, except not mangled as comics have always mangled classics.

At their best, did they ever do anything that was worth pissing on?

Who?

Classics Illustrated.

I can't say because I read them so long ago. I'm sure they didn't, because they were adapting them for children.

I work in film, and there's a problem here that you have to understand. Film, even at its best, is a superficial medium. The word "superficial" is used in a very special way – I don't mean "shallow," I mean "surface." There is no way, short of doing voiceover, to give you the interior monologue that informs so much great literature. So, if you want to do something like, say, *Madame Bovary*, which is one of the great novels, you would be reduced to some very coarse images. Because you could not penetrate the mind of *Madame Bovary*, and you couldn't possibly know what moves her to passion and what moves her to destruction and all of those things. Let's take it at the highest possible level: *Crime and Punishment*. There is no way you can do *Crime and Punishment* or its equivalent.

You couldn't do *Remembrance of Things Past*, either.

Right, or *The Red and the Black*. Or *Moby Dick*.

But I don't see where that negates the potentialities of film.

It doesn't, but this is a definite problem you work with at all times.

What do you think of Bergman?

I find him an incredible crashing bore. I think he's a dreary old man. Would you like to see my imitation of Ingmar Bergman?

Will it sound like Woody Allen's?

It'll sound better. There are two people sitting in an all-white room. There is a vase with one dead flower over there. The man says [*mimics Swedish gibberish*]. The woman says [*more pseudo-Swedish*]. This goes on for a week and a half. Until finally Harold Pinter comes in and kills them. I think there are only seven directors in the world. That's all. Seven. All the rest are craftsmen or women of varying degrees of ability from as high up as Steven Spielberg to as low down as Hal Ashby. But, there are only seven directors.

But, you've got your problems doing great works as comic books.

That's personally what makes it so fascinating to me.

Yeah, if it could be done it would be an interesting thing. You look at it at its best, you look at the Rockwell Kent illustrated books. *God's Man* is a fascinating book told only in pictures by Rockwell Kent, who, God knows, is a brilliant artist. And even it is shallow. Because a picture is not worth a thousand words. It never has been and never will be. A thousand words, carefully chosen, can paint a picture that it would take a canvas the size of the Great Wall of China to compare with. I can spin a more careful and interesting and involved and intellectually stimulating story in a thousand words than the best comics artist in the world could with one picture.

I won't argue with that.

One more thing about Stan, to tie it off about Stan. We've been talking about a lot of other things, but this is the sort of framework of all of this bullshit. I don't see Stan as doing any great deal of harm. I see him at worst – and I don't even know if this is the case – but at worst, as a man with a nice little talent in a specific, little, narrow area, who has built it into a perfectly good, workable, marketable commodity. He's like the Music Man; he sells harmless dreams. I don't think what Stan writes is great art and I don't think Stan really believes it. On the other hand, Stan occasionally makes the claim for the Silver Surfer. It's not great art by any means – it really is not great art – but it may be one of the pinnacles.

That struck me as Stan's only "serious thought," which is that man will triumph over his own humanity, which is an utter banality.

Whatever. There's a universal thing there. There are only three or four characters in fiction that are universally known everywhere, to children in Basutoland, to adults at the North Pole. And none of them are out of Shakespeare. One of them is Sherlock Holmes, the second is Superman, the third one is Mickey Mouse, and the fourth is Tarzan. And they're all trash. They were invented as trash, they never aspired to be anything more than trash, some of them became eloquent trash, but they were entertainments. Cheap entertainments. And yet there was something universal there. There is a transcendent quality. And I think in some way – and I don't want to overstate this or overemphasize it – I get the same resonance from the Silver Surfer. There is something there Stan lucked onto light years – to use the idiom – beyond everything else that Stan has done or that comics have done for a long time. I think that [same quality] was there in Swamp Thing. I think they lucked onto something and went with it as long as they could. It's a fragile thing.

How would you differentiate what Jim Warren does from Stan Lee in terms of what they do to make a living? It could certainly be said that Jim Warren packages dreams.

Well, I'm not sure there is that much difference, if you press me to it. It's obviously colored by the fact that I don't like Warren and Warren fucked me over and Stan Lee has always been a gentleman to me, so obviously I'm going to feel that there's a difference. I don't know why I should, and maybe they are exactly the same. Maybe they are. Except for all the mercenary, transient things Stan Lee has done, from *The Micronauts* and *Shogun Warriors*, to *Star Wars* and *Battlestar: Galactica*, all of that shit which is intended to make money, and all that garbage, Stan has never really published anything like *1984*, and God knows he's had the opportunity. He's had the black-and-white magazines for a long, long time. And if he were as cynical as Warren I think he would have done it.

I wonder if that is not so much due to any sort of moral commitment to his product as it is to the fact that he really doesn't need to.

I don't think there's anything in the world that would keep Stan from putting together something that would make money. I mean, anybody who would put together a Kiss magazine and an Alice Cooper comic book, for Chrissake, would do anything. He doesn't do it. He doesn't do it. There's nothing even remotely approaching that, and Warren goes right for it.

It just seems to me that Lee's is a subtler form of crap than Warren's. Warren's just more blatant about it.

You could well be right, Gary. I don't think about it that hard. I go on my gut a lot of the time, and I've never had the feeling about Stan Lee that I have about Warren. For instance, when I discovered Warren was going to be publishing *The Spirit*, my first thought was, "Oh my God, poor Will Eisner! He's in the hands of the beast-man!" And as it turned out, bad things eventually did happen, I gather, to Will Eisner.

I'd rather not come across as dumping on Stan Lee. I throw them all in the same pool.

No, you make a perfectly good and, I think, valid point. That, yeah, with all the power [Stan] has, and all the abilities he has, and all the things he has at his disposal, why is it all such bland, useless garbage? But then, all of the mainstream comics are bland, useless garbage. Every time something comes along that is worthwhile, a *Howard the Duck*, a *Swamp Thing*, a… Shit, what else? I can't think of anything else offhand. The list stops pretty goddamn fast. The Silver Surfer. The sales figures eventually take care of it. There are some publishers who will publish first novels and they will pay for them with *Jaws* and Jacqueline Susann. They justify the publishing of Jacqueline Susann by saying, "It permits us to publish Jose Donoso or Miguel Asturias or someone who's unknown, a first novelist." Even ABC kept on *The Paper Chase*. You've got to give them that. They at least kept it on a full season in the hope it would pick up. *WKRP in Cincinnati* was kept on, they fought for it, and they won. So it paid off. You like an underdog thing, and Stan doesn't do any underdog things at all, and I suppose you could say, hey, if he did a little of that, it would make him the hero. And it wouldn't be any skin off their noses. I mean, how much could they lose off one comic?

What do you think of *Heavy Metal*?

Here I go destroying my markets again. I have very mixed feelings. They have fucked up everything they've ever done of mine one way or another. I mean, the most incredible fuckin' errors. On one version of "Croatoan," they published the last page first, so the end of the story is there before you read the beginning of the story.

But they apologized for it.

Every month for months their editorial was, "Gee, we gotta apologize to Harlan Ellison because we printed his story in Urdu last month" or "Jesus, we'd really like to apologize to Harlan Ellison for painting moustaches on all his characters," or for typographical errors. I've got very firm contracts with them now. They must send me the galleys now. They're reprinting "Santa Claus Vs. S.P.I.D.E.R." in the Christmas issue, and I wrote a new little introduction for it.

I understand Gahan Wilson is illustrating that?

That's it. But he already illustrated it. They're reprinting the cover for the *Magazine of Fantasy and Science Fiction*. It was six, eight years ago. I sent them the original from my house. It's all framed and everything. It's a wonderful painting. [The story] is a dated piece, but then I've written an updated introduction to it, which is really kind of nice. And I must tell you, they are the third highest paying market I have. *Playboy*, *Omni*, *Penthouse* – but I won't work for *Penthouse* any more – and *Heavy Metal*. They pay me a lot of money for a story. They pay between $1100 and $1500 for a story. For the reprinting of "Santa Claus" they gave me $750. Found money.

But what do you think of their magazine?

I think it sucks. I think it's idiotic beyond belief. I think it is criminal to waste paper and space and artistry like that. It frustrates the shit out of me. I go through it, I leaf through it and never read it. The only stuff they've run in the last year that has been of any value as far as I'm concerned is the Strnad and Corben *Arabian Nights*. That's why I wrote the introduction to the book. Have you seen the book?

No.

They put them all together in a book. It was intended as a book and they ran them in bits and pieces in *Heavy Metal*, and they asked me to write an introduction. I wrote the introduction and I raved about it. I think it's absolutely sensational. First rank. Have you been reading that stuff?

Yeah. I think very, very highly of Jan Strnad. I think Strnad is a fine writer.

And the shame of it is that Jan is not going to get as much publicity off it as Corben. And when they talk about it, they talk about it as Corben's *Arabian Nights*. And Jan has got to be as responsible because that thing is plotted well. It is really well written. And I remember Jan from years ago when he had some little fanzine he wanted me to…

Anomaly.

Right, and he wanted to print something of mine, so I've known him for a long time. But I can't stand that *So Beautiful and So Dangerous*. I think it's stupid. The thing that really drives me crazy is that one that's done in phonetic English, at the back of the book, where people say, "Arr yugo-ing tu thee marr-kett" – Oh, my God, I look at that and I say, That is the pure cannibalization of the acidhead. It's lunacy eating lunacy and producing lunacy. I read it and I go, "My God!" But they have published a lot of interesting fiction. Julie's a peculiar editor. God knows what Ted White is going to do up there.

I was going to ask you what you thought his contribution would be.

I have no idea. I don't even have an opinion. I have no way of knowing what

Ted plans, or if he'll make a contribution or if he'll vanish from there or what. It's a strange magazine. But then, *Metal Hurlant* is a strange magazine. And the reason there's a terrible dichotomy for me is that in France, they're the ones who publish all my books. And they have made me in France a literary sensation. I am very hot in France. I had the front page on *Le Monde*. You cannot get any better than that. One of the quotes was, "Three years ago, it was the time of Bukowski. Last year was the period of Hubert Selby. And this year is the Ellison Explosion." And they went on and treated me – they've done three books of mine. They did *Memos From Purgatory* under the title *Les Barons de Brooklyn*, and they did *Strange Wine* under the title *Hitler Peignait des Roses*, which is "Hitler Painted Roses" – they didn't do it as "Strange Wine" because they thought they'd think it was a wine book – and they've done *Gentleman Junkie* as *Gentleman Junkie*.

Do you know French?

Oui. You may say, "Yeah, but the French like Jerry Lewis too, so what the fuck do they know?" and that may very well be, but they like me and they like me a lot. They treat me with the same kind of high respect as they feel for James M. Cain and Dashiell Hammett and Raymond Chandler and Nelson Algren and that's pretty fast company for me to be running in, because I think Cain is one of the finest American writers we've ever produced. He's virtually unread these days, but he's a great, great, great, great writer. They have done many pieces on me in *Métal Hurlant* and serious essays and interviews and they've picked up pieces from the American version and reprinted them there. They wanted to do a whole Ellison issue. So when you ask me, "What do I think of the magazine?" I give you a very honest answer which could cost me dearly. And I hope this will lead the readers to understand that I have held back very little here. I've done a couple of politic things in this interview, but on balance I did them only because what the fuck's the point in kicking a cripple, or talking about something else that I'm pissed off about out of personal pique. I mean, what's the point? There are certainly enough people I've attacked viciously here to satisfy the most bloodthirsty.

Even *The Comics Journal*.

Even *The Comics Journal*. Right.

I'd like to speak about the writers, novelists, and short story writers you currently enjoy.

[A friend] was asking me before, "Who should I read? Who do you like?" And I said Conrad, and Mark Twain, and...

They're dead.

It was Dickens who said, "A book you haven't read is a new book."

You like Doctorow, obviously.

I like Doctorow, I like *Ragtime*, I like it a lot, I really like it a lot. Oddly enough, most of my reading, particularly of fiction, in the last two years, has been of the Latin-American writers. People you've probably never heard of in your whole life.

You must like Borges.

I adore Borges. He's had a profound influence on my work. But I've been reading Borges for 15 years. I'm talking about Miguel Asturias, about Cortazer, I'm talking about Lhossa, Jorge Amado, Carlos Fuentes, and Gabriel Garcia Marquez. These are giants who are with us now. I met Borges. He spoke at UCLA and I sat there and watched this almost blind old man, and it was one of the most moving and exciting evenings of my life.

I've been fighting for him to win the World Fantasy Award for Life Achievement for three years now, and they've given it to a couple of worthy people and people who are less than worthy. I won't go back to the World Fantasy Convention because, apart from the fact that they treated me shabbily and passed me over – *Strange Wine* didn't even get on the ballot this year; it was the best-selling hardcover collection of the year, which doesn't say necessarily that it's good – but *Strange Wine* is one of my very best books, and it didn't even get on the ballot. Last year, "Jeffty Is Five" won five of the six major awards for which it was eligible, including the British fantasy award, and the fans put it on the ballot. It was the only story that got sufficient votes from the fans to put it on the ballot, and the judges decided to pass it over. The judges were all Lovecraftians, and all that whole Arkham group, and I finally just said, "Well, piss on you." I mean, they weren't all that crowd, but there were sufficient of them to swing it over to whoever they wanted to give it to. They gave it to a nice man whose story was terrible and it did not deserve the award. I'm not ashamed to say that. Again, it may sound like ego-going, but fuck it. If someone thinks it's ego, it's ego, but that's a goddamn good story. "Jeffty Is Five" is a top-flight story and it should have won the award. And I got really angry about it, but more than angry about my loss was the awarding of the Life Achievement Award to Frank Belknap Long, instead of to Borges. last year. Because Belknap Long at his best – at his best, and he's a kindly old gentleman, he's never done me any harm, but I'm talking here about the relative value of a body of literary work – Frank Belknap Long is a hack.

Who is that? I'm not familiar with his work.

It's a science fiction/fantasy writer who was part of the old Arkham circle and who during the '50s in New York was a copy editor for various magazines. He was paid by the word for the changes. I've seen manuscripts of mine that came back from *Fantastic Universe* where he'd change a name from Fred to Burt so that he could get a penny for that change. The manuscripts looked like fine Belgian lace when he got done with them. He had absolutely no integrity at all. He's had a few books published, only one of which, *The Hounds of Tindalos*, is of any consequence as far as I'm concerned. It's not a bad book, but he did it in the '40s. I mean, this minor writer from *Weird Tales*, this minor hack writer, this commercial writer, in comparison to Borges, who is a literary giant. Apart from the fact the man is going blind, and will probably be dead very shortly, and he hasn't been awarded the Nobel, which he long since should have been, here are those *pishers* sitting out in some fuckin' Texas backwater or up in New England somewhere with the World Fantasy Award. I mean, where the fuck do they get off calling it a *world* fantasy award? I mean, they make this up, out of their own fuckin' heads. I mean, the arrogance of fans. *World* Fantasy Award… They are totally unaware of the material being published in the area of fantasy. When I was a judge – I was a judge the second year – we made sure that the awards were significant and that they were worldwide awards. For the novelists, instead of picking up one of these slash-and-hack sword-and-sorcery bullshit numbers, we picked William Kotzwinkle's *Doctor Rat*. When the winner was announced, these people said, "What? Who's William Coxwell? What? Doctor Wha—?" Then they went out and bought the book and read it and said, "Hey, this is a great book." We gave the art award not to one of their own. We gave it to Roger Dean. We gave the short-story award to Russell Kirk, a brilliant writer, for "There's a Long, Long Road A-Winding." The best we could do for life award was to give it to Ray Bradbury. Bradbury was the only name on the list that was really significant. But there was Borges and Collier and…

This year, they were planning on giving it to – I mean, he's a very good writer – they were going to give it to Manly Wade Wellman, and I wrote a letter to the judges and I said, "I've seen the names of the people who are up for this award, they are all very good writers, and Manly Wade Wellman is certainly a deserving writer, and his life achievement should be honored. But before you get to Weilman you must give it to Borges, there's no two ways about it." I talked to one of the judges and I said, "How did it go?" and he said, "I think he got it." So that's terrific.

But do you think they're going to be smart enough to get in touch with Borges's publisher and say, "This man is winning the World Fantasy Award and we would very much like to bring him up"? No. No. One of their own schmucks, one of their own Arkham circle, some asshole from Worcester, Massachusetts, or some place, will say, "On behalf of George Louis Bore-guess, I'd like to accept this award." And then they'll put it in a box with some plastic bubbles and schlep it off to South America and it'll be busted in half and the guy will get it and he'll say, "What the fuck is this?"

What essayists do you admire? You mentioned Geoffrey Wolfe to me…

Oh yeah, I admire Geoffrey Wolfe enormously.

Pritchett?

Pritchett's good. I like Pritchett. Pritchett is a bit high-toned for me, I'm afraid. You remember Harvey Cassill? Harvey Cassill used to do a lot of the stuff that

Pritchett now does. Jessica Mitford. In her new book, *Poison Penmanship*, I went back and read the piece she did on the Famous Writers' School, and she got them closed down. I understand they're back in business now.

That was Bennett Cerf's scam, wasn't it?

Uh-huh. What a marvelous job of muckraking she did. And that's a very honorable tradition, the muckraking thing. I like Jesse Kornbluth occasionally.

Joan Didion?

I do like Didion. There's something there that I feel uneasy with; God knows what it is. I mean, *Slouching toward Bethlehem* is one of the most remarkable books I ever read but *The White Album*... I don't know, I'd have to go back and reread it. There's something that troubles me there and I haven't codified it yet. But that's the kind of thing I like to do, I like to be troubled so that I go back and read something again. You say, "Ahh, I'm onto something here."

I wanted to ask you who, during your life, has most influenced your thought, the way you think, shaped your values, and so on? I'm very curious about that.

I suppose it would have to be Mark Twain. But when you say, "Who has influenced my thought," it's not so much that any one person has influenced my thought as it is that, for instance, the view of my father, a very good and kind man, who died with none of his dreams realized, all of them unfulfilled, was a living example to me of what I was not going to be under any circumstances. So that was very influential.

So it might have been more your experience than...

Oh yeah, I've been much more influenced by experience than by the written word. Even as I have been more influenced by music and painting in my stories than I have by the written word. I'm triggered by painting and by music more than by other people's stories. My experiences – my life has been a very peculiar one, even among the peculiar people I know, and having run away at the age of 13 and been on my own, having experienced vicious anti-Semitism and violence at a very tender age, from 13 and younger, until I finally ran away at 13. At 15, I was driving a dynamite truck in North Carolina and reading voraciously, just reading everything. I taught myself to read very young. I learned very, quickly the one lesson that I think a writer must learn to be of any use to himself or herself and the rest of the world, which is that what they tell you is real and what you perceive to be real and what really is real are three very different things and that the gap between reality and the word-of-mouth word game they play about real is an enormous one and if you can jump it and land on your feet you can probably write about it pretty well.

And I learned to take risks, I learned to be independent, and I learned to be tough, and I learned to trust my own judgment, and I learned a very important lesson that I guess has influenced almost everything I've ever done, which is that I can be wounded, but they can't really hurt me. They can't really do me any lasting damage. That makes you safe. That makes you beyond their reach. In Hollywood, they don't know what to do with me. Except not hire me, except when they need something done that only I can do, then they've got to hire me, so I've got them by the balls. But they cannot figure out how the fuck to get me in line. And of course "in line" means not to give them any shit and to do what I'm told. And I don't work that way; I don't do that. I don't mean to be troublesome. I've got a very low bullshit threshold. They keep trying it with money and as they go up and up and up and up I keep learning that yeah, maybe I can be bought, but, whatever it is, at the moment, the sum is higher than $265,000, which is what they offered me to do a series on CBS, to create a miniseries. And I said "No," and hung up on them.

The words along the way, Hemingway, and Mark Twain, Conrad, Dickens, Dostoevsky, Cervantes, all the right authors – but, and this is something that I said to *Time Magazine*, I said, "You know, I will tell you that my germinal and seminal influences were Conrad and Dickens and Poe and Blackwood" – which they definitely were, I'm not lying about it – "but the truth of the matter is, the things that influenced me the most were comic books, pulp magazines, old-time movies, and old-time radio." Those were the four boundaries of my world when I was a little boy and I had nothing else. Comics were always very important to me. As I said earlier, I was Supersnipe, I had all the comics. I kept them in a wooden box.

How do you think that's affected your view of things, your writing?

I do things dramatically in stories, which is a trick from comics. I write very, very visually, and people say, "Gee, that must come from writing movies." No, I was writing that way before I went to do movies. That's how I was able to break into movies. I'm one of the very few science-fiction writers who can also write scripts. There's me, there's Bob Bloch, there's David Gerrold, Alan Brennert, there may be half a dozen. And why is that? Because writing for print and writing for movies are very, very different and you have to be able to see it to write it and I got that from comics. Abso-fuckin'-lutely. I owe a great debt to comic books. Which is, I suppose, why I feel so betrayed by the condition into which they have allowed the medium to sink. When you don't care, you don't care. When you love something and you're betrayed by it, you get hostile. Which is why I'm hostile. I don't like comics very much these days. I buy them so I don't miss an issue, but I think it's shameful to have to pay 40 cents for a piece of shit that's thinner than anything you ever bought back in the goddamn '40s. I know it's not the '40s and lithography costs more and typesetting costs more and ink costs more and paper, God knows, is out the window, but Jesus Christ, if they're going to charge that kind of money, they really ought to shoot for the moon. But then you say, "Well, would the audience go for it?" Who the hell knows? Try it and see! But they don't.

Do you think that maybe comics haven't changed as much as you have and that's why you're so dissatisfied with them?

I don't know. I've gone back and read a lot of those from the '40s and I feel them still – they're silly, but there's a vitality to them. They had an innocence. The innocence is now gone, but it hasn't been replaced with an accompanying sensibility of intellectual or artistic viewpoint... Whether that sentence makes any goddamn sense I'm not sure, but by this time, I mean, it's now 3:10 in the morning and I feel like someone's sucking my brains out through my nose with a hose. Yeah, I've changed a lot, but I still see a lot of things through the eyes of a child. I really do. I have no time sense. If I tell you I'll be there at six o'clock, look for me on Thursday. Nineteen-forty-one is literally the same to me as this morning. I have a oneness of time sense, which is why I'm always late. That's why I wrote "Repent, Harlequin, Said the Ticktockman," an apologia for my always being late. And that's because I just can't perceive that something is earlier or later. It's very difficult. And so I find it dubious that I've changed so much that I wouldn't see anything that was of value in comics. I really think they are worse now.

Of course, they were worse in the '40s than they were in the '60s. I think the stuff in the '60s is really the Golden Age. When they talk about the Golden Age, they don't know what the fuck they're talking about. It was the '60s, after the "pop" thing and into the era of relevance, '67-'72, and even that is sophomoric stuff, as you said, but I remember that *Green Lantern/Green Arrow* where the guy gets crucified on the SST, and I thought, "Holy fuck!" I mean, that really blew me away. And I must say that *Swamp Thing* was dynamite, just dynamite, the art, the conception, the whole mythic overtone. I mean, I'm not even sure Len and Bernie knew what they were dealing with, with the great legends of all time. I think they thought they were writing the Heap! And maybe that's it. You're not supposed to start thinking, "Hey, I'm gonna do great art," just "I'm going to write one cracking good story."

Let me ask you who is the greatest living writer of fiction right now? [*Pause.*] Maybe I should limit it to the United States?

[*Pause.*] Boy, I hate popularity contests like that. Who's the greatest... I would say Borges is the greatest. I would say so, yeah. Let me tell you something: The way that question is usually asked of me. [*Snotty interviewer's voice*]: "Apart from yourself, who do you think is a great writer?" I usually punch on that line, because that indicates a kind of insulting supposition that I find really annoying.

An interesting thing happened today. Isaac Asimov was recounting a story – I don't remember who the scientists were, but it was a biologist. Say that it was Haldane, if you will, I don't know who it was. This apparently took place in the 18th, 19th century, and he was testifying as an expert witness in the trial, and they had him under oath, and at the end they asked him, "Professor Haldane, who is the greatest living biochemist?" He said, "I am, sir." And everyone in the courtroom was horrified, because this man was known for being self-effacing, modest, quiet, generous. He had never exhibited any ego at all. After the case was over and he came out, people gathered around and said, "Why would you say such a thing?" and he said, "I was under oath. I could not lie."

Today, Isaac said the same thing. He did this deposition. We were talking about a number of writers, and he said – I won't name any names – but he was under oath, and it was the first time I had heard him say anything like this, It was very interesting. He was talking about a writer, who I think very highly of, but who I don't think is one of the greats. Isaac was asked, "Was he one of the important writers?" "Well," he said, "I would not put him in the first rank. Say there are 10 writers in the first rank. I would not put him in that first rank of important writers. If it went to 20, I would certainly say that he would be in there. And this was a name that, if I were to tell it to you, you would say, "My God!" Later on, the same question was asked of Isaac about me, and without any hesitation, Isaac said, "Oh, he is definitely in the first rank. He is one of the ten most important writers in the country." And the other writer was such a close friend of Isaac's that [Isaac] said, "I would be very unhappy if this remark was repeated so that this person heard it," and so I knew he was not buttering me up or saying anything that he didn't believe. And I suddenly realized that Isaac, whose talent I admire in many, many ways and who is a close personal friend, thought that much of me, and I began thinking, "What is my position?" And when you asked me, "Who's the greatest living writer?" for a moment, I heard myself saying, "I am." And I really believed it. Not out of ego, it was just an analysis. Suddenly: "Who? Who is really that important?"

And then I realized that I was talking foolishly.

Michael Moorcock was staying at my house for two months until a couple of weeks ago. Michael spent hours talking to me and explaining why I am better than Borges and Michael is no slouch in terms of literary criticism. I mean, he is hot shit, Jack. And I think he's full of birdseed. I know damn well I am not better than Borges, because I am in absolute awe of Borges. I sit and read his stuff and I say, "Holy Jesus! It's amazing that anyone would attempt that, much less pull it off so well." So I know I'm not. But nonetheless, writers whose work I admire, who I think are extraordinary, first rank, look at me and talk to me that way, as if I am their mentor. I think. Bill Coxwinkle is *sensational* – and he's been reading me for years and I've had a mighty influence on his work. Well, I just about fell off the goddamn chair. I met Tom Chastain yesterday at a wedding. I admire Tom Chastain's books; I think they're awfully good. And he said, "Oh, I've been reading you for years, and I just admire your work." And his wife said, "Oh my God!" and they talked chapter and verse on the stories, and that just blows me away.

So I don't know who I would say is the greatest. I suppose Borges, perhaps W.S. Merwin. If you don't know W.S. Merwin, you ought to look at him. He's only had two books of very very short stories. He's mostly known as a poet, but his short short stories are spectacular, particularly "The Miner's Pale Children" and another book called *The Carrier of Ladders*, and they're available from Athenium, and they're now in trade paperback; you can get them at any really good bookstore. Do you know I'm getting hoarse?

Yes.

My voice is leaving me. Four and a half hours of steady talking can do that to anybody. Anyhow, there's a Scottish writer named George Mackay Brown who's almost totally unknown in this country. I admire his work enormously. I think he's brilliant. The South Americans I mentioned. The German, Gunter Grass, he's really outstanding.

What do you think of our American establishment novelists, like Mailer?

Well, I think less and less of Mailer as time goes by. I probably shouldn't. I haven't read the new book. I just bought it, "The Prisoner's Death," or whatever...

That's Gary Gilmore?

Yeah. I understand it's really, really good and that he's going back to reasonable writing. Styron I like very much. I've always liked Styron. I don't like *Sophie's Choice* as much as I like *Lie Down in Darkness*. I think it's an excellent book.

How about Capote?

Capote? He's a burnt-out case. He's bullshit time.

Vidal?

Oh, he's even bigger bullshit time. Updike: bullshit time. Cheever: mostly bullshit time, except sometimes in the short stories. Updike, sometimes in short stories, but very seldom. I mean, they are masters of the fine point made – the masters of the *mot juste*, as we say. Joyce Carol Oates I admire. I go for a lot of writers that other people have never even heard of. I just finished the Hunter Thompson book, *The Great White Shark Hunt*.

Did you like that? He seems to me to be a real burnt-out case.

Yeah. Exactly. I'm glad you said it first so that I didn't sound as though I was attacking my betters. I had remembered a lot of the stuff as being really impressive and I had loved it, particularly the Kentucky Derby piece that he did, and the Muhammad Ali piece, but going back and reading it – have you read the book?

I've read every other book that he's written, except that one. But I hear a lot of it is excerpts from his other works.

Well, there's excerpts from both the *Fear and Loathing* books, there's excerpts from a lot of other places, but it's the gathering together of all the small pieces, all the "gonzo" papers, and I now realize that gonzo journalism is an excuse for slovenly writing, for getting crashed out of your brain and avoiding writing the story and doing all the spadework and all the research and just doing a lot of fancy footwork. It is an excuse for irresponsibility and it ennobles it and that's dangerous, because there are hundreds of thousands of kids in journalism school all over the country who want to be Rex Reed and want to be Tom Wolfe and want to be Gael Greene, and want to be, God knows! Hunter Thompson. And he is the worst possible fuckin' example. And the thing again – and this is going to sound like, "Oh well, he's serving his own rep" – I was looking at the stuff and I was thinking, "Jesus Christ, all of this stuff smells, waddles, quacks, goes steady with and sheds water like the stuff I was writing for the Free Press."

The TV stuff?

Yeah. And the "Harlan Ellison Hornbook" columns, which you've never seen. That was another column which I did for two years. That's going to be gathered into another book someday when I get around to it. It's the same kind of stuff. It's personal journalism, it's diary, it's confessional that goes to exploring in an investigative nature and. an analytical nature, and yet he constantly avoids the point. He goes to a place to do the job, gets off the plane drunk – if we are to believe him, and I think he's full of shit and lying up to his ears most of the time anyhow. I don't believe anyone can consume dope in that kind of quantity, although a woman I know was just on the set of his new movie, *Where the Buffalos Roam*, and she said he was crapped out all of the time. But I think that's got to be a pose. Nobody can function, nobody can write, with that much dope in him. He talks about, "I dumped six black beauties and I made up a cocktail of three reds and two whites and then I sniffed some ether on top of that and then I chewed some blotter acid and then I shoved a little coke up my snout and then I did my gums with…" whatever the fuck. And he goes onandonandonandon and on and on… This is impossible, man. I've been around enough righteous, ripped-out-of-their-brains, screaming vampire-bat drug addicts to know that you get a certain amount of chemical in you and forget it, Jim, you are *tabula rasa*, that is it! And there are only very few moments in that book where he really gets it on and sustains it and tells you something you never knew before. One of them is in the piece he does on the Salazar slaying in L.A. Another is a very short piece about a guy who was a freelance writer who died unknown and there are some fabulous lines in that. But even in that there is an inaccuracy and a stupidity that is awesome in a man who's so hip and is supposed to know what's goin' down. He's got a paradigm – he's made up a paradigm for this guy dying unknown and he's picked up a record jacket – I can't remember what the group is – and he says, "Here's this group of musicians, their name isn't as big as the producer's. The producer: Tom Wilson. Tom Wilson, who the fuck is Tom Wilson? Who the hell ever heard of Tom Wilson?" He goes on and on and on, Tom Wilson, Tom Wilson, Tom Wilson. I've known Tom Wilson for 25 years. Tom Wilson was Bob Dylan's producer. He's the one who made all the best Bob Dylan records. He produced the Band. He for Chrissake produced Miles Davis. He was the only Black producer at Columbia for 15 years. He went out on the goddamn road and found Lightning Hopkins. He published *Jazz Guide*, *33 Guide*, *Stereo Guide* out of his own pocket. He is the man who put on the Ryker's Island Jazz Festival two years running, for Chrissake. Tom Wilson is a fuckin' giant. And schmuckpuss didn't know him. Schmuckpuss didn't take the time to find out who Tom Wilson is. He used him as a paradigm and happened to pick someone with impeccable credentials. And it invalidates everything else. You say, "This guy doesn't know what the fuck he's talking about." He's just suddenly coming off the wall and sounding like Mr. Whizzbang. He's a drunk and he's a doper who has got a style which is very dangerous for journalism students to pick up on.

You remember, I guess, after his series on the campaign trail in *Rolling Stone* was made into a book, all of a sudden there were all these gonzo journalists out there who aped his style. And of course they bombed, every one of them.

Man, when I go to colleges, I mean, the condition – and I hope you publish this in one of your big call-outs – the state of academic journalism is roughly on the level of the early Cretaceous era. I've never seen so many fuckin' illiterates in all my life. I mean, simple stone illiterates who cannot spell, who cannot take a note, who have to have a tape recorder and then misuse it, who never ask you to spell anything, who never look up dates, who never check back with their source to find out if they've gotten the right facts. And the thing that they do constantly is that they ape your style because they haven't got one of their own. They try for flash and filigree and they come off looking like boobs. They misuse syntax, they trip over their own goddamn analogies. It's just pathetic to look at. They think they're hot shit, and they're being turned out of those goddamn colleges by the hundreds every year. College newspapers everywhere I go are unbelievably bad. Even in the area of sports writing, where you usually get a little fast stuff in there, it's just… Oh, God!

Our universities are turning out illiterates every day.

Slovenly. They don't care. They don't have any sense of professionalism. Well, that makes it all easier for guys like you and me. I find it very easy to be an outlaw. Because the world is fuckin' sheep and drones. Thank God. Thank God for the sheep and drones. They keep the machines functioning, they take out the garbage, they make sure the lights are lit, there's ice in the refrigerator. That permits me all the time in the world to run around and play Zorro.

TCJ

STEVE Englehart

THE CRITICS' CHOICE

INTERVIEW BY RALPH MACCHIO, WITH GARY GROTH, KIM THOMPSON AND MIKE CATRON: Born in the Midwest and educated in the Northeast, Steve Englehart came to Marvel Comics as a writer after a brief stint in the U.S. Army and an even briefer time finding whatever minor work he could as an artist. He enjoyed signature runs on many of that company's most popular titles, including *Captain America, The Avengers* and *Dr. Strange*. He was the thinking fan's superhero comics writer, weaving complex stories that often had at their core an adult hot-button issue or two – disillusionment, or feelings of inadequacy, or the dangers of corporate influence on politics. He was eventually hired away from Marvel by rival DC Comics and revamped several of their most popular characters such as Superman, Batman, and Wonder Woman. Elements of his take on Batman can be found in nearly every popular treatment of the character since, including the successful film franchise.

The following interview with Ralph Macchio, Gary Groth, Kim Thompson, and Mike Catron (TCJ #63, Spring 1981) reveals how deeply Englehart felt about his place in the profession, how he thought many of the major superhero concepts worked best, and how writing for comics might have changed once the concerns of big business entered the picture.

Englehart has kept a hand in comics in the years since, doing creator-owned work and projects for the superhero publishers. He was a driving creative force behind Malibu's Ultraverse concept, and saw his Nightman character make it into syndicated television. He has also written books, provided scripts for television cartoons, and designed games for a variety of companies. His contribution to so many major comic-book characters at key times in their development has only begun to be appreciated.

Writer: Steve Englehart Artists: Marshall Rogers & Terry Austin *Detective Comics*
#471 August 1977 [©1977 DC Comics Inc.]

RALPH MACCHIO: You once mentioned that after having dropped out of comics as a teenager, you got back into reading them when somebody brought to your attention a _Spider-Man_, and at the bottom of a panel, there was a caption that said, "Norton G. Fenster, who is a fulltime nut..." That one line got you back into reading comics?

STEVE ENGLEHART: That's right. I had read comics as a kid, and I had given them up at the age of 13 because I had outgrown them. Specifically, I can remember _that_, for some unknown reason. There was a letter in _Superboy_. Somebody wrote in and said, "Why doesn't Superboy fight the Commies?" and the answer was, "Well, he never gets involved in political situations." And I thought, "Well, this is not reality." Not that I wanted him to fight the Commies, but how can he exist and not get involved in the real world?

So I gave them up, and it wasn't until spring of '66, end of my freshman year in college, when a guy came up and said, "This comic book is nuts. Read this." And it was exactly that panel – the last panel on page two of _Spidey_ #36. "Whoa! This is all right! I'll read this stuff!" And I was living in a college town where they only had a couple of newsstands and they never bothered to really take too much care of the comics, so I was able to buy three issues of everything and got introduced not only to the whole Marvel mythos but also to continuity, and went nuts after that. I went back that summer to Indianapolis, where I was from, and noticed they weren't distributing half the Marvel line, so I called up the newsstand and said, "I want to see some _Daredevil_ and some _X-Men!_" and the said, "OK, we'll send some out." They had them but they just weren't distributing them. I've never gotten my check from circulation for that. [_Laughter._]

I got hot and heavy into it and by the time 1971 rolled around I had a complete collection and I was ready to go.

As an artist.

Yeah. My father's a newspaperman and so I'd always written stories, but it wasn't anything I [was planning to] do when I grew up. I wanted to be an artist. I worked with Neal [Adams] and I got to be a real mediocre Neal Adams imitator, and went out and tried to become an artist. I was able to do some "Do's and Don'ts of Dating" for Murray Boltinoff and some touch-ups in the graphics department at DC. I was slowly starving to death when I got my job on staff here as an assistant editor, and when you're on staff – at least it used to be – when you're on staff they start giving you freelance work to supplement it, and I did a couple of romance stories which were real mediocre.

You drew them and they were published?

Oh, yeah. There was one that John Romita inked that looks like Romita, and one that Jack Abel inked that looks like Jack Abel. I think everybody knew real quick that I had a ways to go on that, so then, totally out of the blue, they gave me a monster story that Gary Friedrich had been supposed to dialogue and had decided he didn't feel like doing.

[*Thompson*] **"The Pterror of the Pterodactyl."**

Right. So they liked that and they said, "Want to write the Beast?" And I said, "OK, I'm not a writer, but what the hell." And then I found out that I liked it, and…

So you had no background in literature in college, or creative writing?

Oh, I'd taken a class in creative writing, I believe, but my B.A.'s in psychology. I was always interested in characters. It's all tied together – I just was always interested in *why*, why people work this way. Later, after I started writing *Doctor Strange*, I got interested in why the universe works this way, and so on and so forth…

I think most people assume that you got into *Doctor Strange* because you had the knowledge before you got into it and just couldn't wait to get into the series to –

Not true. I was always interested in why things work, so a guy who could bend reality to his own ways and knew more about how reality works was somebody I was interested in, but I really didn't have the knowledge arid I think it sort of showed. I'd been writing Doctor Strange in *The Defenders* as basically a superhero who shot rays out of his palms instead of out of his eyes, or whatever. Later, as people remarked, it did turn into a little more scholarly, what-is-magic-all-about. I don't know that that was necessarily the best way to go, but that was the way *I* was going at the time, and as I learned more I wanted to incorporate it.

Well, it must have worked, because the book went monthly under you.

Yeah. I don't know if *Doctor Strange* were being produced with exactly that team and all that whether it would sell today or not, but it seemed to me that it was part of that time. There was a real occult boom, and there were enough people out there who could relate to his difference, just as there were enough people who could relate to Captain America. In the entire history of *Captain America* – or at least since World War II ended – it only sold when I was writing it, as far as I know. Again, the approach I tried to take was, "Why is this guy different from the rest of them?" In *Doctor Strange* I just had to work a little harder to educate myself.

Why don't you tell me about Shang-Chi? Because *Master of Kung Fu* was your own creation – yours and Jim Starlin's – you obviously felt very strongly about it, even to the point of giving it up because you didn't want to ride roughshod over something you'd have to do very quickly. In a certain sense, it achieved a popularity I'm sure you never expected it to achieve.

Not entirely true. It was unabashedly a take-off on the *Kung Fu* television program, which was sweeping the country at the time, and all of the kung fu Bruce Lee movies that were sweeping the country at the time, so we expected it to be real popular. But of course we were aiming for the TV *Kung Fu* series as opposed to the Bruce Lee movies. I saw it as pretty much *Doctor Strange* in a sense, although with a much more melodramatic situation, with Fu Manchu and all that – and I've always liked Fu Manchu, too. I did give it up when they said, "Let's can the philosophy and get into the action." I have to say, most of the time when I give up a strip it's hard for me to follow it thereafter because I've so figured out who I think the guy should be that reading anybody else's version is tough on me, but I would like to say that the stuff Moench and Gulacy did, although not the character that I created, was really good stuff. My Shang-Chi would not have joined up with the forces of the Western secret service, but still and all, that went on to become a real decent series.

When I've spoken to Doug [Moench] about your comments on Shang-Chi, he feels that you painted yourself into a corner with the character.
I only did five issues. How –?

Well, he thinks you had a character who's nonviolent but has to get into fights, so he felt the character had to be nudged toward a more aggressive role, so that he could act rather than simply react.
Well, strips are organic. Stan used to say that they write themselves, and they do. My best example is Mantis, who I introduced to be a slut and a hooker and who turned into a celestial Madonna. So had I continued *Master of Kung Fu,* I might well have come to those same conclusions. As it was, I got off the book long before I felt that I'd exhausted every possibility in what I was trying to do.

You at one point mentioned to me that you were going to have Shang-Chi and Doctor Strange meet for about four issues.
When I left Marvel, the only series that I had a lot of plots backlogged on was *Doctor Strange.* The others were worked out, I'd say, for the next three months. Things were getting more and more oppressive, so I was rapidly losing interest in being a Marvel comics-writer – but with *Doctor Strange* I did have the rest of the "Occult History of America" plot in mind, and then I was going to do a trip with Lord Pfyffe – Chris [Claremont] has now picked up on that, he's doing something different, but I had planned to do a thing with Lord Pfyffe. Basically, the trip I had in mind was that a long time ago the Pfyffe family had been cursed by this demon and in the 10th generation there was going to be hell to pay, and Lord Pfyffe had been the ninth Lord Pfyffe until the world ended and everybody was replaced and all of a sudden he was the 10th lord Pfyffe. I was going to be playing off that End-of-the-World routine. And after that I wanted to do Doctor Strange vs. Fu Manchu with Shang-Chi caught in the middle. We're talking a year after I got off, so I don't

know any more than that. I would have liked to have done Doctor Strange and Shang-Chi and Fu Manchu all mixed together. It would have been decent.

Why did you give up on comics, quit the field when it seemed you could have named your own ticket, you were at the height of creativity, and you decided to pack it in?

Well, because I *couldn't* name my own ticket, basically. I also thought I was doing pretty well at the time, but Gerry Conway called me up and said, "Hi, I have power and you don't, I'm taking the *Avengers* away from you," and I said, "[*raspberry*] forget that, I feel I'm at the point where I don't have to take that any more, and I'm not going to take it."

But I was thinking more like when you were at DC; when you left you seemed to be doing stuff which seemed to be at a peak – *Detective*, the *Justice League*, *Mister Miracle*. You just kept on turning out better and better material.

But that's why I wanted to quit. There were no new peaks to climb in comics. All I'd ever wanted to do was be a Marvel comics writer, and all of a sudden, I found myself on the phone telling Gerry Conway that I wasn't going to be a Marvel comics writer any more. So I went to DC, but I really did decide that this business was going to hell and this was not going to get me anywhere. I was in no position to just walk right then, but I figured, I'll take a year, I'll go to DC, I'll do the damnedest stuff I can possibly do, a) for myself, because it's my last year in comics, I'm going to blow out everything I've got to give; b) for DC, because they were nice enough to take me on and give me pretty much what I wanted; and c) against Marvel – I figured they ought to know that they'd blown it by going through this stuff. So I did go over there and I did the best stuff I could possibly do, because there was no sense that I was going to have to save myself for the next five years. And when that was over, I went to Europe, wrote a book, and so on and so forth.

[*Groth*] Steve, could you clarify what you meant when you said the business went downhill starting in 1973?

Well, the conglomerates bought both businesses pretty much simultaneously in '73. Warner bought National, Cadence bought Marvel, and Stan, who had been at the top of a creative heap that he had founded, that he had initiated, suddenly turned his attention from being at the top of the creative heap to being at the bottom of the corporate heap. And decisions started being made in terms of, "Well, we don't really care up here on the ninth floor what's in the books, but you must make 10 percent more next year." This is not unique to comics; you hear this story about record people, movie people, book people. It's just entertainment in general. It's happened to everybody. But it was happening here and we were all here and that's the one I was involved in. It was like a snowball. At first we had to do these strange books with one page that was blown up to two pages so they only had to pay us for 17 but could print 18. Those things did seem kind of bizarre, but the stuff I most objected to was when they started saying, "Well, let's not be quite so different any more, let's not try to move forward any more, because now we have to kind of circle the wagons, because now we're getting the merchandise." I understand merchandising; it's a business, and it's hip. I can understand why if you buy the Avengers and the book is coming out with a whole group of different people from the ones you've got on your T-shirts that makes a difference. Still and all, it wasn't what Marvel used to be.

I have to say, having come back and spent two weeks here, having heard how it works now, I think it's worse in 1980 [than in 1976]. To me, the Marvel Comics that exists in 1980 is 180 degrees from the Marvel Comics that I joined in 1971. When I came into the business you were encouraged to do stuff. I told Jo Duffy the other day how it used to work and she couldn't believe it. But what really amazed me was that she'd never even *heard* how it worked. They used to say, "OK, this series is yours, we expect you to do it; if you don't do it, we'll take you off it" – and I would come up with a plot, I would send it to the artist, the artist would send it back to me, I'd write it, I'd send it to the letterer, who would send it to the inker, who would send it to the office, where they'd see it for the first time, make minor corrections – because everybody had done his job along the line – and it would go out. Today every one of those steps comes back to the office, I believe – at least most of them do – and everybody sort of depends on everybody else to take care of the things that they messed up. I come from a different school. I come from a school where I was supposed to get it right myself, and I have always sort of gone on that assumption. I didn't like where it was.

There's been four periods in Marvel Comics. There was '62 to '67, which was primarily Stan's energy; '67 to '72, which was primarily Roy's energy; '72 to about '76, '77, which was a whole bunch of us – me and Gerber and McGregor and Wrightson and Brunner and Smith and Chaykin – all these people who came in because we all really wanted to do it. But we were the end of it, I think. I don't see that there's great hordes of people still coming in who have got as much to offer, and people don't seem to find the books as entertaining, the sales are down, and all the rest of it. It's not as if this is happening in a vacuum.

[*Groth*] I understand the sales are up.

It depends on which ones. I've heard some pretty dull things about what's happening at DC. Maybe Marvel's up; I don't know so much about Marvel. I've heard specifically they're down at DC; I've *heard* they're down at Marvel, but Jim [Shooter] has the records and I don't. That's why you and I can hear different things. In any event, by the time I quit, Roy has given up his editorial job because *he* didn't like dealing with those people upstairs.

Although Marvel still has a lot more energy than DC does, it's all on a much smaller scale than it used to be. DC in particular – Marvel to a lesser extent, but still not a whole much lesser extent – would rather function as a machine these days in that people and stories and concepts and everything will fit into a smoothly functioning organism which can be depended upon to deliver X amount of profit. I keep hearing the same stories over and over again about how people got screwed here and people got screwed there and so forth.

It's just dull to me now. I ask people what's good to read and they say the *X-Men*, they say *Daredevil*, and then there's this silence. There used to be hundreds of books, and you used to know that even if this book was no good, if you hung around long enough somebody would come along and they'd make it good.

[*Groth*] I just wanted you to trace the disintegration as you saw it.

Well, I've been in and out of it, so I can't give you a blow-by-blow, but it's been the increasing transformation of a place that was actually a bullpen – really, truly, it was just what they said it was: a bullpen of people who sat around and had a great time thinking up new and bizarre things every month and selling a lot of comic books doing it – to a corporate empire. When I went to work at Marvel in 1971, there was me, Romita, Herb Trimpe, Marie Severin, Morrie Kuromoto, Holly Resnicoff, John Verpoorten, Roy and Stan. We were the Bullpen. It was about twice this size [*gesturing at Macchio's office*] and people were talking and yelling across the partitions. People still do that, of course, but it's all been so spread out and structured, it's just different. And maybe it's just old-timers looking back, all the way back to 1974, but it was a wholly different atmosphere and a different way of operation back then, and I prefer that to this.

[*Thompson*] That editorial conservatism you were talking about, did it start to manifest itself when you were still working for Marvel?

Yeah. I was here until 1976, and it was around '74 that it first began to get noticeable – slowly at first. When I quit in 1976, in the same three-week period, when Conway was the editor, Gerber quit, Starlin quit, Gulacy quit. It wasn't just me – a lot of people went out during that time. It had gotten to the point where a lot of people just didn't feel that it was what they'd signed on for.

[*Thompson*] What kinds of restrictions were put on you editorially?

Well, just "don't be so bizarre, try not to progress so fast." There's that famous meeting that happened just before the quitting time when Stan said, "I don't want progress, I want the *illusion* of progress now. We don't want people dying and coming out of the strips, we don't want new girlfriends, we want to try to keep it the same." That, again, was an extreme case, because I know it's loosened up since then, but everything goes through periods.

Here's an example: I went to work here in the summer of '71 and I started writing in the fall of '71. When it came around to do the books for the summer of '72, they weren't going to publish any new annuals. And I remembered that as a fan I really liked those giant-sized summer specials that Marvel had, so I thought, "Well, what the hell, I'll do an *Avengers/Defenders* crossover," and I came in and

I said, "I want to do this, back and forth, throughout the summer." They said, "Well, I don't think it's really going to sell, but what the hell." That was the attitude – "give it a shot." And it turned out that it *did* sell, and they came back and they said, "Well, this guy has strange ideas, but they seem to sell, so what the heck." And after that, really, they said, "Take this series and do what you will with it." If I want to write eight months of *Captain America* without Captain America in it, "sounds weird to us, but OK, if you can do it, give it a shot."

And I don't really think you can get away with stuff like that any more. Everything has to be more upfront and more immediate. And therefore you start losing the subtleties, and people who are working in an environment where they know they don't really have to think the story through because the editor will rewrite it for them, where they know that they can't really take too many flights of fancy, start to get lazy and start to turn out product rather than push individual creativity to the fore.

It's a lot more intangibles than it is specific instances and what instances there are are all being lost in the mists of time anyway, because I really haven't paid much attention to that part of my life for a while now.

[*Catron*] Looking back at that three-week period, I'd be interested in getting a chronology of what happened. What led up to it and what came down the tubes.

It was a strange three weeks, and what you need to do is talk to everybody who was involved in that time, and then you might be able to put together some sort of tapestry.

All I know is that the first week Conway and Shooter – his Assistant Editor, or the right-hand man – called me up and said, "We really don't like the *Super-Villain Team-Up* you just wrote because you said that the Sub-Mariner's father did or didn't do something." It's on page two of issue six or seven or something. I don't even know what it is now. But they said, "You did this." I said, "No, I really didn't." And they said, "We know you did, because we were told by whoever proofread that you did it." I said, "I've got the script here, and I didn't say that." And it was like, "Yes, you did, and you're gonna' pay for it. You're really in trouble for doing this kind of stuff." So I took my Xerox copy of the script and I Xeroxed off the page and I sent it to them.

The second week I got a call from Conway saying, "We're really sorry. We were misinformed. I see your script, you're right, I went back and looked at it, everything you said was true, hey look, no hard feelings, huh, I'm just getting started and I don't really know how to do all this shit and let's just let bygones be bygones." Jim Shooter was also apologizing and smoothing things over.

And the third week I got this call saying, "I wrote the *JLA* at National, I want to do the *Avengers* here, so I'm taking it." I mean, it was like bam! bam! bam!, night and day. The first week was real strange, the second week was kiss-and-make-up, and the third week was real strange again. And it only lasted three weeks. He also took Gerber's *Defenders* away from him, he canceled both of McGregor's books so he could start new books for himself – It was this total power mania.

[*Groth*] Did Conway "single-handedly ruin the industry," as has been suggested?

No. Well, he *was* sort of the flashpoint. The stuff had been coming down for a while and what it had done was, it had driven all of the good editors out. They'd passed Gerry over a couple of times, because Gerry learned all his vocabulary from TV. He's got a great vocabulary but he can't spell it. And he was always having to be fixed up when the stuff came in. You always had to respell words for him. So a couple of times he asked if he could be an editor, and they said, "No way!" [*Laughter.*]

And then they had nobody. After Marv left, they made Gerry the editor because he was the only one left around here. I'd been the assistant editor under Roy, and if I'd stayed in New York when Roy'd left the first time, I would have taken over as Editor instead of Len [Wein]. But that wasn't what I wanted to do; I wanted to write. I learned only later about office politics and power games and so forth and realized that since I'd never played any of that I had no power when it came down to that. I had assumed that writing a lot of best-selling books for people and not causing them any trouble was just exactly what was expected of me. But when it came down to a crunch, [it came down to] who had more power.

After I'd quit, Starlin had quit, [Alan] Weiss had quit – Weiss wasn't doing a whole lot, but we were sitting around in my house in California one day, and we called up Stan and said, "Stan, I don't know if you know what's going on, but this guy is really screwing up your company. All these people are leaving, and we've all given you faithful service, we've all really done well." Stan goes, "Well, I don't know anything about this, I'll check it out," so he calls me back about an hour later and says, "I went downstairs and asked Gerry and Jim and they say you guys are all lying so I'm sorry, I have to stand behind my editors. Goodbye and good luck."

This was like two weeks after we'd quit. I'd already set things up at DC. But I felt an obligation to Marvel. I really had loved Marvel Comics in those days, and I'd thought, "Well, maybe Stan doesn't know what's going on," and I'm not sure that he ever did, exactly. But I really liked this place once upon a time. Sorry to see it go.

[*Groth*] The late great Marvel Comics.

Well, that's what I consider it. In my opinion the Marvel Comics that I worked for doesn't exist any more, and this is something else.

[*Groth*] What are your impressions of Jenette Kahn as an editor, publisher?

Well, it's been through two phases. When I went to work there, she could not have been nicer to me. Since I was like the first big fish they'd caught, I used to sit around in her office and we'd shoot the shit and discuss things. I remember when they thought they had gotten John Buscema to come over to DC – which got caught and nipped in the bud, but they thought they had it in the bag – and she called me into the office: "Don't tell anybody, but we got this." It was really close

– it was the feeling of a bullpen, in a sense. But I was only in town for a couple of weeks, and I went out to California.

Throughout the year that I wrote for them, I had no troubles. All my stuff was in far ahead of deadline, they loved it all, everything got printed the way I wrote it or with minor exceptions, but nothing I could object to, I got a bonus at the end of the year for having gotten all my work in on time, completed my contract.

But the last couple of times that I've been in New York... first of all, Jenette seems to have much less to do with the company. I mean, she sort of spaces in and smiles and spaces on down the hall, and –

"Spaces"?

That the verb I would use. [*Laughter.*] And this whole trip where I had to take my scripts from DC because they tried to chisel me on a rate. Behind that sort of unfocused smile there is a real hard lady, I think, and when I have negotiated with her since then she's been a lot harder about the whole thing. Once I lost the confrontation, the second time I won the confrontation, but it was definitely a confrontation, it was no longer the same.

But I don't know her, I've met her just in these brief periods, and so I'm not the one really to tell you who Jenette Kahn is. My impression is that she's a cog in the Warner's machine who is more responsive – just like Stan is, I believe – to the people above her than the people below her, and I would say that comics to her is more or less a means to an end, to be part of the Warner's hierarchy. And when her five years is up she'll go to Atlantic Records or she'll go someplace else.

At least, with DC there was none of this stuff that went down when I quit Marvel, these statements about, "Well, Steve's really one of the major talents in the industry and has been doing great work, we wish him a lot of luck, and really, if the syphilis hadn't finally reached his brain, we'd still be..." You know, one of these knife-in-the-side numbers that came out here. Jack [Harris] just says it was a misunderstanding.

[*Groth*] You said you won a confrontation and lost a confrontation. Which one did you win?

I won this one, because they said "Take $31 or die," but it's all part of a thing that I see more clearly over at DC because I've been working there – I suspect that a lot of it goes on at Marvel too, but I don't know specifically – which is basically "Screw the freelancers." That the freelancers have got nowhere else to go and they're going to have to eat whatever shit we feel they have to eat. Ever since the work-for-hire thing became a big *cause célèbre* and there was the big confrontation over the Guild and the Guild lost, and everybody came around and signed their contracts, I think there's a real attitude on the part of management that these guys a) have no option and b) even if they did are too chicken to take it.

[*Groth*] Isn't that largely true?

Yeah, I think it is largely true, but that's still no excuse for screwing people. I realize that I am unique in that I am in a position where I don't have to take it. I think career-wise that I am far past the point where I have to take any bullshit from either of the companies. And I've got another career. Comics was just a sideline for me. I did it because they asked me to do it, I had the time, I enjoyed doing it – if all those factors fall into place, I'm perfectly happy to do a comic.

But there's a bad attitude around. Because I heard later that the same thing happened with Jim Sherman, that Jack promised Jim Sherman a rate and then when Jim Sherman turned in the job he didn't get the rate. He eventually did get paid, apparently, but he had to fight for it. I have no idea if that's just a once-in-a-blue-moon aberration on Jack Harris's part, or whether this is an actual policy: "Promise them anything but give them whatever we feel they'll take." But it was real bizarre because I'd never had any problems with National up until that point. And who could imagine that I would turn in the jobs and be told that I would have to take a lesser rate.

So I came to Marvel and I sat down with Milgrom – Shooter was out of town – and I said, "Here's the story, do you want to buy these?" and he said, "Well, *I* do, but I'd have to ask Jim before I could come up with a definite situation…"

I am sort of amazed that you were actually going to sign the Marvel contract.

Well, I was not real thrilled with the idea, but I was on an incredible adrenalin high that day.

Pulling scripts back is a real bizarre concept, because it means you don't get paid, and you've already written them. But I believed that I had enough stature that I could take them elsewhere and sell them, and I went to Marvel first because I didn't even know about Eclipse then.

[*Groth*] Did you feel that strongly about the Marvel contract?

Well, when I came back from Europe two years ago, I was not in town for more than three days before I stopped at Continuity and walked into a hotbed of revolution, and these guys said, "You're a writer, you help write the new contract." So I sat down with Val Mayerik and we wrote the contract, which basically says we keep the rights, foreign sales, all that stuff, and then they called that meeting where the *Journal* published an accurate record of it as far as I can recall, right up to the point where I told Jim Shooter he was lying and stuff like that. I got up and I gave this impassioned speech about "Workers unite! This is the time, if you don't get it right now, you're going to be screwed forever with this new contract," expecting a groundswell of enthusiasm, and what I got was a lot of people sitting there saying, "Well, but, but, it'll put us out on the street, and where will we find our next job if we don't do whatever they want us to do?" So I said, "OK, fine, I'm, not in this business any more, I gave it my best shot, and that's the end of it."

I really feel very strongly against the contract, but on the other hand it wasn't as if I was planning to do a lot of stuff for Marvel in the future, so signing away all my rights forever probably wouldn't have netted them a whole lot in the final analysis anyway. But at the time I figured, "If it's not going to be sold to DC, I'd better sell it somewhere. I can't write this off." And since it really wasn't going to hurt me too much…

The nice thing I do recognize about the situation is that because I didn't sign anything at DC before this trip came down, I *was* able to take those stories back. I hope this doesn't encourage them to come up with a lifetime contract after this.

[*Groth*] How did you feel about the criticism of the Guild, that it was people like yourself and Adams who had nothing to lose who were organizing it?

I think that's entirely true. But the point is, God didn't come down and say, "You are now magically able to be your own man." I worked hard to get to that point, and so did Neal. I would encourage people to do it, but if comics are your only income, unless you're prepared like me to do something as absurd as going for several years and not make any income, so you can turn something over, you have to take it. Still, criticizing people who have gotten ahead and are trying to help others do the same is the classic victim's mentality.

[*Groth*] Was there anybody in comics who had a great deal to lose who was as gung ho for the Guild as you and Adams and Gerber, who had nothing to lose either, because he was already on the West Coast and out of comics?

Uhhh… well, Starlin, but he was already getting into paperback covers.

[*Groth*] Chaykin, but he was getting out, too.

Marshall [Rogers], at that time, had just done the *Detective* stuff and did and still does want to work in comics…

[*Groth*] But he's done well doing very little comics for quite a long time.

[*Thompson*] Chris Claremont was very noisy at the meeting. And look how long he lasted.

Oh yeah, that was kind of strange to me. When I came back this time, the first person that I really met was Chris. The night I got into town he came over and that's when I first heard hundreds of "How Jim Shooter Screwed Me" stories. "Jim Shooter screwed me this way, Jim Shooter screwed me that way, then he took away my book, but that's OK, I didn't want to fight him on that one because I was going to get this other one, but then he screwed me again…" And I was saying, "Well, Chris, I think you'd better get out of comics." And he's saying, "Well, yes, but I really like it." I'm not criticizing Chris for this, either; everybody's got his own situation.

There's another guy I talked to last week – names are irrelevant, you could fit in names – who was telling me about how he got screwed and he got screwed and he got screwed and I said, "Well, get out," and he said, "But all I want to do is write comics."

And if all you want to do is write comics then you've got to play the game. This is the only game in town. I mean, there's now two games in town but they're not so different and if that's what you want to do then that's what you have to do. Again, in the old days, we were playing this game too. We signed away all our rights. But nobody was really aware that they *could* get anything else, or that anyone else got anything else. That's another real pleasure in dealing with the book business.

Those guys treat you straight across. Comics is so much like parent and child. It's all sort of based on guilt and paranoia and sort of omnipotent authority which you may not question. In the book business they know that if they screw you you'll go to one of the many other book companies and it breeds a kind of thing where they're dealing with you straight across and not from top to bottom. They treat you fairly, they know your talent, they know they'll get rich if you're happy and you stay with them. A real pleasure dealing with people you can just talk to and you don't have to think, "What are they scheming this week? What am I going to tell them so I don't antagonize them?" There are so many games that are necessary for doing comics these days, so many subterfuges and hurt feelings that you have to swallow and shit that you have to eat because you have no option.

[*Thompson*] How did you come to do those three stories for DC, being so disenchanted with comics?

I really thought I was totally out of comics, and for all I know at any given point in time, I may still be, but the way the book business works is that you get a project, you sell a book, you go away and write it for a year and a half, and then you come back and you have to have a month while your editor reads it, and then you discuss it with him, and then you have a month while you're selling your next project. These are the dead periods, and I don't want to sit around idle, so the two times thus far that I've had dead periods since I got into novels – first when I was selling it and now that I'm selling the second one – I wanted to fill my time with something. As it is, the most logical thing was to fill it doing comic-book stuff. If I find something that I can do instead, I probably would, because I really don't think the business has done anything but get worse in the last four years.

Let me ask you how your novel writing was influenced by what you did in comics. Did you have to outgrow it to go into novels, or did you have to veer away from it?

I had to do all those things. It was real interesting, to me at least, as a learning experience. It goes back to when I started going around selling the novel. I had achieved a plateau in comics, I had name recognition, I had a solid seven years of success behind me, I had a fan following, I had really generated a lot of excitement with the *Detective* stuff, and I thought, "Well, great, I'll go to novels and they'll just love me because I'm such a celebrity," and I went in there and I found out real quickly that not only was my credential useless, it was a detriment. They said, "Well, you're a comic-book writer, and comic-book writers can't write." That's the actual quote. An editor up at Jove asked my agent to ask me to come in and I thought, "Oh boy, great, she wants to talk to me." I go in, and my manuscript's lying on her desk, and she says, "Why did you send me this?" I said, "Well, I want to sell it to you." She says, "But you're a comic-book writer." I said, "Well, did you read the manuscript?" She said, "No, I don't have to read it, you're a comic-book writer. Comic-book writers can't tell stories without pictures, and they can't get into depth. It's all superficial nonsense for children." And I said, "Well, that isn't really what I did, and why don't you read –" "No, I don't have to." It was real crazy. It worked against me selling a novel – though I eventually did – so I became real sensitive about the fact that I was going to have to live down comic books when it came to the real world. We all know that when anybody in the real world says, "This movie was like a comic book," they're not saying it was a good movie. They're saying it was cheap and it was no good.

Also, when I decided to do this, I had asked myself, "What mistakes have people made before that I'm going to avoid this time?" And the one I was really aware of was that people always say, "I'm going to get out of comic books," and they do it and after a while, things start to get a little tough, and they sort of fall back into it, and then they never get out of it again. There's been a whole string of people that have said that, and they always come back. So I made real certain. I went around and told everybody, "I'm through with comic books" to make it tough if I ever wanted to fall back, and I stopped reading them, I totally put it out of my head. I really reacted violently against comics. I said, "From now on, that was my past, I have nothing to do with that, I'm a novelist, I'm going to go out here and I'm going to do this new thing."

Then I found as I started to go through with it, that every time I'd get to a point of departure in the plot, I'd say, "Well, my instinct is to do this, but is this a comic-book instinct that I should reject, or should I follow it because it's worked for me?" For several months, I was making decisions without really knowing. It was like flipping a coin every time. "Shall I go this way or that way? I haven't the slightest idea." And I made a lot of wrong turns along the way. When I finally had a complete draft of the novel, then I was able to go back, having mellowed out, not being quite so paranoid about comic books, and say, "Well, now that I've got the entire story, I can see that this is wrong and this is wrong and this is wrong. I will now fix it." So in the end it became a synthesis of the whole thing.

When I went into it, I also thought, "Well, I've never written a novel before, so maybe I'll turn out to be a James Clavell or John Fowles, or Nabokov," or whatever. What I found in the end was that I was always Steve Englehart. The Steve Englehart who wrote this novel is like a guy who's been really able to stretch out and play without restrictions, being able to write stuff as long as it needs to be written. It was fun to be really able to get out there and not have to do anything except what I thought was the right thing to do either in the beginning or after I went back and looked at it. Anybody who reads this novel – which I hope everybody does – since I'm now in business for myself, I have to say those things – if you knew my stuff before, you'll know it's me writing this thing. In the end, it's Steve Englehart. But it's a further-along-the-line Steve Englehart, a guy who's not using a lot of the tricks and restrictions that are necessary in doing 17 pages with six panels a page and so on and so forth.

So the comics – just to tie this up – was like a real learning experience. I learned how to tell stories, I got my taste of having people tell me that I did good stories so that I got a feeling of what was good and what was bad, so for my personal development, after all these ups and downs, I would say it was real valuable. But I would really advise anybody who thinks that "Hey, I'd like to become a novelist, so I'll become a comic-book writer first to learn the trade" to think again. It's much better if you're starting out to just do what you think you want to do. Comics has a bad reputation outside of comic books, and you really have to fight that hard.

[*Groth*] Do you think that's entirely undeserved?

No, not entirely undeserved. There's nothing wrong with comics as a medium, and yet it's been generally badly used in America. We all know that it's a big deal in Europe, but in America it was decided early on that it was going to be children's material, and when in the '50s the EC people tried to break out of that, we ended up with the Comics Code to ensure that it would always be children's material. And even though the definition of children's material is flexible, as we all know to most people who don't read comic books it's a cheap, throwaway art form which is only for children. Most people know comics only from what they read as children. They don't know what *Doctor Strange* and *Master of Kung Fu* and *Howard the Duck* got to be, they don't know how we can all play with the restrictions and slide past them and so on and so forth.

So yes, I would say that the *extremely* bad rap comics have is undeserved. On the other hand, there are still and always have been a lot more bad comics than there are good comics. So, even people who might want to have a fair mind about it, if they just go to the newsstand and start picking up *The Human Fly, Brother Power the Geek*. I like the medium; I'm not real thrilled with the way it's been run by the various companies through the years.

When that editor rejected your manuscript in that manner, did you feel defensive for comics and your background in it, or did you feel an animosity toward it because you had been doing something that was held in such low esteem by the rest of the world?

I probably felt both. I was in a period of transition. I've been in a period of transition for the last two years. I was giving up a successful career where, even if you don't get rights and royalties you still make a decent living, in order to start something new which I understood fully well would take me three or four years before I'd start seeing any return off it. I'd have to write this book, then it would have to get published, then it would have to make back my advance, and *then* I would start to make some royalties on it.

So I'm sure I felt defensive and I felt animosity and I also felt misunderstood and I felt that she was an ignorant fool. If everybody in books had thought comics was a piece of junk I would have been in big trouble. Fortunately not everybody feels that way. Dell and Avon both ended up wanting the book and I went with Dell – those people were willing to take what I was showing them and say, "Ah, this guy *can* write, let's give him a shot." And now the book is over. Six weeks ago I finished it, I mailed it back, I've been seeing my editor at Dell, getting his comments on it, and I'm happy to say that there are very few comments on it. Out of 110,000 words they'd like me to trim about 5,000. They just think the beginning ought to move a little faster. I started out slow, you know. But again, I'm learning, and that's cool. I feel that I've got a lot of things going for me and at the same time I'm real ignorant in a lot of ways about bow the book business works. I'm just starting from the bottom again, working up.

[*Groth*] Can we talk about your novel for a moment?
Sure.

[*Groth*] What kind of novel is it?
The Point Man is an espionage novel with a touch of supernatural in it. Basically, it comes from this true situation: in 1957, the United States military decided to see if they could contact submarines underwater through telepathy, because radio won't go underwater and when submarines went down they were out of contact. Just like in S.H.I.E.L.D. way back when, they got together a group of telepaths and tried it and had some success, but not enough for the military to really feel that they wanted to go around recommending this to anybody, so they gave it up. But the French got a hold of this story and published it, and the Russians immediately leapt up and said, "Oh, we've been doing this for 25 years!" This was a typical thing in the '50s, they were always claiming to have done stuff beforehand. Whether they had or not, they sat down in 1957 and said, "Maybe we can make some military use of this," and since 1957 there has been a place called Academgorodok, which means "Science City." It's a think-tank in Siberia – it actually exists – and it's been given over totally to telepathy, telekinesis, ESP, reading with your fingers, all this kind of stuff. And so it's true. Nobody who's talking knows exactly what they're doing with it now, 25 years later, but I set up a story in which my hero gets his house burgled of something that's very valuable to him. He figures that first it's a robbery, and then he finds out it's Russian spies, and then he finds out it's Russian spies who have got legitimate, proven magical powers. I did not do another *Doctor Strange* – there's nobody shooting rays out of their palms in this – but it's an attempt to play with what is actually physically real in terms of "magic" powers. And the Russian spies not only can do telepathy but they can do a bit more. In a sense, it's sort of an initiation novel; this guy starts out being an average American in 1980 who gets drawn into not only the world of espionage but also the world of magic at the same time.

THE RACE DOWN SHADOWED CORRIDORS IS *SWIFT* AND *SHORT!*

—*UNNH!*—

ALL RIGHT, MISTER: *END OF THE LINE!*

NOW LET'S JUST HAVE A LOOK *UNDERNEATH* YOUR COWL BEFORE—

GOOD LORD! YOU!!

BUT YOU-- YOU'RE--

EXACTLY! BUT HIGH *POLITICAL* OFFICE DIDN'T *SATISFY* ME! MY POWER WAS STILL TOO CONSTRAINED BY *LEGALITIES!*

I GAMBLED ON A *COUP* TO GAIN ME THE POWER I CRAVED-- AND IT APPEARS THAT MY GAMBLE HAS FINALLY *FAILED!*

I'LL *CASH* MY *CHIPS,* THEN!

NO, *WAIT--!*

KRAK!

DON'T...

A MAN CAN *CHANGE* IN A FLICKER OF TIME.

THIS MAN *TRUSTED* THE COUNTRY OF HIS *BIRTH...* HE SAW ITS *FLAWS...*

...BUT *TRUSTED* IN ITS BASIC *FRAMEWORK...* ITS STATED *GOALS...* ITS *LONG-TERM* VIRTUE.

TRUSTED.

THIS MAN *NOW* IS CRUSHED INSIDE. LIKE MILLIONS OF *OTHER* AMERICANS, EACH IN HIS *OWN WAY,* HE HAS SEEN HIS TRUST *MOCKED!*

AND THIS MAN IS *CAPTAIN AMERICA!*

BEGINNING: THE MOST *AMAZING* STORY YOU'LL READ *ALL YEAR!* **CAPTAIN AMERICA NO MORE??**

Writer: Steve Englehart Artists: Sal Buscema & Vinnie Colletta *Captain America* #175 July 1974 [©1974 Marvel Comics Group]

But, although we do have some supernatural stuff in there, it is a realistic novel, it's not intended to be a fantasy. And it was real interesting creating a character who was not a comic-book character. I created Shang-Chi with Starlin, I created Star-Lord; each one of those was destined to live out his life in a comic-book format. This was my first chance to really sit down and do something where I could create the tone and I could create a guy where we didn't have to turn the camera away when he had sex with somebody, we didn't have to worry about language, we didn't have to worry about anything but was he credible?

[*Groth*] Were there things you did in the novel that you couldn't do in comic books?

Oh yeah. First of all – I think it was Nabokov who talked about the O.S.S., the Obligatory Sex Scene. Any novel that wants to sell has got to have sex in it. OK by me; I was quite happy to do that stuff. There's also people smoking dope in this novel. This isn't "Englehart Unleashed" – you know, "I get to write, oh boy! sex scenes and dope-smoking scenes." It's just part of the whole tapestry.

Another thing about a novel is that it's large. Seventeen pages, 22 pages, 25, 34 – you name it – pages. Still broken down into six panels a page. is still minuscule compared to 354 typewritten pages, which is what *The Point Man* came out to be. In three panels in a comic, you can do a little insight that nobody's seen before and they'll say, "Wow, that guy is really deep, he's really gotten into it." That same thing takes about one paragraph on a page and you've got an entire 10-page scene to fill. You start finding out that you get a lot deeper into everybody. In a sense, that lady way back when was right in that comics is superficial as compared to novels. On the other hand, that's not to say a guy who writes one can't write the other, or that I'm the only one who could possibly make that transition.

[*Groth*] Well, when I asked that question, I meant less in terms of Code restrictions and the like, and more in terms of making felt what you couldn't make felt in a comic-book story.

You mean by being able to portray deeper emotions or more complex situations? Oh, yeah. Because once I saw that I was either going to have to get this right or else I was just going to be a superficial comic-book writer like this lady had said, I decided I would get it right, and that became a lot of fun – being able to stretch out and get into somebody's head and make him progress. Writing the *Avengers* you can take Mantis from slut to Celestial Madonna over the course of two years in small sections as a small part of a larger entity, and you get a month between episodes to think over what you're going to do next. When you're doing a novel, a guy's got to carry for that entire time. He can't burn out, he's got to keep going, keep progressing.

[*Groth*] Are there things you could do in a novel that you could never do in a comic-book story?

Yeah. Even if you forget the sex and the dope, it's just the size of it, being able to tell a story on that scale. That was the main trouble I had when I went back to writing comics again, I had to start thinking, "By God, I've got to get this thought into this balloon and into this panel and the whole thing can only last this many panels and has to fit into 17 pages and…" It's like, *ngghhhh!* being *crushed* to death. I found, having gone through this transition we were talking about, that I could go back, having gotten over my paranoia of comic books, and say, "OK, I did a novel, and it worked like this, now I can go back and do what I did before," so it wasn't impossible or even totally difficult to do that, but still, I was real aware of the fact that I could no longer – Well, I plotted the Superman-Creeper story. Julie [Schwartz] never told me how long it was going to be, and I assumed it was 25 pages. So I had a 25-page story plotted. Then he says, "OK, and you know that it is 17 pages, don'tcha?" You know, *crrrunchh!* shoving all this stuff in there. I had to throw out what you usually end up throwing out, which is a lot of character stuff and a lot of development. I wanted – you know, the Creeper to me was a guy who got introduced 12 years ago and has come back every couple of years since and you're supposed to care about him but very few people remember why any more. So I wanted to go back and take this opportunity to re-establish the Creeper. And a lot of what I was trying to do there went. And that's where I kept feeling, I'd really like to go a bit further into the Creeper, what he could continue to do, but no, no, I have to cut it here and move on to the next thing. That would have been true even with 25 pages; it was *real* true at 17 pages.

[*Groth*] **If you wrote *The Point Man* as a comic book story, how many pages would it have to be?**

I haven't the slightest idea. But it would be *real* long.

[*Thompson*] **Do you think that one aspect makes the comics' medium inferior to the prose medium?**

No. I wonder, since it's never really been proven exactly, how long a comic book can be before people – if you did a 250-page comic-book novel, would people buy it or would they just throw up their hands in despair and not touch it at all?

[*Groth*] **They'd have to adjust their thinking.**

Yeah.

How long are Byron Preiss's books?

[*Groth*] **They're over a hundred pages – 110, 120.**

[*Thompson*] **I know of a European comics-novel that lasted over 160 pages, eight-to-12 panels a page.**

Yeah. But that's Europe again. I'm thinking in terms of American audiences. No, but comics, as I said before, is a perfectly viable medium. Sometime I may well try to write a novel and then have it illustrated, but I would want to do it much differently from the way McGregor does it, for example. Don likes to put 10 panels on a page and fill them all with word balloons. If I were going to try and tell a long story I would want to try and get a long book to do it in. Because I believe that the basic comic-book format, six panels to a page, nice balance between story and art, is the most pleasing way of doing the thing. So instead of trying to cram everything into this, I'd just let it run 250 pages, and I haven't the slightest idea whether anyone would buy it.

Still and all, there are some things that look better if they're well drawn than if they're put into words. I got through that, too, when I was writing the novel – learning to really describe stuff evocatively and put it across. At the same time – if you really wanted to sit down and really get into Spider-Man's head for once, you could write decent copy about what it's like to be on the side of a building. But you can only do that in writing. At the same time, in comics, you can show him on the building and put a moon behind him and get a series of nice visuals to go with it, so I don't think comics is inferior.

I wonder because of 40 years of cultural conditioning whether you could do a novel in comic-book form and get people to sit still for it. You can certainly do a comic book in *movie* form. It's called *The Empire Strikes Back,* and people will not only sit still, they'll go to see it five times, but that's a whole new trip.

[*Groth*] That's a real exception.

Yeah.

[*Thompson*] How do you think Eisner's *A Contract with God* ties in with that?

I haven't seen it. I would like to see it because I like Eisner's stuff but I have not seen it.

[*Groth*] Would you say that filmmakers have their art down better than comic-book artists? In the sense that they can actually tell a very complex story in 90 minutes?

I think a good comic-book artist can give a good movie crew a run for their money. There are lots of movies – Ralph and I were discussing *The Shining* earlier – where they didn't pull it off. And there are a lot of comics where they didn't pull it off. But I would tend to think that for example me as a writer and Marshall Rogers as an artist – or any number of people in both those capacities – could do some really fine stuff that would give you a better feeling having gone through it. I would think, if I may say, that people who sit down with the eight issues of *Detective* I did – six with Marshall – are going to get a lot of intensity and good vibes and interesting visuals and nice flashes throughout that book, and you could name any number of movies that wouldn't give you that much enjoyment out of the thing.

They've got a lot more money and a lot more technical expertise at their command in movies, and they can maybe dazzle you better at the same time, but enjoyment's independent of all that.

[*Groth*] Well, I'm thinking more in terms of someone like Bergman, who has no money and doesn't dazzle anybody with special effects, but whose films are infinitely complex. Is that sort of thing possible to do in comic books?

Well, way back when, Alain Resnais wanted Stan Lee to write a script for him on one of his movies. As it turned out, Stan couldn't produce what Alain wanted, but had he been able to do so… I mean, Resnais, in reading Marvel comics, obviously thought that he was going to get something out of Stan that he would be able to use and commissioned the whole project.

[*Groth*] It could have been poor judgment.

Well… To me, moving pictures is just a technically more advanced version of comics, but give a good writer and a good artist a chance to really kick out and…

Also, you can do things in comics that would be almost impossible to convey on film – stuff like Marshall did with the Batman's cape.

[*Thompson*] And you can have juxtaposed images playing off each other, which you can't do in film, because they follow each other.

What might you want to do if you came back to comics – what kind of material?

Well, I haven't given it a whole lot of thought. If somebody locked me in a room and said, "We'll give you $100 a page to write comic books, come up with something fantastic," I'd give it my best shot. I'd see what I could pull out.

But I really have been concentrating, first on *The Point Man*, second on coming up with a plot for the next novel. In the meantime I did do those things for National, which have now gone elsewhere. And that stuff, that was decent. I enjoyed getting back into comics after having not seen any for a year and a half. But it was not a return to comics for me, it was good stories. I've never hacked anything that I've ever written, you know. They said, "Do it," and – we're talking about jobs like *Skull the Slayer*. I just hated that job; I said, "OK, they said, 'do it,' so what can I do to make this strip work, to make it better, to make it come across?" There's nothing that I've ever done that I'm ashamed to say I did.

What about the *Mister Miracle* story credited to "John Harkness"? That was very well-written, by the way.

That was weird. I had a contract, I had to write x number of stories for DC and three of them were supposed to be *Mister Miracle*s. And then the night before I left

New York to fly back to California to get ready to fly to Europe – the night before I was essentially leaving comics behind – Larry Hama came to me and said, "I need this script, I've got nobody to write it, I'll tell you what to do." It was pretty much a real, legitimate work-for-hire number. And I went home and wrote the entire 20 pages overnight, which I had never done before or since – no, I did write a *Doc Savage* once, and the *Prisoner* story, but those were both adaptations – and turned it in. It wasn't what I would have done with the character, it was written overnight, and I said, "Well, I don't really want my name on it. So call it John Harkness." I was surprised that everybody, or almost everybody, seemed to figure out who it was. But even with all those things, it wasn't just a piece of hackwork, it was the best I could do with the time allotted.

[*Catron*] I'd like to ask a question, and this concerns your interest in both Batman and Captain America. I'd just like you to compare those two characters.

OK. They have similar athletic abilities. Beyond that, their heads are very different. Captain America is in a sense naive because he believes in a dream, but he believes in it purely. I don't agree with the stuff that I've read recently in *Captain America*. They treat him as the kind of a guy who goes around and says corny things, and the guy that I wrote didn't say corny things. If he said corny things, it came out of the situation, it was part of what he was believing in – but to my mind Captain America is sort of the slave to whatever happens to America. He's always striving to make America better, and to stand for what's good in America. Therefore he's not fighting so much for himself as for that ideal.

Batman, on the other hand, is totally self-contained. Batman is fighting for justice as he sees it, and I really want to add quickly that The Batman to my mind is not insane, and not a fascist. He is a guy who is right out there on the edge, and if he had any less self-control, might be either insane or a fascist, but the guy's right about what he does. He goes out there, he doesn't beat up innocent people, he doesn't harass the wrong guys, he only goes after the people who deserve to be gone after. He is not insane, either. He is living in an insane world, but he's sort of the element that holds it all together. He's much tighter, much more intense, and he's right there on top of everything right now in order to accomplish this thing that he set out to do when he was a child, his goal to be The Batman, to be the guy who will get retribution on the criminal element in society.

Captain America is much more changeable as time goes on. The guy that I wrote in the midst of the Watergate situation was basically against all that sort of stuff, but I really wouldn't have any sort of quarrel with a more right-wing, patriotic Captain America in the '40s. I do think the Cap I wrote would have been smart enough in the '50s to know that this red-baiting stuff was getting out of hand and wouldn't have been going around fighting the Commies all the time like he did in the books.

[*Thompson*] You wrote a story about it.

Yeah. And if it turned out that the entire government was taken over by liberal pinkos – as an example here, right – and it got to the point where the best thing that could be done for America was to become very intense and very conservative, I would think Captain America would go in that direction, and I would have no trouble writing a conservative Captain America if that seemed to be the best thing for America at the time.

But Batman doesn't change; Batman is exactly what he was in the 1940s because he's not concerned with the outside situation, he's concerned with being a sort of force. He wants to be the force that will oppose the criminal element. I totally disagree with fighting monsters like he did in the '50s.

In both cases, I could almost let the work speak for itself, because they were different characters and I'm satisfied with what I did on both of them, although I only did a year of Batman and three or four of Captain America. Still, that's the differences as I see them.

[*Thompson*] In his interview, John Byrne said Batman was a "brooding psychopath."

Uh-uh. I don't believe that. A lot of people think that Batman's crazy, and I really don't. I don't think he broods. He's so totally sane – it's very crystalline in a sense. He's totally aware of what's going on and what to do about it without any real worries about how it will appear to other people. He'll turn down the woman he loves for the life that he's sworn to live.

[*Thompson*] He's single-minded, then.

Yeah – single-minded. And I have to say that the way I see him I don't believe that the next month he would be seeing Silver St. Cloud's face in other women's faces and going, "Arrgh, my heart is breaking!" I don't think so. He would have said, "That was a bad experience but there was nothing else that could have been done, and I will now go on to the next day." He wouldn't forget Silver St. Cloud, but neither would he go around brooding about it, neither would he go around agonizing over it. I don't think he's crazy, and – I don't think he would allow himself that much.

How about the Vision? Do you see any similarities between the Vision and Batman, aside from the fact that…?

No, because the Vision's not that intense. He doesn't quite have the range that a real person would have. But I don't see him as brooding. I mean, he's very dark and he's sort of single-minded again, but he's not that intense and he's able to get the woman that he loves. No, except for the kind of intensity in their eyeballs, I don't see a whole lot of similarities between them.

Well, I've never liked people referring to him as "Marvel's answer to Mr. Spock." I think they really are dissimilar characters.

Oh, yeah. I don't agree with that. He was quite different from everybody else, as far as I was concerned. The Red Tornado was much more pitiful, and Mr. Spock is much less emotional. I don't know what Roy had in mind when he invented him. Again, you come up with a concept and as you use it you find that it just demands to go in some other directions, so perhaps the whole humanization of him came after Roy had created him to be somebody else, but certainly the way he turned out under Roy and under me was in-between. Spock is too emotionless and the Red Tornado is too emotional.

[*Catron*] I'd like to talk a little more about the various characters. Mister Miracle, for example. I'd like to get your conception of the character – what motivates the guy, how he reacts, and what makes him different from the people around him.

I'm happy to do that, but again, I have to throw in the caveat that I haven't been in the world where I really had to live with it night and day for three years now, so some of my recollections are going to have to be dredged up a little bit, and I may not have everything that I might have told you in 1977.

Mister Miracle was one of those characters where I took it over and was told, "Let's make him sell this time." There were several things that I disliked about Kirby's version, one of which was the Mother Box. The trouble with a lot of Kirby characters, it seems to me, is that they're kind of omnipotent. They can do anything. In issue nine, they'll say, "Oh yes, well, I can also knock down buildings." "Oh. OK." Jack doesn't write characters and therefore he doesn't tend to develop people who will have character problems, who will get into situations where they will have to make a decision: "I can't get out of this sewer, what am I going to do to save Aunt May?" That's not the kind of stuff Jack does.

I liked what I could glean of the consciousness of Mister Miracle out of reading that stuff, but I always had the feeling that there was some great untold part of Mister Miracle's life. Orion seemed to me pretty straightforward. You knew where Orion stood: he was a bad guy who'd been raised by good guys. Mister Miracle, on the other hand, was the good guy who'd been raised by bad guys, and yet he was always kind of an enigma to me. So I was trying to kind of start something off by putting him back on Apokolips, by setting him up back where he'd grown up, where he knew the landscape, but now back as a revolutionary.

I did like the fact that he was quite commercial in his comic-book life, that he'd gotten into selling himself down on Earth, and so I liked the idea of his being the son of God, with lights to proclaim it and all this kind of stuff – running a media campaign to convince people that you were Jesus Christ is an interesting concept, but exactly what he thought is difficult. I gave him a consciousness insofar as I could in the three issues and carried on from where he'd been, but his primary motivation was just to win the war against Apokolips. If I'd continued to write that series I think I would have come up with some great untold concepts about Mister Miracle. I mean, it wasn't clear what he could do. He was a son of Highfather, and yet he was always down on Earth doing escape tricks through the aid of the Mother

Box, and yet he should have some powers; everybody else in the New Gods had powers – so I figured he had something that was going to be so mind-blasting that it would amaze you when you found out what it was he could do. And I set all that stuff up. I mean, he asked all those questions in the book, but I wasn't really with him long enough to say specifically who or what he was.

[*Catron*] Can you compare the Avengers and the Justice League?

Mm-hmm. They operate out of different premises. The Avengers are all Marvel superheroes up front, and that means that they are more human than the DC characters.

They're better. [*Laughter.*]

I would agree with that. I think they are. They operate in a more human environment and they're more caught up with each other. When I took over the Justice League, I sat down and I went back to what I considered to be the best example in their individual series. I went back to the Adams/O'Neil *Green Lantern/ Green Arrow,* I went back to the John Broome/Carmine Infantino *Flash,* the Joe Kubert *Hawkman,* all those guys. The Batman I was already going back looking for the stuff I liked. I find that I'd never really totally warmed up to Superman.

But what I did was: I sat down and said, "This is who they are, and now this is who they should be," because I wasn't going to come in and just write them all the same, as they'd been written for so long. I wanted to start differentiating them, and yet I was real careful: I did not want to make the Black Canary the Scarlet Witch and Iron Man Batman and Superman Thor and so on and so forth. I wanted to find out why they were each different, and as you go along through the series, I was able to start picking out the differences. I started off just getting Flash and Wonder Woman in the thing, and the next issue played off that as it affected more people, and it went on from there – but the DC characters are to start with, DC characters.

The Justice League is not the Avengers. The dynamics are different. They operated on a heavier scale, somehow; there was more mass and more movement and more inertia in anything they did. They tended to be more formal, and again, it reflected the company to a certain extent. They tended to work more as a kind of group of elite people who got together because they were "elite," stars who got together in a kind of communal effort and they had rules and regulations as to who could join and who couldn't join. If Hawkman was in, Hawkgirl couldn't join. I figured we'd take that and play with it.

I don't think the Avengers thought of themselves as being individual superstars, they were just guys who had these powers but they also had problems and the whole Stan Lee schtick. They operated together because they felt like it, because they thought they could do things by getting together, and then once they got together they got into human interactions and so forth and they hung together, because they liked being together, not because they joined a club in a sense. It's those differences which just sort of shape the tone of the whole thing.

I loosened up the Justice League a lot, and yet I really didn't want to make them quite as light as the Avengers had been, because that wasn't who they were. I wasn't trying to write my *Avengers* and call it the *Justice League,* I was trying to write the *Justice League.*

The other group that I wrote for a while was the Defenders, and they were totally different; at least in those days, their rationale was that they didn't even want to be a team, they just got together because they sort of kept running into each other opportunely or one of them would know that he needed somebody, but that was a whole different dynamics, too – they were much more antagonistic toward each other and prickly about the whole thing.

I was amazed at the fact that you decided to give up the *Defenders* because you were doing it so well, and yet on the *Avengers* you hadn't yet mastered the group dynamics. Why did you find one easier to do than the other one?

I don't know. I think part of the fact was that even though Roy had created the Defenders and had just come off four or five brilliant years of doing the Avengers, I took over the Defenders with basically their fourth story, *Defenders* #1 – after three lead-ups in *Marvel Feature.* I never had any trouble with it, probably because I really like the Sub-Mariner, I had some feeling for Doctor Strange, I liked the Hulk a lot, and then I was able to bring in the Silver Surfer and the Valkyrie, people that I had liked, and I was able to just start running with it whereas on the Avengers I tried for a long time to be Roy Thomas, and it took me a while to realize that I wasn't Roy Thomas, didn't really function best trying to imitate Roy Thomas, and that I should better do Steve Englehart instead.

And so after about a year, after I'd done the *Avengers/Defenders* crossover, I looked around and said, "I don't really want to write two group books, and I've done the Defenders right, there's no problem with them, I would rather not drop the *Avengers* while I'm still not successful at it. I would rather sit down and devote all my energies to figuring out how the hell I'm going to do this thing right." That's always been my trip. And again, I don't want to have to apologize for anything I wrote, I don't want to have to say, "Oh well, I didn't mean it." My name's going on it and I want it to be good, and *Avengers* wasn't good yet. So I was going to give one up, I was going to give up the one I *had* gotten right and shoot for the other one.

As for the relative difficulties, I don't know. It wasn't until I brought in Mantis and started doing more with the characters within the group of the Avengers that it really started falling into place. When I was plotting the thing I would say, "What do I want my characters' heads to go through this month?" and then think up a villain who would fill out the issue, somebody who could accomplish whatever I needed the villain to accomplish. I think I'm the only one on that – I haven't asked everybody, but I know that over the years I was told by pretty much anybody I can think of that they always thought of the villain first and then fit in the human interest second. So the first year and a half of *Avengers* I was trying to come up with great menaces for them and not paying so much attention to Wanda and the Vision and that kind of stuff, and it wasn't until I really shifted over that I got the *Avengers* to where I wanted it.

I was going to ask you something about writing DC characters as opposed to Marvel. I suspect a number of people up at Marvel are actually closet DC lovers; that is, they've always wanted to write DC characters but for some reason they're all working at Marvel. With you, you created the Shroud, you did the Squadron Supreme thing in *Avengers*, parodying the JLA. Did you want to write any DC characters aside from The Batman?

No. Well, they *have* some decent characters. The Batman was always the favorite. I wouldn't have minded writing, say, Deadman as a series, or Adam Strange as a series. By and large, though, I was a Marvel fan, and (I'm sure this still continues) we used to sit up in the old Marvel Bullpen and laugh our asses off over the fact that these guys didn't have the slightest clue on how to put out a decent comic book.

If Carmine [Infantino] had remained in charge over at DC, I probably still would have gone there, because I needed a year to get my act together to get out, but I just happened to be fortunate. It seems that a lot of my career has been marked by good fortune – just at the right time, I would get an opportunity opening up.

But I wouldn't say I had always lusted – no, I wanted to write the Marvel Universe. I did that *Batman* with Sal Amendeola, which I only dialogued off his brother's plot and Neal's concepts. It was fun…

That was kind of a classic of sorts.

Well, it was a real group effort, and it was one of those things where everybody knew exactly what he wanted to do. But when I suddenly found myself going to DC, I did take a look around and said, "What would I like to write?" And so when I was negotiating with Jenette, I said, "I want to do The Batman, and I think I'd better be doing the Justice League, because I can really do some nice things for you on that." But it's either coincidence or cosmic, depending on how you want to look at it, that I was writing a Batman character and a Justice League set of characters just before I went over there and did those guys.

How do you see the relationship between the two companies? Do you think they're truly competitors. Or do you think that one does aim for a specific audience?

Oh yeah, I think they do. When you ask me if they're truly competitors you're getting up into decisions that are made at levels far beyond mortal men. I don't know. Obviously, Stan and Jenette or somebody has sat down and said, "Let's do one and now another Superman/Spider-Man team-up." They obviously talk to each other. What else they do I don't know. I think they're competitors, but again, there's so little energy in the business now, it's not as if people are going tooth and nail. When I joined Marvel Comics, they were number two, fighting their way doggedly to become number one. They passed DC while I was there, and after that, they stayed number one and DC stayed number two. The fact that there isn't more interplay and switching back and forth as to who's more popular indicates that if there's a competition it's not real hot and heavy now. It seems to be very settled, that both places have got their routine down, and they would rather have, the routine than the uncertainties of trying to outdo the other guy.

I do know that DC has made a specific decision that their future lies with five-year-olds, and so they're trying to deliberately cut the intelligence of the books so they'll appeal to children. I don't think Marvel has made that decision. I do think that things are more restricted than they used to be, but still clearly the stuff from Marvel is much more interesting than the stuff from DC.

[*Groth*] Do you think that the people at DC consciously aim at a lower level?

Oh, yeah. They told me that. They've decided that their future lies in selling comic books to children. And so they've given up trying to compete really with the real fan-favorite stuff.

Did you work for a certain age level, or did you ever give up a certain storyline because you thought it was too sophisticated for the audience you were writing for?

Uh-uh. I was always pretty much writing for people my age. I got back into Marvel Comics when I was in college, so I figured that if I did and Marvel was as big as everybody said it was, that those people were still out there, and as I grew through my 20s, so would those people. I was of course aware there was a difference between *Doctor Strange* and *Captain America*. The letters that came in on *Doctor Strange* were pretty much all from intelligent people who had intelligent things to say – not cerebral so much, just people like you and me who were there and could relate to it on that level – and *Captain America* had some letters in it like that, and some letters in crayon on brown paper saying, "I like the Falcon. He is nice. Signed, your friend Billy." Which I don't negate. There was a difference in audience, but see, I remember when I was a kid knowing I wasn't as dumb as people thought kids were. And so I went on the assumption, "Sure, they'll understand this." Again, we were encouraged to experiment, and if it turned out that I did something that didn't work, then I'd give it up, because I always understood that I was working for a company. But I never gave up any plotline because I thought it was too sophisticated.

Were you writing for any age level in particular? You said your own age level. You never wrote down.

No, I never wrote down. I knew that younger kids were reading it, and so undoubtedly I didn't quite use all the vocabulary that was at my disposal, but I never tried to simplify it for people. I always figured the kids would understand it.

[*Groth*] Since your comic books are read by kids, do you feel any obligation not to put forth any personal points of view?

Oh, no, I put forth plenty of personal points of view. But always sort of in tune with the characters. *Captain America* probably had a pretty heavy dose of personal point of view in it and yet I don't think anybody ever really came around and said – probably some did, but not very many did – "This Captain America is not really Captain America."

When I took over a series, it's like he existed up until this point. If I want to take him somewhere else there's gotta be a journey involved in that. I've got to take him there. I really couldn't get behind the idea of coming in and saying, "OK, I'm writing it now, everything's different." The character is more important than the writer. Captain America had to go from a right-wing patriot to a guy who could be horrified enough by Watergate to become the Nomad for eight months. And again, I wrote Captain America pretty much as a liberal, I wrote Batman pretty much as a – not conservative, because politics didn't play that much a part in it – but a much tighter character than that. It was endemic in the characters and I was interested in doing the characters right, not in propounding Steve Englehart's version of the world under any guise that I'd get a chance at.

[*Groth*] How much do you think what you personally believe in intrudes upon your writing, unconsciously?

Oh, unconsciously, probably everything. Consciously, as much as I feel works. I take a sort of – to use a sort of overused word – cosmic view of life. I do think that there's more to reality than what you see on the face of it and I do believe that there are forces beyond our comprehension that are out there working, so if I'm writing The Batman I don't start sticking in mystical stuff, but probably a coherent overview of reality creeps into everything that I do. But if the character's not right for it, I don't want to push it on him. There are some people who will buy a book just because Steve Englehart wrote it, but most people are buying the book because they like the character, they want to see this guy in action, and so it's not my job to do anything before I make sure that the character is likable, that the character is doing good.

[*Groth*] You probably have to do this more in the novel than in a comic book, but how well do you think you transcend your own point of view to create characters unlike Steve Englehart?

Pretty well, I think…

But doesn't each one have a facet of you in it? You can't really transcend yourself totally… or you couldn't write it.

Well, it's hard… It's all coming out of me. I encompass all of that stuff. Somebody once said, "I encompass multitudes," or something along that line. I'm a comic-book writer – I don't know all that stuff. But one of the characters in my book is an extreme bitch, a woman who uses everybody she can get her hands on to accomplish her ends and her ends turn out to be a lot more bizarre than you think they are in the beginning of the book. Obviously, I wrote it, so I had to understand all that, but I don't think much if any of that really relates to my personality. I'm not female; I don't think I'm scheming; I don't think I'm trying to shape the world in my image; all that kind of stuff. If you read this book and you believe in Madeline Riggs when you see her, then I created her OK.

[*Thompson*] **For the record, what happened to Mike Friedrich's *Batman* book?**

What Mike Friedrich, Marshall, and I envisioned doing was like our own Batman movie. We wanted to do a thing where you could sit down for an evening with a glass of wine and just go away into The Batman – just get into this whole thing on a long-term story. But we frankly didn't think DC would let us do it.

Amazingly, they agreed to let us do it, but they put a few restrictions on it, the basic one being that so long as we kept the number of copies printed very small, we could do anything we wanted. If we wanted to do a more visible project, they wanted editorial control. The other part of it was that Mike was looking to recoup a lot of losses that he's had and so he was trying to spend absolutely the minimum amount possible. We were both kind of looking toward fashioning our careers at that point, and we wanted to be in Brentano's next to Frazetta. He and DC both wanted us in comic-book stores. The project didn't seem worthwhile by the time it was actually worked out.

We got the thing half worked out, and found that we – Marshall and I – really did enjoy working together. So there's always the possibility of doing more projects, different projects, other things, as it fits in. Novels is really what I'm doing now, but there are going to be break periods in there, and if I get a couple of months' break and I feel like I want to write a comics novel or whatever, I've got a standing arrangement with Marshall that he'd draw it. But *The Batman* just sort of fell apart.

[*Thompson*] **You said in your introduction to the Marshall Rogers interview that Marshall was one of the five artists you'd worked with that you really got along with, that you felt had really augmented your work with their art. Who were the other four?**

Jim Starlin, Frank Brunner, Herb Trimpe, Al Milgrom… but there are a lot of artists that I've liked working with, and very few that I didn't like working with. I mean, everybody had something to offer, even the people that are not real fan favorites. There are a lot of them that I really enjoyed working with.

[*Groth*] **What people in the industry do you admire?**

I would say almost everybody, except for a couple of people who I've already mentioned in this interview, who I really don't think too much of.

[*Groth*] **I was talking about their work, not their personalities.**

But most everybody… There are some people who are just sort of there, but it would be a long list. I admire, for example, Sal Buscema. People dump on Sal Buscema all the time because he's "just a comic-book artist," but when I was doing *Captain America,* anything I told him to draw came back clear and accurate; I really appreciated it. Sal Buscema was a real strong part of *Captain America* as far as I was concerned. Everybody that everybody admires, I suppose. Kirby, Buscema, Roy Thomas in his heyday…

[*Groth*] Gerber?

He depresses me too much. I found that the stuff where he was having to fit in with established characters like the Defenders and the Guardians of the Galaxy I liked well enough. But the stuff where he had created the characters on his own or had free rein with *them – Man-Thing* and *Howard the Duck* – I just don't subscribe to that view of reality. There were several stories where people committed suicide because life was just too terrible. I don't think it is, and I can't watch the world get worse every month. People would write in and say, "Gee, I'm really worried about Steve, he's always so depressed. I hope this isn't…" And the answers were always, "Well, I'm not really depressed. I'm just being real. Life really is terrible. " I think his concepts were brilliant, the stuff that he'd do. I was real impressed with his concepts and his wordsmithing was great, but I didn't like a lot of the stories.

[*Groth*] How about McGregor?

I had a rhythm in which I'd read comics and every time I'd get into a McGregor comic, I'd get to page one and my mind would just skip off. I couldn't take the time to get into it. So I never read McGregor's stuff. And it wasn't until I went down and dug out the *Demon*s to do this *Demon* story a month and a half ago and found that although I'd wanted to throw this stuff away because the writing was so bad, Kirby's art really is worth having. So I said, "What else did I not like before that I might like now?" I went down and read *War of the Worlds*, and I said, "By God, this isn't bad. It is overwritten to an extent, but on the other hand the characters are really nicely developed, the stories are nice," so I notched up my opinion of McGregor quite a bit after that.

But we could go through this and I could tell you what I like and dislike about every comic-book writer. The thing is, I did it the way I did it out of a combination of natural inclination and learning what I found worked for me and didn't work for me. And so there's no one else at this point I'd rather be as a writer; in every case, this means that there is a flaw I find in what they do that I think I've got a better handle on one way or another. But that's not really a criterion because I'm sure there are plenty of people who think Steve Gerber's got it right and *I'm* too optimistic, not serious enough, or whatever.

There's a phrase I always hear bounced around about Steve Gerber, which is that he's the best writer in comics but not necessarily the best comics writer.

It depends on what you define as "writing." I say again, his concepts are brilliant and his wordsmithing is real good. But I think – although you don't want to just give the audience what they're looking for – writing also has something to do with entertaining people, and certainly he did entertain some people. But I think he alienated a lot of people too, and if you consider – I'm serious – if you consider alienating people the mark of somebody with a real strong point of view and the ability to put it across strongly enough to alienate those people, that may be the mark of a good writer. I don't necessarily think so. But that's again a judgment.

[*Thompson*] I have one question that doesn't tie in with anything at all. You colored a couple of stories. How did you get into that and why did you get out so fast? It struck me as very interesting...

I got into it because I was starving to death as an artist and Neal looked around for something else that I could do to make money. And then when I became a writer, I didn't really have the time. I think coloring is real important, but it doesn't pay very well and it takes a long time to go through all those pages and color in everything, and you have to blot it dry in between. It's vastly underpaid I think.

But you did color a few *Avengers*, I think.

Yeah, because I wanted to. I colored the first *Master of Kung Fu* that I wrote. It's a total money-losing proposition, but it's fun to do. I'd scheduled myself to color those Madame Xanadu stories, but... The only reason I got out of it is just because I usually didn't have the time. But then again, I would make the time if I felt like it.

[*Thompson*] You seemed to have a more painstaking, original method of trying to work mood into your coloring than most other people.

Well, I was a dilettante. People who *are* doing it for a job day after day can't be expected to spend as much time thinking about it. They were my stories and I knew exactly what I wanted, and I had been trained by Neal, who works with colors real well. Trained by Neal and sort of retrained by Jack Adler, who didn't necessarily like everything that Neal was doing, but I came to sort of a synthesis between being able to be real arty and real commercial. I would have colored those stories again, just for the hell of it.

[*Thompson*] Have you seen the *Heavy Metal* stuff?

Very little of it. I suffer from writers' bias. Unless there's something there for me to read, all I can do is flip the pages. I can get into the artwork, but I can't get into a whole magazine of nothing but artwork and no stories, so I never really caught on with *Heavy Metal*. There's some brilliant drawing in there, but... It's like when I was in the middle of writing the Celestial Madonna stuff. I was living with Starlin and Orzechowski in California. I got real excited over something I wrote: "Boy, this is *really* coming together nicely, what do you think, Jim?" and he said, "Well, I don't really read the *Avengers*." "Well, why not?" "Because the art is *so* bad, you know, as an artist, I can't look at that stuff." And later on I found that it works both ways for most people. Artists have got to have something to look at and writers have got to have something to read.

[*Groth*] Are you keeping up with the other alternatives-undergrounds?

Oh, yeah. In fact, I'd like to heartily recommend *The Cartoon History of the Universe* to everybody who hasn't heard about it yet. That guy is brilliant and those things are wonderful – the best comics I've seen in four years. And the stuff that Jaxon's doing, like *Comanche Moon,* either in the original three-part version or the collected softbound volume. One of the places I do a little work for is a newspaper called *The Enlisted Times,* which is published for all the enlisted people in the Army – it's kind of a *Rolling Stone* for those people. It talks about records and sports and what the military is up to in regards to enlisted men. It's for the people who are *in* the Army, not the people who are making their career of it. When I got back to California after having sold the book, they had heard of me somehow and asked me to be Managing Editor of the paper and I told them I didn't really have the time. But because I liked them, I took on – originally for free, now I'm getting $20 a month for doing this, it's basically out of friendship – I pick out their comics for them. They're reprinting *Doonesbury,* they're reprinting *Farley,* they're doing new stuff on *Dopin' Dan*...

[*Groth*] *Spider-Man*...

No. But their office is right next door to an underground comics office, Last Gasp, so every time I go in there to pick out the comics for the *Enlisted Times,* I go next door and see whatever is new, so I'm pretty much on top of that stuff.

But comics in general are all sort of fading away in the mists of time. It's a skill that I will probably never lose, like riding a bicycle. I think I'll always be able to sit down and write a salable comic-book script, but a lot of it's in the past now.

TCJ

DENNY O'NEIL

RATIONALITY
AND
RELEVANCE

INTERVIEW BY GARY GROTH WITH MIKE CATRON: Dennis "Denny" O'Neil was one of the most highly regarded comic book writers of his era. His best-remembered work is his run on *Green Lantern/Green Arrow* with the artist Neal Adams, a full-on embrace of various societal issues that felt to many fans like the first step towards an adult superhero literature as far beyond the bombastic soap opera of the early 1960s as those comics had been an advance on the one-dimensional pulp of the 1940s and 1950s. That series was also one of the first times a mainstream comic company had injected new life in a second-tier project by providing a shift in narrative tone, an editorial technique that would come to be used by both Marvel and DC in the decades to come for projects that felt like they could benefit from such a boost.

O'Neil also wrote well-received runs on *Batman, The Question*, and a revival of the pulp character *The Shadow*. His influence was so dominant that at one point O'Neil's comics practically defined how you wrote books for an older and potentially more sophisticated audience. His treatment of Batman as an editor and writer effectively put a final end to his dalliance with camp, and echoes of this approach have been seen in every version since the mid-1970s. He has since the time of this interview conducted in 1978 and 1980, and released in full form in TCJ #66 (September, 1981), become a more significant influence as an editor. His work as a writer has come on occasional projects like the *Batman Begins* videogame.

O'Neil was one of the more formidable thinkers among his peers, and projects an impressive presence throughout the following interview. O'Neil talks about his work but also speaks to general issues about making art and the value of what he does for a living.

GARY GROTH: You've often referred to yourself as a "commercial writer"…

DENNY O'NEIL: Yeah, in that I never started from the standpoint that I have anything to say to the world.

Harlan Ellison said he never writes for anyone but himself. You, I assume, write for an audience.

I never write for myself. I mean, I write for me – if I do a comic, I say, "All right, I'm Denny, and I'm out there and I feel like reading a comic book. What would amuse me if I felt like reading a comic book?" That's as close to writing for myself as I get.

Sometimes I've done stories with specific people in mind, like, "I want so-and-so to read this. This is a story for X." Once, I wrote a story for a specific

Writer: Denny O'Neil Artist: Neal Adams *Green Lantern/Green Arrow* #76 April 1970
[©1970 DC Comics Inc.]

individual and I wanted her to read it and say, "Hey, I'm not mad at you, this is what really happened." I can express myself better in fiction than I can verbally. But, those things are very rare and they're also terrible self-indulgences on my part. Professionally, I can't ever justify writing a short story because I don't make any money on it. But I don't, on the other hand, almost ever, start off because there's something I want to say or even something I want to express.

I think if Harlan has never written a story for anyone but himself, then he's been very lucky that he's found such a large number of people who are simpatico to what he does and that's quite possibly what goes down. But, it's not where I started from at all.

When I left college, I never thought I would create another piece of fiction in my life. I was sure that that was all behind me. I didn't have any desire to write fiction… I mean, I had a niggling desire to do it, but I didn't anticipate making it my life's work. I didn't know what my life's work was going to be, so I went into the Navy to kill time, and I came out and taught for a while. I didn't like that very much, I didn't like the apparatus of the school system. I said, "What else can I do? I have to eat. All right, I've done journalism, I can be a journalist, I know how to write a news story." So I answered an ad in the back of *Editor & Publisher:* "General Reporter Wanted. Small Missouri town." I got the job, and found that I could indeed function as a reporter. Then I came to New York and found I could function as a comic-book writer, that I had whatever it takes to be able to do that, at least on some level.

You've said in the past that when you entered comics, over a decade ago, you had the intention of working in comics only about six months to make some money and then splitting. How come you've stayed about 12 years or so?

Because I had a child sooner than I could have anticipated, and we thought it would be bad, with a baby, to pull up stakes and schlep back to the Midwest. Then we began getting involved in the neighborhood; I began to find an aptitude for doing this stuff that I hadn't had any reason to believe existed. I began to enjoy doing it. I began to pick up other things that were interesting to do – magazine pieces. The first thing I knew, there didn't seem to be anything to go back to in the Midwest – four years had passed and the job that I had come from undoubtedly wasn't there any more. It was more sensible to stay and keep doing comics than to try and go back to journalism. Also I began to really dig it about that time. I began to get reorganized; my ego got some stroking – that didn't hurt – and I found that I could be really happy writing a comic-book script that I thought was pretty good.

Do you enjoy writing comics as much now as you did in 1967?

A tricky question. I enjoy exercising the craftsmanship that I have gained. Ah, to use a word that I don't like to use, creativity – the exercise of that I still enjoy. I don't get as fantastically high as I used to do when I do a good job, but that has as much to do with the field as with me, though…

How so? The field has changed since you've come in and after?

I think it's a duller place to work than it was seven or eight years ago. Seven or eight years ago there was a feeling that we were taking an art form, a minor art form, but an art form, and advancing it. And that we were doing the best stuff that had been done. I mean, not only I had that feeling, but a lot of people. And we were opening whole new vistas, and we were coming up with new ideas and new places to go and new things to try. Now I sense that it has gotten to be very sedate, plain, ordinary… I would expect that it is a lot like working in an ad agency now, which doesn't mean that there is no satisfaction, or no creative kicks involved, it's just not a feeling of working in new areas, of opening possibilities, of *becoming,* you know, in the existential sense. The people who are new in the field don't seem to be having as much fun with it as Steve Skeates and Neal and I did back when we were just starting. It seems to be more of a job to them. It was kind of an adventure for us for a while. There was a tremendous feeling of camaraderie, of feeding off each other, getting ideas constantly. It was a terrific place to be working in 1971.

In '71 you were more or less a real hotshot writer because of the *Green Lantern/ Green Arrow* books.

Yeah.

And now, I don't think you are quite regarded as the same. Would you agree with that assessment?

Oh, absolutely, sure.

How does it feel to come down from that peak?

Well, what happened was that I had about two or three really bad years – personally and professionally. That shouldn't be a secret to anybody. But because of what was happening, I wasn't aware of coming down when it was happening. There has been, I think, a recovery from that, and I'm not at all unhappy with the way things are now. I'm not getting the publicity and the tremendous fame, but I couldn't reasonably expect to continue at that peak. That was, after all, a time and a place kind of thing. I was doing something that was considered daring at the time. If I did the same thing today it would be considered commonplace.

Do you really think so, considering how dull things are now?

Well, they would say, "He's done it before, it's been done." And other people have done it. Other people like Gerber have maybe taken it a step further than I did.

How would you rank your *GL/ GA* books?

All I can say about that is that people still talk about them eight years later, and how many comic books is that true of? I haven't reread them at all. I would suspect that they stand up as comic-book stories. I think there was more to them than just the relevance. At the time, I was very conscious that my first duty was to turn out a story with a beginning, a middle, and an end, and preferably some suspense and some characterization and some imaginative use of the superhero format. That was and still seems to me to be my primary job when I sit down to do a comic book, and I don't think I neglected it back then.

Do you think that was a high point in your comics career, in terms of actual achievement?

No, I think I've done other stories that were technically every bit as good as any of those. In fact, some of the Batman stories were technically quite a bit better. It was a high point in terms of the amount of attention I was getting, sure, but in terms of professional achievement, no.

You said comics were a minor art form. Can you define an art form?

No, I can't. Art is what artists do. Anything that is an expression of something is probably an art form. That goes for racecar driving as practiced by people like Stirling Moss, and any form of music or storytelling or picture-making with paint brushes or cameras or whatever. That's a question that's been argued since the 15th century at least and I'm not about to attempt to wrap it up in two neat sentences here now.

What would you consider a major art form?

Cinema, music, the novel, drama – though comics as practiced by Will Eisner come very close. And I don't mean to denigrate comics because I consider the short story a minor art form and it's certainly respectable and valuable… It's just that not as much is possible with a short story as there is with *War and Peace* or *Hamlet*. It largely has to do with the matter of inherent limitations within the form.

Do you make the distinction between high culture and popular culture?

Yeah, I think it's necessary to make that distinction. But I think it's a distinction that's disappearing, and the sooner the better.

Really?

Yeah.

Why?

Well, because it's a distinction that's largely fostered by people who teach in universities who have a vested interest in terms of their jobs in making the division because a popular culture is obviously something that's accessible to everyone and high culture, *haute culture,* isn't, therefore it needs to be taught, therefore people have to teach it, therefore if you want to get your tenure as a professor… It is self-serving of those people to make the distinction.

But, I think it's largely a matter of inaccessibility in terms of language. I mean, Dostoevsky's novels have to be taught because we are not very familiar with the Russian customs and the popular thought when Dostoevsky was writing, therefore they are not entirely accessible to most of us on first reading, therefore someone has to explain things about them. The same will be true of popular movies in 50 years probably. They will tell you that there is High Culture and it deals with loftiness and so on. I'm not an expert on this stuff, but as far as I can see, historically that is not really true. After all, Dostoevsky's novels were, most of them, published in the popular magazines of the day. *The Idiot* was a serial in a magazine. So, obviously, he was shooting for a big audience. The classic example is Shakespeare who was shooting for the guys who were getting drunk in the pit down there. The passage of time makes a thing a) respectable, b) inaccessible, and c) susceptible to being taught.

How do you see comic books now? Working in the field for 13 years, your views must have changed. What do you try to do in a comic book these days?

Entertain. End of discussion. That's it. I try to be amusing on paper.

There are ways of being amusing. Like a fight is in one sense amusing. And in an equally valid way a revelation of character, which can be very quiet and subtle, is amusing. So, I try and work all the ways there are to work. Even when I was writing *Green Lantern,* I wasn't trying to tell anybody how to run the world. The basic mistake that always gets made about those stories is that they were proselytizing. They were not! They were saying, "These problems exist. Look at them." That's as heavy as I ever wanted to get. If I had solutions to the problems, I wouldn't use a comic book as a vehicle to express them. And anybody who reads that so-called "relevant" stuff that I wrote for *Green Lantern* or before that for Charlton or since occasionally for whatever I happened to be working in will see that I never proposed a solution. I have just said, "Hey, let's not be complacent, because it's treacherous out there." And there are problems that we have to deal with.

Have you grown to hate the word "relevance"?

Yeah, it's not my favorite word any more.

Seven years ago you said, "Beginning writers in comic books should not try to be creative, they should be commercial."

Yeah, I probably said that.

Are the two anathema to each other?

I don't know. I guess what I meant was that you should learn the craft; you should learn the form before you try to transcend it. I absolutely believe that today. And I can't think of a single way to cite an exception.

I will give you some *haute culture* examples, if you want. James Joyce's first book of short stories, *The Dubliners,* is quite a traditional collection of very well-crafted ordinary stories. That was before he did *Ulysses* or *Finnegans Wake*. Picasso's first pictures were very representational and photographic. I think you always have to learn the craft in anything. And in terms of comic books, being commercial is learning the craft. Do what other people did first until you know how to do it as well as they did and maybe you could figure out new ways to go. It seems to me it's a bad thing for writers to try to be awfully innovative early on, and I can give you examples of how that's loused people up, but I won't because I don't want to insult anybody. But, people who come in with a kind of "That's only commercial stuff" attitude, maybe don't realize how hard it is to be commercial. It's what James Agee called "the very difficult task of being merely entertaining." And how many people bring it off? How many Marx Brothers have there been? They're only funny, right. No great messages for the world. But nobody's come close to them at doing their thing. That's what I meant.

How long did it take you to learn the craft?

I don't know. I would guess that I wrote 50 stories before I began to be comfortable with what I was doing.

What were some of the tricks of the trade you had to learn?

Learning to express things very economically; learning to move a story and to not let it lag; learning to compose a story so that there's a small kicker in the last panel, there's some reason to make you turn the page, a mini-cliffhanger, or question that needs to be answered or something like that. Largely it's a matter of learning how to pace a story and I don't know of any way to teach that. Keep it moving; keep it interesting. Work contrast between the high moments and the quiet moments, make them work off one another so that the quiet moments aren't dull, but create a tension between the more active or violent scenes. It's a subtle thing and I don't know of too many people who do it and I don't know of any way to teach it.

Except by doing it.

Yeah. Any kind of writing that's largely true of. The rest of it is craftsmanship – learning how to do characterization without going into a long soliloquy about what the guy is, being able to pin a character in maybe three sentences or one characteristic action so the reader knows everything he has to know about him in a very short time.

Several writers or craftsmen in the industry have said that writers versed in other forms of writing – novelists, for instance – could not necessarily write a comic book. Do you think that's largely true?

Yeah. A couple of novelists I know who have tried haven't been very good at it.

Do you think that the majority of good writers could write a comic book if they have a firm hold on their craft?

No, I think that they need to understand what I, in a recent speech at the MWA, dubbed the *übergrammar* – hey, I was not a philosophy minor in college for nothing – it has to do with the fact that the visual and the copy form one linguistic unit, and you have to have a natural sense of how that language, that peculiar language works. In crudest possible terms, if I say, in a caption, "However…" and the visual is Batman socking somebody, it's analogous to the subject and the predicate of a sentence, one being visual, but they form the same linguistic unit, the same unit of communication even though they're different things. They work off each other, they complement each other, they create tensions within the panel. You have to have an instinctive grasp of what that's all about in order to do this. I think the instinctive grasp comes from being exposed to this particular form of storytelling at an early and formative age, at the time when maybe we're learning English. Most of the good comic book writers I know were seeing comics when they were three, four, five, six years old, at about the time they were learning to speak. And I think they learned the [comics] language along with English. They picked it up subconsciously, and when they went away to college or wherever they went and picked up sophistication, they brought some of that. But, I think those of us who are good at this have at an early age learned it like a second language. And almost none of us, unless we're Vladimir Nabokov or Joseph Conrad, are fluent in our second language. I've reached this conclusion only after talking with dozens of guys and trying to figure out why I can do this and x-novelist, who's a much better writer than I am, can't.

So you would say a visual literacy is a sort of second language?

Yeah. My first exposure to any kind of art was comic books and my second was movies. I didn't *see* a novel until I was about nine years old. I didn't really know they existed. The good writers I know who don't seem to do comic books very well were reading novels maybe at six but did not have comics around the house. And sociologically, we all seem to be from the lower middle class.

What is visual literacy and how does one learn it?

By looking at lots of pictures, all kinds of pictures: Paintings in museums, photographs, comic books, television shows, movies. It is an understanding of how images convey story or emotion or idea.

Should visual literacy be taught?

Yeah, I think it should be taught. It's not news – ever since McLuhan – that we are moving into a more iconic culture, meaning we are more and more visually oriented, and I think it's as important culturally to be able to understand with your eyes as well as the left side of your brain.

How much of McLuhan do you buy?

I haven't read him for years and years. I think he had some insights. The last time I thought about McLuhan I thought this: He had some insights into specific things that he tried to stretch to cover everything, which is a common failing among people who have insights. Martin Buber did the same thing. To some extent, so did Plato, so it's OK.

Where do you think things have gone wrong with comics, economically?

I think that we're 20 years overdue from realizing that Mom and Pop stores don't exist in most places any more, and therefore the main retail outlet for comics has been quietly going out of existence all these years. That's not my problem, that's the problem of the guys who went to the Harvard Business School. They're supposed to know about that. I think that as far as the writers and the artists are concerned, the reason that we are in – and Paul Levitz and a few other people would violently disagree with this – but I think that among so-called creative people we are in the worst economic position. The television writers have a pension plan. Every time you do a TV script, x-number of dollars gets put in that the companies have to match and that's your retirement. We don't have anything approaching that. We don't have very much in the way of medical benefits; what's considered normal fringe benefits for a guy who works on an assembly line we don't have. If I go dry and I absolutely can't write for some reason for a year I'm dead. There's nothing I can live on unless I have money saved. That's not true of anybody else in any other field, especially not with a large backlog of material. But I think that's just because the guys in 1945 didn't do what was necessary to do to get those benefits. As [Steve] Gerber has pointed out, guys who have been working in this field have been just so grateful to the companies for giving them the privilege, the opportunity to work out their fantasies on paper, that they have not worried about simple, economic facts, such as cost of living raises, which I now get, but which isn't usual in the field and hasn't been at all except for about the last three years. I think that's one of the benefits of Jenette Kahn. She began to see that we needed those things that every other stratum of society gets as a matter of course and has been taken for granted for 25 years. But, see, in 1945, *Superman* was selling nearly a million copies a month and that was the time for those guys to demand their rights and they didn't do it, and I think it's too late now.

Would you say that the comic-book industry has been run pretty ineptly, financially, for the past 30 years?

Yeah. I don't know very much about finance or business, but as an interested layman, I'd say that was pretty obviously true. I think there are steps being made to remedy that now. Whether there will be enough and in time, we don't know.

What are they?

Well, I know that there are different distribution systems being experimented with. There are studies being made. There is talk of going to European format, which makes a lot of sense since comics don't have to be periodicals. They happen to be periodicals because that's what they started out being, but there's no reason why the average Superman story won't be as good or as bad five years from now as it is now.

Do you have any idea why the business aspects of comics have lagged so far behind the other entertainment industries?

Yeah. Because I think it was a very *déclassé* business and it didn't attract bright business minds. If a guy's smart and he comes out of business school, he's not going to think about going into comic books. He's going to think about going into television, or into slick magazines or something like that. We simply haven't attracted the talent in that department. I don't know if that's currently true because I have no idea who's running the show in that department now. But it has been true, undeniably. Guys who maybe had a rough, crude kind of shrewdness started the business. I don't have to mention names because anybody who's familiar with the medium knows what the names are. And that was OK when comics were a hot thing. When they were the lowest common denominator entertainment and they were for a long time, therefore they were a mass medium, therefore for a while all they had to do was get 'em printed and put 'em on a stand and the rest sort of took care of itself. Gradually that became untrue, but they didn't realize that it wasn't untrue until they were already in trouble. I don't think comics will even be, by any stretch of the imagination, a mass medium in 10 years. I think it will be a specialized medium. I think that you won't buy them because, hey, this is a simple form of story that's accessible to anybody and it's exciting, because that's television now. I think people are already buying comics for the unique satisfactions of the medium, for the manipulation of the language that I was talking about before. In a sense it's getting to be almost like poetry, it's something you have to have a taste for. It's moving in that direction. I think that's the wave of the future. The comic book will be a genre particular to itself, no longer mass entertainment, but something that, hopefully, 300,000 people in the country will really dig and really like enough to invest money in.

Who are some of your favorite authors?

Currently?

No. The whole gambit.

It'll sound pretentious. It will. Let's stick with contemporary people because if I say Shakespeare I'm going to sound like one of those pretentious assholes who are always culturally name-dropping.

I currently like John D. MacDonald as a novelist who does not write novels for English majors, and I think that is a consummation devoutly to be wished. By contrast, John Updike, who does write novels for English majors.

You have no great love for academics, do you?

No. I'm softening about that. I'm coming around to thinking they're not as worthless as I once thought them to be. I question whether anyone should attempt to teach culture in a college because it seems to me you either respond to a work of art or you don't and what the artist was doing was trying to make you respond emotionally or intellectually to what he was doing. I don't know if you can properly assign grades to that. I was an English major in college and I regret that now. I also taught English for a year in the St. Louis public school system. I think you can teach reading, you can teach language. But how do you say a kid gets an F because he did not respond to *The Brothers Karamazov?* And now comics are being taught in colleges and it freezes my bowels to think some poor kid is going to be sweating over a blue book on a final over some stupid little story that I dashed off in an afternoon to meet a deadline. I want to amuse them, I don't want people to fret over my work, and if it gets very much more respectable than it is that's what's going to start happening.

I spent an evening with a college professor I had had and he told me he was teaching a course in science fiction, which flabbergasted me because he seemed, when I was in school, so opposed to popular literature of any kind. It so happened that he was generous enough to drive me 20 miles out of his way to take me to where I had to be and I was talking to him about science fiction on this drive. It became very apparent to me after about five miles of this 20-mile drive that he had not read it at all – what he was teaching, even – and didn't have much intention of doing so. For example, I mentioned *The Stars My Destination* and he didn't seem to be familiar with it. How can you teach modern science fiction without giving a nod to that book, which is considered by most critics to be the single best modern SF novel? There's a school of thought that you start with *The Time Machine* by Wells and you go to *The Stars My Destination,* and those are the two you have to read. He didn't seem to be too familiar with either one. That made me question the validity of what they're doing at all. A guy gets assigned a science-fiction course because some department head says, "We should have a science-fiction course; who's got a hole in his schedule? A guy who's an expert on metaphysical poets? Okay, we'll give him the science-fiction course because he's not doing anything on noon Monday, Wednesday, and Friday." I think they're assigned just that arbitrarily.

Now if they bring in somebody from outside, somebody like Chip Delany, who's vitally involved with this stuff, and use him as a visiting teacher, I can see that it could conceivably be a rewarding experience. But I don't see how somebody who's the proverbial two chapters ahead of the pupils is going to make them like science fiction or understand it or appreciate it, or maybe do anything other than turn them off it. And by extension that goes to anything from Elizabethan drama to Thomistic philosophy.

Was that the professor that you and Steve Gerber had?
Yeah.

It's ironic that he detested popular culture, and look where you are now.

It's ironic that he turned out not one but two comic-book writers. He hasn't turned out anybody who's done a lengthy, heavy, weighty tome of the John Barth variety. But he's turned out two popular writers.

Did you actually ever learn anything from him?

He gave me enthusiasm. I don't think he ever gave me a single piece of information, a single piece of data, but I think his enthusiasm for poetry made me want to read it. And by the way, maybe that's what a teacher should do, maybe that's how to teach culture. To get real enthusiastic about it. But obviously that precludes teaching it because you have an opening on Monday, Wednesday, and Friday.

How would you define a hack?

One who has no care for what he does. I don't think it has anything to do with productivity. After all, Georges Simenon wrote over 700 novels and most of them are good. It's just someone who does it solely for the money.

How would you rate your contemporaries?

[*Catron*] How many would you call hacks?

I'd have to think about that. Nobody I play poker with or see with any degree of frequency. I know guys who live in other states who in all evidence are hacks. Among my friends I don't think everybody hits the long ball all the time, but I don't think it's for want of trying, and anybody can have a failure. If I have a criticism of my contemporaries, it's that they're too involved in comics. Being a hack has to do with having no moral standards, largely. It was part of my agreement with DC that I will not be asked to write a story glorifying war because I don't believe that war is ever a good thing and I would not feel comfortable with a military hero. I also don't like to write romance stories. I did *Millie* way back when. That's a skeleton in my closet, though. I think the way those stories are handled demeans what happens between a man and a woman.

Do you think DC's war books are pro-war?

No, I don't, no more than anything else that deals with the subject. I'm not attempting to justify this in any terms other than the fact that I don't like military things and I've had a lot of experience with them. I have met *one* career officer in my life that I've respected. I went to a military high school, I was in ROTC in college and I put in my time in the Navy. I have a lot of acquaintance with it and I don't feel like making any of those guys heroes. It's as simple as that. If I were a total hack, sure, I'd write that stuff, because, what the hell, the check comes out to the same number of decimals.

What would you say to the possibility that superhero comics glorify violence?

I think it's something I've lost sleep over.

Do you think Freddy [Wertham] was right, partly?

Well, Freddy oversimplified. The warrior has been a cultural hero in our Western tradition since before Homer. Even if I personally made a big stand against it, it wouldn't change 5,000 years of cultural history. Warriors are heroes; men of action are the ones our culture has chosen to elevate to the status of Heroes. I try to work with that tradition. I don't think I ever glorify violence. I've written a lot of scenes where people regret the fact that violence was necessary in a given situation. In one of the best stories I ever did, "There Is No Hope in Crime Alley," the whole point of it is that the old lady who stayed in the slums and never raised a finger to anybody was a much greater hero than Batman – which he acknowledges on the last page. That's the way I go with it.

On the other hand, I believe boxing is an art form. One man against another with all the skills and intelligence that it takes to be a good boxer. I never met a stupid prizefighter. I think it's an art form the way people like Ali and Norton practice it. What those guys do with their hands and their bodies is an art and I think that's a valid thing. I've been involved in the martial arts and believe that's an art form. So, I guess I'm not against violence *per se*; I'm just against senseless violence. I'm against artillery shells because they'll zap somebody in a village with whom the guy who pulled the lanyard has no quarrel. I'm against high-level bombing where you knock out Dresden. I'm not against one man squaring off against another if they both feel like doing it and I try to get that into what I write. I'm not a knee-jerk pacifist. I used to be once upon a time. It's another way I've changed.

What changed you? Anything in particular?

No. I just changed. I've lived a lot. I guess I've Lived – capital "L" – in the last seven years more than I did in the 30-some that came before.

How do you feel about your profession? I know at least one writer who's embarrassed to say he's a comic-book writer.

I'm not ashamed of it. I use a different form of my name – Dennis O'Neil – on other things, but that is a signal to people that they're not going to get Batman out of this. It's going to be a very different thing.

Do you find that there's a stigma attached to your name if you try to write for other markets?

Yeah. I found that there's a terrible stigma attached to it in television. One of my big bitches – hey, we can get into the things Denny's pissed off about – is that television people are absolutely unwilling to use comic-book people to do the comic-book shows. Alan Brennert did two *Wonder Woman* TV scripts. After he'd done the second one, he happened to mention that he'd once supplied a plot to the

Wonder Woman comic book, and was told that had they known they wouldn't have seen him the first time.

I find that there's a terrible stigma attached to us by people who are doing the same thing we're doing, only in a different medium. I don't know why that is, except maybe it has to do with the Pecking order. Everybody has to have somebody they're contemptuous of. I did a television show [an episode of *Logan's Run*] and I don't think it was the 700 comic-book scripts that got me that assignment so much as the fact that I went in and did what I was supposed to, which was convince them that I could do the script. But I think they were probably more impressed by a handful of science-fiction stories that I'd done, which I consider inferior to the best of my comic-book work. I thought 10 years ago that that wouldn't be true. We were getting respect. That's something good that's going to come out of this respectability, that nobody is going to have to be ashamed of doing comics any more. But there is *still* a stigma attached to it. Even stoic, staid *TV Guide* ran an editorial saying, "Comic books are generally superior to the same characters done on television," and yet there is a stigma attached. You are considered some kind of subliterate because you do comics. I had dealings with a TV producer a couple of weeks ago and he was curious about comics, so I gave him a whole bunch of stuff. He called back a few days later, *astonished* that it was literate and had good stories and characterization and all that. I don't know what he was expecting, but that's a fairly common reaction.

Could that be economic?

It's partly economic, yeah. If you get $8,000 for a script, obviously you're superior to a guy who gets $400 for the same amount of work. Yeah. That brings us to the thing that I'm currently most angry about, having to do with the Superman movie and the TV shows, and that is that none of us guys who pioneered this form or who have been working in it or developing it are reaping any of the benefits, economically or any other way. Warner has released eight books in conjunction with the [first] Superman movie, none of which were written by comic-book people.

One was.

Which? Elliot [Maggin]'s novelization? Yeah. Elliot peripherally, but when they needed somebody to do the novelization of the movie, when they needed somebody to do the calendar, none of us got a shot at that. I'm very bitter and very angry. Not necessarily me, but somebody from comics should've gotten a chance to write some of the *Wonder Woman* TV scripts, the *Hulk*, *Spider-Man*.

It was a natural, logical assumption of mine when I went into this that if I worked well and worked honestly and did the best I could and didn't fool around with anybody that there would be a natural progression, both economically and artistically, and it's very frustrating to me that that has not happened. I know that I'm really going to sound like a crybaby now, but it seems to me that comic book

EPILOGUE

GREEN LANTERN OF EARTH! HEED ME--HEED MY *ANGER!* YOU HAVE BEEN *INSUBORDINATE!* YOU DISOBEYED OUR ORDERS!

WE COMMANDED YOU TO REMAIN ON STATION UNTIL WE DECREED YOUR TASK *COMPLETED!*

I...I'M SORRY...

THAT'S RIGHT, *LANTERN...* APOLOGIZE! *GROVEL* IN FRONT OF THAT WALKING MUMMY!

YOU CALL YOURSELF A *HERO!* CHUM...YOU DON'T EVEN QUALIFY AS A *MAN!*

YOU'RE NO MORE THAN A *PUPPET...*AND THE *GUARDIANS* PULL YOUR STRINGS!

LISTEN...*FORGET* ABOUT CHASING AROUND THE *GALAXY!...*AND REMEMBER *AMERICA...*

...IT'S A *GOOD* COUNTRY...BEAUTIFUL ...FERTILE...AND TERRIBLY *SICK!*

THERE ARE CHILDREN DYING... HONEST PEOPLE COWERING IN FEAR...DISILLUSIONED KIDS RIPPING UP CAMPUSES...

ON THE STREETS OF *MEMPHIS* A GOOD *BLACK* MAN DIED...AND IN *LOS ANGELES,* A GOOD *WHITE* MAN FELL...

SOMETHING IS *WRONG!* SOMETHING IS *KILLING* US ALL...! SOME HIDEOUS MORAL CANCER IS ROTTING OUR *VERY SOULS!*

21

Writer: Denny O'Neil Artist: Neal Adams *Green Lantern/Green Arrow* #76 April 1970 people have done all this stuff and perfected this particular form of storytelling, and when there's finally a chance to a) reach big numbers of people, which is something everybody who writes or draws wants to do – we all work for as big an audience as we can get – and b) get some sort of financial security, we're not even considered. The publicity attending the *Superman* movie – the *Newsweek* story said that Warner also owns a company which is licensed to publish the Superman character as a comic book. That is the attitude of those people. It angers me both because it's stepping on my toes and it demeans what I've been doing for a living all these years.

I'm staying with comics because I'm not ashamed of what I do. I get a craftsman's satisfaction out of doing this thing well – I think it is something I do well – and I need to make a living. I have a lot more financial obligations at 39 than I did at 26. But in a sense – Bob Kanigher talks about the Golden Rut and I used to think he was exaggerating or whining or being a crybaby, and I see what he's talking about now. There are assumptions when you go into anything that you're going to be dealt with fairly. I don't think that's very much true. I think we're used. That's not to say any one specific person – I think both Jenette Kahn and Joe Orlando, to name two people, are not happy about the situation. Corporations simply don't care about people.

What is it about comics people that they can't put together a guild? You hear comics professionals screaming about the injustices heaped upon them all the time and yet they do nothing about it.

I'm not so sure we can't put together a guild. I think, like democracy, it's an experiment that has yet to be tried.

Writers did it in the '40s. The Writer's League more or less forced publishers to give them twice the royalty rate on paperbacks. Every other group of writers has done it. Television writers, novelists have a strong –

Novelists don't have a strong anything. But at least they get royalties and they own what they write unless they're dumb enough to sign away the rights and some of them do that. I have worked for some pretty chintzy publishing companies and I've never found one where, if you made a point of it, they wouldn't give you the copyright.

At this particular – to use a Nixonism – point in time, it's not economically feasible to rear back on our legs and make demands because they don't need us. It's a depressed market, it's just bad economics.

As for why they didn't do it earlier: We tend to be independent people who like working alone. That's part of it. Perhaps part of it is that sense of inferiority which has pervaded comics almost from the beginning. Until recently nobody would cop to working in comic books. If you were visiting your home town and your home newspaper had a "Who's Visiting" column, you'd describe yourself as a journalist, or "work in publishing," something like that.

One of the good things Jenette did was start calling it DC Comics instead of National Periodical Publications, which sounds like something that's devoted to delineating the activities of obscure New Guinea tribes. That letterhead we used to have – "National Periodical Publications, Anal Retentive Publishing Company." There was no fun that you got out of that. And Jenette had at least enough guts to say, "It's comic books that we're doing. Let's call it what they are." So, that sense of inferiority probably worked against forming any sort of viable guild.

The fact is that until my generation of comic book writers, guys tended to be not formally educated very much and weren't maybe aware of the clout they had. I mean, somebody like Bill Finger, who's a great, raw talent, with no polish at all. I think he was just so happy to be writing that it wasn't till the end of his life that he even got angry about the inequities that were leveled against him and it was much too late for him to do anything about it then. I think it's a miracle that Siegel and Shuster got partially what's coming to them. At least they won't have to worry about money for the rest of their lives. On the other hand, if they had been in any other field and had created a character which is known in every corner of the Earth, they'd be many times millionaires. But they were a couple of young guys and they didn't know from publishing, and they probably didn't start out to be publishers. The guys who worked in the pulp magazines had the same deal. They signed over everything, including the rights to their first three children, to their publishers. So, when that stuff gets reprinted now it's pure profit. There are no editorial costs involved at all. I think. Walter Gibson is an exception to that, but one of the rare exceptions. I doubt if Lester Dent's estate gets any money from the Doc Savage reprints or the movie or any of that stuff. That's just been true of pulp literature.

I would say that it's not necessarily that way in book publishing. They're not out to gouge you in quite so avaricious a way.

See, you've got to understand that popular culture is a technological and not an artistic phenomenon. Comic books existed because Max Gaines had presses that he needed to keep busy, and also they had recently acquired a quartering machine, which meant they could take pieces of newsprint and cut them into four pieces. It was a toy that they had, and Gaines had to keep the presses running for one of those obscure, arcane economic reasons that I don't understand. So what did he do? He invented comic books as we know them. Then, having had the technology, he had to find something to fill it with. So he went out to find anybody he could get to tell a story and draw a picture. These people were delighted to be pulled from nowhere and given work, doing something they wanted to do. They didn't think of themselves as artists or creators.

The same thing is true of the novel before that. The high-speed printing press is the reason we have popular novels at all. In the 19th century a bunch of things happened. After the industrial revolution, there arose a leisure class that was not yet the upper class. These were lower-class people who suddenly had time to read because they didn't need to toil in the field 16 hours a day to eat. They only had to work 11 hours a day. That gave them some time to fill up to amuse themselves. At the same time, high-speed printing was invented. The logical thing: You put the two together. You've got a need to fill up those extra four or five hours a day and you have a technological device that can fill the need. Now you begin to go look for somebody to supply the stuff that gets put on the linotype machines. You find somebody that's talented from the same social stratum as the people you're aiming the book toward, which is blue-collar people, lower middle-class people. This guy doesn't come out of the cultural tradition. His grandfather didn't know how to read at all. He doesn't think about the fact that there are royalties and rights due to him as a creator. He thinks that this is a hell of a lot better then working in the factory for 11 hours a day. "And I get paid better than my brother who's working in the factory." That's as far as his thinking goes. Therefore, he signs away all rights to everything. Publishers get used to this happening. There arises a tradition of it happening that's carried through until recently. It's a technological-sociological phenomenon. I think that explains why these people never demanded their rights back. And people like me, we came into this tradition, we came into a structure that had been set for 40 years, and no one person can fight it.

It's the most absolute truism in the world that technology always precedes art. Always. No painter ever said, "Well, I want to make a portrait of the Mona Lisa, so I'm going to figure out a way to do this." He said, "I've got these paints and this stuff, and what can I do with it?" That always happens, and it's something it seems to me that nobody who teaches this stuff in college ever acknowledges. Going back to the cavemen, they had to have the wall and the sharp stone before they made the pictures. And it's especially true of things like comic books, which are low-common denominator art.

So, basically, comics are just bottom-of-the-barrel publishers.

Yeah, and the bottom-of-the-barrel creators, people who did not come from a tradition of demanding their rights, of even knowing what their rights were. People who were basically uneducated, maybe enormously talented, but not formally educated, so they didn't know what was coming to them and they didn't demand it. And Len and Marv and me and everybody have inherited that and that's where we're at.

You've said that the guy who could fix a carburetor is as valuable as a writer or a musician. Just as valuable in what way?

He has something that he does that is valuable and necessary and takes a certain set of aptitudes. Not everybody can do it. The world would not function without that guy, therefore he's as valuable as I am, or as valuable as Mahudin, or as valuable as Gore Vidal or...

Maybe more valuable? Can't the world function without your comic books?

Yeah, in that sense. If the Bomb went off tomorrow and there were only a handful of us, my survival would not have a very high social priority. The guy who knows how to make the fuckin' engine go – him you'd have to save. Yet I think I'm a valuable member of society because I do something that people need. They need to hear stories.

What is the value of culture, then?

It makes us civilized; it makes us something other than animals.

Isn't that its value, then?

That's a very complicated subject that, again, people have been debating for 12 centuries. But I can say that when people get past subsistence, when they know that they are going to eat and have something to keep the rain off them, they need me. They need the shaman, the tribal storyteller. I have an image of myself, if that Bomb did explode, squatting on a hillside surrounded by children telling them stories which is, after all, how I started out. When I was seven years old, I told stories to the neighborhood kids. I wasn't the best football player, I wasn't even the smartest kid in school, but I was the one who could tell them stories, and that's what I'm basically still doing. That's my function. I don't like it always, I'm uncomfortable with the role, and I'll slug anybody that calls me an artist.

Why?

Because that carries all the cultural freight where I'm supposed to be uplifting people. I don't want to do that. I don't know if I'm capable of it. In my best moments I can amuse them.

Another head change... This occurred to me while I was reading the Neal Adams interview you ran. Actually, it occurred to when I was talking to Harlan [Ellison] last Thursday, and he had had dinner with Neal, and evidently they had been arguing about using the medium to Change The World. Evidently, if Harlan is to be believed, Neal was coming down on him for not trying to use television... And I thought, Jesus, do I want to live in a Neal Adams world? No. I don't at all. If I lived in a Neal Adams world, women would not be equal to me; I would have a very authoritarian attitude toward children; I would believe quantity equaled quality; I would value a 747 above a bicycle. (I believe a bicycle is the most beautiful machine there is. It's simple, it's economical, it does exactly what it's supposed to do, and it doesn't hurt anybody.)

And conversely, maybe someone wouldn't want to live in my world if I became King-God tomorrow. Maybe the system we have, as dumb as it is, is better. So, by just taking that one extra little step, I have to believe that I don't have the final answers either. And maybe I should limit myself to squawking about things that I perceive as inequities and trying to let solutions work themselves. If you recognize the problems, maybe the solutions will come. I'm saying I'm a hell of a lot less of a proselytizer than I was at one time. I mean, the Reverend James Jones had solutions to things, right?

This Synanan dude had solutions, and look where both of these guys ended up in a very short period of time. They ended up insane. They ended up corrupting and destroying the very people they set out to save. That seems to be the way of it. As intrinsic as it is to human nature to hear stories, it also seems intrinsic to human nature to abuse powers. Who are the great villains? Hitler was probably the greatest villain of all time. And Mussolini – and they made the trains run, by God. I get very itchy now when people come on very strong about changing the world. And even in the peace movement, which I was close to for a time – my FBI file is probably like that, [*holding up his hands*] not because I ever did anything, but because I testified a lot – and I saw those guys get on fantastic ego trips, which partly defeated what they were trying to do because they got into squabbles with each other and they forgot that LBJ was the enemy, not the guy who was running the other faction of the peace movement. Same thing seems to have happened in the feminist movement. *Ms.* magazine is notorious for ripping off women writers. In the best of times, it seems that people catch themselves in time to keep from going completely around the bend. If they don't, they're James Jones. It's another reason I think I want to deal with me – rather than you – first. Even Shaw, who is maybe the greatest advocate of socialism who ever lived, said somewhere, "The trouble with looking out for Number Two is you don't really know what Number Two needs or wants."

[*Catron*] You wrote something on Manson, didn't you?

Actually I was accused of writing specifically about Manson and what I intended was – I saw within the peace movement and within the comics culture a lot of fascist stuff beginning to happen. I don't know why it happened to come out looking so much like Manson, but he was one of three or four people I had in mind when I was doing that. I also think we copped out on that and used drugs as an explanation. But, you don't need to use drugs to explain that people follow charismatic leaders. They did not put LSD in all the reservoirs of Germany in 1932.

Why do you think people follow cult leaders?

Jesus, I don't know. I could offer guesses, but they would be no better than yours or anybody else's. Personally – looking at me because I can't talk about you – I occasionally feel so insecure about my life that I wish somebody would come along with a neat set of answers. I keep waiting for a telegraph from God and if God happened to manifest himself in the form of a very charismatic human being who calmed my fears, offered me a program, and made life simple for me, I'd be tempted. In modern life you see that more and more because the nuclear family is disintegrating and whatever is good or bad about that, it makes people tend to be scared.

Could you see yourself joining a cult?

I'm not a joiner. I don't even belong to the Writer's Guild. I don't know why

I'm not a joiner. I've never figured that out about myself. But I don't think so, merely on the basis of past history. I had to be talked into joining ACBA [Academy of Comic Book Artists], and really talked into serving on the board. And I declined the chance to run for President of the organization when I was nominated.

I can understand people wanting to follow somebody who has answers. I live a thousand miles from my nearest relative – except for my child – and I feel sometimes at 3:00 a.m. that this apartment can get awful big and awful lonely, and I would like very much to have somebody around that had to like me because I was their relative, somebody I didn't have to perform for. A lot of people are exactly in that situation. Or if they do live next door to their parents they're estranged from them. That happens more and more. It's a very natural thing. We're not solitary creatures. We need to belong to something.

I've written a lot of stories about alienation. I guess one of the reasons I respond to Batman as a character is I think he's basically alienated from everything except his obsession. In "Elseones" [one of O'Neil's short stories] I wanted to write the ultimate alienation story – a story about an alienated alien. That's because I guess I have felt alienated from this society from very early on. I'm at a loss to explain why. I had a normal childhood, I went to normal schools, and I'm currently on very good terms with my parents.

What do your parents think of your comic-book career?

I think they're reconciled to it now. I think they didn't understand what it was all about. I don't think that any middle-class person can quite understand what it is a writer does.

Why is that?

Because sitting down and making up stories is not work. You're not building or selling something. When I was in newspapers, they could understand that and it was fine. They read newspapers; they knew what it was. I don't think they quite understood what I was doing in New York. I think they realize now that what I'm doing is work, it's honorable. I mean, I'm not pushing dope or mugging people.

Roy Thomas leaving Marvel is to your mind fairly inconsequential. Might that be because the comics companies have diminished the individuality of artists and writers in the field to the point where they are an interchangeable commodity, and it doesn't matter where they go or what they write?

That's a complicated question. Here's a sketchy answer. In general, the artists and writers are far more important than they've ever been in the history of the medium because for a long time, you'll remember, we didn't even get bylines. I've published a lot of stuff that went out without bylines, and I've been in the business a relatively short time.

The top 10 artists and the top 10 writers may very well be interchangeable for all practical purposes. Len [Wein] and I were talking about that the other night. I

WIGGINS IS THE FIRST TO REACH SAFETY! DESPERATELY HE CUTS AT THE THICK ROPE SECURING THE BRIDGE...ONE STRAND THEN ANOTHER PARTS UNDER HIS BLADE...

BUT WIGGINS' NEMESIS IS NO ORDINARY MORTAL! NO, THIS IS *THE BATMAN* --VETERAN OF A THOUSAND PERILS, RELENTLESS AVENGER OF WRONGS! WITHOUT HESITATION, HIS SUPERBLY TRAINED MUSCLES REACT; LAUNCHING HIM ACROSS THE YAWNING EMPTINESS...

...HIS CABLED FINGERS FIND A HOLD, CLAMP TIGHT ON A RAIN-SLICKENED BRANCH...

...A HEARTBEAT LATER, HE VAULTS UPWARD, TO FACE HIS FOE-- AND WHEN HE SPEAKS, HIS VOICE IS AS STEEL...

IT'S OVER, WIGGINS! YOU'VE GIVEN ME A GOOD RUN, BUT THE RACE IS FINISHED-- AND YOU'VE *LOST!*

UH-UH, *BATMAN!* I USED TO BE THE BEST KNIFE-MAN IN *HELL'S KITCHEN*-- AND I AIN'T *ABOUT* TO BE TAKEN!

2

Writer: Denny O'Neil Artists: Neal Adams & Dick Giordano *Detective Comics* #410
April 1971 [©1971 DC Comics Inc.]

am now writing one of his characters – Dominic Fortune – and he's writing one I've been associated with – Bat Lash. I don't think either character has suffered because I think Len and I have about equivalent skills. I don't think that any casual reader – meaning reader who does not pay attention to bylines, which is most of them – is going to notice. I think a character will suffer from being taken from somebody of considerable skill and given to someone of lesser skill. But there is a certain plateau that people reach after a while and if they keep their heads intact and they keep their sanity and if they maintain the ability to function at something near maximum effectiveness… well, you know, when Roy takes over *Batman*, it's going to be a different *Batman* than mine. I question whether it's going to be substantially better or worse.

Well, it might not be better or worse, but it might be different and that's the important thing.

It'll be different and that's one of the little joys of the medium.

But, the question is: Will it be different? You just said Len is doing *Bat Lash* and you did *Bat Lash*…

Well, we're talking about some Platonic ideal of quality I guess. Yeah, Len's *Bat Lash* is doubtless different than mine, Len's *Batman* is different than mine and we've talked about that. But, it's probably just as enjoyable. It *will* be different, but I suspect that – if there were some way to measure an enjoyment factor, given 500,000 readers, it would probably come out to be very close.

I wasn't talking about deriving an equal enjoyment out of different writers or artists. I was talking about the sameness that contributes to that interchange-ability. You can derive an equal amount of enjoyment out of Shakespeare and Ibsen, but that doesn't mean they're interchangeable.

The institution of storytelling is vital and important to our culture and any culture. It exists in every culture that we know about and in some of them it is on a par with religion to the collective consciousness of the tribe. I think storytellers are tremendously important, any kind of storytellers to any kind of civilization. I question that any one story or even any one storyteller is that important. I don't know that modern drama would be a lot different if Shakespeare had never existed. I'm prepared to say almost unequivocally that there would be virtually no change in the modern detective story if Conan Doyle had never existed. So it is possible to venerate the institution and still become a little chagrined at the freight that is put upon any one given manifestation of the institution.

Again, you're sort of diminishing the individual artist from which art comes.

Why?

Because you're saying no artist is that important.

In the broad overall, comprehensive picture, no, I don't think any of them are and yet that does not mean –

But haven't they added something precious to the world?
Sure.

Without which the world would be poorer?
Unquestionably. I have certain authors whose books I buy, in hardcover even, and my life would be a lot poorer without them. But, that's my life. The world as a whole would not notice their absence is what I'm saying.

I'm sure that's true of any author, but I'm not sure what that means.
It means that it's possible to get too excited about things that don't have a lot of consequence in a big picture. I've noticed that people tend to get a lot more excited about their pleasures than about their livelihoods. People can come out of a movie vehement in their anger at some poor director or filmmaker, and it's a kind of vehemence that they seldom display at their politicians, or their children's principals. I don't know why that is, but I notice it in myself. When I have an ill feeling about a piece of art, it's almost inevitably more intense than my ill feeling toward a political situation. Possibly because it is the child in me that responds to the art, any art from a Double-Bubble comic strip to a Beethoven symphony. It's that side of me that responds and that side of me tends to get more excited about anything than the calm, mature person that has to deal with politics or family matters. So, I understand why – I think I understand – why all this heat comes from comic-book stories, why people can get so vehement about something that really does not affect their lives.

I don't think that in any way diminishes my regard for the dozen favorite writers I have. I mean, my God, I read four novels a week, and probably see four to five movies a week. I'm as into it as anybody on Earth, just about. A major portion of my life has to do with art. And a major portion of the joy I get from life has to do with it. But, if John D. MacDonald had never lived I would substantially be the same person, and I might have found somebody else to fill that vacuum that he fills in my life. I don't know. But that's the easiest example I have of some whose work I always enjoy.

That's true of any artist or writer, that you can live without him.
That's all I'm saying.

That's inarguable. You talked about storytelling and how important, it is to a society, but that doesn't speak to the differences to a society of good stories and bad stories.
I don't think anybody has formulated an aesthetic for the ages yet. I mean, I think aesthetics is fascinating and I will willingly read anything that anybody has

to write or listen to anything that anybody has to say about it. But, I don't want to get into the question of good and bad because it's so muddled.

Yes, but it's important.

Yeah, I have a gut feeling that it's important, but I'd be at a loss to say exactly why. I do know that, for example, literary fashions come and go. Dickens seems to be respectable now, he was absolutely not respectable when I was in college. So to some degree people's perceptions seem to change about what is good or bad. I don't know anybody who has managed to establish an absolute yardstick, and in fact some very serious thinkers disagree violently. Plato would have eliminated Homer from the Greek culture as being morally pernicious. Nietzsche would have eliminated approximately 90 percent of all art, particularly 90 percent of all music. Strauss was, in his time, vehemently condemned for the waltzes. Obviously, in the case of Nietzsche and Plato, they were very respectable thinkers who were passing those judgments. I don't want to get into aesthetics with a 10-foot pole. I have my own standards of storytelling. They are pretty much mine, but since they seem to find a large area of response out there in that a lot of people apparently like to read what I write and edit, I suspect they are the standards that many people hold.

But, do people hold standards at all?

Oh, I think the average reader picks up a comic book and then puts it down x-minutes later, thinking Good or Bad and does not delve into aesthetics. I think that's generally true of almost any entertainment.

Well, that points out the utter lack of discrimination among the public, which reflects our state of popular culture.

Yeah, but it's an evolving thing. I think it does need to be looked at and commented on. I just think we have to be careful when we talk about elevating the general taste, because elevating it to *what* comes to mind. As I said, that gets changed every 10 years or so. John D. MacDonald is an example. The first book of his that I read I was very angry that somebody had lent this to me and recommended it and wasted my time. That was when I was about 22. A few years later, I read, for whatever reason, a second book and liked it very much. And later went back and read that first one and liked it. So, my tastes changed.

What were your objections? How have your tastes changed?

I think I had a snotty college kid's attitude toward pulp fiction. I think I objected to something about his style, some petty thing. I might still object to it, but now in the context of everything else that's in the book, I would consider it beneath mention.

I once saw an English professor, a guy who taught English in an upstate college, pick up a copy of one of Vonnegut's books, *Cat's Cradle,* and read the first page and the last page, and not having read anything else of Vonnegut's and on the basis of that, pronounce it dreck. Then there is Denny's Adventures in Professorland, meeting some of *my* taste-formers now on a social level where I have some credentials myself, and being appalled by what they don't know about what they're teaching.

Why don't we go back to when we were talking about the interchangeability of comics writers and artists and my feeling that the comics companies encourage this attitude, and it diminishes the value of the material. Could you comment on that?

I doubt that there has ever been a company policy at either place formulated to minimize the importance of artists or writers. That may be the pragmatic result of what has happened, but with one exception, I don't know of anybody whose mind would work like that, who would deliberately minimize somebody's importance for the sake of gaining something.

Bear in mind that it is a mass medium and it requires a lot of material and the presses have to roll. So, for example, if a guy is getting behind, you have to put in work by somebody else in his place. I have to do it myself and I don't want to, ever. There are practical exigencies; try to have an inventory issue of every monthly book and that is simply because everyone misses deadlines, *I* miss deadlines. I just missed one, I missed it big, I missed it by six weeks through circumstances I couldn't help. That happens once in a while. It behooves *my* editor to have something to fill up those pages with. It behooves me as an editor to treat my creative people likewise, so I would be delighted if all of them were in every issue of the magazines they're associated with.

But, think about comic books compared to television. How many people even know television bylines at all? Even people who watch a lot of television seldom bother to read those credits. Television is sort of analogous: It's a mass medium which consumes a lot of material and it has implacable deadlines. And television is a good thing to use as a comparison because the only right that you have with regard to a television script that you've written is the right to take your name off it. That's all. They retain total control of every other aspect of everything you've written. Comics, it's not quite that bad. There's a lot more attention paid to the individual's needs and to the feeling of the readership *for* a given writer or an artist. There are times when we can't pay attention to that stuff.

Now, I don't know about what people at the very top of both corporations are thinking, I don't have dealings with them. I can talk about editors, and I know we pay a lot of attention to that. If a book is a Chris Claremont book we want it to remain a Chris Claremont book, and it is only under pressure of exigency that it will become a not-Chris Claremont book for an issue. In my case it's partially because I still respond to the material, I still read it for pleasure, and to that extent I share the discriminating fans' distinctions and preoccupations. I suspect that nobody at the *very top* of either corporation reads anything and they don't know. That, however, is also true of other kinds of publishing. How many times have

I heard books referred to as "product"? That's just the way it is. So, they may not know, but I don't care – I don't meddle with their preoccupations.

I have a fair amount of autonomy as an editor and, with certain exceptions, most of the decisions, pro or con, that get made having to do with what I edit, are my decisions. With personnel, at least 97 percent of the decisions that get made with who's going to do what are mine. *Pro forma* I frequently consult with an editorial director, but Shooter sort of makes it a point of saying that the bottom line is yours. He will suggest – he has never to my knowledge stated that somebody has to be doing something. In fact, the fights that I've had with him have dealt with my keeping people on books that were giving me a lot of trouble and making my life unnecessarily complicated but I felt the readership liked these people on these particular characters and so I decided to put up with the grief I was getting personally.

I'm sure most people pay as much attention as you do, but the fact remains that in comic books artists and writers are interchangeable commodities. If one of your writers died tomorrow you would simply scoop up another one from your stable with virtually no change –

Oh, but Gary, that's true of all mass media. Look, I just saw a movie called *Hopscotch*. When they originally put the deal together *Hopscotch* was to star Warren Beatty. It ended up starring Walter Matthau. And it's a perfectly good movie. I liked it, and it probably would have been a good movie with Warren Beatty, too. They would have made the adjustments necessary.

All I'm saying is that if x-writer died tomorrow or left the business, the following day I'd have a replacement for him. Because I'm out there entertaining those readers, and I have to have somebody to do the work. It does not mean that there would be no regret attached to that. But, I have been taken off books as a writer myself for reasons I didn't always think were justified, and the books went on, they survived. I don't know if that has anything to do with the importance of the individual artist or writer. Yes, they are interchangeable because we have a given number of pages to produce a month and those pages have to be produced or we're not in the comic-book business. We'd be in the vanity press business or the small press business. But as the business is constituted we are as print media go, a mass medium, and we have those pages and we have a lot of jobs depending on those pages getting filled. So, if X can't do the work for whatever reason, Y has to. In that sense, X and Y are interchangeable. It does not mean that we're not aware of the differences between X or Y or that those decisions are ever ever ever made lightly. Bear in mind that – I'm an exception – most of the people who are now running the comic book world on a practical day-to-day level were once fans.

I understand that, and I understand the exigencies of a mass medium. But, is there any significant difference between writer X and writer Y? And doesn't this sort of thing breed a collective artistic consciousness as opposed to an

individual artistic consciousness? Art has always been the most individual activity possible; now it's being reduced to a formulaic approach where you simply plug into the slot the required participant. I'm talking about the bankruptcy of mass media, and the fact that comics so enthusiastically embrace this bankruptcy.

If indeed it is a bankruptcy, it is one that is built into the nature of mass media. Go fight city hall. Go quarrel with the industrial revolution. That's who you're ultimately railing against here. I could also question that art has always been the most individual of acts, because in pre-literate times…

Well, we don't know much about art before then. We have only sketchy ideas.

We know that for a long time that stories were transmitted orally from storyteller to storyteller and so what you got after 200 years was the equivalent of a mass media product, something that had passed through a lot of sensibilities. Up until the last century, artists wrote for a really tiny audience, all of whom had the same set of preconceptions. Goethe's Weimar had 25,000 people in it, of whom five or 6,000 people were literate. That was his audience. He knew them virtually. So, yeah, it was individual in that it was clearly and definably his stuff, but he knew his audience intimately in a way we can't. Shakespeare's London had 100,000 people. That's a tiny, tiny fraction of the number of people that I have to write for in a given month.

But it is possible to promote an individual vision in today's mass media.

Sure. A few people do it.

So it isn't impossible.

It is seldom done on television, for example.

That's because television is, as you have pointed out, the lowest common denominator mass medium. It panders to audience preconception, and if you pander to a homogenized audience, how is there any room for an individual point of view?

Well, there's not much. I'm trying to think of how we can apply this to other media. I don't know how much of an individual vision, if I understand what you're talking about at all, you get from best-sellers.

Again, I come back to. the fact that there is a greater range of values at play in other entertainment media.

A greater range of…?

There's a far greater range of depth, of insight, of character revelation…

That partially has to do with the limitations of the medium. I mean, in 22 pages you're not going to do *Hamlet*.

Twenty-two pages is a limitation of the industry, not the medium.

If I go see *Game of Death* and I look at the character that Bruce Lee plays, I am not going to come away from that movie knowing anything about why that character chose to become a martial artist, what his political, social, or religious, or moral feelings are. I'm going to know he does one thing superbly, and I either accept or reject the movie on that basis. What those movies are about at their best is the way a man can realize himself physically.

Likewise in comics, anybody that reads anything I write expecting to find out what I think about the forthcoming election is barking up the wrong tree, because I'm not in business to do that when I'm working in that medium. The average TV show isn't in the business to do that. In fact, the thing that's leveled against *Lou Grant* – the main criticism that you hear about it – is that it's too preachy. I don't think it is at all. I think they're dealing with a newspaper and to deal with a newspaper realistically you have to deal with the things a newspaper deals with, which are public issues. But, that's an excellent show that's constantly criticized, because it deals with serious stuff. I don't know if the *Los Angeles Tribune* is a liberal or conservative paper and I watch the show pretty often. They don't even get into it that much but because they get into it at all they collect a lot of flak. Well, I don't know – when I'm doing a comic book I'm not going to get into certain kinds of things because that isn't the place to get into them. But there are in everything I do implied values with regard to things like violence and brotherhood – to use one of those big words.

It's there but it's buried so deeply it's difficult to ascertain.

Because I'm writing fiction, not polemic. People like Rich Howell will disagree with this – and have – but I think there are limitations to the medium, built-in limitations to the format, to what it is. I would be delighted to be proved wrong, I don't see doing Hamlet's soliloquy in a comic book. *Gen of Hiroshima* is a very good example of somebody who looked at a comic book and saw what it could do and used the limitations of the medium and made the copy and the artwork to tell what is a very, very serious story. Yet it's not ponderous, it's not heavy, it's not overblown. It simply takes what a comic book is and uses that to convey this guy's sensibility, to convey the story he had to tell.

But every medium has its limitations. That doesn't mean comics can't have the same profound quality…

Exactly. And you're not going to get from a Shakespearean play the same thing you're going to get from a Wagnerian opera, even though they may be dealing with very much the same kind of subject matter.

Right. So the potential of comics isn't limited just because you can't do Hamlet's soliloquy. Something just as touching could be done in the comics form.

Exactly. And we are still – but, and I don't know if this is a good analogy, the Beatles expanded the parameters of popular music, and yet they could do that because there existed the 33 LP. Al Jolson, for example, on his recording, if he wanted to, could not have expanded the parameters of popular music at that point because of the nature of what phonograph records were; he had five minutes, tops. So, he couldn't do a *Sgt. Pepper.* Very much the same way comics are evolving, they're very much in the process of becoming…

Jolson's was a technological problem, not an economic problem. Comics are an economic problem. There's no reason, technologically, why Marvel Comics couldn't produce a 200-page comic. Their only excuse is economical.

Yeah, and that would mean Marvel, if they did a lot of that stuff and had no audience, would be out of business. Therefore, it would be self-defeating. You would not have a mass medium any more. Remember, we're always talking about a mass medium. That means reaching lots of people, that means finding certain things we can all agree are amusing.

All right, but film is a mass medium and you have Coppola and other film-makers who are doing superior work and who are reaching a mass audience.

Your assumption is that comics people *aren't* doing superior work. Some are, some aren't. We have our losers, but we also have our Coppolas.

The problem as I see it is that you don't have the range he did to play with. You're working in a more restricted, more confined range within the superhero context.

All right. Frank Capra had 90-minute movies to play with. He gave you what he could give you in 90 minutes and still reach the numbers of people he had to reach with the stuff. It's a very close analogy. I have 22 pages. I have a lot of things I have to do that are givens before I sit down to fill those 22 pages. I am not going to give you 22 pages of talking heads even if the conversation is fascinating, for example. So, OK, given that…

I see what you mean. I don't see the page count as much a limitation as the restrictions to the content in those 22 pages that are imposed upon you. It's a limitation but it's a limitation that can be surmounted. Kurtzman did it. Kurtzman told stories in seven pages that were far and away better than the stuff DC and Marvel are doing now.

Kurtzman was Kurtzman. You're talking about a guy who is probably a genius. We ain't all geniuses. Would that we were. And then Kurtzman eventually ran afoul of commercial limitations. The reason he is not editor of *Mad,* if my reading of that brouhaha is accurate, is because he could not make his vision ultimately conform to the mass market. It's unfortunate because the mass market is certainly impoverished and I wish to God that Kurtzman could have made his vision and his discipline conform to the exigencies of periodical publishing. We'd have had lots and lots of great stuff that we don't have if he'd been able to do that. I think *Annie Fanny* is tripe. It's superbly executed tripe, but you have this major visual comedian who's reduced to doing smarmy sex gags. Too bad, man. Don't you wish that Kurtzman could have met those deadline schedules on *Mad* back in 1952?

My question is: Do Marvel and DC encourage the Kurtzmans of today?

They may not encourage them, but they don't discourage them.

Don't they discourage them implicitly by setting an example by the material they publish, which is almost all derivative and banal?

Your opinion, Gary.

Even new artists coming into the field, you can see all their influences are totally from old comic books.

Well, of course. What do you want their influences to be? Rembrandt's chiaroscuro? Come on!

I'm saying they don't bring in any new values. It's all regurgitated Kirby-Lee stuff.

What you're talking about is a lot of the limitation of the talent. Here's something I learned very early in my alleged career. I was writing scripts for Charlton. I was putting in Westerns these terrific action scenes, "Here comes the Loco Kid" – or whatever character I was doing – "somersaulting over this rock, both guns blazing." What I'd get is a picture of a guy with a gun in his hand pointing it at someone. I was furious! I thought, "This idiot is vitiating the entertainment value of my stories!" I later found out that those artists were not capable of drawing what I was asking. They were doing the best they could. A lot of what you're talking about is that artists are not capable themselves. They're capable of doing acceptable work – so are writers, I don't want to limit it to artists – so we use them because, sure, why not? They are entertaining x-number of people by what they do. The reason they are not doing it better is that they can't, at least not at a given point.

Frank Miller is an example of somebody who's come in who is capable of doing better and *is* virtually every month.

OK. Could I talk about Frank for a minute?

Sure.

I've been impressed with Frank's design and panel configurations and his storytelling techniques. Yet he hasn't learned how to draw the human figure. You can see where he's taken from Gil Kane, from Steve Ditko, from Jim Starlin, and from other comics sources. His first story, which I just read, in *Daredevil* #168, just embraces all of the melodramatic formulas of every comic that has

preceded it. So, here's a guy with a very personal approach, but it's almost entirely subsumed by derivation.

All right, there's a number of things you said, and I'll speak to them one at a time. To my eye, anyway, Frank's figures are realistic within the confines of the exaggeration of what is basically a cartoon medium. They're exaggerated, but I would not like it if they weren't. As an editor that's what I want, that's what I'm asking him to do. I think the Elektra story is very good melodrama. It may not be original melodrama, but within its own self-imposed limitations he did it well.

I agree, but we've read it a hundred, a thousand times before.

Well, we have seldom read it that well done. That's the beginning and end of my answer to that. The third point is that Frank is still learning, and one of the things that most impresses me about him is that as good as he is now, he's always willing to learn and always seeking out new information.

I hope this doesn't come across as though I'm dumping on Frank, because he's certainly one of the freshest talents to come along. But I read that story and thought, "My God, he's falling into the rut."

I edited that story and thought it was a very good first story. For a guy who's learning how to write, I thought it was a fine first effort. I defy you to show me very many people's first stories – especially including mine – that were anything like as good.

And everybody always imitates at first. Like, Raymond Chandler was imitating the pulp guys. It's just that he had a much finer sense of language. He was basically telling the same story, he just did it better. He did it with fresh language, with a fresh approach to that archetypical private-eye character. As far as plotting, Chandler brought nothing to the American detective story. He just used the same tools and used them better. In the Elektra story that's what Frank was doing to my perception, using the same tools and doing it better than it's usually done. And I applaud that. And I think that's a way we can raise the level of the comic-book reader. Because you're buying *Daredevil* for a certain kind of melodrama and that's what he gave you. He just has his own way of doing it and, again, I thought it was better than most versions of that melodrama.

I suppose that melodrama is the basis –

If you don't want to read that melodrama, go read Fowles or Hawkes or Thomas Pynchon or those people. You won't get that kind of melodrama. And anybody who does not take advantage of the fact that there is a Pynchon as well as a Frank Miller is impoverishing themselves. And that happens a lot.

As I've said in print before, one of the few very serious reservations I have about my colleagues is that they limit themselves to pulp-derived material. Their work and their souls would benefit from a more constant exposure to a wider range of stuff. But if they choose to limit themselves to pulp-derived material and do it well, I can applaud the fact that they do it well, and I have no right to condemn them for what they don't do and what they don't want to do.

The only thing I'll say about this comic book-type melodrama is that, like all comic book melodrama, it's cheap, obvious, shallow – it doesn't even have the melodramatic qualities that something like *All About Eve* had – it was not deep by any means, but it had involving characters, it had witty dialogue, it had a piquant tone...

All right. Mankiewicz, who wrote the screenplay for *All About Eve,* had 120 pages, probably. Miller had 22. It's as simple as that. I think he's probably capable of the kind of intricacy that you're talking about. But if Mankiewicz had been doing a 15-minute short about a rivalry between two actresses, it would not have been *All About Eve,* because he couldn't have gotten the subplots in 15 minutes. It's just that simple.

I think what is conveyed subliminally in your magazine is an attitude of disdain. A little while ago you yourself used melodrama as a pejorative. Melodrama in my vocabulary is not a pejorative. It is a form. It is the form I predominantly work in as a matter of fact. It is a form with equal validity and weight with tragedy and comedy. It is one of the three modes of dramatic expression. And as Norman Mailer said, melodrama seems to be the natural mode of 20th century America as tragedy was the natural mode of Socratic Greece.

That might say more about 20th century America and its cultural standards than it does about the validity of melodrama as a form.

If, by that, you mean we are living in a melodramatic age, yeah.

In an age that embraces cheap melodrama...

An age that embraces melodrama; why does it have to be *cheap* melodrama? Cheap and melodrama are almost always yoked like that and yet melodrama is in itself neutral, it ain't good and it ain't bad. It's a form. The sonnet is a form; the ode is a form. Melodrama is a form, tragedy is a form, comedy is a form. It's just a dramatic attitude, and there's cheap melodrama and there's not cheap melodrama. There's bad tragedy, there's bad comedy. I will say unabashedly with almost no fear of contradiction that what we do in comics is melodrama, it's broad melodrama, fantasy melodrama. That's what comics are. If you don't like that, go read someplace else, go someplace else. I am not in the business of satisfying the tastes of anybody who is not willing to accept fantasy melodrama as a viable form of entertainment.

Love it or leave it.

It is in a way. You can't judge me for something that I have no intention of doing. What I intend to do is produce melodrama. Why condemn it for something it doesn't pretend to be?

Again, we're going back to Goethe's third criterion: Is it worth doing? Which may be the most important criterion of them all. In other words, why condemn a Russ Meyer movie because it's just T&A and doesn't aspire to anything beyond that? Because it's crap.

Actually, in singling out Meyer – he's one of the few auteurs in that form.

[*Laughter.*] I guess he is.

There is distinctly a Russ Meyer movie and it's not mistakable.

That's true, but it's misogynist trash nonetheless.

All right, by your standards. But I can see where Russ Meyer movies might do a helluva lot more social good than Socrates. If you're a frustrated, sexually deprived little man, and you can crawl under the turnstile into a sleazoid 42nd Street theater that's showing a Russ Meyer movie and you can have your sexual tensions relieved, and you walk out of there feeling better, the Russ Meyer movie that you think of as trash has done a positive social good for that poor, little man. It has alleviated the sum total of his suffering. Which is something that most high art can't lay any claim to. Russ Meyer movies have their place. I would not want Meyer movies to stop existing on the face of the Earth.

I think Russ Meyer movies are demeaning. Speaking of this poor, frustrated little man, a different form of art or entertainment might emancipate him from whatever problems he has in a more meaningful way than a Russ Meyer movie. A Russ Meyer movie may sustain him till the next day, but if he seeks to improve his life in a more satisfying way, he may find life more endurable, even enjoyable.

So, what are you saying? That you shouldn't pander to the very basest part of people?

That's what I would say.

I agree. I don't do any comic-book equivalent of *The $1.98 Beauty Show,* for example, which I think is debasing and immoral. But, I'm not going to accept any condemnation because I do melodrama. And I'm not going to say shows satirizing beauty contests are intrinsically bad, I just think that one is. I feel sorry for the people who participate in it willingly. And I think Chuck Barris is a reprehensible man. But, I don't do that. If I were doing a television show, I would hope I wouldn't do that one. I would be trying to reach the same audience that that reaches, but I would be doing a show with more dignity and more wit.

You're back to two things which we've talked about tonight: The ability of the individual artist – for want of a better word – to do something; and the readiness of people to perceive what he's doing. I mean, it's happened again and again in history that people have been ahead of their time. The Armory Show in 1915, which was the first show of modern painting, was totally lambasted by the critics as immoral among other things. People who get into this sort of thing get into morals a lot, for some reason. Now, a lot of those paintings are considered masterpieces and certainly nobody on Earth would consider any of them immoral any more. I think I have occasionally had ideas – well, like *Bat Lash*, which was a comic book that was 10 years ahead of its time. That's unfortunate that occasionally that happens. Norman Mailer's mayoralty campaign was considered radical in the extreme and now 50 percemt of the mainstream politicians around have incorporated those ideas. It's unfortunate that the guy who breaks the ground is frequently not the guy who reaps the profits from what he's done. James Joyce did not die a millionaire, and he showed people a whole new way to write novels. That's unfortunate, but again that's sort of like railing against earthquakes.

Man-made earthquakes.

Yeah, but when you're dealing with masses of people – and we're always talking about masses of people – you're not dealing with one, perfidious individual, human being. In this case, you're talking about mass taste, which changes with glacial slowness. Of course it does. You have to get four million people to agree on something before you have any significant change in mass taste. Obviously, that's going to happen slowly. You can lament that that's true, but there's not a damn thing you can do about it.

You can lament that it won't change.

So those of us who are working in any mass medium who consider ourselves to have integrity try and do good stuff. Don't always succeed. I won't quarrel if you point to any given story of mine and say, "This is a piece of garbage." I will quarrel if you say that I set out to do a piece of garbage. I have failures of talent and intelligence all the time. My intention is always to produce something that is at least acceptable when I sit down to do it. I don't always make it. Nobody else does that I know, either, but I'm always trying, and I happen to be the guy with the access to the comic books. And if you think you can do it a lot better than me then you should start doing it and start getting yourself in a position where you have access to the same amount of print that I have access to in a given year. You can make the case that in order to get to that place that you will be so compromised by the time you get there that you won't know what your values are any more. That's the thing that's often said of politicians. I don't know what I think about that; I don't think that's necessarily true. I think it's sometimes true. I think I'm relatively immune to that because I'm not very ambitious. I think in a funny way that's true of most people who are in comic books, because if we were ambitious we wouldn't be here. So, I think in an odd kind of way – this has never occurred to me before right now – that we do probably keep our standards intact more than most people who are in mass media.

When your standard is to write *Rom* you don't have to compromise yourself.

All right, if your standard is to write *Rom* and you are writing *Rom* well you've succeeded in what you're doing. Nobody is pointing a gun at your head and making you read *Rom.* And truly you would not deny that people have a right to read and enjoy *Rom.* Or *Betty and Veronica* or *Casper the Friendly Ghost* or anything else. I may not be able to stand reading *Betty and Veronica* – and as a matter of fact I couldn't the last time I tried – but I can't deny the pleasure or even the validity of the pleasure of people who get it from that stuff.

But the original point is comics creators have nothing to compromise in the first place.

So, are you going to hang them because they don't have genius or largeness of soul or whatever? They're doing the best they can.

So's Chuck Barris.

I don't know. I think Chuck Barris is cynical about it. I don't know of any comic-book people who go into it with a dead, cynical standpoint. Even the guys who I think have been damaged by working in the medium – they're guys who tend to be 15 or 20 years older than me – they're not so totally cynical that they go in thinking that they will exploit the medium or the kids reading the stuff. I don't know Chuck Barris, he may be a commendable man, but I have a feeling he goes in intending to exploit bad taste. So, if you say that somebody is not capable of perceiving anything outside the limitations of the kind of comic books they grew up with, and that is the highest standard they have, I might agree with you and say that it's too bad. If we make this quantum leap – if that person might not like *The Spirit,* for example, which is pretty generally regarded as an excellent comic strip – and I know people who do not like *The Spirit* and who do like *Betty and Veronica* – well, what can you say about that? It's too bad? What I perceive as extraordinary quality they cannot perceive as such. I think they are wrong and I think it's too bad their aesthetic grasp is so limited. Y'know, it's too bad. They're not bad people. The people who produce what is within their aesthetic grasp are not bad people for producing it and Will Eisner is not a bad man for exceeding that grasp. There's no blame here.

Another problem with mass taste is that it impairs the ability to make subtle distinctions.

How so?

Because the artistic response is always operating at such a low level. I fail to see how people can make distinctions on a higher level when they can barely make them at a lower level.

All right, if that's true, if there is what you're saying – a coarsening of sensibility – then you blame television much more than comic books.

Of course.

I think you're probably right.

I think it's affected me and telling me to go out and read a good book isn't going to help because the fact is we are bombarded by it all the time.

Then don't let yourself be bombarded by it. I'm a snob; I'm a print man. I don't watch television; I can't watch television. I just published a story in *Fantasy & SF* which is, on one level, a covert shot taken at all of my friends who do watch television a lot. The character, Quentin, in that story, is a composite of a lot of people I know and as a matter of fact, of a lot of people I like, and I don't understand how a guy I play poker with can, on a normal night, sit in front of a television set for five hours. I can't do it. I simply am not physically able to do that and after two hours of television, tops, I run screaming for the nearest book.

I regret the coarsening of a sensibility that cannot respond to a novel as deeply as it can to a television show. But, again, that's fighting city hall. It's too bad. It may be doing, and I suspect it is doing, some kind of harm to our collective consciousness. But, I don't know what to do about it. I can only feel it on a personal level and try not to let that happen to me, and try to expose myself to as many kinds of things as possible. I am currently spending a lot of time with someone who's deeply involved in modern dance, about which I know nothing at all. It's a small effort for me to remain open to what she says, but having made the effort, I am now finding things to like in modern dance.

It's probably a great opportunity to learn about it.

Yeah. I wish more people would do that. And I guess I do tacitly, covertly condemn people for not being open to more kinds of experiences.

You should not just read my *Spider-Man* stories. You should go out and buy paperback books and go to a library and get hardcover books and you should go listen to the free concerts in the park, both jazz and classical music, and you should go listen to the free rock concerts. You, living in the New York-Washington-New Jersey Metroplex, have access to all of the world's culture, to everything that's ever been done, you can get it. And if you don't get it, it's too bad for you. You are impoverishing yourself. You can't blame me because I am not offering you Beethoven because Beethoven is available to you. Personally I read comic books and Russian novels and there are times, with a gun at my head, I would not read a Russian novel, and I want a comic book, dammit. There are other times when I might be in a gloomier or more contemplative mood when a comic book will not satisfy what I'm looking for. One of the few ways we are blessed with in the 20th century, living as we do in interesting times, is that we can get anything we want. It is all available to us. You only have to reach out. If you choose not to reach out, it's too bad. Why don't you?

It's not that mass culture conspires to encourage triviality and mediocrity; it's just

that they think the same way and have the same goals. The result is a cultural dictatorship that encourages people to find the cheapest, easiest form of escape. The people who accept it at face value are being cheated.

They are and they aren't. Did you ever work at a bottle factory?

No.

I worked in a bottle factory. Two summers to put myself through college so I could get *haute culture*. Working at a bottle factory is this: I stood at the end of a conveyor belt. Ten thousand beer bottles came at me a day. The heat was 120° because these beer bottles were being molded in huge blast furnaces about 40 feet up the line. I took them off, I looked at them, I put them on gauges, I flipped them over, I put them in boxes. I repeated that until 10,000 of these bottles had been done. Then I got in my car and drove through a dismally bad East St. Louis neighborhood, and I got home. At that time I was very snobbish about things like melodrama. I was much worse in my prime than you ever were. [*Laughter.*] I mean I was an English major in a Jesuit university, man. If it was popular, it was no good *per se*. That was, for one year, my criterion. If a lot of people liked it, I didn't. End of discussion. Well, I was not capable of reading Dostoevsky after eight hours in that bottle factory. I couldn't do it. I could maybe crawl into the living room and turn on the television and stare at whatever happened to be flickering across it for an hour before crawling up to bed and getting ready to repeat the whole horrible process the next day. To appreciate Dostoevsky, you have to read a book with a lot of attention.

What I like about novels is that they absorb me because I have to bring some of myself to them. I have to make the effort of reading; it's not a totally passive experience. But that's because I'm now in a position where I am not physically exhausted except when I choose to be. If I were still working at that bottle factory I could not read the serious stuff that I do. In fact, I couldn't go to the serious movies I go to. In fact, I couldn't go to the Japanese melodrama that I go to on Tuesdays at the Bleecker Street because I would not have the energy to get past the language barrier, and see what was going on on the screen. All that I could do is to watch television. A lot of people have jobs like that. Their lifestyles sort of limit the culture that is available to them.

That's why the level of culture corresponds to economic class.

Yeah, absolutely. But, it had never occurred to me because I haven't thought of that bottle factory in 20 years.

I know what you mean. I worked in a restaurant taking red-hot dishes that had just gone through a huge dishwasher off a conveyor belt. After eight hours of that I crawled home like a whipped cur.

And yet ironically, probably working in that bottle factory made me a better writer who's able to bring things to my own work that wouldn't be there otherwise.

Certainly my experience in the Navy, as much as I hated it – which was a lot – broadened me. I think that unquestionably made me a better writer. One of the things I often recommend to, what we jokingly call the younger writers, is just to live more.

Experience.

Yeah. Because your work is bound to be enriched by anything that happens to you. One of the few good things about being a writer is that you can use pretty much anything that happens. I am hardly the first person to make that observation.

But if you are the son of that bottle-factory worker, and you grow up being only exposed to that, that will harm your taste. You will never exceed those formative years. And yet you may, because my parents were not cultural in any way at all. And yet somehow or other at about age 12, without any prompting that I'm aware of, I started reading books. And I think probably there was a certain amount of unease in my family at first because I was reading those books.

Eventually, my father, who did not read novels himself, was applauding the fact that I did. And yet the people I grew up with did not ever start to read novels, and to this day, their highest cultural peak is *Laverne and Shirley.* I don't know why I did it and they didn't. I'm thinking of one guy who's every bit as intelligent as I am and is exactly my age. He is a cultural illiterate at age 41. I don't know why it went one way with me and another way with him.

It may have very little to do with native intelligence, and more to do with what you expose yourself to. Once you expose yourself to different things, you'll acquire a taste for them and expand your taste as a result.

Yeah. And if you walk around being open to things in general, you'll have a much richer life. You'll see the way light is shining through the ice on the tree branches, and you will be given a moment of rare beauty that doesn't cost anything. I guess the moral of all this is to be open. In the non-erotic sense, to try to love everything, or at least to be nonjudgmental.

For example, the social stratum that I come from, which is Shanty-Irish lower-middle class blue-collar, St. Louis, there is a tendency on the part of a lot of the people who live in the neighborhood I grew up in to automatically condemn anything that is cultural, that is stamped with that. I sometimes wonder if my own anti-academic attitude is somehow related to that. But, my family would dismiss something as "deep," which means, "We can't understand it, so go away." A lot of the things we were dismissing as deep weren't. But, they were simply being judgmental and therefore closing themselves to a lot of things they would've liked, they would've enjoyed. We're getting quasi-mystical-philosophical, but that's all right because I'm 41.

You've earned it.

It seems to me that one of the primary duties that any body has to themselves is to try not to judge anything, at least not *prima facie* judge. As I'm finding that I can like dance when I didn't know I could once upon a time. I judged, I said, "That's sissy-stuff. I don't want to have anything to do with it. I can't like it because it's a bunch of dodos leaping around a stage. Forget it." And I was wrong. That's an example from my own life of a stupid judgment that deprived me of a lot of genuine pleasure for 40 years. If you want to extend that to the world of interpersonal relationships, it's even more applicable.

God, if we get any further into this line, we will begin discussing the Tao and things that I'm not really qualified to discuss. In an odd way these are things that are right now most important to me, but I don't know what I think about them enough to talk about them.

What you try to do is make some kind of peace with your own life.

That's another problem I have with your magazine. There seems to be an appetite for turmoil and conflict. I once shared that appetite for turmoil and conflict, and I don't anymore. I don't know about you, but I think I have probably had more conflict and hassle in my life than you have, and I guess I'm sick of it. I don't run away from it if I see a reason for it. On the other hand, I don't seek it out as I once did. I had about five or six years that were full of every kind of conflict and hassle there is, from physical violence on down. I've been through that. I've starred in that movie. I don't want to do it again. It was the cause of a lot of pain. And I don't see any point in seeking out pain. All of it was a learning experience, no doubt; I don't know if I'd do it again or not, because it almost killed me a couple of times. But I recognize at least that, yeah, I'm probably a more complex man for having gone through it. But I don't know if anything will be served by continuing to go through it. In any case, I don't have the stamina any more to do those things I once did. I guess I maybe perceive a kind of young firehouse attitude – you smell smoke and you run toward it.

Once when I was working on a newspaper, a kid called in with an incipient drug scandal. It would've smeared egg all over the face of the University administration. And I got on that story like gangbusters. And one of the other reporters said, "Why? Why are you so excited about this?" I didn't have an answer except that I liked conflict and turmoil when I was 25.

I don't know what it is about being 25, but you're hungry for conflict, for turmoil, and you run toward it. When I was a newspaper reporter, a story involving that kind of thing had infinitely more appeal for me than a story, for example, I did about a lovely old Japanese gardener and his wife who were having a wonderful and tranquil old age. That was a real good story I did, and it was very moving, but I didn't enjoy it nearly as much as I enjoyed the time that I got some real heavy dirt on the police department and I showed that these authority figures had really dropped the ball.

Yeah, now that I think about it, I remember really responding in a Pavlovian way, of anything that reeked of scandal, and I went for those stories with my arms outstretched and my teeth bared. I don't any more, and I can only suppose that it's because I've gone through that. I have probably gotten my allotment of conflict, turmoil – *Sturm und Drang* – in my life. I would like to believe that if I perceived something as a clear, visible moral wrong and it involved turmoil and violence to do something about it, I would not back away from it. I would not seek it out any more, but I would like to believe if I were in Berlin in 1932, I would fight Hitler…with a machine gun if necessary. But, I'm not going to go over to a foreign nation and sign up with a mercenary army for the sake of discharging my machine gun at somebody, even though the person I may be snuffing may be a reprehensible person. I just don't need to do that any more. Whatever it is in me that made me that avid, scandal-hungry reporter doesn't exist any more. I've satiated myself with whatever that need is. Which sounds like slipping into mellow old age or senility, whichever comes first, but it's not true because also my life now is, I think, immeasurably richer now than it was then. I enjoy so many more things. I get through weeks thinking, "Wow. I really don't have it so very bad any more." I mean, I do a lot of interesting things all the time now.

Is your life as passionate now?

I think that my relationship with people is far deeper and far more real. It may not have the surface passion. But, it's like a married couple if they can get through the first 10 years. The honeymoon kind of romantic passion is almost always gone, but if they can get through that initial period, they develop a love that takes the place of passion and is a lot more real and ultimately a lot more satisfying. My friend, Richard Hill, came up with a gag on a postcard three years ago, that said "We practice scribble-do," do meaning The Way in Chinese. It's a Zen-derived idea. I saw Richard a few weeks ago and we both realized that it was a very good joke because it was a very true joke. If you are a professional writer, say – and I'm sure that applies to being a professional artist or anything else – for the first six or seven years, I would get enormously elated from my work. It would be five in the morning and I would have just finished a script and, my God, I thought it was good and I'd have to talk to somebody. I'd telephone somebody in California, just out of this need to exalt; but that was almost always accompanied by a crashing low in which I thought that I was worthless, and the world was worthless and all of creation and the hand of God was worthless. Now, I seldom get that fantastic elation any more. And so you can say that there is a lack of passion in my life. I try to do things steadily.

However, I think that there is a constant satisfaction in my life now that was missing back then. It is a kind of day-to-day realization that one does the work and does it fairly well, and that's like the equivalent to the love between a man and a woman I was talking about before. It is not that great, "I cannot wait to get home and touch her again!" It's the "I know she'll be waiting for me and that we will arise together tomorrow morning and that I will start my day having a very pleasant and even meaningful exchange with this woman even though if I don't get home and touch her tonight it's not going to ruin my day." I think you reach some kind of detente with your work like that, which may be the reason that old men seldom write lyric poetry, because maybe lyric poetry is a result of that kind of unbounded, unfettered, youthful enthusiasm. What older men write are serious novels that require a sustained effort, that require going to a desk every day, and putting yourself in a certain frame of mind and sustaining that for, maybe a year. It's what Salinger once said about himself: He said he was a dash-man and not a miler, and I think history has borne him out unless he's writing a great novel. But even at that, it would be true. Salinger must be well into his 50s by now. So, the book he would write now would not be *Catcher in the Rye* which is a dash-man's book, essentially an extended short story.

On an infinitely lesser degree, I think I have reached that kind of feeling about my work. I try to go to it every day and I try to sustain a level of enthusiasm. In fact, I don't have to make an effort most days. If I've been away from a typewriter for three weeks, which has happened recently, I go to it with a great deal of enthusiasm, because I have, on some level, apparently a need to write. I've always written, even when I wasn't doing it for money. The only difference between now and 10 years ago is that I think I'm a lot more sane about the way I do it. And I think that my work is probably more consistent now. I was doing occasional great stories 10 years ago, but read the *Justice League* from that era and you'll see that I was occasionally doing awful. I don't think anything gets that awful any more.

Do you have the highs?

I don't have that mad 4 a.m. exalted feeling, but as I said, I have a general calm sort of feeling of satisfaction. I don't think I'd want the exalted 4 a.m. thing because I think that has to be accompanied by the crash. And the crashes, when they're low, they're real low. But, I think even if that were not true of me and it's certainly not true of everybody who reached this kind of detente, that it is generally better for work to do it consistently, rather than in peaks and valleys. We're talking, of course, about a sustained body of work. One individual story might benefit greatly from being done at the peak. Well, yesterday I read *Thus Spake Zarathustra*, and I also read the introduction by Nietzsche's sister and that whole book was done on one of those peaks – 30 days – and he went insane the next year. You wonder if there is a relationship. I don't know, but it has generally been true that people who have done that – well, you know, Dickens allegedly wrote *A Christmas Carol* in one sitting, but he came down and wept. He obviously was going through some kind of turmoil. I can remember finishing my first novel on one of those peaks and in an odd way it was one of the most exalted and one of the most horrible hours of my life. I finished it at 4 a.m. in a farm in central Missouri and I needed to go exalt and say, "I finished my first novel!" And there was nobody to exalt with. I couldn't very well wake up my mother-in-law. That would have been a fairly unsavory thing to do. There I was, way up there, with no place to go with it. Now what I would do, I guess, is run. I wasn't running in those days, so it was awful in a way. There was all that adrenalin, and absolutely no place to channel it. I don't ever want to go through that hour again. Now that I think about it, it was ghastly.

The rewards aren't satisfactory?

Well, what I'm doing now is that I'm sort of amortizing the rewards. I'm spreading them out over a week instead of trying to cram it all in that hour. When I finish a piece of work now, and if I think it's a good piece of work, I get exalted still. I don't mean to say that that's all gone.

I finished a job – I won't say which one, because I don't want to put value judgments on my own work – but I finished it at 10:30; I was uptown, at Marvel's office, and I thought, "Damn, it's the best thing I've done in years," and I did get a real feeling of exaltation, but it was not that shrill, sharp, hysterical feeling of exaltation that would've caused the accompanying crash. It was almost like a suffusing feeling of satisfaction, at having done what I considered to be an extraordinarily good piece of work. I was not tempted to scream about it. I was tempted to go find somebody and to share it with them and that's what I tried to do. In fact, I didn't succeed in finding anyone, and in the old days, not finding somebody to share that with would've precipitated the crash, the terrible, dismal low. In this case, I was able to sustain the feeling that, all right, so I don't have anybody to talk to. I still liked the work I did and that's nice. It carried through to the next day.

TCJ

GERRY CONWAY

KEEPING TO THE BACKGROUND

INTERVIEW BY ROBERT GUSTAVESON: Gerry Conway began writing comic books as a 15 year old and seized the high-profile gig of writing *Amazing Spider-Man*, the last Marvel comic to surrender its 1960s vitality, at age 19. It was during his run on that title that Conway scripted one of the more renowned comics of the period, where Spider-Man's girlfriend Gwen Stacy was murdered by archenemy Green Goblin. This was shocking even by Marvel's standards, even more so because it was a life-changing event that occurred not at Marvel's chaotic, anything-goes beginning, but right around the time when Marvel's titles were settling into a period of extended, profit-protective orthodoxy.

If you read enough coverage of the 1970s comic-book industry, you discover that Gerry Conway is kind of a touchstone, his ability to get work done and on time at times overshadowing fair consideration of his talent. Conway was also the creator of The Punisher and co-creator of Firestorm, two of a small group of characters created after 1970 that still hold fans' attention today.

This interview with Robert Gustaveson is a rare one for Conway of this period (TCJ #69, December, 1981); he seems both happy for the chance to go on the record and slightly defensive about some of the criticism he's received.

Conway has since gone on to become perhaps the most successful major comics-author-turned-writer for television; his work includes several scripts for the popular *Law & Order* franchise.

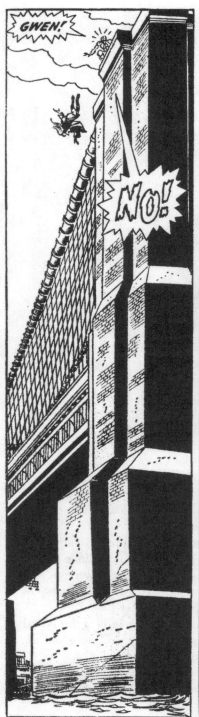

Writer: Gerry Conway Artists: Gil Kane, John Romita & Tony Mortellaro
Amazing Spider-Man #121 June 1973 [©1973 Marvel Comics Group]

ROBERT GUSTAVESON: *I'd like to ask you, Gerry, how long ago you started writing comics and where your first works were published. Perhaps you could give me a brief history of the different companies you've worked for, too.*

GERRY CONWAY: The all-inclusive interview, aye?

Is this your first interview?

Yeah. I really haven't been interviewed very often – very much – by the comics fan press. Well, I began as a fan back in the late '60s. I lived in New York City. At that time DC Comics was doing a weekly tour of their offices. It was run by a man named Walter Herluchek, who worked in the production department of DC Comics. And when I discovered this it was a revelation. It was a way to meet comic-book professionals and people I admired. I just plunged into the fray, and I went in every week on this tour. I became one of the main figures along with Marv Wolfman and Len Wein and Mark Hanerfeld. Eventually we took over giving the tour. [*Laughter.*]

Through that I met Julie Schwartz, Bob Kanigher, and George Kashdan – the basic editorial crew before Dick Giordano and Joe Orlando came in. And I began to make a pest of myself for a year, coming up almost every week with new story ideas, new scripts, and so forth. When Dick [Giordano] came in I began pestering him specifically because he was a very, very nice gentleman, very kind, very outgoing, very free with his time, and after several months I sold my first story – but not to Dick. It turned out that Murray Boltinoff, who was sitting one desk away from Dick, thought I was working for Dick and said, "Say, would you like to do a story for me?" and I said, "Sure, Mur," y'know. [*Laughter.*] "I'd be very happy to do a story for you." It was only after about three weeks of writing and rewriting this same story about six times that Murray finally decided to buy it. He asked me what my rate was, and I told him, "I don't know because I don't have a rate yet." Murray realized that he'd bought my first story. I think that's the only time Murray Boltinoff bought a writer's first story.

What was the title of it and when did it appear?

Oh, God. It *never* appeared… About five years ago Paul Levitz tried to humiliate me by publishing it in one of the books he was editing at that time, putting together for Joe Orlando. It was called "Wake Me up or I'll Die Screaming" or something like that. I don't really remember. It was only three pages long.

Once I'd broken the ice with DC, Dick Giordano gave me some assignments doing short fiction for *House of Secrets*. I eventually took over the introductory page for *House of Secrets* and became an unofficial assistant on the book, assembling the issues with Dick. And that led to work on *Phantom Stranger* for a couple of issues with Joe Orlando that in turn led to some mystery stories for Roy Thomas during Marvel's short-lived mystery book period, *Chamber of Horrors* I think it was, or *Chamber of Darkness,* I don't know. That in turn led to a spec *Sgt. Fury* script and that in turn led to *Ka-Zar* scripting assignments for Roy and eventually to a full-time writing career for Marvel Comics that lasted five years.

So, the very first company you worked for was DC. You worked for them for how long?

I worked for DC from mid-1968 to the early part of 1970. I left the company very shortly after Dick Giordano left. I had stayed there primarily because of Dick. I always wanted to write for Marvel Comics because those were the comics I'd grown up reading. I was really happy when Roy asked me to come over and work at Marvel. It's kind of funny, because at that time there were a few people who said I had sold out by going to Marvel and actually that had been my goal all the time. I don't see that you can sell out to do something that you actually wanted to do very much.

What were the first books you did at Marvel?

I wrote some *Ka-Zar* scripts over plots by Roy. Then I took over *Daredevil* and *Iron Man,* and then a few months after that I was given *Sub-Mariner.* I wrote those books for about a year and kept *Daredevil* for about two years. Then, in '71, I was given a shot at *Marvel Team-Up,* which led to writing *Spider-Man* and *Thor.* From that point on I was writing top books for the company. One of the things we talk about these days is how newer writers in comics now come into the field and start off immediately writing the top title of the line. That's not to say their innate talent couldn't work to their advantage and allow them to turn out a brilliant comic book, but there are reasons why people are eased into writing top titles. When I went to Marvel, they were only publishing about 15 titles a month, so there were far fewer books for me to build up my skills on than there are today. There is just no excuse for people to be thrust into writing name titles before they're ready – and in some cases falling on their faces and being kicked out of the business.

At this time, just before you became editor of Marvel, were you in direct contact with Stan Lee? What was your relationship with him?

Well, I didn't become *an* editor at Marvel until after I had been an editor at DC and I didn't become an editor at DC until I left Marvel...

Why did you leave Marvel at that time?

I had a very good working relationship with Roy Thomas for about five years, a man who I think has been vastly underrated as an editor. His abilities as a writer were very obvious, very apparent. His technique as an editor was always to gather in the best people he could find, bring them into the company, put them into a working atmosphere that was extremely exciting, with a great deal of *esprit de corps,* and then let them go. He would not pick at individual story points. Possibly this worked to his disadvantage in some cases because when a writer takes over a book initially his familiarity with the character isn't as great as it will eventually become, so he's likely to make gaffes and and do things he really shouldn't do. There are a couple of specific instances in my own writing that I wouldn't do today precisely because I've learned so much over the past 12 years. But, Roy allowed you to make these mistakes and I think that is an extremely valuable thing for an editor to do. It requires a great deal of self-confidence on the part of an editor to give his writers and artists that freedom. So, working with Roy was an extremely creative experience for me.

Well, Roy left the company as an editor to become his own editor and the editorial position was handed to Marv Wolfman and Len Wein. Now, I have been friends with Len and Marv for 12 years. I've known them since we came into the business – we came in about six months apart. In fact, I was an instigator in getting Roy to bring Len over to Marvel. We were roommates and we would constantly look over each other's shoulders, look at what we were doing, get excited about various things we were doing, and that would lead to friendly competitiveness. Well, the problem I had was that I had worked at Marvel for a couple of years more than either Marv or Len, and at a point a couple of years previously when Roy was having some personal problems and had to be out of the office for a couple of weeks, he'd had Stan bring me in to pinch-hit for him for the time he was out. When I did that, Stan told me, "Well, Ger," in the kind of friendly, glad-hand sort of way Stan has, "if it ever worked out that Roy leaves the company, we want you to take over as editor." Well, whether I was qualified or not, this was something that was in my mind, and certainly I felt that my qualifications were as great as Len's. Marv on the other hand had had extensive editorial experience at Warren's, and had been an editor at Marvel for some months before Roy left. This sort of cluttered up my relationship with Marv and Len, when they were put in over me. Again, that was a choice Stan made at that time. Later, he told me he'd completely forgotten the promise he made to me and I was probably foolish not to have reminded him of it. But in any case, these things happen, and I think a certain amount of bitterness was engendered on my part. I felt that I had been passed over for the job.

That'll teach you not to express yourself.

I've always had a problem of not expressing myself at the right moment. I'm very good at expressing myself after the fact in a loud, voluble fashion. The problem that I have is that I don't feel as though I'm very articulate in person, so I keep myself back and hold back. I'm a very tall, big person – and since you're also a tall person, you probably find you have a tendency to want to stay in the background in any given confrontation because you're tall. When I was growing up, I was always the tallest kid in the class. I was always picked first to answer the question, so I developed techniques of slouching and keeping myself down and not volunteering information. I suppose that led me to not asserting myself at the right moments. I would assert myself after the moment or I would assert myself loudly at an inappropriate time, but I would not know how to pick that right moment to say, "Hey, this is what I want." As I say, I let this kind of bitterness brew without expressing it. Other things that had been promised me by Roy, Len and Marv they did not carry through on, possibly because I was not articulate in expressing what I was owed. For example, I created a character called the Punisher, and Roy assured me that if and when the Punisher got his own strip, I would edit the book. When in fact the Punisher did get a couple of issues' tryout in one of the black-and-white books, I was not given those books to edit.

That wasn't Roy's fault?

No, because Roy had left the company. Roy did give me a shot at editing *Savage Tales* when he took Conan out of it. I edited several issues. I'm certain Roy would've given me a crack at editing the Punisher. The thing was that Marv and Len were consolidating their authority and really didn't feel that they wanted to fragment their authority, much as Jim Shooter doesn't want to fragment his authority now. So, while I understand now where they were coming from at the time, I was very upset and when the opportunity came to move to DC, I moved. Because DC offered me a fairly full-time editorial position on a freelance basis and I wanted a chance to develop some ideas I'd had while working under Roy, I wanted a chance to either prove myself or not prove myself. If I was not editorial material I wanted a chance to be shown that. I just didn't want to make decisions in an absence of concrete information.

What period of time are we talking about now?

This was about '75 or '76. Jesus, I think it was '75 because I remember a New Year's party that Roy and I were at, at which my toast was that 1976 cannot be as bad as 1975. [*Laughter.*] I was proven wrong. [*Laughter.*] On a personal level my period at DC as an editor was very fruitful. I didn't accomplish as much as I would've liked to, because I was bucking the system when I was there as the editor of a handful of freelance titles.

What were they?

Well, I brought back *All-Star Comics*, I created *The Freedom Fighters*, and I gave them their own book. Well, actually I didn't create The Freedom Fighters. Len Wein had created The Freedom Fighters, but I put them into their own book. We brought back *Plastic Man*, we created *The Secret Society of Super-Villains*, and I created *Hercules Unbound*, which I did for Joe Orlando. It was a very interesting period. I don't think those titles were as successful as they would have been at a company that was geared to do them the way we wanted to do them. But I was grateful for Carmine [Infantino] for giving me the chance to try them at all, because up to that point DC had a particular way in which they were doing their books and when I came in we changed that way of doing books. I don't know whether it was successful, but at least it was moving away from a fairly staid formula – maybe to another kind of formula, but it was an attempt to move.

Now, there are a lot of comics you're working on that are selling incredibly well. I know from personal experience at the American Comic Book Company where I work that we sell out of *Justice League* and several other ones that you work on every month before almost any other comic book. I'd say the only one that's comparable would be the *X-Men* and the first issue of the *Dazzler*. But there are people like Harlan Ellison [*Conway laughs*] who say they don't like the way you write. Can you shed some light on this?

It's a conundrum. It's an enigma. Well, these are two basic topics, because my relationship with Harlan is one topic. As you say, the great difference between the critical appraisal of my work and the commercial success of my work is really rather startling.

Why do you think that is?

Why do my books sell well and not get the kind of critical praise that I think they're due? Well, I don't know if they're due it, because I don't know if I agree with the standards that are applied by critics.

As you say, my books sell well. That's a statement of fact, not an opinion on my part. When I wrote at Marvel, my books sold well. When I took over *Spider-Man*... the last few years under Stan, the book's sales were dropping. Within two years they were up to the top of the line again. Now, a lot of factors enter into that. I think Roy's editing of the line helped bring the whole line up, but I think

Writer: Gerry Conway Artists: Gil Kane, John Romita & Tony Mortellaro
Amazing Spider-Man #123 August 1973 [©1973 Marvel Comics Group]

also that I tapped into some sort of format or some sort of form of storytelling or form of story that the readership was particularly interested in seeing. Now, when I came to DC I did not have initial success on a few of the titles I was working on because we were fighting each other, as I said. But once I was working on books that could utilize my particular talents and once DC changed its direction so there was a support mechanism for the kind of work I wanted to do, we had a good system going and the stories sold well.

Basically, I want to do what is known as the traditional comic book. Let me correct that: the traditional superhero comic book, because I don't think the comic book format is restricted to the superhero form. I think it's a spectrum going from Eisner on the one hand – very realistic, very tight storytelling – to the undergrounds all the way on the other hand. With stops at graphic novels, French comics, *Heavy Metal* sorts of things all the way through. Superhero comics are a particular form within that larger form.

I was reading in one of the fanzines where a writer had analyzed the superhero story into five or six – something like that – basic plots and he was absolutely right. There are five or 10 basic plots for the superhero story. By its very nature. It's a heroic form of storytelling. When you're dealing with the heroic form you're dealing with a myth structure that has been established for 2000 years. [*Laughter.*] That's simply the way it is. If you change the heroic story sufficiently to make it different and new, startlingly different and new, you're taking it out of the heroic form and then it's something else. That's not to say that something else is better or worse than the heroic form. It's simply something else. So, what I'm interested in doing is stories in the heroic form, either using ideas that have been presented before in a new way, from a new angle or a new twist, or in taking something from outside the field and applying it to the heroic form.

And you have reference materials that you've used to do that?

Well, sure. What's interesting about the heroic form –

What are some of the reference materials?

Well, I've probably read the same things George Lucas read when he created the *Star Wars* mythos. There are the books by Joseph Campbell, *The Masks of God, Primitive Mythology, The Hero With a Thousand Faces,* all of which go into an analysis of the heroic form and what we're talking about when we say Heroes. You can't have certain kinds of stories in the heroic form and still have heroic stories.

One of the good things about Marvel Comics in the '60s is that they gave the form a slight change of direction and added dimension to the heroes, which had always been inherent in heroes. The Hero With The Fatal Flaw goes all the way back to Greek drama, Greek literature, with characters like Jason who has a fatal flaw. Characters that strive for victory, but because of their background or because of the nature of their quest are going to be denied their victory. It's heroism in its basic mythic form.

Now we could get really pretentious and say that comic books are a direct, lineal descendant of Greek drama – and that would be bullshit. Comic books are basically an entertainment form designed to appeal to a very young readership, a readership that has developed in its reading skills to the point where they can read something more than "Run Spot Run" and have not progressed far enough to the point where they will be reading adult literature, but still want to read, still want to experience the delight of involvement with characters and with story plot and the situational theme. And this basic, primitive, mythological structure appeals very much to that audience because they haven't started intellectualizing things to the point where they can say, "Wait a minute, this is ridiculous." Because, let's face it, any story that has a guy who leaps tall buildings in a single bound and catches bullets on his chest and sees through walls is basically nonsense. It's on the same level as *Winnie the Pooh*.

I don't agree because if you think of all the technological advances and man's constant quest for technology and science –
But that's science fiction as opposed to fantasy.

But a lot of this comic-book stuff is inspiring scientists of today to create the kind of stuff that Superman can do.
I think you may be stretching a point.

Let me go back. What I mean also is that I don't agree that comic books are only for younger audiences –
No, no, any more than the Warner Brothers cartoons are *only* for kids. In fact, the Chuck Jones-Friz Freleng cartoons of the late '40s and early '50s appeal tremendously to adults because they were written by adults for themselves. I write for myself. But the stuff appeals to a young audience. I'm writing for the youthful part of myself, the primitive part of myself. If an adult likes the books it's because of a nostalgic feeling for that primitive, easy conceptualization of heroic purpose. I like reading – right now I'm into a period of reading a lot of juveniles. I also read Walker Percy and Truman Capote and – y'know, I've gone through a heavy period of reading Conrad. So it's not that I *can't* read adult literature. It's just at this particular moment in my life I find that there's a nostalgic joy in reading *Freddy The Pig*.

Freddy The Pig?
You may well laugh. *[laughter] Freddy The Pig*, yes. Walter Brooks… books written back in the '20s. There's something charming about that material. In fact, I think *Freddy The Pig* inspired *Animal Farm*. That's kind of an interesting thing. I would be surprised if Orwell had not read *Freddy The Pig*, or at least was aware of it because it was a fairly popular series in the '20s.
The thing is, I'm not saying that these kinds of books are substitutes for

adult literature. What I'm saying is that they are a valid expression of youthful fantasies, and there are moments in an adult's life when he wants to experience that youthful suspension of disbelief. Comics provide a way to do that in a fairly quick way. The average comic book story doesn't take more than 20 minutes to read – if that, if you're very lucky. So, you can get a quick fix on your nostalgia and enjoy yourself.

The trouble with the critical fan press is that they sort of miss the point of what this material is supposed to be. They're confusing the form with the particular genre. The comic-book form can be utilized to tell any kind of story from the simplest morality tale up to fairly complex story of interpersonal reaction. The superhero genre is a specific form, a specific use of the form to tell a specific kind of story. Criticizing that just doesn't make any sense. It's like saying, "This peach is not enough like a pear for me to like it." It's just nonsensical.

Now, I can well agree with people who say that these stories are juvenile or not fully developed or anything else, but I don't think that's really relevant to the genre. The genre is *supposed* to be juvenile, it's supposed to be fast-paced and sort of hell-bent for leather and hectic. You're not supposed to sit down and think, "What does this all mean?" It's on the level of a *Smokey and the Bandit* movie. You don't really sit there and say, "C'mon, guys" – do we really believe that Jackie Gleason is going to be able to drive halfway across the Southern states following a guy in a rig and not get stopped by the State Police? No. We accept that because we want the experience of watching Burt Reynolds and Sally Field and Jackie Gleason make wrecks out of half the cars in the Southern states. We just want to experience that because we can't experience it in our real life. And in reasonable moments we know that we can't expect this to be real filmic literature. It's just something that we want to see because it's fun.

If comic books are not fun, there is no reason for someone to read them. Again, I keep saying comic books and I don't mean the comic book form or the graphic art form. I mean the superhero comic book or the mystery comic-book or the horror comic-book.

I wonder if we could create a new title for that?

Well, Stan at one point wanted to use the underground phrase "comix," but was dissuaded from that because it was the word the underground press was using. I don't know. Roy once suggested that Marvel Comics should just call themselves Marvels. Like, "Here's the latest Marvels," which is how some people refer to them. But, I think you're stuck with the term and there's really not a helluva lot that we're going to be able to do about it.

Most comics simply are not funny any more.

No, no, by no means.

But they do entertain.

They're entertaining! I hate to say this, because it may be taken in the wrong way, but the proper place to read a comic book is on the john. [*Laughter.*] Y'know, you're not going to take this into – well, you *could* take it into the UCLA library, but there are so many other things you could do with your time in the UCLA library that it wouldn't make much sense to bring a comic in there.

Let's get into the second part of the question, which is your relationship with Harlan and why he responds to your writing the way he does.

Well, Harlan called me shortly after that article came out and after I had written my response to it, and he apologized for having said the things that he said and the way in which he said them. And he also told me at that time that he hadn't read anything of mine for the past two years and admitted that this sort of made him a very poor judge of what my work may be.

Now, it's entirely probable, knowing Harlan's attitude, that if he did read anything that I wrote in the last two years his opinion would be much the same because I don't really write for Harlan Ellison. What bothered me about Harlan's diatribe was that it *was* a diatribe. He was just speaking off the top of his head, it seemed. I was hurt by it because I've known Harlan for about 10 years and in those 10 years Harlan has *never* said any of those things to me. He chose to say them in a public forum and I thought that was a really unfair kind of thing to do.

I was a little resentful of the way the interviewer kept egging him on. I didn't like the fact that words were put into Harlan's mouth, although Harlan as an adult is quite capable of forming his own opinion and obviously agreed with some of the things said. For example, the reference to Don Heck. Harlan was saying something along the lines of, "This guy, the worst comic-book artist in the business," and the interviewer said, "You mean Don Heck?" Well, the phrase, "the worst comic-book artist in the business" is a statement of opinion; it's not a fact. It's not like saying "the tallest comic-book artist in the business" because that's something you can measure. The interviewer supplied his personal opinion to Harlan *as a fact* that Don Heck was recognized as the worst comic-book artist in the business, and he is by no means thought of as that by the people working in the business. Don's style is substantially different from the style that's currently accepted as good comic-book art, but that doesn't make Don a bad artist. Don is a good storyteller, he's got a technique all his own, he *has* a style, which is more than you can say for many of the artists who are touted in the fan press.

Not to belabor the point, the interviewer showed a bias, a rather blatant bias against several people and egged Harlan into saying things about those people. In another article later, an interview with Ted White, the same interviewer brought up my name to Ted in an extremely negative way. Ted was talking about how publishers have a tendency to take characters that perhaps should only be around for 10 or 15 issues ideally and then continue them *ad infinitum* for the next 25 years and then Gary – oops, the name got out! – "The Interviewer" said, "Yeah, and they'd have Gerry Conway write it," which in the context is an extremely negative thing to say. And Ted just didn't want to pick up on it, apparently, because he dropped it and let it lie there, probably because Ted, having known me for 10 years, knows that I'm not quite the hack some of these people would have us believe. If I was I would be making a lot more money than I do because I can write a lot faster than I do. I choose not to because I *do* care about what I write.

After that interview with Ellison appeared in *The Comics Journal* #53, there were some letters written back and forth and in that Harlan said he didn't really mean that – or that it was interpreted differently.

I think we can look at the context of that interview, 40-odd pages, we can look at the general atmosphere that was obviously prevalent during the course of the conversation and we can make up our own minds about whether Harlan meant what he said the way in which he said it.

I really regret the letter I wrote because, again, I was airing my private feelings in public and I really shouldn't have done that. I really don't want to air too many personal, private feelings here. But, it's a valid question. I mean, Harlan made it a public issue but I don't want to say the same kinds of things that I said in that letter because when I wrote that I was in an extremely emotional state – I was very hurt and I was very upset with Harlan for precisely the reasons I've said – and I probably overstated my case rather drastically, but Harlan's answer was very, very self-serving.

Harlan, like all of us, when attacked, attacks back. I don't blame him for that and I don't admire him for it. It is simply a human response and there it is. I just don't think the interests of journalistic accuracy are served by Harlan saying he didn't mean what he said. He said it and if he didn't mean it he shouldn't have said it. There are very few ways you can take things like, "Gerry Conway should be nailed to a cross." [*Laughter.*] I mean, that seems to imply a certain hostility. Now, knowing Harlan, knowing the way in which he sometimes gets into these excited, verbal put-down sessions, I can see him saying that and not meaning it as a real attack, just as a clever bit of repartee. Still, it gets into print and it's put into large letters in an insert and it's used as a way to justify the magazine's bias against me, as though Harlan, who is not an expert on our field, could really be used as a bulwark for the *Journal's* opinion.

I'm not saying people *should* like superhero comics as great examples of comic-book art. I am simply saying that they are a valid genre within a larger form and too often the reviewer makes the mistake of judging the genre in terms of the form. It would be as though you were judging a mystery story by the logical tenets of a science fiction story. In a science-fiction story you have to provide the reader with information about the social background, the technical background of how' things work. You might be making an effort to extrapolate from a given event in modern history: what will this come to? So, there's a great deal of extrapolation about the society and that is, to a large degree; what makes science-fiction a valid form. But, mystery novels, which are mostly written in a contemporary setting, don't have this same obsession with technological detail, nor should they. Their primary interest is in advancing the twistings and turnings of the mystery plot. Mystery novels that have too intense characterizations can be bad mystery novels because you lose the thrust of the mystery plot. So, it is reasonable to apply literary standards – general literary standards – to a mystery novel, or a science-fiction novel, or an Evelyn Waugh satirical novel, but it is not reasonable to cross-apply the rules of one genre to another genre. In comics, it is reasonable to say, "Is this story written grammatically? Is there a beginning, a middle, and an end? Are there characters that are recognizable? Do they serve the purpose of the story? Is the theme clear?" And so forth. It is not reasonable to say, "You introduce a character and you don't have them *grow* appreciably within this story," because in a serial, format story characters don't grow in individual episodes. They grow over a period of many episodes, many years. And that violates one of the essential rules of literature, which is that the characters have to grow in a story, but in a comic book story or in a superhero genre story, by its very nature the character cannot grow in a particular story unless you have designed the story and the series for that purpose.

So in a series the characters often grow very slowly?

If at all. If at all. And sometimes the growth is circular. Now, that's something that's criticized by comic book critics very harshly. They say, "Peter Parker never grows, never changes." My God, he's not supposed to change. Nero Wolfe never changed over 40 years; The Saint never changed; Sherlock Holmes changed very little; Tarzan never changed. Why is it that Peter Parker has to change? It was the illusion of change that was so good in what Stan and Steve Ditko did and later what Stan and John Romita were doing, but it was an illusion, it was supposed to be an illusion, it was never supposed to be real change.

Possibly the error many of us coming into the field in the early '70s and late '60s made was that we accepted the idea that there was change and we expected to create change in what we were doing. I came in and killed off Gwen Stacy. Regardless of the fact that it was an idea that had been around before I came onto the book, I did it. I think I did it well, although that's open to interpretation by any number of people, but I think I did. I did the story I wanted to do. If it's going to be judged, it should be judged on the basis of what I attempted to do. If I had it to do over I don't think I would've done it, because I know now that it's the illusion of change that's important to maintain and when you critically change a series, you cannot go back, you cannot capture many of the elements that made that series work in the first place.

For example, I'm writing *Wonder Woman* right now. We went through a lot of soul-searching – Len Wein, myself, and I'm sure, Jenette and Joe Orlando – about what the hell we were going to do with this character. She has completely lost her moorings. She has no ties, no background in which to function. How are we going to make it work? What we decided was, OK, let's look back at the original myth, the original structure of the series that worked so well for 25 years and let's see, can we do this? Can we get back to this? And what we decided to do was say, "OK, kids, we're gonna start right from scratch, we're going to go back, we're going to bring Wonder Woman back to Paradise Island, we're going to have her rediscover her love affair with Steve Trevor, we're going to bring her back into the military thing that she was into, we're going to try to recapture that feeling of Wonder Woman as a symbol of the good things in the American patriotic myth." And that's what we did. Now, we've gotten mail that has castigated us for that, but we've also gotten mail that said, "Yeah, OK, we can accept this. We realize you guys have gotten yourselves into a terrible bind and you've just decided to wipe the slate clean and start over." Remember, that's what the comic-book business was able to do in the early '60s; they were able to come in with new versions of old characters.

Captain America.

Captain America. Well, Captain America they did tie into the old stories. They did lose Bucky, which was a terrible mistake. People may not think so, but it was. That relationship between the father figure and the boy was always a very valid myth.

They even brought that back with Rick Jones.

They tried to but they could never recapture that same innocence because Bucky ideally should be about 15 years old, just as Robin ideally should be about 15 years old. They should be on the verge of manhood, they should be on the verge of taking on the responsibility for their own lives, and they should be looking toward Captain America or Batman or whoever as the model on which they want to build their own lives. I mean, Rick Jones is – I don't know – 29 or 30, who the hell knows what he is, [Laughter.] but he was certainly much too old for that kind of role. And Robin now is almost a college graduate in his early 20s, I would guess, or late teens; at the very earliest he'd be 19. So you've lost that essential connection.

In any case, the illusion of change was something that Stan brought to the books and I think much like political thought that is picked up by the second generation and turned into something different from what the original politicians thought it would be, we later writers came in and for about eight or nine years screwed up the field by creating a lot of real change that took the characters further and further away from their original *raison d'etre*. With the result, as you can see, that there is a large and growing hostile fan press that had been led to expect growth and change by the actions of writers in the late '60s and early '70s that was unreasonable for the field even then. Now that we're trying to retrench, now that we're trying to recapture some of that original Golden Age vitality by accepting the myths and working with the myths, they hate it a lot, certain fans hate it a lot. The readers love it because the readers want to know from month to month from year to year who these characters are, how they relate to each other, why it works and why it doesn't work.

Remember the example – there are two examples of this at DC that are kind of startling, disruptions of the myth and then later retrenchment. Alfred was killed off in the *Batman* comic book when Julie Schwartz took over as editor. Julie did that because he wanted a change. It was a mistake. It was recognized as a mistake, not by the comic-book people, but by the TV people, who came along with the *Batman* TV show (the less said, the better) and put Alfred into it, thereby forcing the comic-book people to bring Alfred back into the books. Thank God, because Alfred is a confidante, the one man who you can always turn to, the weak man who has hidden strengths. He's a perfect character.

Jarvis in the *Avengers* is kind of like that.

Jarvis was, I'm sure, patterned after Alfred. Then, later, when Superman was updated in the early '70s by being made into a TV reporter – again, a terrific idea from the point of view of character growth and change. But, ask anybody on the street, "Where does Clark Kent work?" and they're not going to say, "Galaxy Broadcasting." They're going to say, "He's the mild-mannered reporter working at the *Daily Planet.*" Now, it could be that they're just stupid, that they just don't know what's going on. But, it could also be that it hit a nerve, it hit a vital, mythological nerve, the idea of this wimpy guy working for a newspaper, because newspapers, even though they're no longer a mainstay of reporting in our culture, are still symbolic of a certain kind of personality and business that TV reporting is not. TV reporting is show business. Newspaper reporting is studious, scholarly – I say scholarly, what I mean is this kind of digging away, kind of sitting and poring over facts, it creates an image of a bespectacled man sitting at a typewriter while TV reporting does not.

When you actually sit down and write stories, where do the ideas come from? Do they come right out of your head? Are there certain authors you read more than others?

Where do I get my ideas? I'll use the answer George Alec Effinger once gave: People send them to me on postcards. [*Laughter.*] I don't know. You get ideas... for example, take "Lois Lane" – a strip that I really enjoy writing that is not a superhero strip. It's just a straight mystery strip, in effect. For that what I usually like to deal with are problems that are current in our society. I just did a story on waste disposal problems, the disposal of toxic waste. I did another story on the Justice Department's witness placement program. When a particular social issue strikes me as being really interesting I'll want to do a story around it, but not in the way we used to do the old relevant comic books where the entire story revolves around that one social issue, but just generally if a particular problem strikes me as having story potential...

So from world problems you find an angle that sparks your brain into creative ideas.

Sometimes, yeah. Other times what'll happen is I'll come up with an image for an opening scene or I'll come up with what seems like a narrative hook, or I'll do something on a particular fancy or interest of mine, like I'm interested now in the Oz books. I mentioned I was reading juveniles; I'm also reading the Oz books. So, I decided I really wanted to do a *Superman* story that featured in one way or another the Oz books. I talked to Julie about it and we worked out a plot and that's what presented itself. Also, there's a lot of input from editors. Depending upon the editor that I work with, my stories will either be more or less plot oriented or more or less character oriented.

How about when you're dealing with an artist, when you're talking with the artist on the phone; do you actually plan each story?

I haven't spoken to an artist on the phone since I came back to DC, primarily because most of the stories that I've written up until the past year were done full script. I take that back. I did work quite a bit with Al Milgrom when we created Firestorm to do stories he was interested in. We would plot them out together in Jack Harris's office and then I would go off and write up a plot, but that was sort of the exception to the rule. I expect to be doing more actual plotting with the artist now that I'm writing things Marvel-style again. Most of my input, my story input, was from the editors. Julie Schwartz would be more interested in doing a story that had intricate little plot twists, either technologically oriented or logically oriented. Len [Wein] on the other hand I find is more interested in the emotional twists that we can put into a story, the mood twists. And Jack Harris has a good backgrounding in character details, the things that happened in past stories, and sometimes will suggest a story that will be based on something that we had left hanging in a previous issue, either one of mine or an issue written by someone else before that. "Hey, why don't we finally resolve this," and we will work out some sort of way we think is clever to resolve a story point.

When I was working at Marvel, I would, again, depending upon the artist, spend either more or less time plotting with the artist. Ross Andru and I plotted a lot of our work together. We would sit down and talk over hamburgers at Brew 'n' Burger in New York, what we would do in the next issue of *Spider-Man*. When we did the *Superman/Spider-Man* special, Ross and I plotted that in two-page segments practically, over a period of six months. We put a lot of work into that book. We had a general plot, then we worked it out so that we knew what was going to happen on every single page, both from a design point of view – because we had a lot of two-page spreads – and from the story-progression point of view. It was a very intimate, very collaborative effort. Which it has to be on projects of that kind, when you're working with a very strong storytelling artist and a very visually oriented writer, as I am.

It does depend a great deal on the people you're working with. An artist like Ross will give you more input or an artist like John Buscema wants more input from you. An artist like Walt Simonson will have something he really wants to do or a particular way he wants to tell the story, which will then affect the kind of story you will come to him with. It's a collaborative medium and you have to be prepared to either put in more or less of yourself than you would if you were just writing short stories or novels, which I've done.

What do you think of the editor-writer system that Jim Shooter has just wiped out at Marvel?

Well, I've worked in both systems, the system where a writer is directly responsible to an editor, who approves the kinds of stories he does and the way in which he writes them, and the system where a writer has total control of his work.

Which lends itself more to creativity?

Well, let's put it this way: All of the major creative moments in comic books have occurred under the writer-editor system. Harvey Kurtzman produced *Mad.* and *Two-Fisted Tales* under the writer-editor system at EC; Will Eisner edited, I believe, his *Spirit* section in a fairly autonomous fashion. Stan Lee was a writer-editor at Marvel during its heyday as the main creative force in the field. And Roy Thomas produced *Conan the Barbarian* under the writer-editor system. Bob Kane, for whatever people think of him now, was a major creative force at DC in the '50s and '60s as a writer-editor. And Archie Goodwin at Warren was his own writer-editor during that excellent period during the middle to late '60s. I think the evidence is in: the writer-editor system can produce the best work in the field. The trouble is that it has to be handled in a fairly discriminatory fashion. You can't just have everybody editing and writing their own material, which sounds very unfair and elitist. But, as Jimmy Carter said, life is not fair.

The trouble is I believe both companies, at first in an effort not to offend people whom they did *nor* want to edit their own material, created this policy of saying, "Well, nobody can write and edit their own material." Secondly, they had a valid business reason, which was that they wanted to control the actual flow of pages in and out of the office with their own staff in charge. The trouble is that by saying no one can do it, you've eliminated the possibility of someone brilliant doing it. You've thrown the baby out with the bathwater. You've cut off your nose to spite your face. You've done any number of things. And while it works in the short term, you're not building for the future. You've closed off an entire avenue of creative endeavor.

Any chance you'd ever consider going to Marvel with Jim Shooter as editor – or if he leaves?

That's an interesting question. I don't think that Jim would want me back. I don't think Jim would want any of us back. [*Laughter.*] I understand why. He feels more comfortable working with people who he has brought in himself. I think that he feels the only way he is going to make his imprint is to control the creative personnel. I don't think he'd be too interested in bringing back...

I SAY THEE NAY!

'TWAS NEVER THAT WAY-- NEVER!

WHATEVER THOU DIDST SEE WAS IN THY MIND ALONE--

ODIN WAS EVER FAIR-- YEA, AND MORE THAN FAIR--

--'TWAS THY TWISTED VIEW WHICH SAW IT OTHERWISE.

BUT IT MATTERS NAUGHT, FOR THE BATTLE WILL SOON BE OVER--

-- AND THOU IMPRISONED ONCE MORE.

A PLEASANT DREAM, "BROTHER".

A DREAM... AND NO MORE!

ALREADY, THIRTY SECONDS HAVE PASSED SINCE THY HAMMER LEFT THY HAND--

--THIRTY MORE, AND THOU WILT BE THE MORTAL DOCTOR DONALD BLAKE--

-- AND THEN WILL I STRIKE--

--AND THEN WILT THOU END--

AND LOKI WILL REIGN SUPREME!

Writer: Gerry Conway Artists: John Buscema & Vinnie Colletta *Thor* #207 January
1972 [©1972 Marvel Comics Group]

No. I mean your own personal desire.

Well, Jim did me dirt. It's an amazing thing. Jim, if you listen to Jim's interviews and so forth, is a regular font of milk and kindness, but I think there are so many people who have stories of the things Jim has done that we have to weigh the possibility that Jim really is… [*Laughter.*] as bad as they say.

Jim was my assistant when I was editor at Marvel for about a month, and that's really been the extent of our relationship. When I worked there as a writer-editor, I really didn't have anything to do with Jim. When I left, however, Archie Goodwin was on vacation during the week that I left Marvel. It wasn't my intention to make a sudden break, one day I'd be working for Marvel, the next day I wouldn't. It was my intention to give them the option of letting me segue out over the period of a month, to complete the work that I'd already been assigned and paid for on the basis of an advance loan. But Jim, who was Archie's assistant and the person in charge of the office at the time, had Stan's ear and said to Stan, "Well, gee, Stan; do we really want to have a writer who's already decided to leave us working for us over the next few weeks possibly turning out work on an inferior level because he's so disinterested? Let's get that work away from him." That cost me almost $4,000.00

[gasps]

[*Laughs.*] Now I wouldn't want to say Jim did that out of maliciousness or a feeling of ambition, but I do know that several of the stories that were taken away from me were later written by Jim. Jim's motives are his own. I wouldn't attribute to him motives I couldn't possibly know. I was extremely annoyed and not too surprised when similar things happened to Marv when he left. I think Len [Wein] got away fairly easily and I know Roy's not had too much trouble with them, so it's possible that it was just a misunderstanding between Marv and myself and Jim.

Does Marvel still owe you money?

Well, they owe me money for back issues of material that they reprinted. They owe me, I guess, almost a thousand dollars in reprint money. But they didn't owe me money for the work Jim took away – what happened was that I had been paid for the work in advance because I was in the process of moving from New York to Connecticut, and John Verpoorten, who was the production man and the man in charge of making payments at the time, had very graciously helped me out with advance money, fully knowing what my intentions were in terms of doing the work, but Jim pulled it away. As a result, I had to make restitution to Marvel for that money, and it was not an easy thing to do, because it was my intention to write for them and finish up my commitments. And they took it away. They were within their legal rights to do it, but they didn't have any real moral reason to do it.

What are you planning on doing at DC? Are there new things in the offing?

Well, I've been given the assignment of writing both the *Batman* books; Roy

Thomas is taking over *Legion of Super-Heroes.* This is to our mutual advantage because Roy much prefers the straight superheroic action comics, the straight utilization of super powers, and I've already got the *Justice League,* which gives me more than enough time and opportunity to do that kind of superheroic writing. Roy is less interested in doing the Batman and I'm very interested in doing it precisely because it's a different kind of superheroics, it's a different kind of story. So, I'll be doing both *Batman* and the Batman feature in *Detective Comics.* I'm tentatively scheduled to write the Robin backup feature in *Batman* also. And Roy and I want to do a couple of issues of *Brave and the Bold* together. We're doing some collaborations together, which is sort of an extension of what we're doing outside the comics field.

What are some of the good things and not-so-good things about Stan Lee you've witnessed and experienced in your career?

One of the first things I can say about Stan is that when I was trying out for Marvel back in late 1969, early '70, Roy gave me what was then the Marvel writing test, which was four pages of Xeroxes of a story. In my case, it was a *Captain America.* The writer was required to write dialogue for those four pages, and on the basis of that Stan would make up his mind whether he wanted to use the writer. Well, I wrote four pages. I wrote it in the style I was writing stories for DC, which is to say more orientation to mood than to superheroics. Roy liked it and gave it to Stan and Stan's reaction after he read it was, "Gee, this reads a little young." Roy said, "Well, after all, Gerry is 16 years old, and writes very well for a 16 year old," and Stan said, "Well, why can't we get someone who writes as well as an adult?" [*Laughter.*]

He eventually decided I was good enough to work for Marvel. It always struck me as being very funny, this semi-insensitive quality that Stan has. My wife Carla, who worked for Stan, found him to be one of the best employers she's ever worked for in that he was very kind and considerate of her as an employee. But he also dumped a lot of work on her because he would not be familiar with that particular aspect of the work that Carla might be familiar with as his assistant, the legal contracts and the like. Stan has always had that quality of kindly insensitivity. I think he's basically a nice guy, he wants to be a nice guy, he does want to be nice to his employees, but I don't think he's terribly sensitive. If he is made aware of you as an individual, he'll probably be very nice, but making him aware of you as an individual is the problem. He's kind of self-centered in that regard.

His efforts to be one of the guys were always very funny. There used to be something at DC during the period I was working at Marvel – Carmine Infantino, the publisher at DC, would grab a bunch of people and they'd all go out to Friar Tuck's, which was a restaurant directly across the street from the DC offices, and they would hang out for several hours drinking and eating and talking, Carmine holding court, trying to be one of the guys. Carmine, for all of his failings, had many good qualities, and one of them was this real need to be one of the people. It was one of the charming things about Carmine.

Stan, on the other hand, didn't really care to be one of the crowd, but when Carmine was doing it, Stan decided it would be a really neat idea to do the same thing with us. So, one afternoon as the Marvel offices were closing up, Stan came out in a flurry of excitement saying, "Let's go downstairs to the Beef 'n' Brew and I'll buy you all drinks." Well, there were only about five people in the office. There was me, John Verpoorten, John Romita, Tony Mortellaro and Stu Schwartzberg, who was an artist for *Crazy* at the time and worked our stat machine. And Stan gathered us up and brought us downstairs to the Beef 'n' Brew and said, "Why don't we have a round of drinks?" We said; "OK," and he calls the bartender over and says, "Beer for everyone." [*Riotous laughter.*] We're sort of sitting there in this kind of catatonic, stupefied state because Stan doesn't put people at their ease very well. He leans forward on the table and says, "Well, what do we talk about?" [*Laughter.*] This is the normally unapproachable Stan Lee sitting there. We're all sitting there staring at each other and we carry on a kind of desultory conversation and finally Stan, who's speaking, looks at his watch, and decides that he has been a regular fellow long enough and says, "Well, I'll leave you guys to it," and gets up and leaves. We're all sitting there in a state of shock. What happened here? we said to each other. So, that's both a good and bad story about Stan. It shows he occasionally made the effort to reach out and touch and make contact with his employees, but he never had the ability to be warm or to be very sensitive to the people he was with.

Does he ever write comics any more?

Well, I think he writes the newspaper strip, and he wrote the first *She-Hulk*, for what that's worth. Stan, I believe, looks at the comic-book writing thing as something that's totally in his past now. Although he does like to hold it up as a potential bargaining chip in any negotiations with the writers. He has on occasion said, "Well, I could always write the whole line again if I wanted to, you're just ghosting for me," which, of course, came as a shock to many of us since we have, in some cases, been writing the books longer than he has.

How do you view DC's editorial efforts over the last few years?

I think the best thing that's happened to DC recently is the rehiring of Dick Giordano as editor. I can't think of anything that is more encouraging to the creative people of the company. DC has for the past several years been supportive of its creative people in its own way, but it's going to be really nice to have someone like Dick, who has a very good reputation with a very large number of people working there. That's going to bring in people who might otherwise be hesitant to leave their current positions. It's going to reinforce the *élan* of the people already working there. And for those of us who've known Dick, going all the way back to the beginning of our careers, it's a feeling of coming full-circle. We've been away from the house x-number of years now and we're back again. Things may not be the way they used to be: we all progress and move on. My relationship with Dick will be different from the way it was when I was a newcomer breaking in and his relationship with me and with other people will be different from the way it was in the late '60s when anything went. I think Dick is more concerned now with finding the right approach on a commercial basis as well as the right approach on a creative basis than he was then, because we've learned a lot in the past 12 years.

How are Steve Ditko and even Jim Starlin able to work for both DC and Marvel?

Beats the hell out of me! I think in both cases the artist just doesn't care enough where he works for someone to hold over them the possibility that they can't work there any more. In other words, I don't think Ditko really cares if he works at Marvel or DC.

What's Steve Ditko like? To me he is a most mysterious artist.

He's very mysterious to me, too.

Have you met him?

Yeah. I've worked with him. He's in his 50s now, I would guess. He's moderately tall, not very tall, balding, wears glasses. He's a very intense man. Very soft-spoken. But, obviously when he says something he really means what he says. I think he's an artist who is extremely committed to his work, and other considerations just don't matter to him. Money certainly does not matter to Steve because he could have made a lot more money than he has over the past 10 years.

Does he have enough [money]?

Oh, I'm sure he does. I'm sure he makes as much as he needs. But, he worked for Charlton for a long time at a much lower rate than he could have gotten at either of the major companies primarily because Charlton did not give him any hassles whatsoever. DC and Marvel were not about to give Ditko any hassles either, but Charlton allowed him to do whatever he wanted to do.

Besides *Dr. Strange* and some of the early *Spider-Man*s, I think his best work happened at Warren on those early *Creepy*s and *Eerie*s.

Oh, yeah.

Any chance he could get back to that kind of quality, or has he any desire to?

I don't think he does, no. I think… my favorite Ditko story, bar none, including all the *Dr. Strange* stories, was the story he did with Archie [Goodwin], that Lovecraftian story, "Collector's Piece." God, that was beautiful. Or that one where the souls exchange, where someone switches souls and then can't get back into his original body and has to go into a dead body and animate it.

Do you think all that mystical stuff somehow created paranoia or neurosis of some kind and that he had to go to the opposite extreme with the *Mr. A* type right-wing character?

Well, I think Steve as a person is extremely committed to his philosophy. I don't think *Mr. A* was a reaction to *Dr. Strange,* I think *Dr. Strange, Mr. A, Spider-Man, Hawk & Dove, Creeper,* all are of a piece. They are the individualist against the conformist community. Take a look at *Spider-Man,* for example, the way he did it as opposed to the way Romita did it. Peter Parker was far more alienated from the people around him and suffered from being Spider-Man far more than in the Romita strip. People didn't understand him. He was a loner. He was a man who was out there taking the chances himself. There's that classic sequence from the end of *Spider-Man* #12 where Peter and Betty Brant are walking in opposite directions from each other and between them is this ghost image of Spider-Man pushing them apart. If anything says what the theme of that strip was to Ditko, that was certainly it. By the same token, Dr. Strange is the ultimate isolated character. He's isolated from society because he knows more than society does. He's isolated from the alien worlds he goes to because he is not a member of those races. He is totally alienated. He exists in a kind of limbo, between worlds, between societies. That sets him apart. Mr. A is committed to something that sets him apart.

So you think some of these characters are reflections of Ditko the man?

Yeah, I think so. Steve is totally committed to his work. He really doesn't care about anything else. That's why he was so willing to leave Marvel and leave DC when he interpreted their actions as interference with his plans for the various characters. I think Steve is one of the last of the individualists. That makes him an oddity and that makes him the odd man – which, of course, is another one of his character titles – in his environment.

I hear Ditko is a recluse.

Yeah. Likes to be alone. I don't even know where Steve lives. When I was working with him, very briefly – I did that first *Man-Bat* with him, and there was a period where I was the writer for *Shade, the Changing Man,* but I realized very rapidly that it was not my kind of strip – during that period I didn't know where Steve lived, I didn't know how to get in touch with him. He had a studio over in the 40s in Manhattan where he worked. I think it is a tribute to his commitment that he has put so much of himself into his work and is so willing to step away from potentially lucrative deals with the various companies so that he can maintain his commitment.

Is he being treated fairly by Marvel?

I wouldn't know. I really wouldn't know what his financial arrangement is with Marvel. But I doubt if there's any way you could treat Steve Ditko fairly without giving him a major amount of money for the Spider-Man character.

Did he create Spider-Man totally?

Well, he didn't design the character, but I think he set the tone for everything that has gone since... Stan and he working together, side by side, set the tone.

He's getting some credit now.

Yeah, he gets credit, but again, how can you give credit to somebody who for a long time wasn't getting credit? To my mind Steve is as much the cause for Marvel's success as Stan and as Jack Kirby. I think his contribution was far more subtle in that it was an attitude toward the individual that Stan picked up on and carried over into almost every other strip he ever did – the consequences of your superhero actions and how they affect your life.

Let's go onto the next person of the triangle that created the great Marvel Comics, Jack Kirby. I understand he's working in animation. Do you have any more information as to what he's doing now or have any anecdotes about his work in the past?

Well, Jack's another person I worked with at DC. I wrote some *Kamandi*s that he drew. Jack... I don't know if there's really anything to say about Jack in the way that you would say something about Ditko. Jack pretty much exposes himself in his work because he writes a lot of his material now. It's fairly clear where his interests are and where they lie from his work. I think Steve [Ditko] is a better plotter and writer than Jack is, but I think Jack is a better conceptualizer than Steve is. So, they each had their strengths and what they offered to the Marvel universe in the beginning were two separate things. Ditko provided Stan with a framework for plotting techniques, Kirby provided Stan with a tremendous volume of ideas from which Stan could pick and choose and develop new ideas, and new directions for the field. Kirby right now, I think, is so completely disillusioned with comics that he probably won't be returning to it in the conceivable future. I can't see any situation in which he would return, because he wants to write, draw, and edit his own material, and the experience of the companies involved with Jack in the past has been that Jack's books a) don't sell as well as Jack believes they do and as well as they should (but they don't sell as bad as we might think they do), and b) Jack's interest wanes so rapidly that you don't gain anything by having him as the sole writer on a book, because once he makes his statements in the early issues he really doesn't have the interest to build upon it in the later issues. A lot of us writers are what I would call retrenching writers. We look back and see what's been done and how we can amplify on that, how we can explain what's been done, how we can build on it, what we can do to find new meaning in it. Jack on the other hand is primarily an expositor, he puts out his ideas, tells you everything that he has to say in the first six or seven issues, and then he has nothing more to say. That's it! He can keep it up, he can keep being re-involved if he's working with a writer who can say, "Hey, Jack, what about that story idea we had back then, let's do something on that. Or how about this: Have you see this new thing?" Also, the series that Jack started were limited in concept.

I think there are at least two kinds of series that have been created in comics. One is the unlimited but unfocused superhero group or superhero like Fantastic Four or Spider-Man, or Green Lantern, or Flash, or whatever, who is a character who is given or gains powers, is put into a specific environment and let loose. He has no specific goals that he is trying to achieve, there's no mystery about him, there's nothing left for you to learn about them other than, say, the particular quirks and interactions behind the characters.

The other kind of series is the one in which a goal is set up in the very first issue, a goal that has to be achieved eventually, or if it isn't achieved, you're going to feel it's a cheat. In the *New Gods,* the goal was to find out what the hell was going on. [*Laughter.*] Really. We laugh, but you can also say the goal was to find out the resolution of the war between New Genesis and Apokolips. If the war was not going to be resolved, then it's a cheat. If the war *is* going to be resolved, then you have to find a new reason why we should continue reading the book after that war is resolved. The same way with *The Eternals.* Kirby tried to set it up so that it was a longer-running concept, by saying that these Space Gods were going to be there for 50 years before they actually passed judgment. But, by the same token, there's no great urgency to the story as a result. Fifty years is a long time! Most comic books will be lucky if they run 10 years. So, that was a cheat.

But, characters for serial comic books basically say here I am, this is what I do, this is who I am, this is where I am, and anything can happen. Or almost anything. You want to set up certain parameters. But, if you establish a mystery or establish an essential conflict that has to be eventually resolved, you're setting yourself up for disappointing the reader around seven or eight issues into the series. Which is what's happened, unfortunately, with Jack's books.

What happened with your project with Roy Thomas?

Oh boy. We've written a screenplay. It's been bought. A producer is in the process of trying to finance it. He's not having much luck, possibly because... well, I could make the facetious remark that financiers in film are just as foolish as the financiers of comic book companies. There is an element of uniqueness to our idea in this screenplay. But, it's not that unique. It's a horror film and it fulfills the basic rituals of the horror film. At the same time it requires a willing suspension of disbelief on one level and possibly these financiers do not want to suspend their disbelief.

Do you know of any superheroes either from Marvel or DC that are going to be made into movies or TV shows that the general public is not aware of yet?

Well, I know they are trying to sell the Teen Titans as a TV show, probably Saturday morning TV. Beyond that, I know what you know, I read the same trade papers you read. I'm always being surprised when I hear various things. I wrote a *Batman* novel which will probably be despised by certain fan critics because it is wholeheartedly a pulp novel. Which brings up a point that it's always interesting to me that what I call the selective critical facilities of the fan press, that they can admire a Walter Gibson for writing 130-odd or 200 or 300, I don't know, *Shadow* novels, which are basically all the same, which are excellent examples of pulp fiction, and at the same time, they criticize a comic-book writer who basically is writing a new pulp fiction for writing the same kinds of stories as Gibson. Raymond Chandler refers to this as "that form of snobbery which can accept the Literature of Entertainment in the past, but only the Literature of Enlightenment in the present." It's a selective critical facility that says, "Anything that I read before I was 12 years old is good; anything that has been written since I was 12 years old that is the same as what I read when I was 12 years old is bad because now I can recognize the flaws and I choose not to overlook those flaws." That's what it boils down to. It's the choice they make to segment or to compartmentalize their experiences between what they read and enjoyed when they were in their non-critical stage, which is basically the same sort of material, but they love to criticize it now because they can prove they're now in their critical stage. [*Laughter.*] "I'm mature. I can see this stuff is silly." Well, OK, it's always been silly. Gardner Fox was no better a writer than I am and in many ways I think I'm a better writer than Gardner was. Len Wein is no better a writer than John Broome and vice versa, but John Broome and Gardner Fox are deified for their efforts in the '40s, '50s, and early-to-middle '60s, while people like Len and myself, or Cary Bates, who are basically carrying on their tradition, are generally looked down upon, because we're being read by people who treasure their critical facilities.

I assume you read ECs when you were younger.

You've got to remember, I was born in 1952. I was a post-EC baby. I didn't read them until... My first experience with EC was the *Creepys* and *Eerie*s that Archie Goodwin did that were a direct tribute to the Kurtzman and Feldstein-Gaines EC stories.

How about the artwork of Al Williamson and Wally Wood and Roy Krenkel...?

They're wonderful. Ah, Jesus. There's just no comparison between a Williamson or a Krenkel or a Crandall and the people who came in later and were very, very much influenced by them, which is not to say that the later artists, the guys I worked with in the late '60s-early '70s, were bad artists. But, there's just no comparison.

I know for me, when I read comics, and I've read them since I was eight years old, that unless the story had good artwork, I wouldn't read it.

Well, the art is important, particularly if it's a mystery story, or what we call a mystery story, which is actually a horror story. In a superhero comic the drawing can from wretched to excellent and it really makes very little difference in terms of your enjoyment of the comic book because what you're looking for is the superhero experience. When one gets older and starts looking at these things with a more jaded eye, then you start looking for the quality art. Oh, I remember Vinnie Colletta used to get all the best fan mail in the late '60s.

For inking?

Yeah, for the inking. Vinnie is not *my* ideal. I prefer somebody like Sinnott or Dick Giordano. Anyway, the artist is terribly important when you're dealing with horror stories or science fiction – the short piece, the story that's eight pages long or a little bit less or a little bit more – because that's prime storytelling, it requires you to create a world, tell the story, create the characters, get across the theme, all in the space of eight pages – and mostly by what's in the art. Peter Parker is going to look the same no matter who draws him unless the artist is an incompetent. But, a character who was created for one eight-page story is going to have to be specific, is going to have to be recognizable as a Type, is going to have to be the essence of that character, and that's something that only the artist can do.

One of the reasons I'm losing interest in _Savage Sword of Conan_ is because John Buscema or whoever is not adding enough to the backgrounds. Backgrounds to me are incredibly important in comics. One thing I like about your work is in one _JLA_ story you had a maze, a several-story structure you look down to, like an M.C. Escher.

That was incredible. That was Pérez doing that. Pérez is just incredible. That man puts more detail in one panel than many artists put in an entire page. But, he doesn't do it at the expense of the design of the page or the clarity of the storytelling.

That is art.

That *is* art. That is the essence. One of my favorite artists was Carmine Infantino. The fact that Carmine is not appreciated is, to me, prime evidence that fans don't know what they're talking about, because Carmine is the premier layout and design artist in comic-book history. Sure, his draftsmanship is sometimes hurried, his characters are a little bit cold, but the design of those pages is so clear, so dynamic, so structured... There are issues of the *Flash* from the early '60s that I can still conjure up almost page-by-page in my mind. It's funny: I always admired Carmine more than I admired Ditko or Kirby as artists. I recently had the experience of seeing a job Carmine had drawn, the first one that he'd ever drawn of mine, and it's not a great little story, it's not the best mystery or horror story that's going to be published this year, but my God, it looks great. He captured completely what I'd asked for in my stage directions, and gave the whole piece a cohesiveness, a sense of tone, a sense of structure that many artists would not have given. I was very happy to find out that he was drawing a Batman/Firestorm of mine for *Brave and Bold*, and I asked Len [Wein] to let me write a new Space

Museum story for *Mystery in Space* specifically for Carmine to draw. I was very happy that I got permission to do it, and apparently Carmine really likes the story. We're going to do more, so I am in seventh heaven right now in terms of working with artists.

What about [Joe] Kubert, who seems to be incredibly rushed and produces tons of stuff and has all kinds of people working for him? Do you think you could get him to focus on just one high-quality comic?

Kubert is a different kind of artist. I don't know if it would really serve any purpose for Joe to concentrate specifically on one book, to draw it to the best of his ability, because his talent doesn't lie, it seems to me, in his draftsmanship. What it lies in is his overall design.

What about the old *Tors*?

That was years and years ago. I mean, that was...

What would it take to get some of these artists to do that kind of work these days? Pay them more?

I don't know. I mean, Kubert gets a fairly good rate, and he is so fast, if he wanted to put that kind of detail in, he could certainly do it. I don't really know if I think it would be appropriate for Kubert to do that kind of work, because I'm sure he devotes a great deal of energy to the work that he does do. What he's interested in now is layout and design. He's not interested in draftsmanship and rendering.

Well, then, maybe have Carmine and Kubert just do a bunch of books, lay them out beautifully and have some great inkers come in...

That's right, that's what should be done.

Why isn't that being done?

Well, there are not that many great inkers. There's only one Terry Austin, there's only one Bob McLeod. There's a new guy named John Beatty who inked a job of Carmine's.

Couldn't even Adkins help out a little bit?

No. You see, there are different artists with different strengths. Adkins's primary strength as a renderer is in enhancing very detailed work that is already done. An artist whose strength is in doing detailed work first of all requires more money, no big deal as far as I'm concerned, but also requires more time. And when he does take up as much time as he does he's going to produce less and less, and be like Terry Austin who can only do a book and a half a month, so to produce the kind of volume the companies want to produce – how many? – 60 titles a month – you'd need 60 different Terry Austins.

Is there any chance of getting people like Barry Smith, Jeff Jones, Mike Kaluta, and Bernie Wrightson over at DC?

Kaluta does covers occasionally. Wrightson has done a cover recently, I think. I don't really remember. But, they're interested in posters, their own publishing.

Fine art.

Fine art. I don't think they're really… with the exception of a guy like Wrightson, whose work is accessible to the comics format – or Barry Smith – but for the most part, Kaluta and Jeff Jones can better express themselves as artists in fine art. Look at the *Studio* book they did. That's just a beautiful piece of work.

Awesome.

A lot of that would be really wasted in comics because the printing is crappy. I mean, Kaluta's fine lines would be completely lost, they *are* completely lost in many cases in the covers he has done.

How about Craig Russell and people like that, who are doing pretty nicely? And Jim Starlin in *Epic*. I think they could be utilized in comics. Are they busy now in movies, or what?

Well, Barry Smith, I think, has spoken about doing a Conan graphic novel with Roy for the Conan Property people as opposed to Marvel Productions or Marvel Comics. Jeff Jones is primarily into painting. And more power to them. I mean, that's where their talents are best utilized. Why should we want to constrain them to a form they may feel they've outgrown?

What other fans, amateur artists, do you see as heading toward comics or artistic careers?

Well, I don't think many fans want to do comics as a career right now. I think that if they do, they will…

You don't see any that just have high quality that are moving in that direction?

Most fans, I think, are more interested in getting into doing alternative press material than working in comics. There is not really a desire that I can see among the current fan community to work in mainstream comics in the way mainstream comics requires you to work. Nor should they if they don't want to. Certainly there are enough opportunities in the alternative press to express themselves and make a good living and do what they want. But I don't think they want to do mainstream comics, what we call mainstream comics. I hate that word, because it implies that we are the appropriate genre. I mean, we are *a* genre. Superhero comics are *a* genre, horror comics are *a* genre, and they exist as this overall spectrum I see in the graphic form. Trying to fit talents that might be better utilized in the alternative press, or in posters or in cartoons into our genre might be the worst thing you could do to those people. Maybe they should just continue to do what they're doing or find new ways in which to do it. Don't change me; I won't change you.

How old is your baby, by the way?

This baby is one year old and possibly the single most important product of my many years as a comic book writer.

[*Carla Conway*] Roy Thomas is her godfather.

Yes, Roy Thomas is her godfather. And it's only coincidence that she's blonde like Roy is. *[laughter]*

Like your wife is.

Like my wife is.

Who's also a writer.

Who's also a writer, who's written for theatre in New York and written interviews for various magazines, and has been an associate editor for Marvel Comics and has written for comic books and has done almost as much work as I have. [*Laughter.*] We intend to make this child into a thoroughgoing cartoon groupie.

Not hard to do with all these comic-related items and paintings all over the house.

I believe in doing the exact opposite of whatever is the current pediatric fad. Because so many times they reverse themselves anyway. Doctor Spock reversed himself. I don't see anything that they've said that would lead me to believe that they have any inside track… Every time you turn around somebody's saying whatever they used to know they didn't know and now they know something else. So, there's no real permanence to that kind of knowledge.

And what is *your* philosophy of life?

Well, since having a baby, my philosophy of life has changed. I used to believe that being a writer was the most important thing in my life; that dealing with the creative muse was an all-involving continuous life struggle. Whatever. Since having Cara, I have seen that basically my primary purpose in life is to live, to be, to be myself, and to watch this child grow and to help her grow, and to enjoy life through her eyes. To see that things are never permanent, that no goal is a permanent goal, that everything is beautiful, that nothing is a perfect ideal. Being a writer is just what I do.

TCJ

CHRIS
CLAREMONT

GENIUS IN
THE DETAILS

INTERVIEW BY MARGARET O'CONNELL: Chris Claremont's best-selling *Uncanny X-Men* defined comic books for the period 1975-2000 the way that Superman defined the industry in its initial decade. Working first with Dave Cockrum, then John Byrne, and eventually a series of superstar and about-to-become-superstar illustrators, Claremont in his initial 16-year run harnessed elements of soap opera to comics' traditional action-adventure in a way that emphasized the life-threatening danger involved and played to fans' desires to see relationships between their favorites unfold. Claremont also utilized a declarative way of speaking that left little doubt as to what each character was experiencing at every possible second. He emphasized strong female characters and sexually attractive males to great effect. The X-Men were complicated and corny and an industry-defining hit; writers as diverse as Grant Morrison and Joss Whedon have since written in tribute to Claremont's approach.

Claremont has written additional runs on the X-Men characters he made so popular, has published science fiction and fantasy novels, and written for DC Comics and Dark Horse.

This interview (TCJ #50, October, 1979) with Margaret O'Connell finds Claremont building on an already-considerable popularity; the discussion speaks to specific details and character moments in the unfolding *Uncanny X-Men* saga as if everyone was already familiar with them. That's because for a very long time, anybody who read comics *was* familiar with the details of Claremont's stories.

SHE DIED. AS AN X-MAN.

I COULD DIE.

I WISH I'D KNOWN HER BETTER -- *HUNH?!*

BRRRANG!

THAT'S THE *BURGLAR ALARM!* THE HOUSE COMPUTER SHOULD BE PRINTING OUT THE DETAILS ON THE WALL SCANSCREEN -- AH. THERE IT IS!

POSSIBLE INTRUDER ZONE 4

ZONE 4 IS UPSTAIRS-- *ORORO'S ATTIC!*

IF THERE'S AN INTRUDER WHEN I'M BY MYSELF, I'M SUPPOSED TO CALL THE POLICE, BUT I THINK I'D BETTER CHECK THINGS OUT FIRST.

I CALLED 'EM LAST SEPTEMBER DURING A BIG WINDSTORM...

...AND IT TURNED OUT TO BE A FALSE ALARM. A TREE BRANCH HAD BLOWN THROUGH THE SKYLIGHT. THE COPS TOOK IT IN STRIDE BUT I FELT LIKE A JERK.

THIS TIME I'M *GOING* TO MAKE *SURE!*

RUNNING UP AIR MOLECULES IS A LOT MORE *FUN* THAN WALK-ING UP STAIRS!

EVEN IF I *DO* FIND A BURGLAR, THERE'S NOTHING TO WORRY ABOUT. WITH MY *PHASING* POWER, THERE'S *NO WAY I* CAN BE HARMED.

GEE -- IT'S GOTTEN AWFUL *COLD* ALL OF A SUDDEN.

AND *NO WONDER!* MY COSTUME'S INSULATED, AND I CAN *STILL* FEEL THE COLD. ICICLE CITY.

OH, NO! ORORO'S FLOWERS!

THEY'RE ALL DEAD, POOR THINGS. BUT--THIS ISN'T RIGHT. GRANTED, THIS ATTIC WAS LIKE A HOTHOUSE AND THE WINTER AIR OUTSIDE WILL KILL THE PLANTS BUT... NOT SO QUICKLY. SO COMPLETELY!

YUCK!

WHAT THE HECK IS *THIS?!*

THE FLOOR'S COVERED WITH THIS GOOP!

THAT SOUND--! SOMEONE'S IN HERE! BUT *WHO--?!*

Writer: Chris Claremont Artists: John Byrne & Terry Austin *The Uncanny X-Men* #143 March 1981 [©1980 Marvel Comics Group]

MARGARET O'CONNELL: Your writing in comics seems to have been heavily influenced by science fiction. For instance, in the "Xavier's Dream/Intergalactic War" storyline in *X-Men*, I found references to things like Marion Zimmer Bradley's *Darkover* books, where the Princess says "Lady Sharra!"

CHRIS CLAREMONT: Well, yeah, I've got damn near every book Bradley's had in print. I wrote SF before I wrote comics, and I've read SF since I could read. Yes, 90 percent of the comics work I do I consider SF – *StarLord*... the *X-Men* I consider a science-fiction series: a book about a telepath, a guy who fires eyebeams, someone else who can turn his body into steel, a two-toed, two-fingered, pointy-eared, blue-skinned, fork-tailed elf who can disappear in the dark, an elemental/telekinetic, which is what Storm is – yeah, that's science fiction. I mean comic books is science fiction, in its purest sense. Superman – that's a science-fiction concept. Guy comes from another planet, powers and abilities far beyond those of mortal men –

Yeah, but that's really pseudo-science.

Pseudo-science, sure. There's a sequence in one Superman story where he pushes the Earth six inches to save it from destruction. To anyone with any degree of scientific training, that concept is mind-boggling. First of all, that you could find a point of the Earth which could take that much stress, and second of all, the geophysical upheavals that would result – tidal shifts, crustal shifts; earthquakes around the world. But on the other hand, it's science fiction – it's space opera, maybe.

To me the FF, for example – what do you call Galactus? The Silver Surfer. That's science fiction. Perhaps it isn't in the same league as Fred Pohl's *Gateway*, or Heinlein, or Chip Delany or John Campbell, or Larry Niven. But it is SF.

But you do seem to consciously refer to things that have been done in literary science fiction.

Well, I think I refer to SF things in the same manner that Roy [Thomas] refers to Golden Age.

That's what I mean – most comic writers don't seem to refer to literary SF and comic-book SF as if they were equally familiar with both.

Well, you refer to what you know. Roy has a phenomenal amount of knowledge of the so-called Golden Age of comics. I know nothing about it. That's why I don't refer to it. I do have a lot of knowledge about SF, 'cause that's what I write when I'm not doing comics. I'm doing this Tom Corbett series for Dell Books now, a series of novels. They're juvenile science fiction, but my ambition is to do a juvenile which is as good as the Heinlein stuff I grew up with – books like *Citizen of the Galaxy*, and *Have Spacesuit Will Travel*, which is my favorite, I think.

It's also expressed in visual bits. Dave [Cockrum]'s and my one-page homage to *Star Trek* in *X-Men* #105, that whole bridge scene. Throwaways here and there. The mention of Sharra, who in my Princess Lilandra's lexicon is a benevolent deity, whereas I think in Marion Bradley's *Darkover* stuff she is not.

It expresses itself more, I think, in concepts. I've been dealing in my SF writing with telepathy ever since I started, just picking at it, exploring it. I found, partly to my chagrin, that Marion Bradley and I have a lot of the same ideas, the problem being hers saw print first. [*Laughter.*]

They express themselves – have expressed themselves, are expressing themselves, will express themselves – in the characters of Jean and the Professor [in *X-Men*] Not so much up 'til now, because we haven't really focused on Jean. We will be, though, in issues to come.

It's analogous to Dave Kraft's inclusion of rock figures, rock music. That's what he knows. This is what I know. Other people put in what they know. If I were a mystery fanatic, I'd be throwing in references to Philo Vance and Nero Wolfe and Archie Goodwin. [*Laughter.*] Yes, there's been a running joke around the industry about that for years. People follow Archie home, trying to see if he lives near Nero Wolfe.

Were the Starjammers in that "Xavier's Dream" storyline inspired by Poul Anderson's *The Trouble Twisters*?

I don't know. Dave Cockrum is really the one to hassle about that. They're his concept. He came in with the visuals, it was something he'd been wanting to do, I saw it, flipped, and said, "Let's do it in the *X-Men*!" And he said, "Sure."

As far as who the Starjammers are – well, I don't know what their derivation is. As I understand it, Dave's been playing around with some of the concepts for years. They're not the Fatal Five.

No, I didn't even think of that. They did remind me of the Trouble Twisters because that team also has a female sort of cat creature.

You're talking about David Falkayn and Adzel and Chee Lan, the van Rijn books, the Polesotechnic League. Yeah, I noticed the similarity myself. Again, I've got half a shelf-full of Poul Anderson, at least. I don't know. It may be.

The origins that we had in mind, that we tossed back, are – well, obviously, Corsair is Scott's father, he's human. Hepzibah was from a feline race that was conquered by the empire and pretty much decimated. We weren't sure where C'hod came from, or his little pet. And Raza – Dave had a theory that he was the Emperor's brother, or related to the Imperial throne, and that he had been almost assassinated and resurrected as a cyborg.

If we ever do a proposed two-part *Premiere*, where we will explain all this – you may find some of the answers. But again, it's a situation where however we resolve the Starjammers, it's only fair that Dave pencil it, simply because they are quintessentially his creations. When I knew that Dave would not be penciling #108 I suggested that we just drop the Starjammers from the plot altogether, we could make do without them, simply because I thought they were a great idea and I didn't want him giving it away. At least if they hadn't appeared in *X-Men* he'd have a bargaining point with Marvel, he could sell it as a series and perhaps get a percentage. This way, they've appeared, they're Marvel characters, Dave has no claim on them any more. But he wanted to do them. So I said, "Fine."

But as I said – we thought, if there was an *X-Men Annual*, of resolving it there, but Jim [Shooter] felt there is too much in that sideline plot to just throw away as two or three or four pages of an annual, or even 10. It deserves a book of its own. Again, it's purely a matter of when Dave has time to do it. It's not even a question of whether I write it. As far as I'm concerned it hinges entirely on Dave. But as I said, any question about who they are or where they came from – you should ask Dave.

Does the Princess and part of that whole storyline have anything to do with *Star Wars*? Because it does seem to have certain similarities.

Yes, it does, but also bear in mind that we introduced that plot in #97, in February '76, which means that the issue was plotted somewhere in late summer '75, which was a little under two years before *Star Wars* even appeared. The same thing happened to an extent with *Star-Lord*. People were saving, "Well, you ripped off *Star Wars*!" failing to remember or to realize that I plotted *Star-Lord* a year before *Star Wars* opened, at a time when no one knew what Lucas was doing. There were vague hints and intimations, but he was being very secretive about it, and even we who were doing the adaptation didn't know what was going on. And that *X-Men* storyline started more than a year before. People forget that empires and giant starships and battles in outer space and missing princesses have been stock-in-trade in adventure SF and adventure fiction for as long as people have been writing words.

I kind of figured that, but when in the actual confrontation with the Empire you mentioned death stars and there were a couple of references to a force, it seemed as if it had started out as a coincidence but you were throwing in a deliberate reference because you had seen the adaptation that Marvel was doing.

The death stars – well, what do you call nine stars that could bring about the death of the universe? There's a limited number of names. Forces – well, you've got forces there, you've got Kirby's Source – at the time I was also knee-deep in *Iron Fist*, which is involved with the martial arts, which is also involved with the Zen aspects, with force above and beyond the human plane of existence. So is magic. I was gonna do some work on *Doc Strange*. Marv had picked me at that time to take over, but then Starlin came back, and got it.

I was not consciously trying to exploit *Star Wars*. I'm sure subconsciously, but then again Lucas has said that a lot of *Star Wars* was an homage to the adventure films that he loved in his youth. If you stretch the point long enough, you could probably wrap my story and Lucas's up together, the idea that whatever it was that Jean tapped into as Phoenix is analogous to whatever it is Obi-Wan Kenobi taps into. All I can say is, it wasn't a conscious expropriation; it was just there.

Talking about the X-Men, I gather that Dave Cockrum is more responsible for their origins and for the original concept than you – you came in on the second issue, didn't you?

The series was created by Len Wein and Dave. Some of the visual conceptions Dave had been carrying around for years. His sketchbook is filled with them – various incarnations of the characters, Nightcrawler, Storm with a shorter cape and an Afro, black hair, no disappearing eyes.

That's one thing I wanted to ask about. The first time I saw Storm – she looked like a white woman dipped in brown paint. I wondered whether there was any real explanation for that, or –

What Dave was trying to do was draw her – she has cat's eyes. They literally slant up.

Yeah, they're at a 45 degree angle instead of horizontal and parallel to her mouth, the way most people's are.

John [Byrne] doesn't do that, which I suppose you have to file under the heading of artistic fiat, in the same sense that any artist always does a character fractionally different from another [artist].

But Dave's intention – I think he was trying to create someone whose features were not classically black or classically white. A lot of it also depends on how the book is inked. Terry [Austin]'s interpretation of Dave's pencils is different from Grainger's is different from Frank Chiaramonte's is different from Bob McLeod's is different from Dan Green's is different from Bob Layton's, all of whom have inked Dave at various times in his life.

Anyway, what happened as far as the origin is that Len and Dave created it. They did *Giant-Size X-Men* #1, which introduced the new X-Men. But right after that book hit the stands, Len was appointed Marvel Editor-in-Chief – that's when Roy left. And he couldn't handle his workload. And I had sat in on the plot sessions for both the first two issues – the first issue that saw print, and the second issue, which became #94 and 95. So he asked me if I'd handle it. And I said, "Yeah!" The second issue was essentially plotted – all we did was break it up into two parts and revamp it slightly. And from there on Dave and I were on our own.

Number 96 I scripted as a full script when I was in England on vacation in the Spring of '75. And there you have it. The original conceptions are a mixture of Len's and Dave's concepts. Everything that has happened since is a synthesis of me and Dave and by John, and or Roger [Stern]. He helps me out some [as editor].

If Len Wein and Dave Cockrum had plotted both *Giant-Size X-Men* #1 and what became the next two issues, why did they introduce Thunderbird? He seems to have been introduced almost in order to be killed.

He was.

Why?

Well, with a 34-page quarterly book, there's a limit to the amount of issue-to-issue continuity. I can establish something – for example, in #116 we have Storm looking at Wolverine and saying, "Wolverine, there is more to you than meets the eye," and he says, "At my size, that ain't hard." Fine. But in #118, the first Japan story, we establish that Wolverine can read Japanese, and Scott says, "You never told me you could read Japanese." "You never asked." "Oh." And then we go on, a few pages later, to the whole scene with him and Mariko, where he's walking through Sunfire's house, thinking to himself that he doesn't fit in with humanity, he'd like to stay in the Savage Land, blah blah blah, sis boom bah. But each builds on the issue before. I can throw in a piece one issue, another piece the next issue, a piece the third issue. There's a scene in #149, the issue after that, where everybody's happy, it's a Christmas party, they've defeated Moses Magnum, saved Japan, saved the world, Banshee's all right, everyone's happy – except Colossus, who's standing out on the porch; looking miserable, and Storm goes out and says, "What's wrong?" And he says, "Well, it's Christmas. And I miss my folks." He's homesick. And this will be built up over the next few issues, culminating in his quitting the X-Men. The character nobody anticipated quitting.

The point is that [with the book a] monthly, I can hint at things and build on them from issue to issue, 'cause it's only a four-week break. Len had to deal with a three-month break, even though he had twice the space. Which meant that he couldn't so much build as make each issue self-contained. If he'd taken the time for people to get to know Thunderbird, it could've been two or three years. So he decided, BOOM! Shock value! The team has barely gotten together and bang! Never happened in 12 years of [the old] X-Men! They'd never lost a character. And then, blam! Right off the bat, Thunderbird gets axed.

Len probably would've made that a major subtextual element for the next 50 issues, whereas I just dumped it in #96. Scott does his obligatory mope scene, and that's it. Though it affects him from time to time. This team of X-Men seems a lot more prone to getting killed than the last batch. But that basically was it.

It was a different schedule, which results in a different way of thinking. The same way, for example, that – one of the mistakes I made on Captain Britain was plotting it as if I were writing a regular Marvel book, but doing it in six-page increments. And the pacing just kept screwing me up. Because I'd just get started on an issue, and all of a sudden it'd be over. I just couldn't get my head into that. Likewise, I'd find it very difficult to do a daily strip. If they ever came up with a daily *X-Men* strip, I'd find it almost impossible to do it. Simply because it's a different way of thinking, which requires a different approach, a different way of pacing, a different way of doing the characterization. Shorthanded shorthand.

If the *X-Men* were still a quarterly, giant-size book, it would be a far different series from what it is now. Simply because it would be unfair of us – it was bad enough for us to ask readers to stick around on a bimonthly book for the stuff that we were doing. Stay tuned next month for the cliffhanger ending which is only Part II! Ha ha! Imagine if that were a quarterly – they'd come after us with lynch mobs.

That's basically why Thunderbird was killed. There are two ways of killing a character. One is to set up a very strong emotional connection between him or her and the audience, and then bump him off. The other is just killing him for shock value. Actually, there are three ways. The third way is for convenience.

For example, in *John Carter, Warlord of Mars*, I introduced certain of Dejah Thoris's relatives – her mother, her grandmother – mentioned but never seen. The mythical brothers and sisters that she mentions in *Princess of Mars*, and in *John Carter* #11, Marv's issue, but have never been seen in any of the books. So Mike Vosburg and I introduced them, specifically for the purpose of getting them killed, so as to give Carter a reason for his lifelong hatred of the Guild of Assassins. And also to give the story some emotional point.

Unfortunately, we ran into the same problem that everybody runs into on anything that's a series – television, magazines. This kind of makes a lie of a promise I made in a recent letter column that *X-Men* would become a suspenseful book, you wouldn't know who would live or who would die. Of course you know that the X-Men are never gonna die. I mean, that would be kind of stupid. Though I would like, I would dearly like, to have the freedom to kill one of them. Unfortunately, I like them all too much. So the only people who are really in danger are the supporting cast. And, unfortunately, even they're not immune. I mean, look at Gwen Stacy. Here today, gone tomorrow, back the day after.

So it's a matter of treading a fine line. Unfortunately, being a pulp medium, our stock in trade is putting our heroes in situations which should cause their death, or the deaths of one or many other people, or worlds, or universes, or the like. At the same time, because we are a pulp medium, and a continued pulp medium, the reader knows the hero will get out of it. But how, and will it make a difference? That's where the suspense comes in, hopefully.

I like to think that one of the differences between, to get specific, *X-Men* and *Star Trek*, is in terms of continuity. If something happens to an X-Man in one issue, it affects them for the rest of the run of the book, at least as far as I'm concerned. Whereas toward the end on *Star Trek*, Kirk was falling in love and losing the girl every week, and it was a great emotional trauma, but next week he acted as if nothing had happened.

It's one of the things, I think, that makes Marvel what it is, that attracted me when I was a kid: the fact that Stan created characters who were real, whose lives did affect those who came after. There's a sequence [in] *FF* #50 [where] Johnny Storm goes to college. But he drops out almost immediately. But then 50 issues later – I don't know if Stan wrote it – he goes back for the graduation of Wyatt Wingfoot and is sitting there thinking, "God, if I'd just had the guts to stick it out, I could be up there." Which is something unheard of in *Superman*, at least 'til recently. An action occurring 20 or 30 issues – that was four or five years before – would never affect what's happening today. Each issue was complete unto itself.

In Marvel everything always affected everything else, from book to book. And it's still happening.

Unfortunately, the books I write are so out of the mainstream that it's hard to come up with an off-the-cuff example of a seminal event – well, the death of Gwen Stacy. It affected Peter Parker for the next bunch of years and to a certain extent still does. Which is something you never used to expect from a DC book.

If somebody close to Superman died, it [affected] only that issue. It never extended.

It was usually a character that was only introduced for that issue, too.

Yeah. And if it were a major character like Ma and Pa Kent or somebody, it was either imaginary or they came back to life. Which kind of limits the suspense. And at the same time limits reader involvement.

Marvel characters can be hurt physically and emotionally. And you could relate to them because of that. Again, one of the strikes against Ms. Marvel for so long, I think, was that no one had a sense that she or Carol Danvers could be hurt or be vulnerable. I think that sense was what made the introduction of her folks in #13 and that whole sub-conflict with her father in #14 that was elaborated on in #19 work. In terms of the character, not so much in terms of popularity, but I think also in terms of popularity. We finally gave Carol an existence, and we showed that she could hurt, that she could be vulnerable, that there were people she cared about, people she needed, for whatever reasons. The idea being that she is someone who cares for her friends, that those she accepts as friends, she cares for and will do anything for. There's a sequence in *Ms. Marvel* where at the end of the book, she's just rescued Salia from fates worse than death. And Salia is in hysterics. She has been subjected to mental control, brainwashing, all manner of horrors for the last year or so, has been forced to do things that made her nice person's soul just cringe, and she's walking the fine edge of madness, to coin a phrase. And Carol's trying to calm her down and Salia's going, "No, no, no, no!" Salia just doesn't know who this person is. So Carol takes off her mask and says, "Hey, it's me, Carol – calm down." And Salia goes, "Ohh," and calms down. The idea being that it was a calculated risk, that Salia wouldn't remember, which is probable, the way her brain was fuzzed out – and that Vance Astro doesn't know Carol from a hole in the wall, and he can't go down to Earth. He can't ever leave Drydock, so even if he knew, what could he do?

But the more important element is that Salia, Carol's friend, needed help that Carol could give her. And weighed against that need, the imperative of her "secret identity" just didn't count for anything. To me that's an important point. It's something that is carried through. I started it in *Iron Fist*, continuing to a large extent in *X-Men*, who don't really have secret identities. Byrne and I have toyed with an amusing scene of Storm trying to stuff all that hair under an Afro wig. We figured if she ever did have to wear a wig it would be a variation of Rastafarian dreadlocks – just long black hair with the white stuff pinned underneath.

But it's the idea that used to be in comics that a hero's secret identity was the most important thing in the world. Superboy and all those would go to incredible lengths to preserve their anonymity. Spider-Man does today. There's a scene in *Marvel Team-Up* where a girl that Parker's on a date with is about to be murdered by a werewolf, and there's simply no time for him to change to Spider-Man. So he just tackles the werewolf and they go rolling into the lake. Luckily the darkness and the confusion and the lake obscure the fact that he hits the guy with webbing and he's far stronger than he ought to be, but the idea is that there are certain needs that outweigh the secret identity imperative. With Spidey I'm treading on thin ice because he's not my character, because losing his secret identity would make much more of a difference to him than it would to a lot of other characters.

But someone like Iron Fist, for example – it didn't really matter to him. It's a convenience, nothing more. It's not the big be-all and end-all of his life. To a degree it's the same with Ms. Marvel. If the need is there, she'll blow her cover. Because there are more important things: To help a friend in need is, to her, of paramount importance. And the reason I think it's important from a characteri-zational standpoint is that it's a very human thing to do. And as I said before, humanity is something that, as much because of the way I've been writing it as anything else, has been lacking from Ms. Marvel's character. Her temper was a good element because it's something people could relate to,

Yeah, that scene where she smashed a steel girder in a fit of temper and said, "I don't know my own strength!"

Yeah, there's a sequence in #21 where a lizard just backhands her and she says, "That's it! I've had it! You're gonna hit me? Boom! I'm gonna hit you!" And the next second she's going, "Why the hell did I do that? I mean, I'm supposed to be an adult. I'm supposed to think my way out of situations, not hit people! Anyone gets killed now, it's my fault!" And of course the story goes on from there. But the idea is that with her, hopefully with all characters, there is more than meets the eye, because the more you have, the more a kid, a reader, can relate to, hopefully better.

How did they react at Marvel when you started proposing these big changes in *Ms. Marvel*, even in the costume and the other visuals?

The costume was the last. Well, what happened was, I plotted the first couple issues off the top of my head and then sat down and tried to figure out what the hell I was doing and where I was going. And I didn't know. And it got worse and worse. It's like trying to plug the hole in the Titanic with a box of cotton and a few Band-Aids. Everything was just slipping through my fingers, and I went in to Archie [Goodwin] on a number of occasions and said, "I can't relate to this book; maybe it's better if you took me off it." And he said, "Well, maybe it is. You sure?" I'd sit down and we'd pick the thing apart. Luckily, everyone agreed with most of my objections – to the concept, to the characterization. We just began fixing it, bit by bit, finding out who she was, where she came from.

Part of the problem was that Jim Mooney and I did not mesh as well as we could have. It happens, sometimes. And it isn't always a case of an artist and a writer not meshing, it might just be an artist and a writer not meshing on a particular book. 'Cause he and I did a *Spectacular Spider-Man* that was a lot of fun, had no problems with it.

Somehow, though, on *Ms. Marvel*, we were [at] cross-purposes. I would tell him something, and he would hear something subtly or completely different. The same words – it would just push a different button in his head. And unfortunately I had such a specific visual conception of what I wanted that it became an surmountable roadblock to me. I mean, Jim is a marvelous person, an incredibly nice guy, and a very good artist. He has, as I think his work on the *Man-Thing* strip showed, a very good visual imagination. He was doing some really extraordinary things – what comes to mind is Danny's eyes in the "Scavenger of Atlantis" series. Just very nice stuff. But somehow I could never pull that out of him with *Ms. Marvel* – my plots didn't inspire him or something. And finally with the eighth issue he went off to *Spider-Man* and other things. Keith Pollard came in for an issue, which had its up and downs.

The sequence in the first – this is an example of what can happen sometimes when you're working on the plot. The sequence in there was two pages – one page of Carol walking around – from the moment Carol changed to Ms. Marvel and realized that her whole house had been burned out to the arrival of the police. In the plot, that was supposed to be three pages. And the missing page was critical. There's a half-page sequence I wanted of Carol walking through the apartment and picking up things. Burned scraps of manuscript. Rossi's picture half burned up. Clothes, keepsakes, mementos – all destroyed. Just to focus the reader on a human reaction in her. And unfortunately, as some pencilers are wont to do, Pollard added an extra page to the fight and compressed [the earlier scene] to two. And I was forced to shorthand it.

Then Sal [Buscema] came in, and Sal is a magnificent storyteller just in terms of action. But again, we were playing musical inkers. I think for a six-issue stretch, the book didn't have the same two people working on the art two issues in a row. Same thing happened in *Carter*, unfortunately. And that always hurts, because first of all, especially when you're dealing with continued stories, the new people might not know what the hell's going on. Second of all, it's very hard to build any kind of momentum, especially if the visual style is demonstrably different from issue to issue.

What happened with Ms. Marvel is I just started evolving her very slowly, getting rid of the circuitry field, so that her powers were her own. Most importantly of all, evolving an origin. How did she become Ms. Marvel? And in that origin, as it turned out, we explained that her powers were always her own, that she is more than just an Adam's rib-style superheroine. And we just evolved her – a little bit here and a little bit there. I would talk to Archie, or Jim [Shooter], and weep, scream, yell; Archie would look depressed: "Why won't this guy just go home and write the damn book!?! Why does he keep pounding on my desk? You're supposed to be a writer, Claremont; write, don't kvetch!"

And there's a point, a realistic point, where you begin to wonder. We all have an ideal, a thing our books would be like. Even on the *X-Men*, there are things I could wish were better. There are compromises that have to be made. (This is an industry whose byword is compromise.) Not in a pejorative sense, but the writer's initial plot conception is compromised insofar as the penciler's interpretation of it. Then the writer has to look at that penciled interpretation of it, and figure out how to take his plot and fit it, the things he wanted to say. in the space available, in the pictures available. Then that is further compromised by means of the inker. If he's a good inker or a bad inker, if there's three weeks to ink it, or three days, or three months. Very rarely is anything exactly the way you wanted it to be when you set out. Sometimes it's better. Sometimes it's worse. But there's always a balancing act that has to be maintained. With *Ms. Marvel*, I kept pushing in that direction. I knew I was right. But there was a part of me that kept saying, "Well, I could be wrong. Maybe it would be better to let someone else take over the book, give it a fresh set of eyes, ears, minds."

Finally with the first Carmine [Infantino] issue and the second Carmine issue, it all started knitting together. Actually, the four Mooney issues in between were essential also. It was all build-up. I couldn't have done the second Carmine issue if I hadn't had those four middle issues to kind of work things out. As far as the costume went, I'd been bugging Archie about the costume since I took over the book, 'cause I thought it was a mistake. Because Captain Marvel had never sold well enough on his own to justify tying a character to him, and worst of all, Cap's costume is designed for a man. It's designed to accentuate narrow hips, broad shoulders, the V-curve of a magnificently built male specimen. Unfortunately, the female body is not a V-curve; it's an S-curve, it's a guitar.

The point is that we have this costume which has a V over the crotch, this big blue V, on Ms. Marvel, accentuating the wide hips, which is wrong. And then you have this blue shoulder thing sitting right on top of her breasts and shoulders, emphasizing the broad shoulders. And she looked like a wrestler. And questions of femininity aside, she did not look attractive to me, especially with that damn cut-out. And again, the problem with the cut-out was that it was very hard to draw. No one could do it right two panels in a row. So I'd been bugging Archie about it; Archie'd been saying no, and finally he just said, "The hell with it. Ask Stan. If Stan says it's okay, fine with me." I wore him down, I guess. So Dave and I went in to Stan, and it turns out Stan hated the costume too.

So Dave and I sat down and went through literally a hundred sketches, all variations, and finally arrived, after three weeks of work, with the one we got — which was originally supposed to be a white costume, with no highlights, but then we decided upon a black costume with white highlights à la Storm, simply

because – the reason the coloring on #20 looks screwy is 'cause it was colored originally with the white costume. And they looked at it, and it didn't work. The main criticism was that she dropped out against pastel backgrounds. So they just colored it, but unfortunately the backgrounds weren't keyed for that, so it looked kinda screwy. I think it works fine.

Again, my own personal feeling is that if I were a superheroine, if I were doing what she's doing, especially with her powers, which are involved in punching and hitting, I would cover every square inch of my body – Phoenix's costume, essentially. 'Cause scraping bare skin on rocks can be very painful. But again, it's the aesthetic that we want to portray as attractive a physical image as we can, and it was felt that – even though to me, a well-drawn female figure supposedly covered with a skin-tight costume is as attractive as a well-drawn female figure in a G-string, it was felt that we ought to show some skin. So, we compromised again. She isn't Red Sonja. It isn't slit to the crotch. It's the best compromise between what Dave and I were going for and what we were being asked for. We gave a little, they gave a little. Like all compromises, it leaves a little to be desired on each side. I'm sure it's not as sexy as some would like us to have it. And it's not as practical as Dave and I wanted. But it's all right. It's a damn sight better than what was there before.

People are always talking about how you are the writer for women in comics. Do you feel that you're being pigeonholed in that category, that people aren't paying any attention to anything else you do any more?

Well, there has evolved a cliché in the office, the so-called "Claremont woman." That is to say, a gorgeous, attractive, nonwhite – no, actually, any kind of woman who, at the drop of a hat, will machine gun the hell out of anyone in her way. This description having been coined after *X-Men* #96, where Moira MacTaggert picks up a machine gun and starts blasting away at the monster.

Writer: Chris Claremont Artists: Paul Smith & Bob Wiacek *The Uncanny X-Men* #173
September 1983 [©1983 Marvel Comics Group]

In retrospect it might have been a bit more realistic to have her pick up the gun and swat the guy on the nose. But on the other hand, I wanted to do a woman who knew how to use a gun and wasn't scared.

I don't know if it pigeonholes me in terms of so-called fan reaction. At Marvel – the reason I created Harmony Young in *Power Man* was that Shooter challenged me to create a dip, a woman with no mind. Or at least a woman who, when faced with danger, would not pick up a gun and shoot people. Archie qualified that by saying he would like her to be an interesting character. So what I did was I created a woman who was a fashion model, whose primary asset was her body and how it looked. A woman who'd clawed her way to the top of her profession, or at least to the top rung of her ladder of the profession, which is probably just below Cheryl Tiegs, Farrah Fawcett, Lauren Hutton – superstar status. And who liked the good life. There's a scene, I think in *Power Man* #51, where she says that. She likes what she is and she isn't going back. Within the dictates of her profession, she knows everything there is to know about lights, camera angles, make-up, clothes – everything that revolves around her profession. But that's it. Drop her in the wilderness, she'd probably starve to death.

Unfortunately, most of the other women I have created, or have embroidered on in this business, have been of necessity major supporting characters: Misty Knight, Colleen Wing [from *Iron Fist*], Jean [Phoenix], Ms. Marvel, Lorna [Polaris], to a lesser extent, Storm. Nobody in *War Is Hell*. Nobody really in *Satana*, other than Satana herself. Dejah Thoris. Oh, [in] my very first story, *Giant-Size Dracula*, I introduced this lady cop, Kate Fraser. The basic gimmick upon which the story is hung is that she is a spitting image of Dracula's murdered wife, Maria. And there could even be a loose question as to whether she was the reincarnation of Maria, many times removed. And boy, was I gonna have fun with that. [*Evil chuckle.*] Luckily I had gotten taken off *Giant-Size Dracula* before I could – oh, I had plans. And Marv [Wolfman] was ready to wring my neck.

But all I have ever really basically done in creating women in my strips – and, to an extent, in the work I do outside my strips – the central character of the first science fiction story I ever wrote, "Psimed," is a woman – was to create characters who are believable, who are likeable, who work. Notice in all this I haven't mentioned Carol Danvers.

If I have a rule of thumb in creating lead characters, good guy characters, it's people that I would like to meet, people that I would like to know.

At the same time, when I began in the business, I deliberately set out not to write – everyone was writing women who were backups who at the drop of a hat would fold. Sue [Storm] took a long, long time to come into her own, and even then she's –

That's really weird. Now she can fight a villain just as well as the others, but she still talks as if she's helpless.

See, therein lies the problem, because you'd have a writer on the FF – I don't speak in terms of specifics, as in Marv or Len or Roy or Gerry or Stan – you've got a person, Person X, who's writing the FF, anyone, even me, wanting to turn Sue Storm into Wonder Woman. But you can't. You've got 15 years of Sue Storm. You've gotta go back and judge who this woman was.

Sue Storm grew up in that amorphous time before whatever war it was that Reed and Ben went off to fight. She grew up in a time when women were not self-assertive. I think from a writing standpoint one of the fascinating aspects of Sue's character is that here's this woman in her 20s when it happened, if that, who's all of a sudden turned into a woman who can turn invisible, can shoot out force fields, and things like that. And she's part of a team that has fought Galactus, that has been from one end of the universe to the other, blah blah blah sis boom bah, all of this. And it's like having the ability and the responsibility to act with the team, and yet having the cultural conditioning to be in the background, to be protected. That's something I think we've probably lost over the past 10 years. When you talk about Sue Storm, I think that has to be taken into consideration.

One of the things I felt was wrong about Ms. Marvel was that Carol Danvers has always, from *Captain Marvel*, been a pushy bitch who folded under pressure. But she's always been a self-assertive woman. And Ms. Marvel is a self-assertive heroine. So wherein is the conflict? It's the same side of two different coins, as opposed to two different sides of the same coin.

For my money, it would have been a far better initial choice to make Ms. Marvel's human persona – this is something Steve Gerber came up with that was very well received initially but the final analysis, I think, was that it wasn't saleable – was that she be a divorcée with two kids, a lousy job somewhere in Podunk, Iowa, living in a trailer if necessary, or a house, trying to make ends meet. And escaping from that into the glamour and the power and the self-assertion of Ms. Marvel.

And therein the possibilities begin to boggle the mind. I mean, "What happens to this woman when the thrill of being a superheroine is like – oh God, I don't want to go back to the drudgery of dishes, and changing diapers, and Johnny's late home from school," and all that stuff. Therein you have the germs of some really meaty character conflict, and the potential of saying something relevant and important to the reader. Whereas with Ms. Marvel, Carol has got it equally well made as Ms. Marvel or Carol.

Yes, in fact, at the May Creation Con, it was said that one of the reasons Marvel was so dissatisfied with the character and let you change her was that initially she had it better as Carol Danvers than as Ms. Marvel. She had no reason, no incentive, to be a superheroine.

That's one of the points I kept making to Archie. The classic Marvel character is a hero because of something that he can't be in his own life. Peter Parker originally was a schlump. As Spider-Man, he still made mistakes, but he could thumb his nose at the Flash Thompsons of the world. Iron Man as Iron Man could do things that Tony Stark couldn't do because of his bad heart. Daredevil was a hero who didn't have to obey the unconscious restrictions of blind Matt Murdock. You go on down the list. Captain America is the antithesis of 98-pound weakling Steve Rogers. Ms. Marvel is great, but so is Carol Danvers.

Going back to just how I write women, essentially I approach them the same way I approach men, which is I want to write an interesting character. I would not approach it any differently if, for example, Storm were the only male X-Man in a team of women. It's just a matter of being true to their characters. It's an accepted given that there are some facets of being female that we can never touch on, simply because of the Code, physiological things. But people who accuse Ms. Marvel of being nothing more than a guy in drag – well, she's a hero, a person who does heroic things. The people who object to her punching, to her knocking down walls, to her penchant for going into action, would not be making the same judgments, the same critiques, if she were a man, which is in itself a kind of reverse sexism. [They] assume because she is a woman that she must have feminine powers. In the same [vein], why, because a character is a man, must he have masculine powers? Doc Strange has punched someone maybe twice in his life. Yet no one would accuse him of being non-masculine. I think that argument is a straw horse.

It's merely, for me anyway, a matter of writing characters as truly as I can, whether they're men or women, adults or children. And if I'm doing it right, and the character's interesting, whether it is a man or a woman, or an adult or a child, or if I'm doing it wrong. Unfortunately, perhaps – well, from Shooter's standpoint it's probably unfortunate that most of the women I create tend to be very self-reliant. Unfortunately at this point there's no one in the X-Men – except maybe Amanda and Betsy – and no one in *Carter*, and *Team-Up* doesn't really count, and no one thus far in *Ms. Marvel* anymore who cannot cope with any given situation at any given time. They're all very capable people, both male and female.

I agree that that does tend to get kind of limiting, that there is a danger of, as Roger [Stern] points out, creating my own new cliché. But I think in *Iron Fist*, for example, one of the things I had done with Joy Meachum was that, although she is head of a major corporation, she's still very much a normal person. I'm trying to do that with Phoenix, as well – remind people that although she saved the universe and is very powerful and has experience in godlike epiphanies, she is still very much Jean Grey, with Jean Grey's experience of the world, and, to an extent, Jean Grey's reactions to it.

Another example is Mariko – Sunfire's cousin – and she'll become the great love of Wolverine's life. She is exactly what she looks like – a daughter of Japanese nobility, trained in the idealized art of a geisha. She is there; she acts as Shiro [Sunfire]'s hostess, she is a woman. There's a line she has – when she first sees Wolverine, she nearly jumps out of her socks. He says, "Don't be afraid; I'm one of the X-Men."

She says, "Oh, you startled me, I'm sorry. I am not like my cousin Shiro, I have no courage, and I'm only a girl."

Which for her, for her character, is right. She has courage. She won't run. There's a scene later where an android comes after Sunfire, and she's sitting there trying to pull him out from under some rubble. The girl has guts, but she's by no means – let me put it this way: If a villain charged into a room and in the room were Colleen Wing and Mariko Yoshida, Colleen would grab a sword and Mariko would dive under the bed. She is not a fighter. She is a daughter of nobility. Her duties are, as she has been taught to believe them, centered around managing the home, and presumably eventually having children.

One thing I have noticed about the way you write women is in general you seem to like to delve into the characters' emotional reactions and attitudes more than a lot of other writers do. And even in your writing, the fact that women have been traditionally expected to be, or permitted to be, more open about their emotions than men is reflected in the fact that you have Ms. Marvel having these epiphanies of by when she suddenly discovers that she does have an identity and she's exclaiming, "I'm me and I'm beautiful!" Phoenix does the same thing in the "Xavier's Dream" story, when she enters the crystal, and she sees the whole pattern and says, "I never realized how beautiful I am," as well as everything else. But even then you don't have the male characters doing anything quite that emotional.

Oh, I don't know. In *Iron Fist* #8, there's a whole three-page scene which is nothing more than Danny Rand walking around his house, remembering the last time he was there, which was his youth. And as he's walking through the house, there's this magnificently drawn house – but he just walks around, and John [Byrne] did these outline figures of the ghosts. And the nicest compliment I ever got was Byrne called me up after that book hit the stands and he said that – he penciled it, he read the plot, he knew what was coming – and he read that scene and it made him cry. And that was when he figured that I knew what I was doing as a writer.

But again, that was specifically there – I did that scene to make Danny Rand human to the reader. Which hadn't been done very much before that. He was nebulous. All we knew of him at that point was here was this kid who'd gone off to K'un-Lun, come back with a vengeance quest, become Iron Fist, farted around for 10 or 11 issues, gone off to rescue Colleen Wing, gone through this, gone through that, and we'd never really locked onto who is this kid who saw both his parents killed before his eyes at the age of nine. What that must have done to his head, God only knows. He spent half his life just hating someone. That was what that was there for. And also, we very rarely see heroes cry.

Well, I don't know. There's more of a convention of the one-panel shot of the hero with one tear coming out of his eye –

Well, yeah, that's dramatic effect, it's always considered better to be subtle. But that wasn't; that was go for broke. We knew he was sobbing his guts out. Let's see

– the scene in *X-Men* #101, where the X-Men are all cheering, Jean's all right, and everybody cheers, and Nightcrawler sees Scott go into another room, and he peers in and there's Scott, just with his head in his hands, sobbing.

I don't *per se* have my women characters any more or less emotional, given their specific characters, than the men. Again, in the Daughters of the Dragon story [in *Deadly Hands of Kung Fu* #32-33] there are two specific instances in the second part where first Misty comforts Colleen, just before Colleen tries to go cold turkey on the heroin withdrawal, and at the end, after the fight, Colleen comforts Misty. I think, given characterizational imperatives, I would've done the same with two guys, considering what they went through in that story.

Nobody is really omnipotent. You try to do the best you can, and every so often you'll hit a rock. Something will trip you up. I think all of us in this industry, even on the best books, have our dud issues. All you do is pick yourself up and go on from there. I think, for example, the two-part Japan story [in *X-Men*] is really well done. And the Canadian Avengers issue – *Alpha Flight* – #120 and 121, [are]

Writer: Chris Claremont Artists: Paul Smith & Bob Wiacek *The Uncanny X-Men* #173
September 1983 [©1983 Marvel Comics Group]

equally good. The issues that are upcoming I think will work out really well. But – my first clunker was #95, my second one was #115. At least they're 20 issues apart. My next one shouldn't be due 'til sometime in 1980. One clunker every two years I'll settle for.

Okay, I want to talk about Storm some. Storm always kind of bothered me until issue #113. Everyone else seemed to love her, but to me she always seemed a little too self-consciously good to be true. There was just this whole goddess image. When she would refer to her friendship with Jean or something like that, I didn't believe it, because Storm didn't seem to have any real human feelings; she was just there to be impossibly rational and try to reason with people even when they were obviously in such a berserker rage that they weren't going to listen to anything. She just seemed like a sort of cut-out of nobility. Even her claustrophobia seemed sort of grafted on to give her some sort of human weakness so the reader would feel a little less totally removed from her.

Yeah, that unfortunately comes from the too-much-happening-off-panel syndrome. We didn't have the space to cover it in the book, so we let the reader infer it from the dialogue. Unfortunately, there are cases where the reader needs to see. You need a visual establishment that Jean and Storm are good friends. We established that Jean and Misty are roommates, and that seemed to work well, in that scene in #105 with her folks. Or even earlier in #101. Or roughly the same time in *Iron Fist* #11.

What was it that made you change your mind about Storm? That scene where they've all been captured by Magneto and they're strapped to these chairs –

The lockpick?

Yeah. You'd had flashbacks to her childhood before, but that was the first time it seemed to mean anything.

Again, it's a matter of evolution. Len [Wein] thought of her as a goddess. My own feeling is that she's more, in terms of pure characterization, a princess, who 99 percent of the time is royal. She has a sense of propriety, a sense of dignity, a sense of unflappability. Nothing will faze her. Of course, every 1 percent of the time she'll break out into this incredible grin and go, "Gotcha!" just because she's human.

The difficulty unfortunately with Storm is, being the only woman in the group – and God, there's a sequence in #119 where she's looking at the X-Men, suddenly realizing that they're her family, that when they came together x-years ago, they were all loners, and now they're a family. And she feels really good about it, so she walks up to Nightcrawler and says, "Kurt." "Yes?" "Nothing. I just wanted to give you a kiss, because I love you very much," and walks away. Everyone will say "Wow! You mean Kurt and Storm are in love?! What about Amanda?" Kids write in and say, "What happened to the affair between Storm and Colossus?"

That seemed to be more in Colossus's mind than anywhere else.

No! It wasn't in Colossus's mind at all! He wouldn't dream of touching her – in that way. [*Laughter.*] The relationship is brother and sister, pure and simple. She says it in the next book, in #119. "Is something wrong, little brother?" Again, that's the royal aspect. For someone who's lived alone all her life, she's very socially centered. Nothing knocks her off-balance. Even when something disgusts her, she will do it in a dignified way. In #116, just the way she drew her cloak around her and looked. Wolverine went "Faugh!" at the smell. And it was a real ripe smell. I told John I wanted scum city.

But she seems to take it for granted that everyone realizes that what she does is just what she says it is. I guess this is what would be logical for someone who had lived alone or been worshipped as a goddess for most of her life. But she doesn't seem to realize that if she gives someone a kiss like that, they won't automatically assume it's just a brother-sister relationship. They'll read more into it.

Oh, well, the X-Men won't. The reader will.

But the poor reader wonders why the X-Men don't. If anyone else did it, you'd expect there to be more to it than that.

Well, I dunno…

If anyone else kept walking up to her teammates very scantily clad and saying, "Do you like this outfit?" [as Storm did in #114, page 17], you'd think there was some kind of flirtatious intent behind it.

I don't think so. Again, a disadvantage I have as a writer is that, being trained as an actor, I hear my dialogue as I write it. I can hear people saying it. And I know exactly how she'd say it. "Do you like this dress?" Eyes wide, not a thought of the sexual implications. And because she's not thinking of it, the X-Men really are sensitive enough not to pick it up. I don't think there's an X-Man in the team who is in Hawkeye's class of emotional klutz. Wolverine, simply because he's too animalistic – if she's not interested, he'd know it. He'd sense it. Banshee's too much of a gentleman. Scott has the biggest potential for getting his signals crossed, but he's occupied elsewhere. Nightcrawler is too sensitive, I think, and Colossus is too young.

Storm's emotional role in the X-Men is that of a sister. And also the royal aspect of her, the princess aspect. It's like she puts her emotional feet exactly right. We may shake her up a little in issues to come. I don't know yet. There's a line in #118 which kind of says it. From 10 miles away, she tells Scott, "Nightcrawler's signaling from shore; he's all right." And Scott says, "It's awfully far away; are you sure?" And she says, "If I were not, I would not have said so." That's it. She means what she says.

Presumably if she ever wished to have a physical or emotional liaison with anybody, she'd come right out and say it. Neither John nor I foresee her having anything like that in the near future, simply because we have yet to find or create a character who is worth it for her. If we ever do a story in which Storm falls in love, it will signal an event in her life, I think, as Gwen's being killed was to Spidey. Regardless of how it turns out, Storm is not of the Supergirl school, where every third issue she meets a guy and falls head over heels in love, and is rejected and picks herself up and falls for the next guy. In that sense, Storm is both tremendously secure and tremendously vulnerable. 'Cause if the right guy comes along and he screws her up — emotionally speaking, please — the damage could be inconceivable. Because I've seen it happen. And to an extent, I think some of the blame is mine, because I wrote her ambiguously, deliberately so, but I think people may be taking things a fraction too literally. There are red herrings — I see nothing overtly sexual in a scene of two people sitting on a blanket talking about their homelands [as Storm and Colossus did in one issue].

I do not understand, I think, the need, this imperative in readers, that the moment any character does anything remotely kind or reaching out to another character, that it is an instant sexual liaison, emotional liaison. People were saying, "Gee! In issue #99, when Storm showed up all right, Colossus was going, 'Yay! You're all right!'" Of course. They're teammates. They're friends. He cares for her a great deal. But that is not to say that he is in love with her, or loves her. Both Kurt and Colossus in #101 flirt with her as they're going down to dinner, and she tells them both, "I make up my own mind." I fail to understand this need. I used to think that comic book writers were probably the horniest people in the world, next to comic-book artists. But this reading of sexual implications into even what seems to me at the time I'm writing it the most innocent scene I've seen, gets now and again to be a little absurd.

I grant you that in certain respects some of the ambiguity John and I, and Dave and I, have deliberately played on, to kind of get people going. But the relationship, as far as Storm is concerned, with Colossus is brother and sister. And to an extent I think that carries on to the rest of the X-Men. They're her family. She knows them too well to — she loves them all and is in love with none. And that's about where it really rests. It's like — she understands Wolverine, because he is the kind of being that she has lived intimately with for half her life — the great cats on the veldt.

It's hard to say, because Storm, like all the other characters, is evolving. They are different people now, to a large extent, from when I started the X-Men three and a half, four years ago. I hope they will be different people in four years. I think if there is an aspect of the book that may cause trouble, that could be it, because they are growing, and they are changing, and there are certain respects — for example, what will become of Colossus's growing realization that what he is doing as an X-Man may be to the detriment of his homeland, the Soviet Union. He leaves the X-Men. He comes back, but there are times when perhaps the characterizational imperative is to make a more permanent break.

We had a lot of letters from people saying, "Why don't Jean and Scott get married? They've been together for 13 years!" But they haven't. They book has been in print for 13 years. Scott and Jean have known each other for three, maybe four years. It's been barely that amount of time since Xavier formed the school for gifted youngsters. Four years into a relationship, especially considering it's probably only been about two since he admitted to her how much he cared for her, and vice versa, is not a very long time. Relationships are very, very, very fragile at that point. Especially when one of the halves of the relationship changes dramatically, and Jean has. She began changing with #98, visually – well, #97, actually. She was a different person. She left the X-Men; she's more independent. She has needs – she has a life outside the team. Scott still doesn't.

But to assume that a relationship that is two years old, even three years old or four years old, is set for life, is absurd. They're nowhere near ready to be married yet. Banshee and Moira are nowhere near ready to be married yet, and they're the closest we've got. The problem here is the fact that you've got someone who's been reading the X-Men since he was 15, and he's now 28, and these two kids are still bemoaning the fact that, "Gee, does she love me? Doesn't she love me?" You've got to bear in mind that it's been 15 years and Peter Parker's only now graduated from college. Dick Grayson is still a teenager, and that's been 40 years. Comic books run, unfortunately, on a slightly different timeline. Only *Conan* can really have the luxury of one year of issues being one year of real time, and, as Roy pointed out, by the time he gets to the point where Conan is in his 60s, it'll be the turn of the century, and Roy will be in his 60s, and who'll give a damn – if he's still writing the book. God. He has time to spare, in other words. We can't really do that with the X-Men. They get older very slowly.

But the whole point behind the break-up of Jean and Scott is that people change. Jean has changed; Scott has changed. The whole foundation upon which the older relationship was built no longer exists. Much as I would prefer to have it different – and this is why Phoenix isn't on the cover or in the title logo – is that in the opinion of Roger and John, she isn't an X-Man.

Why not?

Because – well, she isn't, really. She is part of the team, but she is not. She's an X-Man in the sense that Thor is an Avenger. She's around all the time, but – what I wanted to establish before, when I originally created Phoenix, is that she is almost forced back to the team. She has – though we haven't had much chance to show it – a life, an existence, a job, friends outside the X-Men. Scott doesn't. Phoenix is not Jean. Jean doesn't even know what she is any more. There's a whole sequence in the Phoenix story in [#125] where Moira is examining her, trying to figure out, is she Jean? Is she Phoenix? Is she human? Is she a mutant? What is she? What happened to her when that solar flare hit? And she doesn't know. And there's a line at the end of #117 where she's watching Misty fly off to Japan – this is the Xavier origin issue – it goes something to the effect of, she realizes for the first time since she joined the X-Men, she's on her own, with no one to help, no one to turn to or give her support. And that scares the hell out of her. She's still, for all that has happened to her, a very young woman.

Phoenix is actually Marvel Girl at her ultimate extent. Phoenix in #108, when she saved the universe, was Jean Grey achieving her fullest potential as an entity. Maybe not as a person.

But this is again an interesting insight into the way things work. Dave and I kind of liked the idea that we had a female character who was cosmic. No one else did. Len [Wein] objected strenuously to our using Firelord if Phoenix beat him. We couldn't have a lady character who's cosmic, because – well, his argument was that it made the rest of the X-Men superfluous.

You could say the same thing about the Avengers and Thor.
Yes, we did. Quite often.

We got around it by having the fight be a draw. And by making sure that Phoenix got the last shot, which is blasting Firelord 10 or 12 miles into New Jersey.

So anyway, we were told, Dave and I, that Phoenix could not be cosmic. And when the editor passes down an edict, you're stuck with it. What we did then was sit down, and – we had to cut her back. So we decided to cut her back to roughly where Storm is, which is fine. Now I had to think of a rationale. Okay. I put my head together, and we figured that Jean – this is my own personal interpretation. You will hear disagreements among other members of the editorial staff if they hear it. You'll hear disagreements from Byrne if he hears it, 'cause they think – well, they think it's a mistake. The potential to become Phoenix is still within Jean. But without the necessary increase in her awareness, in her perception. If her consciousness, her soul, whatever, is not enlightened, if her consciousness is cosmic, then she can't handle the power. It's like Doc Strange could not become the Sorcerer Supreme until had achieved a certain psychic and emotional balance, awareness. Neither can Jean. She'll burn herself out, she'll be warped, twisted, turned into an evil person. Ergo, what happened was her mind shut her down, as safety mechanism. To prevent her from hurting herself it just dropped a wall down.

Of course, one of the character elements Byrne and I are working on is she really enjoyed being cosmic.

She wants to be cosmic again. It's like a drug, a very strong, very irresistible drug, and she wants more. The more she gets, the more she wants. But the thing is she can't handle it. She's too young, in evolutionary terms, as well as physical terms.

So there's a case of a perfectly logical rationale coming in ass-backwards. We're given the situation, we invent a rationale, rather than inventing the rationale and then applying it. Which is how things happen around here.

The X-Men are all young. You tend to lose sight of this, 'cause Banshee's in his 30s, and Scott's in his mid-20s, but that's still comparatively young. They're very capable of making mistakes, of sticking their feet in their mouth, and questioning, and of being unsure. Scott is no longer sure – he thought Jean was the most stable thing in his life, the center of his life, the thing that gave his life purpose. That's what he said in #102. But the Jean that he was talking about to a large extent no longer exists, and he has to come to terms with the new Jean, just as she has to come to terms with herself and with the fact that Scott is changing, too. Part of the reason we [got] him involved with Colleen is to give him some new perspectives on life, to broaden his emotional and physical horizons some, to get inside his head.

It's unfortunate – I could write volumes about what's going on in that book, just describing, getting into the emotional details, nitty-gritty. But in the issues there isn't room. It's a matter of choosing which element we'll focus on this panel or this page or this issue and building on that. It's a matter of my own instincts to be subtle versus how much of that subtlety the audience will pick up on, and nine times out of 10, they won't. Though they appreciate the subtleties. Again, the letters on #114 were just incredible. "You have broken my heart! You have killed Scott Summers' character. You have violated it from one end of the – " Another saying, "What a brilliant move! Jean is different, and Scott's reacting to it!,' Granted, it wasn't the most ideally written scene I've ever done. I wasn't satisfied with it and Byrne didn't like it at all. But it got people interested.

But it's like, Scott is a person. Scott is changing, even as Jean is changing, and I don't really know if they'll get back together again. I would like it, in my own heart of hearts, because I think that relationship's really good. On the other hand, it will take a lot of work and understanding and changes in both of them to come to terms with that. I don't think, for example, Scott understands who the hell Jean is. I think she may understand him better simply because he has less facets. Scott Summers is basically the leader of the X-Men. But is he? Wolverine is coming up pretty fast on the outside track in that regard. So is Banshee. I want to do a couple issues where Scott isn't there and the others are leading effectively. Scott himself may come to doubt, "Am I just the leader of the X-Men?"

The possibilities are infinite, for just exploring the interrelationships of these two characters, let alone the other 12 or 15 or God knows how many we've got in the silly book. The possibilities are mind-boggling.

But that's, to me, what it all comes down to – the emotional relationships. To me the fights are bullshit.

TCJ

ARCHIE GOODWIN

THE HEART OF
AMERICAN COMICS

INTERVIEW BY STEVE RINGGENBERG: Over the course of his long and illustrious career, Archie Goodwin became one of the most well-liked, respected figures in the history of American comic books. He began as an assistant to comic-strip artist Leonard Starr before moving onto Harvey Comics and then Warren Publishing in the early 1960s. At Warren he made a name writing stories reminiscent of the genre-driven EC Comics of the 1950s for magazines such as *Eerie*, *Creepy* and *Blazing Combat*. He would continue with a variety of writing assignments in the '60s and '70s, including *Secret Agent X-9* with his good friend Al Williamson and various titles for both Marvel (*Fantastic Four*) and DC (*Batman*). In the mid-1970s Goodwin became a key editor for Marvel, and briefly the editor-in-chief, helping to negotiate extremely difficult waters during an extended, fallow sales period. He wrote the *Star Wars* movie adaptations and series that were the rare strong-seller during this period. Moving into the 1980s he would help launch *Epic Illustrated* magazine, the Epic Comics imprint, and the Marvel Graphic Novel series – some of the few experiments in format and creator-owned work ever attempted by that publisher. He would finish his career as an editor at DC Comics. Archie Goodwin died in 1998.

The following interview (TCJ #78, December, 1982) with Steve Ringgenberg and, occasionally, Kim Thompson, finds Goodwin talking in a friendly, matter-of-fact way about his accomplishments and some of the critical decisions he made along the way. It's as complete a picture of a life working in mainstream comics of this era as one is likely to find.

EVEN IF HE HAD DONE WHAT YOU THOUGHT, KILLING HIM DOESN'T MAKE IT ANY BETTER! I HATE THE GERMANS FOR WHAT THEY DID TO THAT PATROL, BUT KILLING THIS MAN MAKES US JUST AS BAD AS THEM, SARGE! IS THAT WHAT YOU WANT!

PURVIS, YOU GIVE ME A PAIN!

THIS IS WAR, PURVIS! OUR JOB'S TO KILL KRAUTS! DOESN'T MAKE ANY DIFFERENCE HOW OR WHY! JUST ONE MORE DEAD KRAUT!

HE'S STILL A MAN, SARGE. LIKE YOU AND ME.

HE'S THE ENEMY, PURVIS, AND *NOBODY* CARES WHAT HAPPENS TO HIM!

END

Writer: Archie Goodwin Artist: John Severin "Enemy!" published in *Blazing Combat* #1
October 1965 [©1965 Warren Publishing Co.]

STEVE RINGGENBERG: OK, let's start at the beginning. Were you interested in comics as a child?

ARCHIE GOODWIN: Yeah. As near as I can remember, I was always interested in comics. Any time we would travel anywhere, we'd buy comics for me to read on the trip. At that time, there was no TV; there were only horse-drawn radios, things like that. So I think you tended to read more anyway and there were a lot of comics available.

What comics do you remember reading?

Oh, everything. I think the earliest things I remember reading were *Donald Duck*, funny animals – things like that. As I got older I'd read anything, superhero stuff, anything. I even collected *Classic Comics* for a while. I stayed interested in up until I got really fanatical about them as a young teenager and gravitated toward the EC stuff.

What do you think had the most lasting impact on you and your work?

Oh, obviously the EC comics. When I became an EC fan, they were printing the biographies of the artists and all. Reading them, it just dawned on me that there could be something like comics that you could be interested in and yet obviously be able to earn a living – What did I know about living at that time? – but people were finding employment, doing something that I really liked and enjoyed reading and being involved with. So this was about when I was 13 or 14, I got it in my head then that "Why couldn't I work in comics?" I liked drawing, I liked making up stories. Once I saw that there were actually real people who they wrote about and promoted in their books that were doing these things, it sounded good to me, and I went along with doing it.

Didn't you originally want to be an artist?

Yeah, I came to New York, originally, and I went to what was then the Cartoonists and Illustrators School. It eventually became the School of Visual Arts. It was run by Silas Rhodes and Burne Hogarth. Again that was through EC: In several of the artists' biographies they mentioned the School.

So that was like Mecca for you?

Yeah. Really. So I headed here for that. Unfortunately, at the time I went to the school, this was 1956, and the comic business had pretty well been beaten to its knees, maybe even to its waist. There was almost no comics work, and the school was kind of retooling. And whereas the cartooning course had once been the reason for the school's coming into existence and all, that department was now actually shrinking. Illustration and design were coming into the forefront. I stuck with cartooning, and consequently I wound up being a writer.

How did that come about?

Well, mostly because I was more adept at the writing. It came much easier to me than the art ever did. I think I would be maybe a struggling mediocre comic-book artist now instead of a rich and successful mediocre comic-book writer.

So how much training as a cartoonist did you actually get?

Well, it was a three-year course. And I didn't really complete the full three years. I came close enough to doing it. But other than working in a [*pointing to one of his humorous comic strips hanging on the wall behind him*] stylized cartoon style like that which I was more adept at, I never really did anything in the way of straight drawing.

What about that fishing page you did?

Well, a friend of mine was an art director at a fishing magazine and he knew I did cartoon stuff like that. At one point I couldn't afford to go to school any longer, this was after about 2+ years, so I was looking for work, and he said "Gee, we're revamping the magazine, we'd like a cartoon page." But I knew nothing about fishing, so I came up with these weird, vaguely fishing-oriented cartoon pages. That was right after art school. And I did a little more when I was working at *Redbook*; I did a few cartoon-style spot illustrations for them. But that's really the only published artwork I've ever done. That and "Sinner," which I'm going to keep publishing until somebody picks up the movie rights and I can retire. Oh, and my two-page underground strip for Flo Steinberg's *Big Apple* comics.

What did you do for Stan Drake?

For Stan Drake, nothing. For Leonard Starr, I helped him with writing the *On Stage* strip. I got involved in this through Al Williamson who's been like… well, he's largely responsible for getting me into comics. It was through Al that I wrote my first published comic book script.

For Harvey?

Yeah. And I did that while I was at art school. Al had seen some of the stuff I had done for class and thought I could write. And it's been one of the few flaws in Al's career for quite a while. He keeps thinking I can write.

Evidently he's thought it for about 17 years.

Yeah, well, I keep fooling everyone. [*Laughter.*] But never myself.

How did you and Al start working together?

A friend of mine in art school named Larry Ivie was also a big EC fan, and a big cartooning fan. He later published and edited a magazine called *Monsters and Heroes*, which I think predated *Castle of Frankenstein* and a lot of the fantasy/comic book-oriented magazines. Larry was a lot less shy about trying to get in touch with people than I was and somehow through a mutual friend got Williamson's home phone number and called him up and said, "I'm an EC fan, and admirer of yours, and I'd like to meet you." Al thought he was kidding. Back then very few people working in comics knew that there were fans; they were like a novelty then. So instead of hanging up the phone, he invited Larry out to see him. Eventually, Larry got around to bringing Al around to the apartment building where he and I and a lot of other guys who went to school at Visual Arts, were all living. And Larry is a fairly secretive guy, would never let anybody know what he was doing. I came home from school one day and he was sitting out front. And I said, "What are you doing, Larry?" And he said, "Well, I'm waiting for a friend of mine." "Oh, is it another comics fan?" And Larry said, "Well, I guess you could say that." "Oh, who is it? Is it somebody I know from school?" "No, he used to go to this school." "What's the guy's name?" "Oh, it's Al." "Well, if you feel like it, drop by, if you want to sit around and talk comics." So a little bit later he drops up with this guy and he says "Hello, Archie, this is Al." I figure this guy's a comics fan, let's kid around with him a little. I said, [*Sarcastically.*] "Oh, Williamson?" And he said, "Yes." And I went, "Oublublub." And that's how I met Al. And we've been sort of friendly ever since.

As a result of knowing us, Al got kind of interested in pushing Larry and me to do stuff. He was working for Harvey then and unhappy with his scripts. I guess they weren't paying much for scripts then. But they offered to let Al come up with his own scripts, so Al suggested we try writing some. And the story "Hermit" that I wrote eventually was, I think, drawn by Reed Crandall and Williamson inked it. That was my first published story.

Was this before of after you went to work for *Redbook*?

Oh, this was before. And then, after I got out of school, when I quit for lack of funds, I was just desperate to get some kind of work. Through the school I heard that *Redbook* was looking for someone to do paste-up and mechanicals. I went up and got the job, which was just going to be a temporary job, but after working with them for a couple of months as a temporary, they decided to hire me. So I started out at *Redbook*, doing paste-ups and mechanicals, and worked up to doing layout and design for them. In the meantime, while I was working at *Redbook*, I was still friendly with Al and he began working with John Prentice on *Rip Kirby*. John shared a studio with Leonard Starr. Leonard happened to mention one day that he would like to get someone to help him with the writing on the strip. And Al said, "Hey, I have a friend who writes."

And Al showed him some stuff I had written and Leonard said, "This will do." And so I started working for him on *On Stage*.

How long did that last?

That lasted, oh, I guess I worked with him for a couple of years, until I was drafted for the Army. And, chiefly, very little writing that I did [for] *On Stage* ever made it into print. Leonard sort of used me to sort of take care of in-between steps that ordinarily would take him time to do.

Sort of a safety net?

No, more or less I think, he let me make the mistakes [*Laughter.*] and I became a lot of Leonard's rough drafts. We would get together and he would have some idea of what character he wanted to do, and maybe a vague idea for a story. We'd talk it around a little bit. I'd do a synopsis and kind of turn our initial plot discussion into a written story. He would take that, tear it completely apart. I would then take whatever we had reconstructed, and do a weekly breakdown, take it back to him. He would rip that apart, and then I would take back whatever remained, and write the actual continuity with dialogue and all. And then he would take that and usually totally rewrite it. And each time, totally improving it. It was really like on-the-job training for me. I learned a lot about writing. Not enough to ever write as well, or at least to write continuity strips as well as Leonard, but certainly it helped me.

Do you think Starr's a good writer?

Oh, I think Starr and probably Milton Caniff are the two best writers of dramatic continuity newspaper strips.

What did you do after the Army?

I went back to working at *Redbook*. I worked for them a couple of years before I went into the Army, and for a couple of years after I got out. While I was working at *Redbook* the last time, Warren started up *Creepy*. The guy who was going to edit the book talked to Al and through him to a lot of the other people who worked for EC about doing the books for him. And, again, Al recommended me and Larry Ivie to do writing for the books. And we were fast and we were cheap. So they used us.

You wrote a lot of those early *Creepy*s.

I wrote a lot of material, yes. I guess the artists seemed to like the scripts I was doing and having read ECs and a lot of '50s horror comics, it was a nice break after I'd come home from *Redbook*. It was sort of a lark, knocking off a Warren script at night. And that's how I sort of drifted into it.

Did it come pretty easy to you?

Oh, very easy. The first year of doing it, it was incredibly easy. It hasn't been that easy since and it gets harder every year. But back then, I wasn't really approaching it as any kind of self-conscious writing. I was just generally amusing myself. "Hey, this is almost like writing real comics." And I had no sense again, of fans, or anyone reading the stuff, or anything. But later on, when it became a full-time job, then I began taking it a little more seriously. I met more people in the business, became aware of my peers. Once you are conscious of peer pressure and pleasing people that you like, and things like that, that starts making it tough.

You took over as editor…

With the fourth issue of *Creepy*.

And even then you were still writing most of the material. I was wondering why you were still writing it. Was there that great a shortage of writers?

Well, back then, yeah. I think Warren was paying $5 a page for scripts. The better writers in the field were probably getting twice that. And then, I don't think there was anybody around who was into doing that kind of material. Comics were just starting to creep out of about a 10-year dark ages, the Wertham era of the '50s. A lot of comics went down the tubes and they never really got back any kind of commercial inroads to sales until the superhero stuff began to take off, which was just about that time. The Marvels were really starting to get hot…

Around '65, '66.

Yeah. But until then, nobody new had come into the comics field. So I think probably the first fan to become a comics professional was probably Nelson Bridwell. And then shortly after Nelson, I was getting into it through Warren. And Jim Shooter was probably starting to do stuff for DC. And then in the next six months or a year, Roy Thomas had stuff. *Vulcan* for Charlton.

When you were working for Warren you got to work with some of the best artists in the business, like most of the old EC gang. Who are some of your favorite artists, and why?

I never particularly play favorites that way. With the people working at Warren, I think I liked them all in one way or another. Al is a friend of mine and certainly one artist that I would stop doing everything else for a chance to work with. But I like working with Gray Morrow, Angelo Torres, and Reed Crandall, because they all could do different types of stories. And I would more or less try to do like I had heard they did at EC, where they try to tailor the scripts to each artist. I think one of the things that pleased me most was getting Alex Toth to do stuff. Calling him up and finding that he was interested. Because I always liked his work a lot, from my days as a fan.

He always did his best work for Warren, I thought.

Well, he did some really good things, yeah. The "Monument" story that he did was very good. I always felt that sometimes my stories were not quite up to what Alex did. I could never find a horror story that worked as well as a story as his artwork would work out on the stuff.

Did you write "Overworked" with Wally in mind?

Yeah. Again, Al introduced me to Wally Wood. And what I would do with any artist was to ask them if there was any story that they'd like to do, either some kind of character, or some kind of setting, a type of story. And he mentioned that he always liked that story "My World" that he did in the EC science-fiction books. It was tailored around "My name is Wood and I'm a science-fiction artist." So he said, "Maybe we could do something that would give me a chance to draw everything." So I sat down and tried to come up with something that would give him a chance to draw all kinds of different stuff. So yeah, that was tailored with him in mind. In fact, that one… Usually at Warren, I was doing everything full script. That was the first job I ever did in what they call Marvel Style. Because what I did was just do thumbnail breakdowns of how I thought the story would be, and then I showed that to Woody and kind of explained to him what was going on, and he said "This is great, don't give me anything else." And he took my thumbnails and just didn't follow them at all in terms of layouts or anything, but it gave him enough of an idea as to what was happening in the story that he penciled it and I took it and dialogued it and had it lettered. Then Woody and Dan Adkins, who was working with him at the time, did the finishes.

I guess that story is sort of ironic considering what happened to Wood.

Uh… It is and it isn't. In retrospect, any time anyone dies, you can go back and say, "Oh, this is ironic. Gee, only four and a half months before he died, he had this dream about coffins or something." But no, that could be anybody in comics.

Do you think most of the pros work pretty hard?

Yeah. I think that was always the thing with comics. Both the curse and attraction of comics is that you generally love doing them, are obsessed about doing them to one extent or another. You lose yourself in the work. Sometimes to the detriment of your personal life. But I think most people doing comics are obsessive about it. There are exceptions. There are some people that can apparently come in at 9 o'clock, draw three pages, and go home at 5 o'clock or whatever. But I think most people really tend toward obsession, putting themselves and their fantasies into the material.

Are you that way?

Yeah. I definitely tend to get wrapped up in the stuff that I'm writing. I like to think that I also stay somewhat professionally removed from it. But if I didn't really enjoy it and could kind of escape into doing it, I probably would have stopped doing it a long time ago.

So you still enjoy it. It's not just your job?

Yeah, I enjoy it. What happens now is that I enjoy it before I start doing it and then as I start doing it I go "Oh, this is work. I'd forgotten. That's right. This is hard to do." So I always fool myself a little bit. Like you go through a spell where you are talking about what you are doing next and getting enthused about it and all, but there comes the moment when you sit down to do it and you start to remember "Oh, yeah, this is work. I'm going to have all this fun, but first I've got to write this first caption." And then you start sweating it. Or at least I do.

[*Kim Thompson*] Going back to *Creepy*. That was pretty much the first comic book to go outside the Code. Did that cause any problems, with retailers, censors... ?

I don't know. They might have caused Warren problems in that it may have been a little harder for him in the beginning to get decent distribution, but in the beginning he was distributed by Kable, I think, which was hard to get decent distribution from anyway. They were a small distributor. It's hard to tell. The only thing I can remember is that in a few of the fanzines there was a kind of reaction against them. This fear that these guys were going to fool around with our comics and bring about a new era of repression and ruin the good comics we already have. There was a little bit of that, but not very much. And really, you go back and look at those things, they are pretty mild.

[*Thompson*] Compared to *1994*.

They are very mild compared to that. I think even compared to stuff done under the Code now. You could probably take most of the early ones, put color on them and run them with out much problem. If you think about it, you tan probably cite a couple of examples to prove me totally wrong, and embarrass and make a fool of me. But you won't do that because you are too nice a guy, Kim.

[*Thompson*] Of course.

And I can make a fool of myself without anyone's help.

Whose idea was *Blazing Combat*?

Let's see. Russ Jones was the editor who did *Creepy*. I don't know if it was his idea or Warren's idea to do *Blazing Combat*. When they first came to me about working for it, it was before Russ departed. My feeling is that probably between the two of them, they were talking about doing more titles and they thought if there seemed to be some interest in the EC horror-type material, why not also try something like the EC war stuff. They first came to me just about writing the material, and then Russ departed and I took over just before the book came but.

Your approach was as pretty eclectic like Kurtzman's in terms of depicting all the time periods.

Well, obviously I'm very influenced by Kurtzman's war comics. I think they were probably my favorites of the EC material. It was the only way I could think of to do a war book. What Kurtzman had done was so heavily set in my mind, that it probably wouldn't have occurred to me to do them any other way. I didn't care much for the DC war comics coming out at the time. That was back in the period when they could barely let anyone fire a rifle in a war comic. Sgt. Rock and his squad would bump into a squad of Germans and they would have fistfights. [*Laughter.*] Which didn't seem like the right way to do war stuff. Plus I found that I like doing all different kinds of stories. I liked going out and digging up research on a story. I would usually read one or two books on a historical period and try to see if something would come out of the actual period that would suggest a story and then build a story around it.

Blazing Combat was odd in that it was basically an anti-war comic at a time when that seems to have been an unpopular political stance.

I think that's like getting credit where it isn't necessarily due. I didn't sit down to do a hard-hitting anti-war book. Just mostly from the influence of Kurtzman's stuff. And probably from the influence of seeing movies like *Paths of Glory* by Kubrick that had come out before then. I had read *Naked and the Dead, From Here to Eternity.* Fiction about war. And it seemed that logically it would be hard to do a pro-war book, that anybody sensibly would be doing anything pro-war. I think if you go back and reread the *Blazing Combat* stories, you'd find some stories that—if definitely not pro-war—they are certainly not anti-war either.

But the overall tone…

Yeah, the overall tone. Knowing what Kurtzman had done, what could I do to make it any different? Anytime I tried to sit down and tried to think up a plot for a war story, it would seem that Kurtzman had covered the ground one way or another. There doesn't seem to be an infinite variety of war stories that you can actually do. It seemed that the only logical thing you could do was make them a little stronger in the anti-war tone. And I think there was a certain amount of making war a little more hell, than he was able to do at the time.

You were also working outside of the Comics Code…

Sure, which also helped. And this was, what, 10 or 15 years later. So that helps too. When Kurtzman was doing it, he had stories set in the Korean War, which was certainly not as popular as World War II, but was certainly nowhere near as unpopular as the Vietnam war proved to be. So there was that difference in tone too. Had Kurtzman started immediately doing stories like we were doing in *Blazing Combat,* in the '50s, he would have been branded a Communist, and hunted down and dragged before the HUAC. So I think just the passage of time made a difference.

I was also conscious of the fact that as Kurtzman did more stories, they became more technically oriented. And the human element began to disappear. The characters almost ceased to exist as characters. They became more like illustration points for whatever technical thing he was doing. The earlier stories had a little more human interest for me. And I think I wanted to keep that a little more in my stories, although I could find the same thing happening. I only did four issues of *Blazing Combat,* and I think they had seven or eight stories each. Whereas

Kurtzman only had four stories in each issue. But by the time I was doing the fourth issue, it seemed that to me I was straining to find new stuff. And what I was finding was that you become more and more enamored with the research material, stuff about the weaponry, the planes. I find it to this day tremendously fascinating. I love going to a hobby store and looking at the books they have on different aircraft and war machines. I find it tremendously seductive. I have no interest in having my own army or waging any battles, [*Laughter.*] but I find the equipment and the idea of it all fascinating. And I think it's easy to get caught up in that. I didn't have a chance to. With the Vietnam stuff, since things were just heating up in Vietnam when we were starting *Blazing Combat.* It seemed okay that we should do Vietnam stories. It was very hard to find out anything about Vietnam. There was not a great deal being reported about it. Just a few newspaper articles, a column or a page or two in *Time* or *Newsweek,* and it was only like a year or two after we stopped doing the book that it became easy to get Vietnam reference material. Some things are accidental. The story that according to Warren got us knocked out of army PXs was, I forget the title of the story, but it was a story that Joe Orlando did…

The one about the old peasant…?

"Landscape." And actually, the thing that upset the Army was that it looked like on the last page that the South Vietnamese troops, our guys, shot the old man. And I think the way I originally did the story was to have him shot from the rice paddies. He was standing up arguing in the middle of this fight and a shot from the rice paddies from where the other side was, got him. And the way Orlando drew the panel, he did it close in on the peasant so you see the shot hitting him in the back from somewhere. You don't know where. Whoever looked at it that was judging books for the PXs thought that it was the "good guys" who had shot him. And was offended. I don't know if that's actually true but at least that's what Warren said caused the books to be knocked out of PXs.

Where would you have taken the book if it had a longer run?

I don't know, because as more material about Vietnam began coming out, I definitely would have taken a more anti-Vietnam stance. So I probably would have stepped up the number of Vietnam stories, and probably have gotten into trouble sooner or later down the line because of that.

How political are you?

Not very. Kind of a fallen away, knee-jerk liberal. [*Laughter.*]

Is it important for you to make a statement with your work, or are you just content to entertain people?

It's not important to me to make a statement. If the occasion to make a statement arises, I think it's nice to. It's nice wherever you can to – if not make a statement – at least supply some information that people reading comics might not ordinarily get. Maybe show them how to do something… that *could* be misinterpreted. [*Laughter.*] I was thinking in terms of a guy named Rick Leonardi who sent me a sample script. He's now drawing for Marvel, but earlier he sent a sample script and artwork. And one of the things I liked about it was that he had a sequence on mountain climbing that really took an almost Kurtzmanesque war comics approach to mountain climbing, showing people struggling against the elements, clearly showing the technical aspects of mountain climbing and making it exciting and interesting. It's one thing I think comics should do and don't always do as well as they could. One of the great things I think that Kurtzman was able to do is to show you how things work and are done and make it come alive for you. Any interest I had in history came from reading his comics. It never came from any history class I ever had in high school, which always seemed tremendously dull. But the EC historical comics actually sparked my curiosity about reading more about the Revolutionary War, the Civil War, things like that. And it's something I would like to see comics do more of.

[*Thompson*] This is going to sound awfully self-serving coming from me, but have you seen *Los Tejanos*?

Yeah, I think Jackson has definitely picked up on what Kurtzman started doing. And I think that the nice thing that Jackson does is to humanize the historical characters so that somebody now can relate to them. Some of it throws me a little bit, like when he had the Sioux in *Comanche Moon* speaking street slang and all. But it has a logic to it, and I imagine it probably worked for a lot of people. And I think that's good, I'd really like to see more of that.

Have you ever written any prose?

Who's to say for sure? [*Laughter.*] Yeah, I wrote a novelette for the first *Weird Heroes* for Byron Preiss and I had a short story published in *Ellery Queen's Mystery Magazine* eons ago.

Under your own name?

Yeah.

[*Thompson*] To the consternation of everybody I guess.

When they wrote me that they were going to buy it, they said, "Can you verify if this is your real name or a pseudonym? If it is, we think you've chosen a bad one." [*Laughter.*]

Well how does Nero feel about your moonlighting?

I don't know. I've often wondered how he felt about my mother. [*Laughter.*]

Do you have any plans for a novel in the future?

You probably can't be a writer without at some time sitting down and saying,

"Gee, I better work on a novel." I suspect that if I haven't done it by now, I may not be likely to. But, yeah, in the back of my head, it would be nice to sit down and write a novel. Of course, it's not that simple. To even write 500 pages of gibberish is not as easy as it might sound. Not without speed.

Are you talking about the chemical?

Yeah. [*Laughter.*]

Why did you write *Savage* and *Blackmark* under pseudonyms?

I wrote *Savage* under a pseudonym because at the time I guess I was writing *Iron Man* for Marvel...

... and you were contractually obligated ... ?

No, I wasn't contractually obligated. I just felt that *Savage* was going to be violent atypical comic-book material. It seemed professionally bad to put myself in a situation where if someone picked up *Savage* or somebody's girl picked up *Savage,* and they or their parents were offended by it, to have them saying, "Oh, this is by Archie Goodwin." I didn't want them throwing any onus on Marvel. "If you're supposed to be such a decent comics company, why do you hire this sick, violent, depraved guy?"

Did you like doing *Savage*?

I enjoyed getting together with Gil when we were plotting it out, doing page breakdowns, going over all that stuff. That was fun. The actual writing of the stuff... by then everything was under the gun. We were all under pressure to get the thing done by then. The leisurely part was all over with. The fun part of the breakdowns, finding new ways to split teeth and splatter brains; that was all done. And just sitting down and writing it I found hard. And unfortunately, there wasn't time to go back and rewrite, or to let it sit and edit out every three adjectives and four adverbs, which I think the book really needed. And on *Savage* I felt, at least with the written material, no one functioned as editor on it. Gil and I talked about doing what Feldstein did with the EC stuff, but I wrote it, thinking "Well, if it's too much, he'll tell me and I'll cut back." He never told me, because he never had time. When I would deliver it, it was like going into some emergency center or a camp under siege. Gil, Roger Brand, Michele Brand, Frank Giacoia, and Gil's partner Larry Koster were all holed up in Gil's apartment on E. 63rd, grinding day and night to get the material done. And the only good thing about it was that I could walk out. I could deliver my pages, someone would start typing it on the typesetting machine, and I would run out free to go to my own apartment. But the rest of them were sort of trapped there, trapped with those pages and having to get them done.

What were the differences between working with Gil and working with Williamson?

The two projects [*Blackmark* and *Savage*] were Gil's projects. I was brought in usually at the 11th hour. What would happen is that Gil and I would talk about working together. We would talk and talk and talk about working together and we never would quite get around to doing it. And then Gil would get into a situation where he was ready to begin a project, I would find myself in other situations so I couldn't work on the project. He would begin getting other people to do stuff. It wouldn't work out totally to his satisfaction. He would ask me "Gee, can you come in on this thing." And on both *Savage* and *Blackmark*, I came in on them after they were started.

On *Savage*, the initial storyline was set up and on *Blackmark*, I think someone like John Jakes had actually done a synopsis and several chapters of writing for Gil. Then Gil and I would get involved in the breaking down and laying out of the stuff and reshaping it. But we would always be reshaping as we would go along, because by then the deadline was on us. We've never been able to get together on a really "ground-up" collaboration, and do it leisurely. Our problem is that unless there is really a deadline hanging over our heads, our pace would be *so* leisurely that it wouldn't get done. And that once there was a deadline, there would usually be enough pressure that one or the other of us wouldn't be able to involve himself. Anyway, that's the circumstances under which *Savage* was done. On *Blackmark*, again, I got called in to work on it later on. With *Blackmark*, I didn't do it under a pseudonym, I just didn't get credit for doing it. Gil felt that he would have problems with Bantam because it had been sold as having been done by Gil Kane…

So he just gave you a piece of it?

He paid me a flat rate on it.

How does your approach differ from what you perceive as a money job and one that you really want to do?

As I said, talking about it with Gil and I, if it's a non-money project, I think you spend a lot more time talking around it, and leisurely approaching it. Basically, I don't know too many projects that I consider just money jobs. I want to be paid the best rate on anything I involve myself with, but I try to give the same level of involvement on everything. If I don't feel that way, I'd rather not do it. I suppose that if you are doing a regular monthly book for two years, your level of involvement on some individual story might not be as great as on one of the other stories in the same series of comics. But I think I get just as involved. I think it's just as exciting when I'm working with an artist that I can work closely with, like Williamson or Alex Toth, or Walt Simonson.

[*Thompson*] You were involved with the short-lived Atlas Comics Group, right?

I did *The Destructor* and I did *Sgt. Striker's Death Squad*. [*Laughter.*] And I was also the Editor-in-Chief at Marvel under whose aegis The Human Fly, Godzilla,

Devil Dinosaur, and all those good folk came to be. [*Laughter.*] I don't know if there's really a lot to tell. I did them, I don't think I did them fast enough for their schedule, so they became a little disenchanted with me. The best thing about Seaboard was that Simonson and I did a story for one of their black-and-white books called *Thrilling Adventures,* "Temple of the Spider," which was a very well drawn Simonson story and not a bad story by me.

That I remember fondly.

In fact, that issue of *Thrilling Adventures* is actually a pretty prime issue. It has Russ Heath, Alex Toth, John Severin. It was like whatever good black-and-white stories they had done all wound up in that same issue.

That magazine only lasted two issues.

Right.

[*Thompson*] You were Editor-in-Chief at Marvel for how long?

About 18 months.

[*Thompson*] You were the last editor before Shooter.

Right.

Was that a strain?

Yeah, I don't think I was psychologically or temperamentally suited to be Editor-in-Chief at Marvel, at least not Marvel as it existed then. I think Marvel at that time had gotten just big enough that you couldn't comfortably handle it with one editor. Marvel had expanded enough and there was a big enough workload that having one editor responsible for everything was no longer a viable system. And one of the best things I think that Shooter's done is to come in and totally reorganize. And because of that he's been able to get much more done for Marvel.

[*Thompson*] The last couple of editors didn't last too long.

Gerry Conway lasted about three weeks. Marv Wolfman for a year or two. Len Wein for a year or two. I think for a while they were talking about Roy coming back, but then Roy changed his mind. So it was really a hassle. And what was needed was a total reorganization. I could never get far enough away from the problems to even be capable of that kind of reorganization.

Do you find it easier to work with someone whose style you really like?

Oh, yeah, always. I assume if we were all bricklaying, it would be easier with someone whose gouting and groveling I was in sympathy with. [*Laughter.*] Rather than someone who wanted them to go vertically while I wanted them staggered.

How do you cope with what I assume must be a heavy workload – *Epic*, working with Al on the *Star Wars* strip...

Very badly. I cope with it very badly. I'm a little disorganized, and I'm probably a little bit later than I should be on some of the stuff. And that's generally kind of the way I cope with it. I keep plugging at it until I get it done.

Well, what's your work schedule like?

I try to save writing the strip for weekends. In a good time, I should be able to sit down and write a week's worth of continuities for the strip in... say, three to five hours. If for some reason I'm having problems with it, which sometimes happens, I'll start seeing little plot complications that when I thought of the story hadn't occurred to me. "Oh, yeah, he should have explained that more." Or I may get stuck on something—a tricky escape or exact character revealing bit—in which case if I won't get it done over the weekend, I'll get up early in the morning and work on it. Same way if I'm doing some kind of comics project, I'll get up early and start on the stuff and then come in from nine to five and do the *Epic* stuff.

What are you involved in besides *Epic*?

Well, Williamson and I and Carlos Garzon are gearing up to start the adaptation of *Revenge of the Jedi* [later renamed *Return of the Jedi*], which will be a *Marvel Super Special,* and then a series of four comics.

Will it be in the same format as the *Empire Strikes Back* book?

I don't think there will be a Treasury Edition or paperback. That's all stuff that will happen down the line if it happens at all, but it will be in the *Super Special* format. And the four comics.

Can you describe how you work with Al, how you break down the work on the newspaper strip?

With Al I'm doing essentially full script. Since we've worked together for a long time, I don't do a lot of thumbnails or anything like that, and I don't do a lot of panel descriptions. He knows the characters and is pretty good at coming up with backgrounds so I don't have to worry about that. Or giving him really intricate descriptions. If it's on a new planet, I'll offer some suggestions as to what the planet should look like. Stuff like that. But it's actually pretty much straight script.

How about on the movie adaptations?

For the adaptations, my experience has been that I go out to the movie studio, pick out the reference stuff. We've been getting anywhere from 1000-1200 movie stills. I'll go through the script a couple of times, trying to figure out how much space I've got to work with, making notes on where I think breaks will fall in the script. And how much script I think will fit into how many pages of comics. I try to get that all worked out if not on paper, at least in my head. Then, I go through and try to put the stills in chronological order, breaking them down section by section. Then, I start writing the script, which if I'm working with Al, I'll do thumbnails [*holds up hands*], a little page like this and break it down into panels and do very rough little drawings. And I actually write in the dialogue then too, with little balloons. One of the bad ways I think I work is that I tend to write it in pencil and edit and change my copy as I go, which I think is probably a slow way of working, but it seems to work for me. So essentially what I wind up with is looking at the stills, and doing panels, and pull out several stills that I think might fit a particular panel or something. I try with Al to do pages that are five panels or less. And when Al gets the stuff, he'll look at the stills find some that he can use, some that maybe don't work as well, he may not use everything that I suggest but it gives him a starting point from which to go from. He may then decide that there's too much dialogue in one panel and break it into more panels. He may see a way of combining a panel that I didn't see. So we have that sort of give and take.

How much lead-time do you have?

On the *Star Wars* stuff, a pretty good lead-time, but it's always slower getting started on these things. We're just starting *Revenge* now [in September], the book I guess will have to be completed in March. So that's a fairly decent amount of time in which to do it. The problem with any movie like *Revenge,* or even *Blade Runner* or any of the others is usually that they are all movies that involve special effects, and the special effects are still being done on them.

Do you have any idea what they are going to look like?

We do on some of the stuff. But you never know on everything. You also don't know with any movie what they are going to change their minds about as they assemble rough cuts and have previews. At some point you wind up with a final version that you have to go with because of your printing deadlines. Inevitably it's never the exact version that winds up in the movie theaters, unless it's just an extremely well put together movie. Like with Lucasfilm, on *Empire,* they have the film pretty well doped out before they begin them and everything. Even then, they still had stuff in the script that I'm sure for purposes of screening time and such that they wound up leaving out.

Are they pretty good about getting you the stills, and script and such?

Very good. But with *Empire,* and I'm sure with *Revenge* there are also some things that they withhold till later on and it's something that you've got to be prepared for and ready to roll with when it does happen.

How much freedom does Lucasfilm give you on the *Star Wars* script?

I think a good deal of freedom. I try to check out the storyline with them in advance and let them know vaguely what we are going to be doing. But they don't really sit over each thing. I send them a copy of my script when I'm done with it. But they've been really good about it.

Do you have any idea what Lucas thinks of your stuff? Do you ever hear from him?

On *Empire,* when we finished that, I got a letter from him just saying that he liked it and thought it was a nice job, and I think once that Al may have gotten a phone call from him. On the *Blade Runner* thing, Ridley Scott phoned Al, to thank him for the job he did on *Blade Runner.* But just that one letter is all I've gotten from Lucas. What kind of amazes me is that he even has time to see this stuff.

How satisfied were you with the way the *Blade Runner* book turned out?

It would have been nice if Al and Carlos had been able to finish everything themselves, but that I think was a good deal my fault. If I had had the complete script to them all at once, maybe they could have gotten more done, or been able to get more done themselves. In general I was pretty well satisfied with it, considering that I'm never satisfied with anything by the time it's actually printed. Nothing appalls me more than the latest issue of *Epic* when I get it back from the printer. And I go through and see all the stuff we didn't catch. Every flaw reaches out and grabs you by the throat and says "Aha! I'm a flaw! I'm a flaw! And you let me get through!" You never see it until after it gets printed. And I feel the same way about the *Blade Runner* book, there's always something I wish I could have done, or had known about.

Did you like the movie?

I liked it but I found quibbles along the way with it. I thought, and I know what they probably had to go through with this stuff, trying to tack on a happy ending in the narration, bothered me. A lot of the narration bothered me.

[*Thompson*] When you were writing the script, did you take anything from Philip K. Dick's original novel?

No.

Had you read it?

No. I still haven't read it. I'd like to now but I really didn't want to at the time. We were doing the adaptation of the *movie.* It's their decision as to how much of the book they are going to be using and all. Our decision has to be to represent the movie version as well as we can.

What do you read for pleasure?

Probably more than anything, I read detective fiction. But I read eclectically. I'm trying to think of what I've read recently… *Cujo* [by Stephen King], *The Glitter Dome* by Joseph Wambaugh. I just read one of the Robert Parker *Spencer* detective novels. Occasionally I'll read a biography or historical thing. I like to vary it a bit. But mostly I tend to read popular fiction.

[*Thompson*] Do you read any comic books for pleasure?

Not a whole lot. Back when I started working for DC as an editor, I had always read every Marvel that came out. And maybe about a third of the DC books. And I felt that if I was going to work at DC, I better read all their books. And I tried reading all the Marvels and DCs for a couple of months, and I think right about that time, they both doubled their output too. And I think I OD'd on comics back then, and I've never gone back to regularly reading comics. I'll go through the bundles we get now, and if an issue looks interesting to me, or if a new team is starting it, I'll usually pick it up and read it. The *Daredevil* book I enjoy very much, and I read that regularly.

Is there anybody else in the American comics whose work you really like?

Yeah, I read every issue of *Cerebus the Aardvark*. But the rest of it I spot read or if something unusual comes out... the *X-Men/Teen Titans* book I looked forward to. But I don't read a lot of the titles on a month-to-month basis.

[*Thompson*] Do you follow any of the undergrounds?

Undergrounds I don't see that often. Sometimes at a convention, I'll pick up something. I'm trying to think what the last underground I got was. It's been quite a while. The *Omaha* book. And I don't know if you'd call *Bop* an underground or not.

[*Thompson*] It's been axed. It was pretty much a bomb.

That's too bad. It was a good idea, but probably like everything else, everybody has their own idea about how a book about music and musicians should have been done.

What about the Europeans?

Just what I see in *Heavy Metal* and leaf through at Forbidden Planet [one of the biggest New York comics shops], there aren't a lot that I follow regularly. Again, I try to keep up with what's coming out, but I don't read or speak any foreign languages, so it's kind of hard, but I try to keep an eye out on the material. Anyone I'd name would probably be fairly obvious. Most of the people in *Heavy Metal* I like. I have *Tintin* books at home. I have some of the Asterix books. Albums by Victor de la Fuente and Giraud. Jo [Duffy] buys a lot of the Japanese material and I like looking at that.

Are there any artists that you feel are really important to the medium now?

[Jean] Giraud I guess is pretty important now because of the influence his work is having both in Europe and the United States. I think we've kind of gone through

Writer: Archie Goodwin Artist: Walt Simonson Manhunter in "Cathedral Perilous" from
Detective Comics #441 June-July 1974 [©1974 DC Comics Inc.]

phases where in American comics you had Ditko-, Kirby-inspired artists, you had Neal Adams-inspired artists. You are beginning to get Frank Miller-inspired artists. I think for the late '70s and '80s a lot of the artwork is going to be Giraud-inspired artwork. He's such an incredible draftsman. And what I find interesting about his work is that he's worked out particularly with the stuff he's done as Moebius a rendering style that almost makes it look to anyone like, "Gee, of course. If you do it that way, you can draw." It looks like had you but known, you could sit down and draw that way, too. Of course you can't because he's tremendously good. It's so good that it almost looks like he's revealed it all to you right there. And you need but to imitate that contour line drawing and rendering style that he has and then it would all be there, all very easy.

What do you see as the most crucial flaw in the American approach to comics?
Is there one? [*Laughter.*]

To put it another way, what are you dissatisfied with? What would you like to change?
I don't know. I'm a nuts-and-bolts person. Present me with a problem…

Well, you said you would like to see more emphasis on character, the little guy instead of all the glitz and hardware.
Yeah, but comics do that. There are comics doing that. Miller would do it very well in *Daredevil*. He would, as Eisner did, have his main characters and all, but bring in other characters, drag in everyday people, and let them be affected or unaffected by what's going on in the story. I tried to do it to a certain extent in the "Manhunter" stuff. One of the things I enjoyed doing was a chapter we did called "Cathedral Perilous," which took place in a mosque in Istanbul. One of the things that was the most fun for me was writing the introductory paragraph, which in effect gave a history of the Cathedral. I had read several things on the history of Constantinople and Istanbul and was able to incorporate some real history along with this kind of pseudo-history that I imposed on it. And there are always opportunities to do things like that.

What do you think about superheroes?
Being an EC fan I've never been 100 percent comfortable with superheroes…

You've certainly written your share.

At the time, that's what you had to write to be a comics writer, and I very much liked what Marvel was doing with the characters. At the time I was writing *Iron Man,* it seemed to me that Stan and Roy could write them so much better. Roy especially was really very innovative at taking what Stan had done and going one step further, like when he did the Kree-Skrull War, and when he was working with Neal on the *X-Men* material and a little later with Buscema on the *Avengers* stuff. And some issues of *Daredevil* with Barry Smith, to say nothing of their *Conan.* The influence of everyday life on a superhero, Roy was able to heighten it and do more with it.

But I never felt quite as comfortable with superheroes. Manhunter was probably the best superhero character that I worked on, because he was a lot less a superhero, he was more normal. It was like he was really a spy, or a detective or a soldier of fortune in a funny costume, which I was more comfortable with.

How closely did you and Walt Simonson work on *Manhunter*?

Very closely. I had some ideas about what we were going to do. Walt and I would sit down and discuss the stuff very closely. I gave up writing synopses or anything after the first couple. I would suggest sequences to him and he would take the stuff and run with it from there. But it was an exceedingly close collaboration.

Were you surprised at the critical response?

No, I think when we were doing it, we knew it was good. I think we were a little disappointed in some of the response to it. Mostly reader response. It takes comics readers quite a while to discover something. You need about a year for them to really begin to start finding stuff. And *Manhunter* was only eight pages in 100 pages of essentially reprint material. I'm sure most people didn't even notice it if they were interested at all in picking up the stuff. For fans and even comics critics, of which there weren't a great deal back then, to even get them to notice something, you have to do a regular monthly book, and do it for a good year or so.

[*Thompson*] That was a strange year at *Detective* you had there. How did that come about?

I guess I was a strange editor at *Detective* for a year. [*Laughter.*]

[*Thompson*] It was a very striking change from what had gone before. You hauled in a bunch of strange new artists and strange old artists and gave it a different look, different kinds of stories.

When Carmine [Infantino] asked me about being editor at *Detective,* he said the book wasn't really going anywhere. It hadn't been doing well in sales, and he wanted to do something a little different with it. On the other hand, I felt that the handling of Batman had pretty well been set by the Neal Adams/Denny O'Neil stories, and a lot of the Frank Robbins-written Batman stories. They set the tone for Batman. Jim Aparo was supposed to be the regular Batman artist, and what I found was that Jim is one of the precision artists. He does a page a day, he pencils, inks and letters a page a day. He only commits himself to enough work so that he always has that page to do. But he also doesn't like to be caught without pages to do. What I found was after working on a couple of stories was that I could never get my writing schedule to match his drawing schedule. He would, by the time I had the script done, be moving on to the Spectre or the *Brave and the Bold,* or else he might have time for the *Detective* stuff and I wouldn't have the script ready. So I began first just trying to get a couple of fill-ins done, and then gradually realizing that I was never going to coordinate with him well, and seeking other people to do this stuff. And I think I was consciously looking around for another regular artist and part of the experimenting was that I hadn't found the regular artist yet.

[*Thompson*] There were at least one, maybe two Sal Amendola stories.

Two Sal Amendola stories, one of them Sal had already penciled and just brought to me, and it was such a nice story that I couldn't turn it down.

[*Thompson*] Was that the one that Adams plotted?

Yeah. I think Sal and his brother actually plotted that story and I think what Neal came up with was the idea of Batman popping up out of the water, and Sal and his brother had come up with a story around an image like that. Sal was sharing a place with Steve Englehart at the time, so they got Steve to write it. And then I tried Sal on another one. And at the time, I think Sal, had he been able to work with an inker like Giordano consistently probably would have been a good replacement. But I don't think he was quite ready to do his own inks on full comics stories, at least not under our tight deadlines, and Dick was available to help out on a couple of stories but not able to guarantee full time. So I was casting around. I used Howard Chaykin, Alex Toth…

[*Thompson*] That was a strange one. What was the reaction to that?

The Toth story? Most regular Batman fans didn't like it. It seems to me that the average comics fan will complain about Alex's stuff because it looks simple to them. They say, "Oh, it's too cartoony."

And yet, the very same people rave about Frank Miller.

Well, Frank's stuff is very stylized…

As Toth's is…

Sure, but Alex's approach to a face or figure, I think, gets a lot more geometric and maybe a lot more basic than the Miller stuff. But then, Alex wasn't writing his own material either. Probably if Alex were dealing with content as emotional as say, a lot of the *Daredevil* stuff got, then that might make the difference. But where he was just filling in on one story, and I tried to keep the stories with at least one supernatural element and then to have some kind of mystery, and all in 12 pages. So the stories tended to be fairly mechanical. Without a lot of characterization. Intellectually they might have been interesting to read or fun to read, but they weren't real emotional grabbers or anything.

Do you like Batman?

Yeah, very much. From my point of view, he's interesting because he doesn't have superpowers. It seems like there's a lot to play around with. Although now I feel that it's ground that's been worked pretty heavily. I don't know how much I'd be interested in doing Batman now, but it was certainly fun to do a few Batman stories. It would have been nice at that time to be able to do them and to have a little more input on what was going on in terms of the continuity and things like that. The drawback to working at DC at that time was that I was doing Batman, Julie Schwartz was doing Batman, and Murray Boltinoff was doing Batman. So you had three similar Batmans, but not totally similar. And I tried, since I was doing the shortest of the Batman stories, I didn't feel it was my place to really pack up and run with Batman's characterization. In fact one of the most embarrassing things was that when I took over the book, Carmine sat me down and said "Now Julie and I have been talking and to get a little more interest in the Batman character we are going to try to make him a little more like the Scarlet Pimpernel where Bruce Wayne is this foppish character and Batman is sort of the dashing creature of the Night." And if that's what they wanted to do, I'd do it. And I was doing it and nobody else did it. [*Laughter.*] And I got all these strange letters saying, "Why are you doing this stupid thing with Bruce Wayne's character?"

[*Thompson*] **Like being invited to a come-as-you-are party and really showing up as you were.**

Right. Exactly.

[*Thompson*] **How many issues of *Detective* did you do?**

It was seven issues, just over a year. It was bimonthly and I think it was a seven-issue run.

[*Thompson*] **Why did it end so soon?**

Because I quit DC to go and work for Warren. I've always had a pretty limited attention span and if I had tended to work on any one thing for a couple of years, I'd begin to feel a little stale on it, and written out or edited out and want to move on to something else.

Do you feel that way about *Epic* yet?

No, not really. The thing I really like about *Epic* is that it isn't really one thing. It's constant variety. We may run one continuing thing for a long time, but we can also fill out the issue with a number of other things, and although it's got to be either fantasy or science fiction, that is such a broad loop that I don't really feel like it's doing the same material over and over again.

What do you perceive as *Epic*'s basic editorial thrust?

I try not to have too limited an approach on it. Basically I'd like it to be more story-oriented than a lot of the *Heavy Metal* material seems to be.

Do you think you are getting that from your artists?

Not always, but I think gradually as we go along, we are getting it more and more. When we first started out, we were trying to build up a backlog of material and working from a backlog that Rick Marschall had already built up. We were a little more limited in the material we could buy. But as we go along there's a little more chance to sit down with an artist or an artist and writer and talk a bit more about what they are going to do before they do it. However, since it's all creator-owned material there's a point at which you can give them input, but it's up to them to accept or reject the input. And then it's up to us to either accept or reject the project. If they seek help as the project is going along, we give it, or offer advice. But it's a little different than editing a regular book because you are dealing with creations that other people own.

Do you find that more stimulating?

Yeah, it is, because whereas there's a chance of getting something that might be less than successful, there's also a chance of getting something a little more out of the ordinary and off-the-wall than you might come up with if we just sat down and said "OK let's do a science-fiction comic," or "Okay, let's do a fantasy comic, what should we do?"

Is there anybody out there you would like to work with but haven't had a chance?

Yeah, there are reams of them.

Name some names.

Name some names… I'd love to work with Jack Kirby… OK, where are all these names. A lot of the European artists. De La Fuente, [Esteban] Maroto. Certainly guys like Giraud, [Enki] Bilal would be nice.

Have you approached them?

Not really, because the situation with *Epic* is that Marvel also buys the rights to represent the material overseas. We share overseas reprints with the creators. But we are looking to establish overseas editions of *Epic*. With most of the European artists, they've already had material printed overseas and what they are looking for is just an opening into the American market, not a worldwide situation. So that makes it a little more difficult.

[*Thompson*] Does that mean there's not much chance of seeing European material in *Epic*?

Not as much, but as we go along and do more issues as the publishing situation changes over there, I think you will gradually see more people, even if they can't do a full series. Eventually you may see short stories.

Well, John Bolton did *Marada*. But that's not a reprint of European material.

Well, John is a British artist and I guess a lot of people don't think of England as part of Europe, even though it is.

[*Thompson*] You did run some stuff by Mirko Ilic in early issues.

Yeah, who's Yugoslavian.

So you really have no plans of approaching people like Giraud…

If the opportunity comes up, we will. I have feelers out to some people in Italy and others in Europe. The odds are now that we may use European artists, but they might be more of the up-and-coming artists, rather than someone who's as well established as Giraud, who can probably write his own ticket and find someone to punch it.

[*Thompson*] How about Jacques Tardi? I understand he was up for a visit at Marvel a month or two ago.

That was kind of in and out. He went through *Epic* fairly quickly, and I didn't even get a chance to talk with him that long.

Are you after any up-and-coming American artists for work?

Oh, we are still twisting Miller's arm, Michael Golden's arm… boy, are we tired of twisting arms. John Byrne. There are a lot of people. It would be nice to get Corben to do a story for us. But I feel that we are going to be around for a long time. Eventually, we'll get together.

Do you think you have a pretty stable base of readers now?

Yeah, the sales on the magazine seem to keep going up. They are even starting to talk about making it monthly, but so far it's only talk, but I think that could happen if the sales hold up.

Are you dreading that since it will increase your workload?

Yeah. [*Laughter.*] I feel like to be a totally arrived, successful magazine, eventually it will have to be monthly. It is a very expensive magazine to do. And to go monthly would involve getting a much bigger staff.

It's just you and Jo [Duffy]…

And the Marvel Bullpen. And I think to do *Epic* monthly and the Epic comics, we'd probably need a little Bullpen all our own just to handle our stuff exclusively. But those are things that will have to be talked about and ironed out before we go monthly. But right now if sales keep going the way they are, it will certainly be justified.

Are you given total editorial freedom?

Within reasonable restrictions. I think because of our interest in having copies of the book in racks at the 7-Eleven stores and having them appear in direct sales shops, we hold back from being totally graphic in terms of sex.

Well in the issue with Marada, where she's raped by a demon...

Yeah, but that's done...

Well, they didn't show it, but the idea itself could be construed by some people as offensive.

Sure, but we don't have that many demon readers. [*Laughter.*] Anything can be construed by somebody as being offensive. But what generally seems to make most people nervous are full-frontal male nudity, real hardcore penetration shots...

Rather than seeing someone being decapitated or disemboweled?

Sure.

Arthur Suydam has entrails flying right off the page. Even though it is funny.

Well, I try to judge it in context. Even though sex makes people more uptight that gore does.

How do you feel about that attitude?

Well, I find that a little stupid. But it's something that someone who puts out a magazine has to make a decision on and deal with. I try not to compensate for the lack of sex by increasing the amount of gore. I think we've had stories that are gory, but you can go back and find stories that are not gory. And I never feel that we have to do gore to sell the books. Or sex to sell the books.

[*Thompson*] How about the language? Has that caused any problems?

No. Once in a while, we will get a letter from someone, who might complain a little about the language.

But it hasn't really affected sales?

No, the sales seem to be gradually going up.

Is there any resentment from the regular Marvel Bullpen because of the more adult material that you are allowed to do?

No; I don't think so. I think one of the nice things about doing it is that everybody is very supportive. They seem happy that Marvel is doing it and they like it when we run around throwing out new copies to the Bullpen area. And I think that everyone has a pretty clear idea in their mind about what they can do if they are doing a regular comic book, what they can do if they are doing a Graphic Novel or an Epic comic, or what they can do when they work for *Epic.* And the opportunities are there for all the different things. And I think generally that everyone is pretty happy with all the different things available. But most people, first coming into comics, what they really want to do are draw regular comics. And first coming in, it's probably a good thing to do. Getting used to the idea of doing a monthly comic book is a great forge for learning how to do comics better and for getting really good at doing comics. And when people are talking about comics, they don't mean *Epic,* and they don't mean a Graphic Novel, they mean a monthly pulp comic book, and it's still right now, the primary form of comics. And if everybody stopped publishing those things tomorrow, comic book shops would dry up for product, and dry up for customers. That's what the bulk of the interest is. It's nice that those form a base from which we've been able to expand and do things like *Epic.*

[*Thompson*] There's a train of thought that regards four-color pulp superhero comics as the only really true form of comics. Everything else is pretentious distortion of what comics really are. I've heard that both from professionals and our own critics.

I would think that people…Say you got an editor at the *New York Times Book Review* who was even interested in comics, I think they would find *Epic* a bastardization, and what they would be interested in would be the true comics form. But I see it as a magazine called *Epic Illustrated,* which should primarily be a comics format, but not necessarily entirely comics format. I like playing with the idea of what exactly an illustrated story is. Some of the things we've run…

Illustrated poems, text stories…

Or stories that work as poetry… visual poetry of one sort or another. It's nice to play around with that. I think the bread and butter, meat and potatoes of *Epic* have to be well-drawn, well-rendered and well-told stories, but there's room for other things.

[*Thompson*] Has any critical attention been lavished on Epic from what science-fiction fans call the "mundane" media? The non-specialized press?

Not that I know of. That's not totally true. I think when the first issue came out, in some of the Canadian papers and some of the smaller American papers, they did little articles on the first issue. Things like that. But generally, no. And I don't expect there to be.

[Thompson] **I've seen articles about *Raw* pop up here and there.**

Yeah, well, I think *Raw* gives the appearance of being very with-it, very current. It may not be directly associated with punk or new wave, but you can see correlations with *Raw*. I think *Raw* is good and it's nice that *Raw* is there. There are people who will bring me material, and I could run maybe three or four pages of it, but I really know the general run of our readers are not going to be interested. Whereas they might really be right for *Raw*.

Where do you see comics going in the future?

I think pretty much the direction they are now. There's going to be a lot of experimentation with formats, paper, printing processes, a lot more with direct sales as a market. I don't think any one knows the limits of that market yet. I don't even think they know how many comic-book stores the country can support. There are so many areas that don't even have comic-book stores that probably could have them. That's going to become more and more an influential part of the market. I think the next couple of years are going to be interesting. A lot of the new comic companies are forming because of the Direct Market, and the kind of response there has been in the Direct Market. It will be interesting to see which ones of those will hit, whether there's enough talent existing now to supply that many companies with good product. And to see if reader taste will broaden to take in more than a superhero or a fantasy character who is not too terribly removed from being a superhero. That still is such a main thrust in comics. It's both interesting, and I find a little depressing, that with the Marvel Graphic Novels, the main interest from the audience has always been that if it's about one of the established Marvel characters, there's a much bigger response than if there's a new, unheard-of product.

It seems like the Epic comics are going to be superhero-oriented.

Well, we've only got two in the works so far. But chiefly if not a superhero, at least a strongly fantasy-oriented character.

... a mythic figure?

Yeah, a mythic figure. And I think that's still a limitation. There's going to have to be some poking and prodding to see if we can expand that.

Do you really feel that's creatively inhibiting?

No, I think someone can always come up with a new and interesting way to do it. There has to be some reason why mythic figures are as popular as they are, and I think they say something to all of us. I'm not sure if they say the same thing to everybody. Yes, there is always going to be someone interested in doing it. But I would like to do a detective story, a cowboy story... a fireman story. [*Laughter.*]

More like the EC material, perhaps?

No. I don't have any desire to go back and write short stories with shock endings any more. It would be nice to do stories that are more like novels and focus, not necessarily on non-heroic people, or people who aren't heroic; but on people at least who are not superpowered. People who are working at regular jobs, or living at least regular lives. I don't think I have any great desire to do a Great American Novel in comics form. I think anything I'd be interested in writing would probably be adventure-oriented in some way, because I get off on that. I'm enough of a Walter Mitty, whereas in real life I cringe from winos and look the other way as the mugging is going on, it's nice to be able to write adventures and stuff like that about people who don't.

What are you going to do with Epic Comics?

Right now, we are looking and talking to a lot of people, but beyond *Dreadstar* and the *Coyote* book by Englehart and [Steve] Leialoha… I think over the coming year we might add two more titles. And by then we'll know how the others are doing and take it from there.

Are they all going to be direct sales?

Yes, as planned right now. They are both bimonthly, 32 pages, Baxter stock on sale at your local comics shop for a dollar and a half. Buy two, save one, read one. But I suppose it's possible that some of the stuff we wind up with might be a limited series, depending on what the actual project is. But I'm hoping as we go along we can experiment with some of the stuff different from what you're used to buying.

Experimenting with content or format?

More in terms of content. We may not. If something that was very traditional but done by people I have a great deal of confidence in and was something that I liked a lot, I wouldn't turn it down because it *isn't* experimental. But I think we'd like to look into some different areas. We'll see as time goes by. Right now, they are bimonthly and a lot will depend on the abilities and the work schedules of the people involved in doing them, what they feel they can commit themselves to.

Do you feel better working where creators retain their rights?

I think it's nice to be able to and I'm really excited about this because so far I'm working with people I like working with anyway. And it's certainly a more exciting time to be doing that than doing the regular books that everybody's gotten used to. The thing with me is that I don't think I'd be too happy doing a regular book for too long. And I wouldn't want to have to do what any good [Marvel] editor does, which is run six or eight titles, monthly. Because if my workload seems bad to me, that just seems incredible.

Of course, if I start counting pages, between *Epic Illustrated*, Epic Comics, and the graphic novels we've handled, it may *be* that much. Luckily, Jo Duffy is hardworking and dedicated. And so far she hasn't noticed that I shift piles of work from my desk to hers.

[*Thompson*] As you look back over your long and multifaceted career, which of the things that you have done are you the proudest of?

Blazing Combat, the "Manhunter" series, probably a lot of individual stories, and probably the same thing with different stories and issues of *Epic. Epic* I'm still a little too close to tell. I'm very happy about the numerous collaborations with Al Williamson. Everything I've done with Walt Simonson. I have a great deal of fondness for the *Hulk* books I did with Herb Trimpe and John Severin. That's a personal thing, but I like the way a lot of those turned out. I like the *Flash Gordon* books that Williamson did that I did some of the stories on for King Features. But basically, *Blazing Combat,* "Manhunter," and anything done with Williamson and Simonson. Anything done with Toth, particularly "Burma Sky" in an issue of *The Losers.* A couple of stories when Louise Jones was editor at *Creepy.* I did a science-fiction story there with Williamson that I like a lot, that I think a lot of people tended to overlook: "Homecoming." It was about a guy lost, traveling sideways in time. I liked that. I did a story with Wally Wood that Paul Kirchner helped pencil and John Severin inked called "Creeps" that I thought was a very good story and I liked a lot.

You've been very fortunate in that you've gotten to work with some of the best artists in the business.

And I feel awful when pressed and I'm unable to think of all these people I'd like to work with. But generally there are a lot of people I'd like to work with, but I can never dredge up all the names.

Are you going to be doing any more writing for *Epic* beyond the story with [Mike] Kaluta?

Probably, we've got this *Generation Zero* series that Pepe Moreno is doing, that I will probably dialogue. Barry Windsor-Smith is doing a story for us that I'll probably wind up dialoguing for him. And as we go along I'll do more stuff. I still intend to do a story for Williamson that we can do for *Epic.* And, as with all good intentions, before *Epic* folds or I grow senile, I want to get a story out of Alex Toth.

What do you think is the most important aspect of writing comics?

Probably, it's characterization. Good character bits, coming up with material that reveals the character and informs the reader a little more about the characters. And my perception is that what comics readers generally respond to are an intensity of effort, a sense that the people doing the comic are just as intense about it as they are about reading the material. And giving them intense and involving character moments. Having said that, it always seems that one of my weaknesses is characterization. It's the thing I have the most trouble with when I write. Character bits do not flow trippingly either from my tongue or my pen. Or my electric typewriter. I tend to think of myself more as a plot person and sometimes I think I overplot and come up with too complicated a plot for a given number of pages. That's a strength that becomes a weakness. I do tend to lean towards doing a heavier plot. But basically I think in comics you can get by as a weak plotter. But as long as you can do good characterization or revealing character action, I think you are in pretty good shape as a comics writer.

What advice would you have to offer someone breaking into comics as a writer?

Stay out of the field, you'll only take work away from me. [*Laughter.*]

TCJ

LEN WEIN

NO SUCH THING AS A TYPICAL DAY

INTERVIEW BY ROBERT GREENBERGER: Among his many accomplishments, Len Wein had a hand in building three foundations of modern American comic books: Swamp Thing, Wolverine, and the 1970s *Uncanny X-Men* series. That alone should be enough to guarantee Wein a place in the comic-book pantheon. He's also enjoyed a long and fruitful career as a writer and editor.

Wein began writing comics in the late 1960s, moving to Marvel Comics in the early 1970s where he began a productive period as a writer-editor on such titles as *Amazing Spider-Man* and *Fantastic Four*. He also, like so many others featured in this collection, served briefly as Marvel's editor-in-chief.

Wein eventually moved back over to DC Comics where he focused on his editorial duties. He offered Alan Moore the chance to write *Swamp Thing*, edited the groundbreaking series *Watchmen*, and provided oversight on money-generating fan favorites like *New Teen Titans* and *Crisis on Infinite Earths*. He has since spent more of his time writing for animation and television.

The following interview with Robert Greenberger (TCJ #100, July, 1985) captures Wein's ability to verbalize the concerns of both writer and editor.

ROBERT GREENBERGER: **You just became an editor at DC. What led to this?**

LEN WEIN: They offered me the job. That's basically what led to my becoming an editor. They had been offering it to me repeatedly over the past several years, and I kept turning it down, while standing on the sidelines as a freelancer, kibitzing about "the editors should do this, the editors should do that." Finally, they came to me and said, "Why not put your money where your mouth is? If you think this is the way things should be done, become an editor and do them!" So I said, "OK." And did.

But you had been the editor-in-chief at Marvel, and had given it up because you felt it was affecting your health. How does that compare with the experience at DC?

Writer: Len Wein Artists: Herb Trimpe & Jack Abel *Incredible Hulk* #180
October 1974 [©1974 Marvel Comics Group]

Well, at Marvel I was technically in charge of 56 titles a month. At DC I was in charge of eight. It was a lot simpler. At Marvel everyone was pretty much working for himself, which was fine. It was working pretty well that way. At DC, I had a full-time assistant, whose purpose in life was supposedly to help organize my life, keep things moving, and make it simpler for me to sit here and essentially be creative, rather than spending all my time running around in a panic trying to figure out who was doing what.

Having edited in both companies, is there any fundamental difference in editing?

As editor at Marvel, on the entire line, as their editor-in-chief, the principal difference was that I wasn't really doing anything. I was sort of standing there, checking out the covers, overseeing vaguely what everyone was doing, and the writers were in essence editing themselves. At DC, I was actively editing. I would sit down with every writer. We'd discuss the plots in every story; I'd go over every step of every book from plotting through scripting through penciling through lettering through inking through coloring through production. I was an active hands-on editor. At Marvel I was just overseeing the line.

In the seven years you've been here, has any of that changed?

No. Good editing is good editing. I don't think the approach changes. I change the specifics of how it works on a person-to-person basis. I always have. Some people require more editing, some people require less. You just go with the flow, whatever works best to produce the book.

You commented that, at one point, when you entered DC as a writer back in the late '60s, there were individual fiefdoms. Many people still hold that feeling about DC today, with very little cross-continuity between the books. How is that changing?

It hasn't, as much as we'd like it to.

I think something like *Crisis on Infinite Earths* is an attempt to consolidate the company. It's one of those things where you have to meet one another halfway, and hope everyone is willing to go that distance and try to interrelate. Right now, I've spoken to Doug Moench, for example, and we're doing an issue or two of *Batman* where Doug is going to use one of the *Flash* villains. Just as an attempt to try to integrate the universe more, to prove that, just because you're a Batman villain that doesn't mean he's the only one you fight. You just can't deal with Batman. The books and the characters will have to cross over more, become more of a singular universe. We hope. That's part of why we did what we did.

In the case of *Batman*, where you at one point were the writer on the book, and you've been editing it for the past several years, how much of the writer in you wants to speak out, versus the editor in you, when it comes to storylines and the

way characters are handled? Is there an internal conflict at all?

Minimal. I've been fortunate in that, as editor of the book, I have only worked with writers that I have enjoyed working with, and who have generally shared the same view of the character. There have been differences, but one of the first things I learned as an editor was that an editor *edits,* he doesn't write. A writer writes, an editor edits. And if I was going to sit there and be a writer over other writers and impose my writing style on them, I wasn't doing my job well. Once I started to sublimate the virtues of the other people with whom I was working, then I was not giving them a fair shake. If had hired writer A, I had hired him on the assumption that I liked his work, and should let that work shine through. So I've always worked very hard at never putting my own creative stamp as a writer on work I do as an editor.

Batman, being one of DC's oldest characters, has been accused of being a tired character, which is why the book is not among the top sellers DC has. What can be done to resuscitate that perception?

I think that perception is wrong. I don't think you need to resuscitate the perception. The character is a fine character and works well. The reason *Batman* isn't a top seller is because you can't go out and collect all 583 issues of the book. *Batman and the Outsiders,* which is in its fashion neither any better nor any worse than any of the other *Batman* books, sells much better, because it's a collectible *Batman.* It's a book that the reader can go out and get the first issue of. Unfortunately, too often we are dealing with a collector's market rather than a reader's market. I think in the reader's market, the character does as well as he ever did. But among the collectors who want five copies of something they can sell 15 years from now for 10 times the money, it doesn't do as well, because you can't go get the whole set. I think if we cancelled *Batman* tomorrow and started with the exact same book the month afterwards, *The New Adventures of Batman* #1, it would sell 50,000 copies a month more.

Back here in your old interview, you said, "the comic-book readership is transitory." And you say that readers stick around for only two years. How has that changed?

That hasn't changed a whole lot. Readers still stick around for two years. Fans stick around forever. And part of the problem I think we have as an industry is that we cater to the fans that stick around forever, and tend to ignore the readers who only stick around for a few years. As I said in conversation to somebody earlier this week, some of the best character bits of characters like *Batman, Superman, Spider-Man,* the *Hulk* – *any* of them – get left behind and ignored by writers who go, "Oh, God, that old bit – we've seen it before," never realizing that most of the readership hasn't seen it before. We've been around long enough to remember it. Most of them haven't. And we keep cutting out the heart of what makes these characters work, because we're tired of seeing it. And the readership that the characters would appeal to at a primal level isn't there, because the primal level keeps being submerged.

The fan market is making a lot of demands on the publishers. We're publishing a lot of books now specifically for the fan market. In addition to our deluxe format books, when we're looking at creating new properties, there's a lot of attention paid to what the fan market will want. Are we ignoring the newsstand audience to the detriment of the industry?

Always. We've done it for years. When the Direct Market first reared its furry head, everyone said, "Oh, good, the salvation of the industry, comic-book shops. As long as all they sell is comic books, we've got to be their most important product." And we started to ignore newsstands, which was the only place many of the readers across the country could get their comics. Sales dropped off there, and... we cut our own throats. Now, all of a sudden, the entire industry is trying to regain that lost newsstand audience. We're changing our format in terms of the way we distribute the books, we're reallocating things so that popular books get more copies out to the newsstand than unpopular books. We made a boo-boo as an industry, and now we're trying to fix it.

Is it salvageable?

My God, I hope so. If not, we'll all be out doing something else for a living someday.

Back to editing for a moment. You had said to me in a previous interview elsewhere that, hopefully, people would be able to pick up a comic and know it was a Len Wein-edited comic, much the way that people used to know a Julius Schwartz-edited comic. What elements make up a Len Wein book?

Attention to detail, as much as possible. Having been in this industry as long as I have, I've done a little bit of everything, I've worked in production, I've done coloring, I've done lettering, I've done penciling, inking, writing and I'm aware of all the reproduction techniques, of everything that needs to be done. I'm a nitpicker. And I put a great deal of care and attention to detail. To making sure the costumes are right. To making sure that all the correction and proofreading things are done. The little aesthetic touches that can't even be described verbally that are just things I'm aware of when I've worked over a page. Adjusting balloon shapes, adjusting little things here and there. And an attitude in terms of the characters, in terms of the writing. I like to write about people. I like to read about people, so that's the sort of story I look for in my writers.

Do you think you've achieved that Len Wein look yet?

Certainly, other people at the office think that's true. I think so too, to some degree, by allowing the writers freedom to write in their own styles and not forcing my own writing style on them. Certainly less so than Julie, who used to rewrite the work of virtually all his writers, so that it had a uniform feel to it. Without that particular aspect, I don't think you're gonna find that sort of thing today; on the other hand, if you look across the industry, there isn't any other editor besides Julie, of the current school, who has an identifiable look to their books, be it here, Marvel, anywhere.

Since your return as a writer to DC, you have written _Superman_ and _Batman_, and you've written one or two _Legions_ and you've written _Green Lantern_ and _Deadman_ and all sorts of _DC Comics Presents_, and _Flash_, among others. Which has been the most creatively satisfying?

Of the new stuff? _Deadman_, probably. It's people stories, again. Working with artists like Jim Aparo and [Jose] Garcia-Lopez. That stuff has just been beautiful to be part of. I think that's probably the stuff I've most enjoyed.

One of the other things you were involved in creatively was the revival of _Swamp Thing_. First with Marty [Pasko] and then picking Alan Moore. How did that feel to edit your baby, as opposed to writing?

I had enough distance by the time I came back to it that it wasn't any bother at all. I'd been away from the book for, God, almost 10 years, probably, at that point. And it was a different character. I had given up writing Swampy because I had lost that particular point of view that I had in the earlier stories, and I was not going to try to force that point of view on anybody else. A writer ought to feel he is free to write whatever kind of stories work best for him. So long as they're true to the character, whatever the character may be. And I let Marty go his way, and I've let Alan go his way to the point of recreating the character while I was still the editor of those books.

Issue #21, "The Anatomy Lesson," was the pivotal change. Did you know that was coming when you picked Alan for the book?

That he was going to rearrange reality, so to speak? No, I had no idea. He came in, we talked about doing the book, and then he presented his ideas after I'd hired him.

Well, what led you to Alan?

Reading everything in the business, I'd seen a lot of his work in the British magazines, on _Captain Britain_, on _2000 A.D._, various stories here and there, and I liked very much what I'd seen.

Speaking of revivals and other changes, there was your taking over _Green Lantern_, first as editor, then as the writer, with Dave Gibbons as artist. How did all that come about?

I wanted to do it. That's really how it all came about. I edited _Green Lantern_ probably more often than any other book I've ever edited. I'd do an issue here, two issues there, three issues here, an issue there; they would come and go off my desk sort of like the prodigal son. It just kept popping up. When it had gone through a particularly odd period of its incarnation, and the creative staff was about to change, I went in and said to Dick [Giordano], "Hi, if you need to find new people to do the book, I want to be it. I want to write this character." And Dick said, "OK." And I looked at some samples of artists' artwork, liked very much the work I had seen of Dave Gibbons, and called him up and "Hi, want to do Green Lantern?" He said, "Oh, boy!" and we did.

He gave you a one-year commitment. Did you feel any sort of strain that in one year you had to turn the book around, hoping to keep him on beyond that?

No, I'd hoped that he'd enjoy the content enough to stay with it beyond a one-year commitment. But I knew that was dangerous when I took it, from the beginning. I knew he had promised one year, and I had no qualms about him leaving at the end of that year. He didn't surprise me; he didn't pull the rug out from under me, he told me. And as it was, he stayed actually 14 issues, I think.

You had a rather sticky situation in terms of the book's continuity straighten out when you took over as a writer. And then, after straightening that out immediately changed your lead character from Hal Jordan to John Stewart. Did you in particular need to do that?

Yeah. I didn't feel the book working. I wasn't as satisfied with the kind of stories I was able to get out of the Jordan character at that point. He been turned into something, I suppose partly by me and certainly by my predecessors, into a character I didn't feel was at that moment viable. And I figured what he needed was a breather. Green Lantern could be anybody, unlike Flash, who had to be hit by all the chemicals and the lightning bolt, or Superman, who had to be born on Krypton. Anybody who wore the ring, who was fearless and honest, could be Green Lantern. And Stewart fit that bill; he'd done the job before and struck me as a character with a different type of personality and something I might get better use of.

What about the obvious complaint raised in the fan press about that it was imitating what had happened in *Iron Man*?

I thought about that and I worried about that. I talked to a number of people about it before I went ahead and did the thing, and everyone said it was something that could not be helped. John Stewart had been the second-string Green Lantern for 10 years before Jim Rhodes ever came on the scene over in *Iron Man*. And to avoid making him the next Green Lantern when he had been specifically designated as the next Green Lantern should Jordan ever fall in battle was unrealistic and unfair. I didn't get much mail, actually. Maybe I got a handful of letters who complained about the similarity. Most of the readers did not see it as an *Iron Man* rip-off. They knew better. A number of people were specifically saying, "Well, obviously it had to be John Stewart, because he was the next guy in line."

RAIN: SOME SAY IT CLEANSES THE ALL-TOO-IMPURE *EARTH*--OTHERS PROCLAIM IT THE SORROW OF THE *GODS*, REGRETTING THE *TRAGEDY* THEIR GOLDEN HANDS HAVE WROUGHT...

...THE TRAGEDY THAT HAS LONG BEEN KNOWN AS *MAN!*

BUT THOSE WHO DWELL IN THIS TIME-LESS LAND CARE NOT FOR IDLE *OPINION*. THEY ARE CONTENTED TO BASK IN THE TEEMING *TORRENT*...

...UNTIL SOMETHING SUDDEN *DISTURBS* THEIR REPOSE...

...SOMETHING THAT *CLAWS* ITS WAY OUT OF THE GRASPING *MIRE*...

...AND INTO THE *LIGHT* ONCE MORE!

SOMETHING THAT PULLS ITSELF *UPRIGHT* ON UNSTEADY LEGS, SEARCHING ITS CLOUDY MIND FOR A FRAGMENT OF *MEMORY*...

...THEN *PAUSES*, STUDYING ITS GNARLED MISSHAPEN *HANDS*... EXAMINING THE CLUSTERS OF *ROOT*, THE CRUMBLING CHUNKS OF *MOSS*...

Writer: Len Wein Artist: Bernie Wrightson *Swamp Thing* #1 October-November 1972
[©1972 DC Comics Inc.]

It was interesting to note in the letters that so many people really didn't want to see Hal go. Regardless of how you creatively felt – Hal Jordan worked; they still liked the character.

They liked what they were familiar with. Readers always like the familiar. Nobody ever wants to see change, no matter what it is. When we first proposed the revived *Teen Titans* and the readers found out they weren't going to be Bumblebee and the Golden Eagle and all the characters they had known, and two or three had probably loved, everyone wrote in to protest. Then they saw the *New Teen Titans,* and they all shut up. "Never mind. We're sorry. Go ahead and do what you want to do. This is nice." Nobody ever wants to see change. It's always preferable to work with the devil you know than the devil you don't.

At the same time Dave left the book, you ended up leaving the book. You want to discuss the circumstances?

No.

Okay. Since then, you have been concentrating on *Who's Who*. When are you going to do more writing?

I'm doing a "Tales of the Gemworld" backup story for Karen Berger, I've got four or five *DC Presents* approved by Julie, waiting for me to get a couple of free minutes to write, including the final introduction of the Image character I was going to introduce in *Green Lantern,* and the return of *Brother Power,* which I've been promising for years now.

Threatening.

Threatening, whichever, choose any or all of the above.

At one point you really wanted to concentrate on the writing more than anything else. It was about the time of the *Swamp Thing* movie, where we had spoken for *Comics Scene,* you had said you really wanted to do more writing. And since then, the writing's almost tapered off. Are you finding it difficult getting the work done?

With a full time job, about the time of the *Swamp Thing* movie, I came down with the worst case of writer's block I've ever had, and just didn't write for virtually a year, just absolutely unable to get anything down on paper, and it's been slow and hard coming back, but one of the reasons I took *Green Lantern* was to have a regular, ongoing book that demanded my time, and wouldn't allow me to sort of sit back on my hands and go, "Well, I'll get to it next week." Knowing there had to be a next issue out, because the book was already in the pipeline, and being produced monthly. And that helped a lot. I still have the *Zero Man,* too, which someday in my lifetime, maybe, Paris Cullins will finish doing a brilliant penciling job on. What he's done has been stunning, and if he ever finishes it, the book will be wonderful. I have another superhero team book that's sitting on the backburner that was going to be drawn by George Pérez and now heaven only knows who's actually going to end up doing the art.

When you worked with Dave, did you find it difficult working transatlantic?

Not at all. We'd get on the phone once or twice a week, as the screams from down the hall when they saw the phone bills will attest. We had no problems. My plots are very concise, very page and panel breakdown-y, easy to follow. Dave never had a complaint that I'm aware of, and I never had a complaint with him. I had a marvelous time working with him.

How much input did he have in the actual plot and setups and the creation of villains like the Demolition Team?

Minimal. For the most part. Except for the few occasions where either he was in the States or I was over in London, where we got together and plotted out issues one-on-one, together. There are a couple, in fact, that have co-plotting credit for Dave, which are the ones where he actively participated in. Certainly, all the visuals are his. He designed the Demolition Team and the Predator and the Image, when you finally get to see him. All by his lonesome. We kibitzed a little about some concepts, but the gist of what they look like are all his, and marvelously so.

One of the other things that's been happening in the industry, that has affected the comic books is the increasing influence from licensing. For a while, everyone was concerned that you couldn't change characters because of the way that would affect licensing. How do you feel licensing has been affecting actual comic books?

The same year we came out with a Green Lantern doll with Hal Jordan's head, I changed Green Lantern to John Stewart. That should answer your question.

Do you find it's beneficial to be working with the licensing people to have editorial input? You were involved in the Kenner minicomics that went with the toys.

Well, I don't think the two forces should be diverse. I think we need to work together, and I have no problems with that. I just don't feel that it's up to licensing – I don't want to imply that they do – to dictate to the creative and the editorial people what the contents of the book should be. I think once the tail starts wagging the dog, you're in desperate trouble.

OK. The superheroes have been the mainstay of comics for the last several years, but we all know comics are very cyclical. Do you see the cycle coming to an end?

No, damn it, I don't.

Why don't you think it's not coming to an end yet? It seems to be unusually long this time.

I think because of the Direct Market. I think that so long as the Direct Market tells us they want variety and then only buys superhero comics, we're not going to be able to give them the variety we'd like to give them. God knows there's nothing I'd rather be editing than a Western, or a science-fiction title, or a mystery book, à la *House of Mystery* or *House of Secrets*. We don't publish those any more because all they buy is superheroes. Then they tell us, "Well, we're tired of nothing but superheroes, give us this." But when you give them a *Night Force* or you give them a *Captain Carrot* or you give them *Thriller* or a half-dozen other things that try to be different, nobody buys them. If it's not wearing a big blue suit, a big red cape with a yellow "S," or something like that, they just aren't interested.

Is there something the publishers collectively can do to change that?

Not that I can think of. I think if we'd been able to figure out what to do, we'd have done it by now. Because I know mine is not the only voice crying in the wilderness. Half the creative people in this industry, and certainly many of the people in the hierarchy would like to see that kind of variety.

Do you think we're keeping talented people away from contributing to our comic books because they don't want to draw superheroes?

Yes, certainly. That goes with the territory. There are people I've spoken to who have said, "Gee, I'd love to work with you, as long as it's not a superhero."

And that ends the conversation.

Pretty much.

In addition to the fan marketplace, do you think it's because there are the smaller, independent publishers, Eclipse, Aardvark-Vanaheim, WaRP, First, and Pacific and Capital when they both were around? Do you think that's helped just fan the flames by feeding the kids the superheroes they want without trying anything else?

No, actually, most of the independents don't produce superheroes, mainline superheroes. Unfortunately, most of the independents don't sell terribly well, either. That's part of the problem. I think if we could find an independent publisher who would publish an off-genre title that was commercially successful, it would start opening the way for other people to do that sort of material.

The closest that you really get is something like *Jon Sable*.

Not even there. Mike [Grell] was smart enough in the beginning to make him look like a superhero in the black jumpsuit with the mask, to do all the trappings that made people think they were buying another superhero. By the time they realized that it was a book that wasn't really a superhero, he had hooked them. And he got them to buy the book for its own merits. I hate to have to cheat that way. I'm not blaming Mike. I think it's a brilliant move by doing it, but it's unfortunate that you can't just go, "Here, this is good." And they won't even bother to pick it up and find out if it hasn't got an "S" on its chest.

Now, you said in *DC Releases* that you were developing a white-hat Western, *Dakota*.

Still am! Still at the drawing board. I've gone through two artists before it's even been put to paper. When I find the right guy who can do the series justice, I'll do it. Dick wants to do it, I want to do it.

Well, do you think that if you have the right creative talent on the book, despite the genre, that it would work?

I think if we have the right creative talent on the book, we have a shot at cheating the genre. And I think, there are people out there who want these things. But not enough to warrant publishing them, unfortunately. The company can't see its way clear to publish a book that'll make it a 10 percent profit when they can publish a book that'll make it a 30 percent profit. And that's unfortunate.

If we're stuck with superheroes, what can we do to keep them interesting?

Damned if I know. I think eventually, anybody reaches a saturation point on any particular character. What happens eventually is you just keep changing creative staffs. People get burned out doing whatever it is they're doing, and they go with other things, and you get a law of diminishing returns. Certainly, in several cases a new creative person on the book has increased its sales, increased its image, increased the quality of the book radically.

Frank Miller taking over *Daredevil*, that's almost the best example, or lately, thank heavens, Alan Moore on *Swamp Thing*, where a writer, for the first time in years, has made a difference.

You have said in the previous interview that you have a short attention span as a writer and you feel that that's been part of your problem sticking on books for long runs. Does that apply to your being an editor? Do you find yourself losing interest in a title after editing it for a period of time?

I've been editing *Batman* for a couple of years now, and I don't see any end in sight. I don't think that's much the case. Many of the books that I have given up as an editor, I have not given up of my own choice. It was company decisions to do some juggling, to supply work to various other people. I've generally been very happy with the books I've edited, and stayed on them for quite a long time.

As a writer, do you still feel you have that short an attention span?

It depends on the character. Again, I could have stayed with *Batman*, when I was writing it years ago, for three years more. I had stacks of stories in my head that I hadn't gotten a chance to do yet. It wasn't my choice at that point to leave the book.

With the expansion into the Direct Market with the hardcover-softcover type of titles and with the graphic novels and the miniseries and stuff, do you feel that you're going to get your shot at getting back to that, and tell some of those stories?

Eventually, I expect. In this industry, who can say? When I left here to go to Marvel, I didn't expect to go back here necessarily, doing the same characters again, 10 years later. Everything changes.

Now, while you were at Marvel you had the opportunity to work and write as well as co-edit the line of prose novels featuring the Marvel characters. Have you had any chance to do any outside type of writing since you've gotten back to DC?

A couple of items here and there. Not very much, actually. Nothing anyone's seen. I'm potentially involved in all sorts of things. I'm working out some short stories. I have a novel sitting in the back of my head, waiting to get out.

Do you then see a career in comics for the foreseeable future, or the possibility of branching out and moving on to other matters?

I'm not inclined. I've had more opportunities to branch out into things like television and movies than most people probably get in their lifetimes. So far I've stayed here, because I'm comfortable here. I haven't got a lifestyle that demands upward mobility constantly, and I think I'm happier for it. The more you get into higher-paying brackets, things like television and movies, the more insane the business you work in becomes. And I would rather work where I can be creative as I'm inclined to be creative, than to have to answer to people who I have no respect for, just because they pay me lots of money.

As an editor, do you enjoy the office atmosphere, the constant lunacy where people have to take a number to get into the office, and –

I'm responsible for chunks of it, so of course I enjoy it.

You want to describe what a typical day is like here for you?

There's no such thing as a typical day here for me.

Conjure one.

I don't think I can. There are days where I feel like the Pied Piper. Since my office is the last office at the end of the hall, I come in through a reception area and start to collect people behind me. As I pass their offices, they say, "Len, I need you! Len, listen, Len, can you check this, Len, I need an approval on... Len..." By the time I get to my office they're lined up behind me like rats behind the Pied Piper.

I shouldn't use the analogy, but it's close. They're all stacked up, taking numbers, and arguing that their problem is more important and needs to be checked and approved first. There are days when I will come in and actually not get to sit down on my desk for two or three hours after I've gotten there.

As one of the few senior editors here at DC, you're working with the newer ones. Do you feel that you're going to be making a contribution or have been making a contribution so far to shaping the future of DC Comics?

Absolutely. I think that's one of the reasons I stay, and I've gotten enough feedback from many of the newer editors to believe that I am making a contribution, that they have learned things from me. I'm old and crotchety enough, I've been here long enough to have done a little bit of everything, so there's a lot I have to teach. I was fortunate, I think, in being probably the last writer to come into the business who was taught by a number of editors who then left the business. Not because teaching me was the end and that's all, but because companies were starting to fold at about the time I came in. Like Tower, Gold Key, various companies I worked for, are no longer around for people to learn from those editors. So I've got a wealth of information that was passed on to me that I'm hoping to pass on to others. "Buy low, sell high," there's all kinds of things to remember.

Editing seems to be one of the more transitory jobs in comics, I mean, you know, people will continue to write books, and people will continue to draw them, but editors just come and go. So many of them come on staff, edit for a year, and then go freelance as a writer or an artist. What do you think it is that can't keep an editor at a company?

Because a lot of people don't see editing as the job they want to do. They see editing as an entry-level job to the things they actually aspire to. As you said, they come in as an editor, and then go off to become a writer, to become an artist, to become a taxidermist, whatever it is they want to become next. They don't want to become editors. I think one of the major differences in the industry over the past couple of years is that we're now hiring people who are editors by trade, who have edited in book companies and various other forms of publishing, so that their aspirations aren't to become the next Neal Adams or Frank Miller or Alan Moore, but the next Julie Schwartz.

Have you yet to see that have any sort of positive impact on the books we are publishing today?

It's a little too soon. I think most of the people are still in the learning process. God knows, it took me a long time to learn how to do all this stuff. Julie claims he's still learning it, and he's been doing it for 40 years.

What about breaking into comics? How has that changed since you got in?

Well, in the old days, I used a hammer and chisel. But now they use a laser.

[*Laughter.*] How about in more practical cases?

It's easier, and thus less effective. One of the problems this industry has suffered from in the past 10 years is that on a sheer talent level – a level of skill, level of capability – the level has gotten lower. I don't think the overall creative capacity of the industry is as good or has as much potential as it did 10 years ago. Or, let's say 15 years ago. We're not getting in the industry people like Bernie Wrightson, Mike Kaluta, Jeff Jones, Neal Adams, the list goes on. Denny O'Neil, Roy Thomas, Marv and myself as writers, and half a dozen other people who were all coming to the fore. Who were all people who were going into the business.

Many of those guys aren't here any more. They've gone into other arts. Comics didn't satisfy their needs, unfortunately. They left the industry before things like royalties and much of the approach changed and the people who are coming in don't have the background, don't have the same set of creative skills that the previous ones did. It's the law of diminishing returns again. Everyone learns from their predecessors without having the scope of education the predecessors had. And step-by-step, it gets lower. I don't think the industry is as talented as it was 10 years ago. Overall. Certainly there are high points, don't misunderstand me. There are still people who are brilliant, but I think there are fewer brilliant people and more mediocre and adequate people than before. People used to come in and spend years learning their trade, who would start as a writer or an artist in the backup features in mystery anthologies, where you just learn how to write a story, how to tell a story visually, how to ink, how to color, how to get all of your mistakes out of your system before you could even think of aspiring to a regular, major front-feature. Now these people come in and... I remember when I was a writer who'd been in the business for 10 years and was a major name, and had won awards, and when it looked like I was about to take over the reins on *Spider-Man* I was intimidated. This was *Spider-Man,* which had been written by two or three people, tops, before me in its entire history, and all of it brilliantly. And here I was about to take over the mantle and responsibility of doing *Spider-Man* well. Now *Spider-Man's* an entry-level book. People come into the industry and the first assignment they get is *Spider-Man.* How do you learn your craft?

TCJ

MAN OF TOMORROW

INTERVIEW BY MARK BURBEY: The English writer Alan Moore is such an immense figure in comic books today that many forget he was once just another writer with a work-for-hire gig seeking to make a name for himself in the faltering North American market. Because of the changes he would bring to comics writing through a body of work that would one day include *Watchmen, From Hell, League of Extraordinary Gentlemen, Promethea, Top Ten* and *A Small Killing*, Moore can be viewed as a transitional figure between the learn-through-comics generation of the 1960s and 1970s and the more cerebral scriptwriters of the 1980s and 1990s.

This early interview [TCJ #93, September, 1984] begins with Mark Burbey fairly admitting he was unfamiliar with Moore's work in England. Most people were, and it was Moore's growing popularity that shed a light backwards on features like *V For Vendetta* and *Marvelman* that have since become as big a part of Moore's legend as that initial run on *Swamp Thing*. And *Swamp Thing*, well, Moore's extremely sensitive and immaculately crafted work on that title, smart horror of the kind never seen in comics before, exploded among the fan community like a bomb.

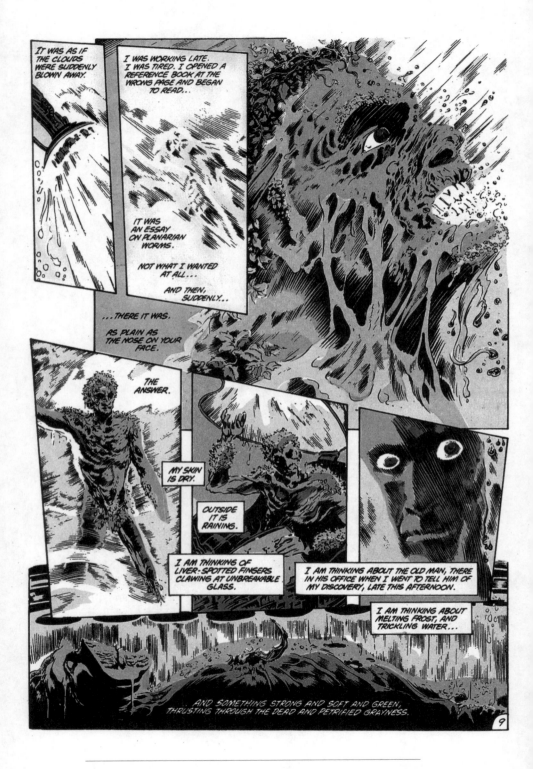

Writer: Alan Moore Artists: Stephen Bissette & John Totleben *Saga of the Swamp Thing*
#21 February 1984 [©1983 DC Comics Inc.]

I AM SITTING IN MY APARTMENT. OUTSIDE, IT IS RAINING.

I AM LAUGHING. LAUGHING VERY LOUDLY.

FRIENDS HAVE TOLD ME IT IS NOT A SOUND CONDUCIVE TO TRANQUILLITY.

I AM THINKING ABOUT THE OLD MAN.

HE'LL STAY LATE, WHEN EVERYONE HAS GONE. PERHAPS HE'LL READ THROUGH THE NOTES HE WOULDN'T PERMIT ME TO KEEP...

...SKIPPING THE BIG WORDS...

...AND THEN MAYBE HE'LL WANT TO TAKE A STROLL, LIKE EVERY OTHER NIGHT. A STROLL AROUND THE BIGGEST DOLL HOUSE IN THE WORLD.

HE'LL PUNCH ONE OF HIS LITTLE BUTTONS TO SWITCH THE DOOR MECHANISMS TO MANUAL, SO THAT HE CAN CONTROL THEM WHILE HE'S AWAY FROM HIS CHECKERBOARD.

AND THEN HE'LL STRUT PROUDLY DOWN THE HALL AND THINK HOW LUCKY HE IS TO HAVE ALL THIS.

HE SHOULD HAVE LET ME FINISH. HE SHOULD HAVE LISTENED.

THEN I'D HAVE BEEN ABLE TO EXPLAIN THE MOST IMPORTANT THING OF ALL TO HIM.

I'D HAVE BEEN ABLE TO EXPLAIN THAT YOU CAN'T KILL A VEGETABLE BY SHOOTING IT THROUGH THE HEAD.

Writer: Alan Moore Artists: Stephen Bissette & John Totleben *Saga of the Swamp Thing* #21 February 1984 [©1983 DC Comics Inc.]

MARK BURBEY: Let me start by saying that, despite knowing virtually nothing about you, except that you've done a lot of writing for England's *Warrior* magazine, I was thrilled when Steve [Bissette] told me that you'd be taking over *Swamp Thing* from Martin Pasko. I was digging the art Steve and John [Totleben] were doing, but Pasko's stories really bothered me. Now that I've read a fair number of issues written by you, I really think the whole package has come together. Everything is clicking to make *Swamp Thing* an interesting book again.

ALAN MOORE: Thanks a lot, and I'm glad that you're enjoying it. From the writing end, I'm pathetically relieved to discover that it seems to be turning out OK. Starting out on the book I was gripped by all sorts of wild and xenophobic anxieties concerning working with American artists for an American audience, but most of these have dissipated since I started writing to Steve and John and learned that they were almost human.

If the book seems to be hanging together well, I'd say that was largely due to the pair of them being so incredibly bloody easy to work with. My scripts are generally sprawling and incoherent items that wander off on totally undrawable tangents and yet Steve and John are able to hack their way through all this foreign gibberish and somehow come up with a lucid visual narrative.

Also, we seem by some miraculous quirk of circumstances to have arrived independently at almost identical ideas about how the character should develop, how he should look, what sort of stories we should use and so on. There's a lot of energy being generated. In fact, some of John's letters are so energetic that his ballpoint pen goes through the page in certain passages. All in all, I'd say that what we have here is one of the most significant meetings of English and American thought and intent since you invaded Grenada a short while back.

Indeed. How old are you, by the way? I'm always curious about one's age.

I was 30 in November [1983]. My teeth are gradually turning a noctilucent shade of ochre and my stomach is trying to eat my knees. I fail totally to understand how this knowledge will increase your enjoyment of *Swamp Thing*, but I suppose I'm dealing with a different culture now.

How did you start writing comics? Comics collecting, I gather, is somewhat different in England than it is in the United States. Were you a typical fan? Were you into collecting and the whole bit?

I've been reading comics of one sort or another since I was about seven years old, back in the late '50s. Homegrown English comics during that period were largely given over to football stories in which a steadfast and plucky multiple amputee goes on to score the winning hat trick in the F.A. Cup by sheer determination and stick-to-itiveness. Conversely, there were war stories in which the main point in each week's episode seemed to be coming up with some new term of abuse to hurl at the Germans. Naturally, coming across items like the first few issues of *The Flash*, *Justice League of America*, and later, *The Fantastic Four* was a tremendous source of relief.

Fandom proper wasn't established in England until the late '60s, when I was in my mid-teens. I seem to remember it being a lot less intense than it is now, but this is probably just a defense I've thrown up to avoid remembering myself as the foaming, obsessive comics-bore that I probably was. At around the age of 17, I started to get a bit depressed about the way in which the whole fan thing seemed to be centering more upon the minute trivia of certain characters and their histories, and paying less attention to comics as a medium. Remember, by this time I'd seen things like Bill Spicer's excellent *Graphic Story Magazine*s and liked to think of myself as an aesthete and intellectual with no interest in the content of Batman's utility belt.

Anyway, I drifted away from fandom, even though I managed to more or less keep up with what was happening with the comics themselves. I didn't really have anything to do with fandom again, until I started working as a writer and developed an almost sexual thirst for the sight of my name in print. The intervening years were passed working with various people and projects, some of them connected with the Northampton Arts Lab, some of them involving stage performance and stuff like that.

In the late '70s (by which time I was married and my wife Phyllis was expecting the first of the malformed brutes from the pit that we laughingly refer to as *children*), I'd decided to make a serious attempt at working with comics and getting paid for it. I started off as a mediocre and elaborate cartoonist, handling a half-page weekly strip for the English rock weekly, *Sounds*. I did two complete sagas for them, working under the name Curt Vile. The first was a Raymond Chandler satire entitled *Roscoe Moscow*, and the second was a Sex-Madness-and-Meteors SF comedy called *The Stars My Degradation*. They ran for somewhere approaching 200 episodes between them and although for the most part they were repulsive bilge, I did manage to learn a little bit about the possibilities for telling a story in pictures.

I also started doing a five-frame gag strip for a local newspaper around this time, something called *Maxwell the Magic Cat*, under the alias of Jill de Ray. In fact, I'm still doing it to this day, and I don't really know why, I suppose it lends me the right touch of humility.

On the whole, though, it became horribly apparent that I couldn't make any decent kind of living from drawing comics. Firstly, I was too slow. Secondly, I was barely capable of drawing even simple objects in a way by which they might be recognized. Since I'd known the very excellent Steve Moore (no relation) for a considerable while and since he was having fun writing comics and earning a living at the same time, I asked his advice on how I should go about pulling off the same scam.

Steve taught me all that I needed to know about style and presentation and managed to bribe Marvel U.K. into accepting one of my stories as a backup in their

Dr. Who weekly. At more or less the same time I managed to sell my first couple of short stories to I.P.C. for use in *2000 A.D.*

Since then, I've been pretty busy. With Marvel UK I've worked on *Dr. Who*, the *Star Wars* books, and, most recently, had a lot of fun working with Alan Davis on the British version of *Captain Britain* for Marvel U.K.'s *The Daredevils*. I've done innumerable short stories and a couple of serials for *2000 A.D.*, and for Quality's *Warrior* I've handled *Marvelman*, *V for Vendetta*, *Warpsmith*, and *The Bojeffries Saga*. Apart from *Swamp Thing*, that's pretty much the whole story.

What sorts of influences do you draw from when you're writing?

I really wish I could answer this by saying something decisive and opinionated like, "I only listen to Cuban jazz from the 1940s and I only read obscure Portuguese poetry in the original text." Sadly, I'm as boringly catholic as most people and tend to absorb just about everything I read, see, or listen to.

I suppose one major point is that in writing comics I don't really absorb too much influence from the comics that I read unless it's something inexpressibly brilliant like Frank Miller's stuff, or *American Flagg!*, or *Love and Rockets*. Mostly I'd say that my influence comes from novels that I read or the occasional film that I see. If anything, I'd say that what I'd like to do as a writer is to try and translate some of the intellect and sensibilities that I find in books into something that will work on a comics page. Although I've obviously read and been influenced by most of the classics work of comic art like Eisner and Kurtzman, I can't help but feel that if you're influenced too much by your forebears in the comics field then a sort of process of dilution results, in which each succeeding generation of artists and writers is a little paler and more anemic than the generation before.

For my part, it seems to smack too much of inbreeding (something we British have a terror of, probably brought on by the state of the Royal Family). I like the idea of bringing fresh ideas and approaches into the field, and although I seldom succeed in these objectives, they're what I'm aiming at.

As far as actual influences go, any list would be long, boring, and inconclusive. For what it's worth, however, I like Cordwainer Smith, William Burroughs, Harlan Ellison, Angela Carter, Stephen King, John Gardner, Flann O'Brien, Thomas Disch, William Faulkner, Damon Runyon, Truman Capote, Dorothy Parker, Peter Carey, and so on and so on. I suppose a major influence would have to be musician Brian Eno; just in the precise and mechanical way he approaches the idea of creativity I've been able to find a vast amount of inspiration to how I structure my own work.

I had wondered if the title of *Swamp Thing* #23, "Another Green World," had been inspired by the Eno album of the same name. I think you've brought *Swamp Thing* down to a more human level, where the reader can more readily identify with what's happening to the characters. Despite its fantastic nature, it seems less like a "comic book" than most comics. The people and their feelings

and reactions seem very important, more so than the so-called obligatory action sequences. What is your approach and attitude about writing *Swamp Thing*, and comics writing in general?

I suppose that overall my feeling about comic writing is that it should be a lot more effective and visceral than it is. I find myself reading humor books that don't make me laugh, adventure books that don't excite me, and horror books that don't scare me in the slightest.

I think that what's gradually happened over the last 30 or 40 years is that each of these genres have gradually built up an arsenal of clichés that have totally overwhelmed and smothered the original concepts. In humor books, for example, if you look back to Kurtzman's *Mad* you have something that was genuinely funny and that would actually make people laugh. Since then, however, it's as if the producers of subsequent humor mags have only had to conjure a little of *Mad*'s style in order to evoke the appropriate response. They cram a panel with largely mundane sight gags, they assume that is sufficient to change a couple of letters in the name of whatever they're satirizing, the pacing is always on a breathless *Laugh-In* level... the assumption is that if you throw in enough items that are recognizable as something approaching *funny comics*, then the end product will somehow be funny. It's a big like the approach that the Cargo Cultists had to practical electronics: if you get a wooden box and stick knobs on the front then it's a radio, and who cares if it makes any noise or not.

The same thing applies to horror. It's been reduced to a form of shorthand. "If a werewolf jumps out from behind a tree and growls at the girl then this will be frightening." But of course, it isn't... The shock or horror and the similar shock of humor are to some degree based on the sudden recognition of something totally unfamiliar. A werewolf jumping out from behind a tree is such a stock image that there isn't the merest frisson of terror in it for the majority of the audience.

So, basically, what I try to do when approaching any genre is to try and sort out the original idea from the accumulated silt of tradition. It's what I tried to do when approaching the superhero strip by way of *Marvelman*, and it's what I'm trying to do with the horror strip by way of *Swamp Thing*.

Specifically, when approaching *Swamp Thing* I could see a number of problems. The first was that Len [Wein] and Bernie's [Wrightson] original conception of the character, while it had worked perfectly back in the early '70s, couldn't really cut it for an '80s audience. The audience has changed, their environment has changed, and their notion of horror has changed. It's like something that I believe Stephen King said in *Danse Macabre* while comparing Val Lewton's *Cat People* to the version by Paul Schrader: he said that the reality set had changed, and that scenes that would have gripped and convinced an audience 20 years ago would be laughed out of the cinema today.

For one thing, a large percentage of our audience now has some sort of access to video equipment. If they wish, they can watch glowingly explicit films showing a woman having her nipples torn off with a pair of pliers. On a more acceptable level, they can watch John Carpenter's *The Thing* and see vivid, godawful weirdness far more real and far more imaginative than anything ever experience in comics… despite the notion that comics have an "unlimited special-effects budget." You see, the problem is that while we might be able to approximate an unlimited special effects budge with out lines on paper, people like Spielberg and Lucas actually *have* an unlimited special effects budget.

We have to accept that this sort of stuff is what we're competing against for the attentions and money of the audience, and we have to work out what can be done about it. Now, obviously, we couldn't compete in the gore stakes even if we had any inclinations toward this area. Similarly, we can't rely upon our *sensa wonder* to pull us through, not when we're up against something like *Poltergeist*, or *Alien*.

For me, the only areas in which we can successfully compete are in the novel things that we can do with our storytelling that cannot be successfully duplicated by other media and in the weight, depth, and moment of our actual stories.

This last point is probably the most important angle from my point of view… much of the culture that I find surrounding me seems to be composed mostly of flash and surface. There very seldom seems to be any sort of depth or meaning or importance to the films that I see, irrespective of how good the special effects are. This is a weakness that I think the comic industry would do well to exploit: people cannot maintain infinite enthusiasm and affection for a bunch of explosions. Sooner or later, to paraphrase a remark I believe was originally uttered by the estimable Jeff Jones, they're going to ask for a donut to go with the hole.

With *Swamp Thing*, we're trying the best we can to construct stories that have some sort of real human resonance and some moments of genuine unease. From my end, this comes down to what I do with the characters and how I set up the story. I find that my general line of approach is to build up the characters, often in woefully slow and monotonous sequences, so that when the action *does* finally arrive, the readers will have some sort of real sense of what is at stake both physically and emotionally. This isn't a perfect approach, in that sometimes I seem to end up with a story in which practically nothing happens and I plunge into a morass of guilt over not having given Steve and John anything interesting to draw. On the whole, though, I think we're on the right track. The alternative is to cram a book with action, which, due to the fact that the characters and events that make up the action have not been properly explored, comes over as empty and lifeless. I've no idea whether all this pretentious pondering will actually amount to anything, but it is at least an attitude. Having somewhere to stand is very important in the 1980s.

Are you doing lots of research into plant science, now that you've turned the character away from being a mutation of Alec Holland into being a genuine plant creature?

No, I'm not. I know I should be and wish I was, but I have a spine-twisting terror of doing anything that even remotely approximates hard work, such as research.

I tend to confine myself to the old fragments of information that I already possess and to whatever reference books are within five minutes walk of my typewriter. If I get caught out on something tricky, there's usually someone that I can ring who has the information somewhere; it's a very sloppy and haphazard process, but it's all that I have time for. Steve and John keep sending me huge parcels full of all sorts of oddities and information, and I generally find that I have all the reference I need for any given story. If any botanically minded reader finds himself getting irritated over my vast array of factual inaccuracies, then if they care to send any unwanted biology textbooks up to DC, I'm sure Karen Berger would be delighted to pass them on.

How did you come to be the new writer of *Swamp Thing*, especially living in faraway England?

Christ alone knows. The phone rang one afternoon and it was Len Wein on the other end asking if I wanted to write *Swamp Thing*. I gather he'd seen some of the stuff I'd done in *Warrior* and *2000 AD* and figured I might not be too atrocious on *Swamp Thing*.

Working with Len on the book was an absolute dream. Everything seemed to come together with tremendous ease, and the only thing that disturbed me was that my editor was the person who'd done so much to establish *Swamp Thing* as a workable and successful character during the book's first run. I mean, if anyone were to take over something that I feel responsible for, like *Marvelman* for instance, I'm reasonably certain that I'd carp and nitpick so much that they'd be afraid to do anything in case I didn't like it. With Len, however, there wasn't the least shred of the proprietary, for which I'm eternally grateful.

Now that Karen's taken over, things are every bit as copacetic. The only major difference so far is that Karen has a much better telephone voice than Len. (Sorry, Len. I know the truth hurts sometimes, but these things are better out in the open...)

How did you feel about having to work the Justice League of America into *Swamp Thing* #24?

Hmmm. This one needs sorting out... I *didn't* have to work the Justice League into *Swamp Thing*. The whole thing was entirely my idea and my decision. It was probably the wrong decision, but it was something that I felt I ought to do at the time.

I find the DC Universe a pretty fascinating place, as a concept, and there are a hell of a lot of things that I'd like to do with it. To this end, I was anxious to avoid giving the impression that *Swamp Thing* existed in some nebulous backwater of the DC continuity, away from the main action. As far as I'm concerned, all this stuff is happening in the same world and the only difference is that the world doesn't look quite the same from Swamp Thing's perspective.

Obviously, this causes problems, the major ones being connected with the ambiance and atmosphere. In context of the sort of mood we're attempting to build up around Swamp Thing, a character in a garish leotard could look just incredibly stupid, with a few notable exceptions; Batman could fit quite easily into Swamp Thing's world, for example, whereas with the Flash there'd be problems.

What I decided to do was throw myself in at the deep end and feature the Justice League of America right up there in the first three or four issues. After all, if the Justice League can work in *Swamp Thing*, then there should be no problems for the rest of the DC cosmos. I think that after the JLA bit, the reader will accept a guest shot by, say, Hawkman a lot more readily, should we ever wish to use him.

Making the Justice League fit into a horror book was largely a problem of approach. What I decided to go for was a more oblique and shadowy representation of the JLA. They appear a little weirder and ominous and more frightening, unknowable entities of immense power that sit up there in space in which we don't get to see any of the Justice League face on in the strong light. Added to this, nowhere in the sequence are any of the League members referred to by their superhero names, nor are the words "Justice League of America" mentioned. My intention was that by stripping the characters of a few of their familiar reference points, I could get the reader to look at them in a slightly new way. Make them a little less cozy, if you want.

On another level, given that I want the book to work within the DC Universe rather than outside it, it's logical that the Justice League would be involved. This is something that used to bother me about the superhero comics that I read as a kid… if Luthor came up with some scheme for offing Superman and taking over the world, it seemed logical that he'd next have to take on Green Lantern, the Flash, the Atom, Hawkman and so on and so on. If it's all happening in the same world than everything must be connected. If the Floronic Man wants to wipe out all traces of animal life on the planet, it isn't only going to be Swamp Thing that has an interest in thwarting him.

Finally, and perhaps most crucially, I wanted to try and establish a *need* for Swamp Thing within the DC Universe, a *raison d'etre* that would hold up under examination. Because on one level, Swamp Thing is just a reasonably strong humanoid. This, in the DC cosmos, is nothing spectacular. What I wanted to explore were areas of difference in Swamp Thing, the parts of his nature that set him apart from all the other characters, the things that he can do that they can't. The basic plot situation that I used… the Justice League being faced by a situation in which they are useless while Swamp Thing emerges as the hero of the hour… was, I supposed pretty clumsy and obvious. Hopefully, though, I at least achieved a little of what I was setting out to do.

Do you have any plans or desires to write other American comics, now that you've got your foot in the door?

Well, yeah. It's pretty much the same situation for me as it is for the American fans who've become professionals. You've been brought up upon these particular comics and characters and you've got a vast web of nostalgia and associations connected with every one of them. Much as I might affect to despise the archetypal dribbling fan mentality, I have to admit that there's a tremendous puerile buzz that comes from being let loose on this sort of material.

The only other thing I've actually written was "Mogo Doesn't Socialize" for *Tales of the Green Lantern Corps*, which I suppose is quite nice in a stupid sort of way. There are also a couple of synopses that I did that I believe are with Julie Schwartz at the moment; one is for a Superman/Swamp Thing crossover for *DC Comics Presents*, and the other is an idea for a three-part Superman/Lois Lane story which might possibly be appearing in the regular *Superman* books.

The Superman/Swamp Thing crossover was interesting to work out, mainly because there were such a lot of difficulties involved in making a story like that work. The Lois Lane story was just an idea that I'd had kicking 'round in my head for a long while; it sort of explore the Superman legend from a funny angle and at the same time is a kind of tribute to the old Mort Weisinger Imaginary Stories. I've not heard back from DC yet, and I'm not sure if I might have been a little radical in my ideas for Superman. I suppose we'll have to wait and see.

As far as future projects go, I've expressed an interest in The Metal Men, J'onn Jonzz, and The Challengers of the Unknown. On the other hand, I quite like the challenge of having a character thrown at me out of the blue and being told to make it work. Of course, if Karen phones up tomorrow and tells me that she wants me to handle a revival of Dobie Gillis or Scooter then I may wish to revise this last statement.

Basically, though, as long as I'm allowed to carry on working with Steve and John and Karen on *Swamp Thing*, I'm not going to be too depressed.

TCJ

To Be Continued...